A. D. Williams.

Aug 16th 1868.

LIFE:

ITS

NATURE, VARIETIES, AND PHENOMENA.

BY

LEO. H. GRINDON,

LECTURER ON BOTANY AT THE ROYAL SCHOOL OF MEDICINE, MANCHESTER;
AUTHOR OF "EMBLEMS," "FIGURATIVE LANGUAGE," ETC.

FIRST AMERICAN EDITION.

PHILADELPHIA
J. B. LIPPINCOTT & CO.
1867.

PREFACE.

THE object of this work is two-fold. First, it is proposed to give a popular account of the phenomena which indicate the presence of that mysterious, sustaining force we denominate Life, or Vitality, and of the laws which appear to govern their manifestation; secondly, will be considered those Spiritual, or Emotional and Intellectual States, which collectively constitute the essential history of our temporal lives, rendering existence either pleasurable or painful. The inquiry will thus embrace all the most interesting and instructive subjects alike of physiology and psychology: the constitution and functions of the bodies in which we dwell; the delights which attend the exercise of the intellect and the affections; the glory and loveliness of the works of God, will all come under notice, and receive their fitting meed of illustration. Especially will the practical value and interest of life be pointed out; the unity and fine symmetry of the True, the Beautiful, and the Good; the poetry of "common things," and the intimate dependence of the whole upon Him in whom "we live, and move, and have our being." Man, as the noblest recipient, upon earth, of the divine life, will naturally be the principal object of consideration; not, however, the only one. Seeing that he is the Archetype of the entire system of living things, the principles of a true doctrine concerning *him* become the principles of Natural History in every one of its departments. Animals, plants, even the inorganic world of minerals, will all, therefore, be taken account of, in so far as will be needful to the general purpose of the volume. To those who care for the illustration which physical science casts upon the science of mind, and upon the truths of Revelation, there will probably be much that is both novel and inviting. In fact, it has been sedulously aimed to show how intimate and striking is the relation of human knowledges, and how grand is the harmony of things natural and divine. Some readers may regard the combination of physiology, poetry, and theology, so eminently characteristic of these chapters, as detrimental to their value, since the subjects in question are commonly regarded as incongruous. It is sufficient to say, in anticipation of such criticism, that one great aim of the entire work is to show the essential consanguinity of every form of human thought and human feeling. There has been no hesitation in dealing with some of the most sacred of topics. The physical and the spiritual worlds are in such close connection, that to attempt to treat philosophically of either of them apart from the other, is to divorce what God has joined together. Though the authorized teacher of holy things undoubtedly has his special office, it is no invasion, therefore, of his prerogative to speak "religiously" on themes so high and beautiful as the attestations of the divine love expressed in nature. Science without religion is empty and unvital. True wisdom, finding the whole world expressive of God, calls upon us to walk at all times and in all places, in the worship and reverent contemplation of Him. Wishful at all times to speak modestly, and upon sacred matters always most reverently, if a single sentence in the volume can be shown not to be in accordance with, or can be proved contrary to a right and true interpretation of Scripture, it is here, once for all, acknowledged false, and declared unspoken.

The views which are set forth lay few claims to originality. They are such as have been held by select thinkers in every age, though perhaps never before expressed connectedly, or in similar terms. Not that the book is a mere compilation of time-worn facts. Several of the chapters, such as those upon Rejuvenescence, and the Prefigurations of Nature, deal with subjects hitherto scarcely touched. Neither are the views here offered final, or binding on a single reader; they are offered as opinions and convictions rather than as dogmas. Certainly, most part of the work is written affirmatively, but this must be taken only as indicating earnestness of conviction; anything like dogmatizing is altogether disclaimed. They are views which have brought inexpressible happiness to the writer; and they are offered in the hope that, while they may render the strange mystery of life less perplexing, they will help to render others happy likewise.

That the book is in many respects greatly deficient, no one can become more sensible than the author is. It would be remarkable were it otherwise, when the vast extent of the subject is considered, and the impossibility of compressing it into moderate limits. Ordinarily, those subjects have been preferred for consideration which are least commonly attended to. Some may seem to call for more lengthy treatment than they receive; but they are designedly curtailed, because already discussed *in extenso* by authors of repute. Such are Sleep, and the Brain. The incompleteness of the remarks upon others is compensated in the author's separate writings. A large number of quotations will be found, ample reference being made to the authorities in all the more important of them, and the remainder acknowledged in the usual manner. The reader who is acquainted with the authors cited will not regret to meet old friends; and to the younger student, they may be valuable as pointing to new sources of information. Inserted, as a considerable portion of them have been, purely from memory, exercised over a long and diversified course of reading, it has been impossible always to authenticate minutely. For the benefit of the younger reader, copious references to the literature of the subject are also introduced; the book forming, in this respect, a kind of index.

Appended will be found an appropriate adjunct to the subject of Life, in the shape of a little essay on "Times and Seasons."

CONTENTS.

CHAPTER I.

CHAPTER II.

CHAPTER III.

CHAPTER IV.

CHAPTER V.

CHAPTER VI.

CHAPTER VII.

CHAPTER VIII.

CHAPTER IX.

CHAPTER X.

CHAPTER XI.

CHAPTER XII.

CHAPTER XIII.

CHAPTER XIV.

CHAPTER XV.

CHAPTER XVI.

CHAPTER XXVI.

CHAPTER XXVII.

CHAPTER XXVIII.

CHAPTER XXIX.

CHAPTER XXX.

LIFE.

CHAPTER I.

GENERAL IDEA OF LIFE, AND UNIVERSALITY OF ITS PRESENCE.

1. LIFE is the loftiest subject of philosophy. There is no place where life is not present; and there never was a time when life was not. In the great composite fact of a CREATOR are involved the elemental facts of Omnipresence and Eternity of existence; and these, in turn, involve Infinite Creative Activity, which is the production and sustentation of arenas of ever-renovated life. To suppose the Creator ever to have been inactive or unproducing, would be to suppose him inconsistent with himself. Doubtless every one of the innumerable orbs of the universe had a *beginning*,—some, probably, were created long subsequently to others, and are comparatively in their childhood; but a period when there were *no* worlds,—no terraqueous scenes of the bestowal of the Divine Love, the mind is incapable of conceiving. Ancient as our own world is, there were "morning stars" which "sang together" at its nativity. That such scenes of life do really exist, certainly we neither know, nor is it probable that it lies within the power of man scientifically to determine; but the affirmative is congenial alike to reason, philosophy, and enlarged ideas of God. Truth in such matters is determined by balancing probabilities, rather than by rigid, mathematical demonstration. If the

former proposition be admissible, namely, that an inactive, unproducing Creator is a contradiction in terms, the "plurality of worlds" is a corollary almost inevitable. "Life was not made for matter, but matter for life. In whatever spot we see it, whether at our feet, or in the planet, or in the remotest star, we may be sure that life is there,—life physical to enjoy its beauties—life moral to worship its maker—life intellectual to proclaim his wisdom and his power." Doubtless, too, every shape of organized existence had its own special era of commencement, as illustrated in the sequentialism of the fossils beneath our feet;* but those very fossils show at the same moment, that organic life is contemporaneous with the consolidation of the worlds which it embellishes, and thus with the dayspring of Time. The very purpose of a world's creation is that it shall be at once clothed and made beautiful with life. "For thus saith the Lord that created the heavens,—God himself that formed the earth and made it; He hath established it; He created it not in vain; He formed it to be inhabited."

2. Under the term Life, however, rightly regarded, is comprehended far more than it is ordinarily used to denote. We err, if when thinking of the habitations of life we associate it only with ourselves, animals, and plants. Life, in its proper, generic sense, is the name of the sustaining

---

* The non-geological reader may be apprised that the petrified remains of animals and plants, which form so large a portion of collections of natural curiosities, are not mixed indiscriminately in the earth, but always occupy the same relative places,—that is, every layer or stratum, or at least every group of strata, has its peculiar fossils, showing that there must have been as many distinct creations as there are changes in the character of the relics. When plants and animals *first* appeared upon our planet, geology will probably never be able to point out, nor even to calculate. Azoic *rocks* are no proof of azoic *periods*.

principle by which everything out of the Creator subsists, whether worlds, metals, minerals, trees, animals, mankind, angels, or devils, together with all thought and feeling. Nothing is absolutely lifeless, though many things are relatively so; and it is simply a conventional restriction of the term, which makes life signify no more than the vital energy of an organized, material body, or the phenomena in which that energy is exhibited. Though in man life be at its maximum, it is not to be thought of as concentrated in him, nor even in "animated nature," outside of which there is as much life as there is inside; though not the same expression of life. "The life which works in your organized frame," said Laon, "is but an exalted condition of the power which occasions the accretion of particles into this crystalline mass. The quickening force of nature through every form of being is the same."* "The characteristic," observes another quick-sighted writer, "which, manifested in a high degree, we call Life, is a characteristic manifested only in a lower degree by so-called inanimate objects."† Hufeland, Oersted, Humboldt, Coleridge, in his "Theory of Life," Arnold Guyot, in "The Earth and Man," and many others, express themselves in similar terms, none, however, more explicitly than the distinguished Carus:—"The idea of Life is co-extensive with Universal Nature. The individual or integrant parts of Nature are the members; universal nature is the total and complete organism. The relations of inorganic to organized bodies exist only by reason of this; hence, too, the universal connection, the combination, the never-ceasing action and re-action of all the powers of nature, producing the vast and magnificent

* "Panthea; or, the Spirit of Nature," by Robert Hunt, p. 50, 1849.

† Herbert Spencer.—*Westminster Review*, April, 1852, p. 472.

whole of the world;—an action and re-action which would be impossible, were not all pervaded by a single principle of Life."* Strictly speaking, every atom of the constituent matter of our globe is alive. "Inanimate matter," "dead matter," often vaguely spoken of, matter waiting for the breath of Deity to give it life, exists only in fable. Matter is not a hearth existing anteriorly to life, and independently of life, and upon which the flame of life is sometime kindled. In its very simplest and crudest forms it is a sign that the flame is already burning. The language of poetry, or rather of the poetic sentiment,—the golden key to the essential meanings of words, and the teacher of their right applications, has from ages immemorial shown that life is no mere term of physiology; and Scripture, which is the sum and immortal bloom of all poetry, pronounces, in its usages, a divine confirmation. In the force and multiplicity of its figurative applications, no word takes precedence of Life,—a fact which mere accident or conformity to other men's example would be quite insufficient to account for; the reason is that what we ordinarily call "Life," namely, organic, physiological life, is the exponent and explanatory phase of a principle felt to be omnipresent, manifold in expression, but uniform in entity. The profound, unerring perceptions of the harmonies of nature, which were the original architects, and are the conservators and trustees of language, acknowledged no private property in words; and though conventionalism and contraction of view may seek to enslave particular terms, Life among the number, ever and ever do those perceptions free them from their bonds, and pass them on to their rightful inheritances. Hence it is that on the

* "The Kingdom of Nature: their Life and Affinity," by Dr. C. G. Carus. Translated from the German, in Taylor's Scientific Memoirs, vol. i., p. 223. 1837.

lips of the poet;—that is, on the lips of every man who is in closer alliance with God, and Truth, and Nature than are the multitude;—words which with the *vulgus* have but one solitary, narrowed meaning, are continually found serving varied and brilliant purposes, which Taste appreciates and relishes delightedly. Strange and unnatural as its phrases may sound to the unreflective mind, figurative language, rightly so called, is Nature's high-priest of Truth. "Rightly so called," because metaphors and similes founded upon mere arbitrary or far-fetched comparisons, though often confounded with figurative language, are generally but its mockery and caricature. True figurative language is an echo of the divine, immortal harmonies of nature, thus their faithful expositor, the vestibule of Philosophy, and an epitome of the highest science of the universe.

3. When it is popularly said, then, that one thing is animate, and another inanimate; that life is present *here*, but absent *there;* the simple fact of the matter is that a particular *manifestation* of life is absent or present. Such phrases come of confounding Expression, which is variable, with Principle, which is uniform. A particular presentation of life is contemplated, and thus not only is the principle itself misconceived, but everything which does not conform to the assumed impersonation of it is pronounced contrary to that which in reality has *no* contraries. Just as with popular notions of what constitutes Religion, which it is impossible rightly to apprehend and define, so long as it is confounded with the forms of faith, and the modes and attitudes of worship, by which it is locally sought to be realized. It is a mere assumption, for instance, that life is present only where there are physical growth, feeding, motion, sensation, reproduction, &c. Life confines itself to no such scanty costume; and as if it would rebuke the penuriousness of a doctrine which so limits and degrades it, often forbears from all the

more striking phenomena of the series, in the very departments of nature of which they are asserted to be characteristic; and expresses itself so slenderly, that science needs all its eyes and analogies to discern it. In the fungi, for example, and in the sponge, both of which forms of being, by reason of their attenuated presentation of life, have been regarded in time past as belonging to inorganic nature. Fungi have been thought to be the extinguished relics or corpses of the beautiful meteors called "falling stars;" sponges have been deemed mere concretions of the foam of the sea. "There is found," says old Gerarde, "upon the rocks neare vnto the sea, a certaine matter wrought together of the fome or froth of the sea, which we call spunges." It is proper to remark, however, that by Aristotle, the father of natural history, the animal constitution of sponges was at all events anticipated.* So with the beautiful frondose zoophytes called Sertularia, Thuiaria, Plumularia, Flustra, &c.† So late as a century ago, the mineralogists disputed the zoological and botanical claims to the possession of these beautiful organisms, contending that they were "formed by the sediment and agglutination of a submarine, general compost of calcareous and argillaceous materials, moulded into the figures of trees and

* For a long and eminently interesting account of the opinions and discoveries of the nature of Sponges, and of their situation and rank in the scale of organized being, see the admirable "History of British Sponges and Lithophytes," by the late lamented Dr. George Johnson, the Gilbert White of the sea.

† Though these names may not be familiar, the objects they designate are known to all who have interested themselves in the curiosities and wonders of the shore. Resembling sea-weeds in their general aspect and configuration, and commonly confounded with them, they are, nevertheless, readily distinguishable by their semi-crystalline texture, and whitish brown color; the prevailing colors of true sea-weeds being pink, green, or dark olive.

mosses by the motion of the waves; by crystallization (as in salts), or by some imagined vegetative power in brute matter. Ray himself seems not to have made up his mind about them, for though in some of his writings he indicates a correct apprehension of their nature, in the "Wisdom of God manifested in the Works of Creation," he includes them among "inanimate, mixed bodies," or "stones, metals, minerals, and salts." "Some," says he, "have a kind of vegetation and resemblance of plants, as Corals, Pori, and Fungites, which grow upon the rocks like shrubs." The fact is, the notions of life and of what lives, as of the whole, genuine, truth in any matter, are things essentially of growth, and modification for the better. The popular notion of life is not a censurable one. It necessarily precedes; the error being to *remain* in it after it has been shown to be only *part* of a truth. Partial truths everywhere form the beginnings of knowledge. In science, in philosophy, in theology, it is neither so much nor so often that positively *false* doctrines are held, as defective ones. The difference between the intellectual conditions of childhood and maturity, and thus between their counterparts, the uncultivated and the cultivated mind, consists, mainly, in the ability to discriminate between what is *less true* and what is *more completely true.* Unfortunately, we are all of us too prone to rest content with our little glimpses, and to deem them the absolute total. Tell the dull-witted, uninformed man that the gray, leatherlike fungus upon the old paling lives as veritably as he himself does, and he will laugh at you. To *him*, eating, drinking, and movement from place to place alone indicate life. You may get his assent perhaps to the proposition that the beautiful tree swaying its branches there, is alive; but to make the same demand on behalf of the lichens, is to quench all his belief in your sincerity, if not in your sanity. To the perception of this higher theorem he must *progress*, as his teacher did before him, and as that teacher also himself further progresses, when not shackled by a mistaken deference, to the perception of a sustaining life even in inorganic things. No estimate of facts in nature can be regarded as just, consistent, and complete, which confines itself to a fixed circumference, calling everything beyond, barbarian. In his sphere, the philosopher who sees life only in organic things, is no more advanced than the rustic and the child, who allow it only to animals.

4. It needs very little observation of nature to perceive that life does not necessarily imply consciousness or feeling. If it did, the whole vegetable creation would be lifeless, together with many animal structures of humble kind, as the sponge and allied beings. So with the mere circumstances, separately taken, of volitional movement, feeding and growth. As regards movement, for instance, no observation or experiment has rendered it even *probable* that plants ever move volitionally, and the same may be said of the humble animal organisms just alluded to. This might be presupposed, indeed, from the utter absence from plants and the sponge, of consciousness and sensation, seeing that without these there can be no volition, and therefore no impulse to move. The fascinatingly curious examples of movement furnished in the different kinds of Sensitive-plant,* may

* There are many kinds of sensitive-plant besides the species commonly so called, though nearly all are comprised in the great family of plants called *Leguminosæ*. The veritable *Mimosa sensitiva* is a very different thing from the beautiful little *Mimosa pudica*, the species ordinarily known as the sensitive-plant. The other examples of sensitiveness occur in different species of *Oxalideæ*, a family of which our English wood-sorrel is the type; and in the extraordinary plants known as the fly-catchers, comprehended in the family of *Droseraceæ*, the most remarkable being the North American Venus' fly-trap, or *Dionæa muscipula*.

seem to be exceptional, but the whole of these are referable to causes which involve no degree whatever of volition. The most curious of all, namely, the play of the leaflets of the Moving-plant,* may be compared with such movements in the animal body as that of the heart, which is constantly pulsating, yet quite independently of the will, and even out of its control. Exceptions may also seem to occur in the closing and opening of many kinds of flowers, commonly called their sleep and their waking; also in the folding and re-expansion of the leaves, and in the advance of the stamens of certain flowers towards the pistil. For all of these, however, there is adequate explanation. Causes exciting from without, manifestly elicit the chief part of the respective movements; while others are purely mechanical. Nothing is easier to perceive, for instance, than that the leap of the stamens of the Kalmia from their niches in the corolla, comes of the wider expansion of the flower, which unfixes the anthers, and thus causes the filaments to exchange their constrained curvature for the straightness of freedom.† The only other kind of vegetable movement apparently volitional, is that of the minute aquatics called, from the nature of their motion, *Oscillatoria*. Carpenter compares this to the ciliary movement in animals, which is

---

* The Moving-plant, or *Desmodium gyrans*, is a native of Bengal, and one of the family of the Leguminosæ above mentioned. Its leaves are somewhat like those of the clover, and the leaflets, under given circumstances, keep moving up and down. An excellent colored drawing of it may be seen in the "Icones Plantarum Rariorum" of Jacquin, vol. iii., tab. 565. Similar movements take place in the *Desmodium gyroides* and *D. vespertilionis*.

† For particulars of various plant-movements of this nature, see Balfour's "Class-Book of Botany," pp. 492–500; and on the subject of plant motion in general, Carpenter's "Principles of General and Comparative Physiology," chap. xv.

so independent of volition as often to continue after the organism itself is dead.*

5. That the mere act of *feeding* is not an indispensable testimony to the presence of life, is shown in deciduous trees, or those which cast their foliage in the autumn, and hybernate till spring, seeing that without the presence of leaves, no true vegetable nutrition can proceed. Insects, while in the chrysalis form, exemplify the same thing, as do all kinds of hybernating animals. So with the phenomenon of *growing*. That this is not needed in order to betoken life, is illustrated in every egg before it is placed under the hen, and in every seed before put into the soil. Contemplating "latent life," as the physiologists call it, or that which supports the egg and the seed prior to hatching and germination, we discover in fact, that behind the scenes there is, if possible, even *more* life than in front. Millions of beings enjoy complete

---

* For descriptions and colored drawings of the *Oscillatoria*, see the "British Fresh-water Algæ" of Hassall, (1845), wherein is shown reason also for supposing the motion of these plants to have been "misunderstood and exaggerated to such an extent as to have surrounded them with an unnecessary degree of mystery.

"Ciliary motion" is that of the *cilia*, in animalcules the principal organs of locomotion and of obtaining food; but best to be understood, perhaps, from what these organs and their movements are in our own bodies. The human cilia are minute, transparent hairs, ranging from 1-500th to 1-5000th of an inch in length, and covering various interior surfaces, with which water, or other more or less fluid matters are commonly in contact. They abound about the eyes and ears, and cover the whole extent of the respiratory mucous tract. Their office is to assist in propelling onwards, and usually outwards, the fluid matters brought into contact with them; and they do this either by constantly waving backwards and forwards, or by whirling round on their bases, so that the extremities describe circles—the natural result being a continuous current in a determinate direction. The waving and whirling are the "ciliary movement."

and active life; tens of millions lie *potentially* alive, crowding with intense vitality the very places which to appearance seem most empty. When excavations are made in the ground, the earth brought to the surface speedily becomes covered with plants, the seeds of which, as they could not possibly have been conveyed there at the moment, must have been lying in the soil, accidentally buried at some remote period, too deep to be acted upon by the rain and air. This is rendered the more indisputable by the curious fact that plants of different species from those common in the neighborhood, not infrequently spring up among the others. Ploughing deeper than usual will occasion similar resurrections, and the same when the surface soil of old gardens is pared off. Often has there shone a lovely and unexpected renewal of choice blossoms on removing the turf under the walls of old, gray castles and abbeys, which for ages, ivy and the faithful wall-flower alone have solaced.* The water contains similar stores, holding in suspension myriads of germs of algæ, ready to grow as soon as they meet with a

---

* For remarkable instances of the tenacity of life in seeds, especially when buried, see Jesse's "Gleanings in Natural History," vol. i., p. 138, and ii., p. 135; Hooker's "Companion to the Botanical Magazine," vol. ii., p. 293; Loudon's "Magazine of Natural History," iii. 418; viii. 393; x. 447, &c.

The well-known story of the grains of wheat taken from the hand of the Egyptian mummy, germinating after thirty centuries' captivity, though doubted by many, Schleiden at least is a believer in. "How long," says he, "the vital power may slumber in the seed, is shown by the fact that the late Count Von Sternberg raised healthy plants of wheat from grains which were found in a mummy case (which, therefore, must have reposed for three thousand years), and laid them before the Assembly of Naturalists at Freyburg. This experiment has also been made in England." ("The Plant," p. 71.) Eggs have been found in a perfect state no less than three hundred years old. See "Gardeners' Chronicle," August 20th, 1853, p. 54.

suitable resting-place. "Before we have kept our Aquarium a fortnight," says Mr. Gosse, "its transparent sides begin to be dimmed, and a green scurf is seen covering them from the bottom to the water's surface. Examined with a lens, we find this substance to be composed of myriads of tiny plants, some consisting of a single row of cells of a light green hue, forming minute threads which increase in length at their extremity, and become Confervas; while others display small, irregularly puckered leaves of deeper green, and develope into Ulvæ and Enteromorphæ." Even the atmosphere is charged with seeds—those minute bodies produced in such amazing numbers by the aërial cryptogamia, and which indicate their presence, like the algæ in the water, the instant that circumstances enable them to vegetate. Where-ever vegetable mildew makes its appearance, it is owing to the germination of these invisible floating seeds, the vital energy of which, lying in abeyance only till a fitting sphere of acting shall be offered, is one of the most wonderful things in nature. The genera most largely represented are Penicillium, Oidium, Chætomium, Sporodyce, &c.* Not only do the seeds of these and other microscopic fungi, along with those of mosses and lichens, thus float in the atmosphere, waiting their opportunity to grow; there can be little doubt that associated with them are myriads of *germs of animalcules*, especially Rotifera, which find a suitable *nidus* in water containing organic matter in a state of decomposition, one kind following another, according to the stage to which the decomposition has proceeded, but which remain inactive until such a *nidus* is afforded. It is not improbable that the glittering motes seen in the sunbeam when it shines through a small aperture into a dark room, consist in part, of these

* Mildew does not *always* consist of minute vegetable growth. Sometimes, perhaps usually, in woven fabrics, it is referable to an action purely chemical.

otherwise imperceptible eggs and seeds. Light, we well know, is the great and universal Revelator. Give light enough, and it is impossible to imagine what might not brighten into human view. The difficulty in microscopics is not so much in obtaining lenses of increased magnifying power, as in obtaining an adequate amount of light. It may be added that as life does not necessarily imply volitional movement, feeding, sensation, &c., so neither is any one of the instruments through which life is manifested, universally present. No one instrument in particular can be deemed therefore, as essential to life, or as absolutely characteristic and indicative of life.

6. That life does not necessarily imply organization or reproduction, is shown in what may without impropriety be called the Life of the World. Doubtless, there is an impassable chasm between the mineral and the vegetable, as between the vegetable and the animal, and between the animal and man. But this inorganic nature, which is represented as "dead," because it has not the same life with the animal or plant, is it then, to quote Guyot, destitute of all life? "It has all the *signs* of life, we cannot but confess. Has it not motion in the water which streams and murmurs on the surface of the continents, and which tosses in the waves of the sea? Has it not sympathies and antipathies in those mysterious elective affinities of the molecules of matter which chemistry investigates? Has it not the powerful attractions of bodies to each other which govern the motions of the stars scattered in the immensity of space, and keep them in an admirable harmony? Do we not see, and always with a secret astonishment, the magnetic needle agitated at the approach of a particle of iron, and leaping under the fire of the Northern Light? Place any material body whatever by the side of another, do they not immediately enter into relations of interchange, of molecular attraction, of electricity,

of magnetism? In the inorganic part of matter, as in the organic all is acting, all is promoting change, all is itself undergoing transformation. And thus, though this life of the globe, this physiology of our planet, is not the life of the tree or the bird, is it not *also* a life? Assuredly it is. We cannot refuse so to call those lively actions and reactions, that perpetual play of the forces of matter, of which we are every day the witnesses. The thousand voices of nature which make themselves heard around us, and in so many ways betoken incessant and prodigious activity, proclaim it so loudly that we cannot shut our ears to their language." Equally, too, may we recognize life as the central, governing force of everything comprehended under the names of Intellect and Will. The particular phenomena of animal and plant life may not be present, but they are replaced by phenomena no less truly vital. Indeed the life of the soul, or that which is played forth as the activity of the intellect and the affections, is the highest expression of all. Compared with *this* life, the life of animals and plants, and the life of the globe, are but mimicries and shadows.

7. It is this full, generic significance of the word life, which we propose to recognize and illustrate in the following pages; physiological life taking its place, not as life absolutely and exclusively, but as one manifestation among many. The doctrine which it involves is no mere hypothesis of the fancy. It is dictated by nature; it commends itself to common sense, to do which is the chief glory of all that belongs to *un*common sense; it is eminently practical; it is promotive, in fact, of the highest aims of science and philosophy, metaphysical no less than physical. Here is the great certificate of its soundness. For while the ultimate characteristic and test of every true doctrine concerning nature is that no phenomenon in the universe is absolutely beyond the range of its powers of interpretation, the immediate and

proximate test lies in its capacity to illuminate every path of human inquiry, whithersoever it may lead. Such a doctrine has not only a local value and application, but is, directly or indirectly, a clue to the whole mystery of creation. Other doctrines may help more largely in particular provinces, but no doctrine is so generally efficacious as this grand and comprehensive one of the omnipresence and the unity of life. Life it is which gives to the universe all its reality as well as splendor, so that the larger our conception of life, the more nearly do we approach both to a just appreciation of the magnificence of nature, and to the solution of her stupendous problems. Not the least of the advantages accessary to the doctrine here set forth, is that the physiologist who adopts it, instead of entering on his inquiries with the sense of a great, unnatural gap between physiology and physics, finds the latter not only adjoined, but an instructive introduction. He ascends, as all rational philosophy advises, from the simple to the complex. Coleridge clearly exhibits this in his "Theory of Life," above cited; Dr. Radcliffe well exemplifies it in his "Proteus, or the Law of Nature." "As an earnest," he observes, "of the rich harvest which is to come when the current separation of physiology from physics shall be forgotten, several phenomena which were once deemed peculiar to living bodies are now explained by ordinary physical influences." Looked at through a single science, Life is unintelligible; for the sciences, separately taken, are but like the constituent portions of a telescope, we can only see properly by connecting them. Physiology, for the same reason, becomes a pathway and preface to psychology, which inquired into without reference to physiology, as its material representative, is but an intellectual *ignis fatuus*. Every true law in metaphysics has a law corresponding to it in physical nature, and the latter is often the surest clue whereby to find it.

CHAPTER II.

THE SOURCE OF LIFE, AND THE RATIONALE OF LIFE.

8. Life is no part of God's *works*, no created and therefore finite *substance;* neither is it in any case detached from him, or independent of him. As the rivers move along their courses only as they are renewed from perennial springs, welling up where no eye can reach, so is it with life. Genuine philosophy knows of no life in the universe but what is momentarily sustained by connection with its source, with Him who "alone hath life in himself." The popular notion, which sees an image of it rather in the reservoir of water, filled in the first place from the spring, but afterwards cut off, and holding an independent existence, is countenanced neither by science nor revelation. How can independent vitality pertain even to the most insignificant of created forms, when it is said so expressly that "in Him all things live, and move, and have their being?" Even man has no life of his *own*, though of nothing are people more fully persuaded than that they live by virtue of an inborn vital energy, to maintain which, it needs only that they shall feed and sleep. Not that men deny the general proposition that life is from God, and in the hands of God. Every one is willing to allow that he received his life originally from the Almighty, and that the Almighty takes it away from him when he pleases. Few, however, are willing to regard themselves as existing only by virtue of his constant influx, which, nevertheless, is the

only way in which it can be true that "in Him we live, and move, and have our being." It is wounding to self-love and to the pride of human nature, to think of ourselves as so wholly and minutely dependent as we are, moment by moment, day and night, the senses all the while insinuating the reverse. Moreover, in the minds of most men there is a strong aversion to recognize physical effects as resulting from spiritual causes. Towards everything, indeed, which involves a spiritual element—which lifts us above the region of the senses, there is a deep-seated dislike, such as mere argument is perhaps incapable of overcoming, and which can only give way, it would seem, under the influence of higher moral feelings. Truly to understand anything of God's government and providence, we must first of all be faithful to his revealed law. We can form no right estimate, either of nature or of life, till we strive, with his divine blessing, to become in ourselves more truly human.

9. Uncreate and infinite, it follows that of the precise *nature* of this grand, all-sustaining principle, this Life as we call it, man must be content to remain forever uninformed. Man can obtain knowledge only of finite and created things. No philosophy will ever be able to *explain* life, seeing that to "explain" is to consider a phenomenon in the clearness of a superior light, and that life is itself and already the *highest* light. However it may be manifested, to man life can never be anything *but* life. This is no misfortune; perhaps it is an advantage. It is impossible to become either good or wise unless we can make ourselves contented to remain ignorant of many things; and the grander the knowledges we must learn cheerfully to forego, the more useful is the discipline. As there is "a time to get and a time to lose," so is there a time to seek and a time to refrain from seeking. The hypothesis of a "vital force," by which some have sought to account for life, does no more

than push the difficulty a little further back, since the question immediately arises, What is the "vital force," and whence derived? Whether we contemplate it in inorganic nature, or in organic, and by whatever name we may choose to designate it, force is nowhere innate, nor is it originally produced or producible by any combinations or conditions of matter, visible or invisible. Everywhere in the consideration of force, we are told of a power within and underlying that which we are contemplating. Nowhere do we find the power itself, but only the continent of the power; perhaps merely the sensible effect by which its presence is indicated. No force, in a word, in the whole range of material nature, is *initial.* The utmost point to which science can convey us, even when dealing with the most occult and recondite phenomena—those of electricity for example—never shows where force *begins.* There is always a still anterior force, which cannot be found except by the light of Theology. In philosophy, as in trouble and in death, willing or unwilling, we must go to God at last.

10. Others refer life to the "laws of nature." This, within certain limits, is perfectly proper. Life, in all its varied phases and manifestations, *does* come, most assuredly, of the "laws of nature." The error is to *remain* in the laws of nature, and deem that life comes of these only. Laws of nature, in themselves, have no more efficacy than "vital force," and have as little independent existence. "In all ages of the world," says Hitchcock, "where men have been enlightened enough to reason upon the causes of phenomena, a mysterious and a mighty power has been imputed to the *laws of nature.* A large portion of the most enlightened men have felt as if these laws not only explain, but possess an inherent power to continue, the ordinary operations of nature. But what is a natural law without the presence and energizing power of the law*giver?* Who can show how

a law operates except through the influence of the lawgiver? How unphilosophical, then, to separate a law of nature from the Deity, and to imagine him to have withdrawn from his works! To do this would be to annihilate the law. He must be present every moment, and direct every movement of the universe, as really as the mind of man must be in his body in order to produce movement *there.* The law hypothesis supposes law capable of doing what only Infinite wisdom and power can do. And what is this but ascribing infinite perfection to law, and making a Deity of the laws which he ordains?"* Law of itself could not cause or maintain the existence of a single thing, though it was according to law all things were created, and though it is by the same primitive, immutable laws, that all phenomena, both material and spiritual, are effectuated. It is the life underlying the law which causes and sustains. The law is merely the mode of the putting forth of that life; the rule of its action; the definite method in which the internal, Divine, dynamic principle is projected. Nature has no independent activity, no causality of its own. God is the only independent existence, and he is the cause of all causes. He alone hath life in himself. Proximately, the universe, and all that it contains, is *law*-governed: but it is at the same time fundamentally and essentially *God*-governed. Animals and plants, in their vital processes, the external world and all its changes, alike declare a Divine beginning. God it is who displays the manifold lovely phenomena which render the earth, the air, the sea, and their vicissitudes, pictures so vivid of human experience. The tossing of the white-crested waves; the gliding of the clouds before the wind; the daily illumination, and the morning and evening painting of the sky; the glitter of the stars; the rainbow,

* Religion of Geology. Lecture ix.

these, and all other such things, come of the watchful and benevolent activity of our living Father in the heavens, who is never a mere spectator, much less an indifferent one, either in terrestrial or in spiritual things; still are they in no case exercises of mere lawless fiat.

11. The very existence of the earth as a planetary mass depends, but in a proximate sense, on the "laws of nature." The same is true of the various materials which compose it; water, for example, formed under the influence of the natural law which science calls "chemical affinity." Let the affinity be annulled,—in other words, let the Divine life cease to act upon the constituent oxygen and hydrogen, no longer impelling them to combine,—and every drop would instantly decompose and disappear. Under a similar withdrawal of sustaining energy, every solid and fluid of nature, even the solids we call simple and primitive, would depart; massive and impregnable as it seems, the whole of this great globe would dissolve into thin air and vanish. For just as water is resolvable into oxygen and hydrogen, so are these latter, along with the solid elements, the metals, phosphorus, iodine, &c., resolvable into yet finer elements, into which, unless supported by the Divine life, they would similarly decompose. The actually primitive elements of our earth, instead of fifty-five or fifty-six, are probably only two. The tendency, without doubt, if we look only at one department of chemical inquiry, seems of late to have been towards an increase of the number rather than to a diminution; the profounder investigations of natural philosophers dispose them, however, more strongly every day, to refer back the whole to a simple flagrant or inflammable body, and a pure conflagrant body, or supporter of fire; in other words, to an active substance and a passive. The analysis of one will lead to the reduction of all the rest, and establish the true *principia* whereby the science of chemistry will be consum-

mated. Science, be it remembered, has never made a single step except in the wake of imagination; the practical ideas of one age have all been begotten of the impractical of a former; the morning star of all philosophy is poetry. Gold, silver, oxygen, &c., probably come each one of them of a special play of affinity between the molecules of the two primitives, having a corollary in the resulting products of absolute and relative ductility, elasticity, &c., such as causes gold to be where we find gold, silver where we find silver, as accurately and inevitably as the affinities which take place between the atoms of gold, silver, oxygen, &c., give origin, in turn, to oxides, acids, earths, alkalies. Whether there be any yet earlier conditions of matter than these two can only be reasoned upon from analogy. It is not within the ability of man to compass with actual knowledge either the *maximum naturæ* or the *minimum*.

12. Though the Divine, by means of his life, be thus the basis of all nature, even its minutest atom, we are not to *confound* him with nature;—this would be even worse than the ascription of everything to "Law." Superfluous as it may seem after the distinct references that have been made, it is well, perhaps, that upon this great and sacred point we should have, before going any further, a full and explicit understanding. The ancients described the world as a huge animal, vitalized by an impersonal *ψυχη χοσμου*, or *anima mundi*. Even in modern times we have seen it taught that—

> "All are but parts of one stupendous whole,
> Whose body nature is, and God the soul."

Commonly termed "Pantheism," this is, properly speaking, *Atheism*. Pantheism, rightly so called, is the doctrine which sinks nature in God. "This was the pantheism of the famous Spinoza, which some people have been so foolish as to call atheism. Spinoza was so absorbed in the idea of God, that he could see nothing else." Pantheism is the most unreasonable of doctrines; atheism the most mean and gross. God is God, and nature is nature. Intimately connected with each other, yet are they absolutely distinct. Nature is an utterance of the divine mind, clothed in material configurations and phenomena,—flowing from it as words from the underlying thought, or the deeds of friendship from its sentiment; God himself reigns apart from it, in the heavens. No true conception of nature can be attained, any more than a true doctrine of the grounds and uses of religion, till this great truth of the separateness, and therefore the *personality* of God, be acknowledged and felt. For even to think only of wisdom, power, omnipresence, &c., is not to think of *God;* it is but to think of a mere catalogue of abstractions; the terms are meaningless till impersonated, till we connect them, in short, with Him who said,—"He who hath seen *me* hath seen the Father,"—"the man Christ Jesus, who is over all, God blessed forever." It is the immediate consciousness of a supreme and eternal unity, as Carus finely remarks, which enables us to distinguish the just, the true, and the beautiful; so that demonstrations of true science exist, in fact, only for those who set out with the idea of God in Christ as the beginning; studying nature *from* him rather than *towards* him. It is good to "look from Nature up to Nature's God," but it is better and best to look at nature from its framer and sustainer. There would be no falling into pantheism, no forgetting the Creator in the creature, were this always made the starting-point in the survey. The humanity of Christ is the true beginning of all wisdom and philosophy, no less than the immediate avenue to redemption. Not that the idea of God can be entertained irrespectively of nature; each idea is needful to the apprehension of the other. "He," says Franz Von Baader, "who seeks in nature, nature only, and not reason;

he who seeks in the latter, reason only, and not God; and he who seeks reason out of or apart from God, or God out of or apart from reason, will find neither nature, reason, nor God, but will assuredly lose them all three."

13. In the "laws of nature," accordingly, we have not "blind, unintellectual fatalities," but expressions of Divine volitions. They *appear* to us independent and sufficient, because God never discloses himself directly—only through some medium. The world is full of *apparent* truths; they enter largely into our very commonest experiences; a stick immersed in water appears to be broken; the banks of a river seem to move as we sail past; the coast seems to recede from the departing ship; a burning coal swung quickly round seems a ring of fire. So with the "laws of nature." To the eye of the senses they are one thing; to the eye of true philosophy quite another. Seeming to accomplish *all*, in reality they accomplish *nothing*. Oersted never wrote a finer truth than that "the conception of the universe is incomplete, if not comprehended as a constant and continuous work of the eternally-creating Spirit;" nor Emerson, in relation to the same fact, that "it takes as much life to *conserve* as to *create*." Because of these great verities is it that to study the laws of nature is in reality to study the modes of God's action; that science is simply "a history of the Divine operations in matter and mind;" that the world, with all its antiquity, is every moment a new creation, the song of the morning stars unsuspended and unsuspendable to the ear that will listen for it, a virgin to every fresh wooer of the Beautiful and the True.

14. How close does it bring the Creator to us thus to regard him not so much as having *made* the world, as still engaged in *making* it; *i. e.*, by supplying the life on which its laws, and thus its being and incidents, depend. It is an ill-constructed theology which regards God as having created

only in past ages. A gorgeous sunset, the leafing of a tree in the sweet spring-time, betokens the Divine hand no less palpably than did the miracles which provided the hungry multitudes of Galilee with food. "Depend upon it," says an eloquent preacher, "depend upon it, it is not the want of greater miracles, but of the soul to perceive such as are allowed us still, that makes us push all the sanctities into the far spaces we cannot reach. The devout feel that wherever God's hand is, *there* is miracle, and it is simply an undevoutness which imagines that only where miracle is, can there be the real hand of God. The customs of heaven ought surely to be more sacred in our eyes than its anomalies; the dear old ways of which the Almighty is never tired, than the strange things which he does not love well enough to repeat. He who will but discern beneath the sun, as he rises any morning, the supporting finger of the Almighty, may recover the sweet and reverent surprise with which Adam gazed on the first dawn in Paradise; and if we cannot find him there, if we cannot find him on the margin of the sea, or in the flowers by the way-side, I do not think we should have discovered him any more on the grass of Gethsemane or Olivet."

15. Uncreate and infinite, it follows, in addition to consequences specified, that Life as to its essence is no subject for scientific consideration. All that science can do is to investigate the circumstances under which it is manifested, and the effects which it produces. Carefully studying these, and along with them, the processes of life, we may learn, however, the *rationale of its action*, next to the nature of life, the grandest fact in its philosophy, and the centre and foundation of all true and great ideas of life; therefore a benign and animating compensation. Narrowly looked at, underlying every phenomenon of the material world, and underlying every psychological occurrence, there is found a fixed,

causative relation of Two things, or Two principles, as the case may be, different and unequal, yet of such a difference, and such an inequality, that like man and woman, who constitute the type and interpretation of the whole of nature, both visible and invisible, each is the complement of the other; one being gifted with energy to act, the other with equal energy and aptitude to *re*act. All phenomena, alike of matter and of mind, resolve into this dual *virtus*. Whether physical or spiritual, animal or vegetable, Life always presents itself as communicated through this one simple formula, *the reciprocal action and reaction of complementaries.* Where there are greatest variety and complexity of action and reaction, all the results converging at the same time, to one great end, as in plants, animals, and man, the presentations are the grandest; where there is least of such variety, and no such immediate reference, as in the phenomena of inorganic chemistry, there the presentations are the humblest. The great cosmic phenomena induced by Gravitation, Electricity, &c., comprising everything studied by the astronomer, the meteorologist, and the electrician, form no exception. Binary causes lie at the base of all. The sun and moon cast their light upon us; the rain falls and the waves roll; the spheres preserve their rotundity, and persevere in their motions, all as the result of underlying *dual* forces. The Fabric of nature, like its phenomena, resolves, everywhere, into dualities. Land and water, male and female, the straight line and the curve, do but express prominently, a universal principle. The Elements, we have already seen, are probably, only Two.

16. The ground of this wonderful, all-pervading dualism, and concurrent action and reaction, producing the magnificent results we call Nature and Life, lies in the very nature of God himself, who is not so much the ingenious deviser and designer, displaying in the world the contrivances of

Skill, as its Archetype and Exemplar. That is to say, the world is what we find it, not so much because he *willed* it to be so, arbitrarily, as because of his containing, in his own nature, the first principles of its whole fabric and economy. It pictures in finites, what *he* is in infinites. Infinite Wisdom and Infinite Goodness, or Love, as we have seen in another place,* are shown both by natural and revealed theology, to be the all-comprehending essentials of the Divine; omnipotence, omniscience, justice, mercy, and every other attribute, inhering in, and manifesting and fulfilling these two. In these two principles all things have their beginning; in all things therefore are they embodied and represented. Wherever there is life, the Divine Wisdom and Goodness are consentaneously and fundamentally declared. In one we may fancy the Divine Art shows most conspicuous, in another the Divine Power; but the true seeing finds these no more than outer circles, enclosing Love and Wisdom as the inmost. In that admirable adaptation and aptitude of things to act and react, and thus to enter into a relation of which marriage is the highest exponent, consists, accordingly, the whole principle of living action. There is no other source of phenomena, either in the animated or the inanimate world, and wherever it brings things and natures into contact, reciprocally adapted each to the other, life immediately appears, beautiful and exuberant. God made things complementary on purpose that they should unite, and open channels wherein his life should have new outlet; until conjoined, and they have opened such new channels, they are everywhere restless and erratic; everywhere in earth and heaven, equilibrium comes of well assorted marriage, or union of complementaries, and there is no equili-

---

* "Sexuality of Nature," wherein the whole subject of the dualities and reciprocal principles of nature is exhibited and illustrated.

brium independent of it. Nothing, moreover, so surely brings disorder and unhappiness, as interference with natural affinities, and neglecting to be guided by them. Using the word in the high and holy sense which alone properly attaches to it, *i. e.*, as signifying the conjunction of principles and affections, and only in a secondary and derivative sense, the conjunction of *persons*—the union of the prototypal, all-creative Wisdom and Goodness in the Divine, is itself a marriage; so that Life might not inappropriately be described as the playing forth of the principle of which corporeal marriage is the last effect. The development of a new living creature, that is, of a new incarnation of life, when there is externalized love between man and woman (who in matrimony rightfully so called, constitute the finite picture and counterpart of the Almighty), is the very symbol and emblem of the development of life. What the babe is to its parents, such is life, as to its presentation in phenomena, to the action and reaction of the two things or two natures underlying it.

CHAPTER III.

THE VARIETIES OF LIFE—ORGANIC LIFE—THE "VITAL STIMULI."

17. PRIMARILY, the manifestation of life is *twofold*, physical and spiritual. Physical life is life as expressed in the constituents of the material or external world, giving existence to whatever is cognizable by the senses. Spiritual life is that which gives vitality to the soul; underlying thought and feeling, animating the intellect and the affections, and sustaining all that is contained in the invisible, non-material, or spiritual world. Spiritual life, so far as it is allowed the finite mind to perceive, is expressed in only *one* mode: Physical life is expressed in *two* modes, namely, as observable, (1) in the inorganic half of the material creation; (2) in the organic half. The latter, which may be called Organic or Physiological life, presents the further distinction of life as it is in animals, (including the material body, or animal half of man;) and life as it is in vegetables. Put into a tabular form, the several distinctions may be apprehended at a glance:—

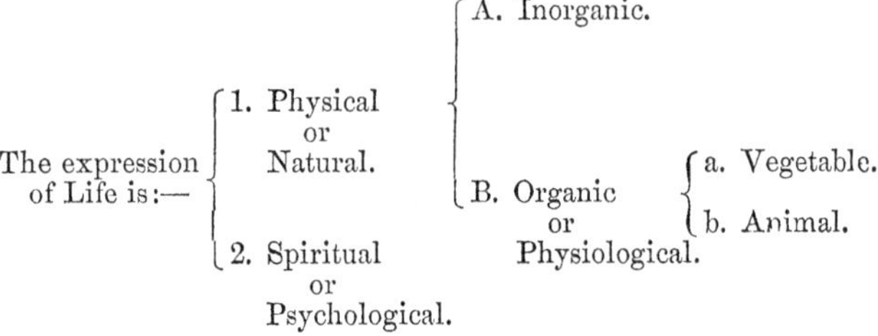

Inorganic life is the lowest expression; Vegetable succeeds; Animal life comes next; and highest is the Spiritual. Wonderful and truly miraculous is it that a single and purely simple element should be presented under such diverse aspects, the extremes far apart as earth and heaven, though it is not without some striking illustrative imagery in objective nature, where the same substance is occasionally found under widely dissimilar forms, as happens with charcoal and the diamond, both of which consist essentially of carbon. There is a grand and beautiful law, however, in the light of which the whole matter becomes intelligible; namely, that the communication of life from God is always in the exact ratio of the Use and Destiny of the recipient object in the general economy of Creation. The more princely the heritage of office, always the more beautiful and complex is the Form of the object, and commensurately with this, the more exalted is the presentation, and the more noble the operation, of the life which fills it. This is the great fundamental principle to which are referable all diversity of structure and configuration in nature, all dissimilitude of substance and organization, and all variety in the force and amount of Life. It may be illustrated by the operation, under its various opportunities, of *water*, which in composition and inherent capabilities, is everywhere precisely the same. In connection with machinery, which is like the complicated and elaborate structure of organized bodies, we see it either turning the huge mill-wheel by the river; or heated into steam, making a thousand wheels whirl in concert; and in either case promoting mightiest ends and uses. Away from machinery, and merely gliding as a stream towards the sea, it serves but to carry onwards the boat that may be launched upon it. Lying as a still lake, among the unpeopled and silent mountains, its energy seems depressed into inertia, though at any moment that energy is capable of being played forth, in all its astounding plenitude, give it but the adequate medium. So with the Divine life in the universe. In the words of a powerful writer, "The material world, with its objects sublimely great or meanly little, as we judge them; its atoms of dust, its orbs of fire; the rock that stands by the sea-shore, the water that wears it away; the worm, a birth of yesterday, which we trample under foot; the streets of constellations that gleam perennial overhead; the aspiring palm-tree fixed to one spot, and the lions that are sent out free; these incarnate and make visible all of God their natures will admit," that is, all of his LIFE they are competent to receive and play forth, by virtue of their respective offices in the system of the world, and the forms they hold in harmony therewith. Carbon in the shape of diamond has a nobler destiny than carbon in the shape of charcoal; therefore it receives that intenser communication of life which is so exquisitely phenomenonized in crystallization, and the concurrent translucency and brightness. The soul has a nobler destiny than the body; therefore has it the imperial life whereby it travels whither it will, piercing space to its utmost bound, centrifugal as light.

18. Inorganic life, the first-named of these three great varieties or manifestations of the vitalizing principle, has been illustrated in the preceding chapters. It will suffice to add here, that it has nothing *in common* with organic or physiological life, much less with the spiritual; nothing, that is to say, except the Divine origin and sustentation. The recipient forms occupy a plane of their own, in every sense subordinate and distinct, and the phenomena which they exhibit bear not the slightest similarity to those manifested upon the superior planes, as regards any strict and essential resemblance. The generalization by which it is associated with the higher varieties, proposes to view it as that particu-

lar expression of the universal Divine energy whereby inanimate things "have their being," just as under another expression, animate things have *theirs*, and nothing more. The second variety, the ORGANIC or Physiological expression of Life,—that which vitalizes plants and animals, and the material body of man,—is so called because of the playing forth of its phenomena through the medium of special instruments or organs, as in animals, the limbs, the heart, the brain, &c., and in plants, the leaves, the flowers, the stamens, &c. Mineral substances, though they sometimes possess a very beautiful configuration, and even a kind of internal arrangement of parts, as seen in agates, never possess distinct organic members. These pertain peculiarly to plants and animals, the sole subjects and recipients of organic life. Taking the word in its literal and most general sense, the phenomena of the Spiritual life are organic, being played forth like those of physiological life, through special instruments; the very *same* instruments in fact. It is legitimate, nevertheless, to restrict the name to physiological life and phenomena, seeing that the latter take precedence of the spiritual, both in extent and diffusion, and in order of manifestation. The race of beings alone recipient of spiritual life constitutes (as regards earth) the least part of living nature, and every member of it is animal before human. The Organic is the expression of life which, as the prime instrument of all man's temporal enjoyments, has in every age allured his intensest interest. Its facts and mysteries have commended themselves to his intellect as the peerage of science and philosophy, the alpha and the omega of all natural knowledge. If, says Aristotle, the knowledge of things becoming and honorable be deservedly held in high estimation; and if there be any species of knowledge more exquisite than another, either upon account of its accuracy, or of the objects to which it relates being more excellent or wonderful; we should not hesitate to pronounce the history of the animating principle as justly entitled to hold the first rank.* With all enthusiasm and assiduity accordingly, have chemistry, anatomy, and physiology, toiled at the splendid theme. Theories innumerable have been devised with a view to its elucidation; all however, in vain, because framed in the sunless chambers of an exclusively secular philosophy. Esteemed by some the cause of organization, by others its consequence; imagined at different periods to be fire,† light, oxygen,‡ electricity,§ and galvanism, "still the exulting Eureka has not been uttered, either in the laboratory, the dissecting-room, or the schools of the *savans*. The enigma has continued to baffle all the propounders of solutions;—the heart of nature's mystery has not been plucked out, even by the most vigorous of the wisest of her sons." Pursued as a matter of purely scientific inquiry, researches into

---

* *των καλῶν καὶ τιμίων κ. τ. λ., περι ψυχης*, Book i., chap. 1, the opening sentence.

† Among those who held this very ancient doctrine was Hippocrates. He considered heat not only the foundation of life, but as the Divinity itself, intelligent and immortal.—*Δοκέει δέ μοι ὅ καλέομενον θερμὸν ἀθάνατον τε εἶναι, και νοειν μαντα, κ. τ. λ.* Works, sec. iii., p. 249. Fœsius' Edit., 1621. Relics of this belief survive in the phrases vital spark, the flame of life, &c. See for curious illustrations, Bishop Berkeley's *Siris*, sections 152 to 214.

‡ As by Girtanner, Journal de Physique, &c., tome 37, p. 139. See also Bostock's Elementary System of Physiology, vol. 1, p. 209, 1824.

§ This has been a very favorite hypothesis, and still meets with approval. Abernethy, for one, regarded electricity "not merely as the prime agent in sensation, but as even constituting the essence of life itself." See his "Inquiry, &c., into Hunter's Theory of Life," pp. 26, 30, 35, 80, &c., 1814. It is singular to find this intelligent writer sliding into materialism at the very time when he is directing the force of his genius against it.

the mystery of life cannot possibly have any other termination, seeing that to follow such a course is to attend merely to Effects, and to entirely disregard and disown the Cause. Look at the results of the countless strivings to contrive a descriptive name for the wily Proteus;—vital principle, *vis vitæ*, vital spirit, *impetum faciens*, spirit of animation, organic force, organic agent, *vis plastica*, *materia vitæ diffusa*, &c., &c.;—what do they amount to beyond a tacit confession of total inability? Look at the attempts, scarcely fewer, that have been made at a definition of life. If they have not been mere substitutions of many words for one, adding nothing to our previous knowledge, they have been similarly fruitless exercises in a *few*. When Bichat, for instance, opens his celebrated "Recherches Physiologiques sur la Vie et la Mort," by defining life as "the sum of the functions by which death is resisted,"* what is it, as Coleridge well asks, but a circuitous way of saying that life consists in being able to live? As little to the purpose is Dr. Fletcher, when he says that "Life consists in the sum of the characteristic actions of organized beings, performed in virtue of a specific susceptibility, acted upon by specific stimuli;" or Richerand, when he tells us that "Life consists in the aggregate of those phenomena which manifest themselves in succession for a limited time in organized beings." Neither of them *explains* anything. Even the attempt, last in point of time, and from the lesson of others' errors, presumable to be best

---

* "*La vie est l'ensemble des fonctions qui resistent à la mort.*" See the remarks on this much criticized sentence in the edition of Bichat by Cerise. *Nouvelle édition*, Paris, 1852, p. 274. Auguste Compte, a mere bookman in such subjects, devotes a long argument in his *Philosophie Positive* (tome 3, p. 288,) to what he calls, with most amusing complacency, the *profonde irrationalité* of his great countryman.

in execution,—that of Herbert Spencer, who devotes the whole of the third part of his masterly Elements of Psychology to the consideration of the subject, bringing up by careful and steady steps to the conclusion that "the broadest and most complete definition of life will be *the continuous adjustment of internal relations to external relations*,"—even this deals but, like the others, with the *phenomena* of life. It is no "definition,"—merely a statement of certain signs of life. If we are to understand by the word "Life" simply the attestations of its presence,—the signs, and nothing more,—these several authors have done as well, perhaps, as the subject permits. But in that case we are left precisely where we were. Life itself, the thing attested, has yet to be defined, and requires a distinct and superior name. Some "definitions" have been couched in a single word, "Assimilation" for example. But as in the preceding cases, what is assimilation more than a *circumstance* of life? Were assimilation life itself, we should know all about the latter so soon as we had noted the assimilating process, by means of a little chemistry, in the green duckweed of the standing pool. In no way is it more paramount than reproduction is. As well might Life be defined to be Death, seeing that death is the universal end.

19. In the phenomena just adverted to, namely, the Assimilation of food internally, and Reproduction of the species in direct descent; followed after a given period of activity, by Death, consist the grand characteristics of Organized beings. However plants and animals may differ among themselves, this threefold history pertains to every species without exception. Functions, accordingly, even more decidedly than organs, distinguish the members of the Vegetable and Animal kingdoms from the Mineral. It is important to observe this, because in many of the humbler kinds of animals and plants, organs strictly so called, are

not developed. In the *Protococcus* or red-snow plant, the whole apparatus of life is concentrated into the compass of a single microscopic cell. Assimilation and Reproduction are performed there nevertheless, proving that separate and complex organs are non-essential to them. It follows that the absolute, unexceptionable diagnosis of organized bodies consists not so much in the possession of distinct organs, as in the presence of *vital tissue;* that is to say, cells filled with fluid, at all events in their younger stages, and possessing, every one of them, full powers of assimilation and reproduction; so that although no more than a single cell may be developed, it is still, to all intents and purposes, an organized body. This latter condition is what we witness in the red-snow plant. The body of man is a vast mountain of cells of precisely the same intrinsic character as those of the *Protococcus,* only built into special members, and endued with a more powerful vitality. Whether members be developed or not, "vital tissue" is the basis of the entire organic world, as markedly as it is absent from the mineral, and forms the *sedes ipsissimæ* of the whole of the vital processes. That they are destitute of vital tissue is the reason, accordingly, why minerals perform no functions. Wanting its sensibility and expansiveness, the stone, the metal, the crystal, once formed, lie forever afterwards in perfect stillness, until assailed, that is, by new chemical agencies from without, tending to decompose them. No alterations take place within their substance; they neither feed, nor breathe, nor procreate; their once active life has subsided into simple, stationary existence. With the organized body it is exactly the reverse. During the whole period of its tenure of life, it presents, more or less evidently, the phenomena of growth, and of change of form and substance, many of the most important changes recurring in definite cycles of succession. Things, in a word, which are recipient only of the inorganic degree of life, are marked by but *one* phenomenon—that of the accretion of their particles into the mass; those which receive the organic degree, present an *assemblage* of phenomena, and these are both simultaneous and continuous. The active life of the mineral ceases as soon as the mineral is formed; that of the organized body goes on unabatedly, and is even more vigorous after the completion of the form proper to it, than before. The diamond ceases from active life as soon as it *becomes* a diamond; whereas the corresponding period in the history of an animal is precisely that of its highest energy commencing.

20. Animals contrasted with plants show distinctions equally sharp, though in many points these two great classes of beings are most intimately allied. In the former, the organs, and therefore the functions are more numerous and varied, and all those now appearing for the first time, have peculiarly noble offices. Such are the eye and the ear, with their respective powers of sight and hearing. The latter kind are distinguished by physiologists as the "Animal" functions; those which are common to both classes of beings, are called the "Vegetative."* In man, for example, the Vegetative functions are feeding, digestion, respiration, &c., (all of which he has in common with the plant), their central organ being the heart, or rather the heart and lungs coöperatively; while the animal functions are those which depend upon the brain. In animals, the organs of the Vegetative functions are generally single, as the heart, the stomach, and the liver; those, on the other hand, of the

---

* Some authors call the Vegetative functions the "*Organic.*" The former is by far the better name, being definite and strict in its application, whereas "Organic" properly denotes *both* classes of functions. The latter is the sense invariably intended in the present volume.

Animal functions, are for the most part arranged in pairs; that is, they are double and correspondent, as in the two eyes and two ears; or they have two symmetrical halves, parallel with the mesian line of the body, as in the nose, the spinal marrow, and the tongue. The functions of the Vegetative organs continue uninterruptedly; the blood, for instance, is in continual circulation; those of the Animal organs are subject to interruptions. Still it is everywhere the *same* life, essentially, which is played forth. The higher and lower presentations come wholly of the peculiar offices, and thence of the capability of the recipient organism to disclose it. The lowest degree of expression is in the simplest forms of vegetables, such as the microscopic fungi, known as moulds and mildew; the highest is in the material body of man. Between these are innumerable intermediate degrees, all referable, however, either to vegetable, or to animal life. In the Vegetable, by reason of its less noble destiny, the operation of life is seen merely in the production of a determinate frame-work of roots, stems, leaves, and flowers, and the maintenance of these in a state of self-nutritive and reproductive activity. In the Animal, it produces analogues of all the organs that the vegetable possesses, after a more elaborate mode, and superadds to them, Nervous matter. This gives sensation, and the power of voluntary motion, and introduces the creature into social communication with the objects around it, such as to the vegetable is utterly unknown. We shall see, further on, how such widely parted extremes are yet consistent with singleness of idea; also, in considering Discrete degrees and the Chain of Nature, how along with the most beautiful serial progression and development, there is absolute separation and distinctiveness, both as regards species, and the great aggregates we call the Kingdoms of nature.

21. To the support of Organic life are needed Food, Air,

and the great dynamic substance or substances known as Heat, Light, and Electricity.* The latter are what authors call the "vital stimuli," their operation, either singly or combined, having long been recognized as the first essential to the manifestation of vital phenomena. Properly speaking, the whole suite should be included under the name of Food, seeing that they equally contribute to the stability of the organism. They are not merely *stimuli*, or excitants of vital action; definite quantities of them must be introduced into the organism, of which they are the *im*ponderable aliment, as food commonly so called, is the ponderable. This is strikingly exemplified in the history of the Cerealia, or Corn-plants, to which a long summer or a short one makes no difference, provided they receive the same aggregate amount of heat and light. Every one knows that if the supply of natural, wholesome aliment be reduced below a certain level, there is alike in plants and animals emaciation and loss of vigor; and that if totally deprived of food, they speedily starve to death. Debarred from regular supplies of Air, Light, Electricity, &c., though the supply of food may be adequate, plants no less than animals, suffer as severely as in the former case. Respiration, the circulation of the blood, the flow of the sap, digestion, assimilation, all stand in need of their united and complementary service. Equally and as absolutely essential is it to the very genesis of the organism, whether we take the child in the womb of its mother, or its counterpart, the embryo seed in the pistil of the flower, excepting, in the former case, the immediate presence and operation of atmospheric air. We shall first

---

* To this list will perhaps have to be added *odyle*, the extraordinary agent to which attention is invited by Reichenbach. See his Researches on Magnetism, Electricity, &c., translated by Dr. Gregory, 1850.

consider the "Vital Stimuli;" secondly, Food; and thirdly, the Atmosphere, in relation to life. This will prepare us to understand the proximate causes and nature of Death; which will lead in turn to the consideration of the great compensating laws of Renewal, and to the curious mysteries of the diversity in the leases or specific terms of life.

22. The most striking illustrations of the importance of Light to the play of life are furnished by the Vegetable kingdom. Secluded from the solar light, plants, if they do not soon die, become wan, feeble, and sickly. What few leaves and shoots may be painfully put forth, are pale-yellow instead of green; and the ordinarily firm and solid stem becomes watery and semi-translucent. If there be an effort made to produce flowers and seeds, that is, to become parents, after self-preservation, the foremost, though it may be unconscious, desire of all living things, it is but to fail miserably. The qualities of a plant are no less weakened by want of light than its constitution is. The acrid become bland, the deleterious innocuous. In gardens and orchards, flowers and fruits accidentally shaded by dense foliage, fail to acquire their proper tint; while of the full sunlight come all the glow and brilliance of the blossom, the purple hue of the peach, the rosy one of the apple. Who has not observed the longing and beautiful affection with which plants kept in parlors turn themselves towards the window; and how the large, broad leaves of the geranium will even press their bosoms to the glass? The sunflower, the heliotrope,* the

* The delicious, vanilla-scented, lilac flower, which now bears the name of Heliotrope is in no way specially deserving of it. Neither is the great golden Sunflower of our autumn gardens, which is so called, not, as often thought, because of remarkable sensitiveness to solar attraction, but because of its vast circular disk and yellow rays.

turnsole, the salsafy, are celebrated for keeping their faces always fixed on "glorious Apollo." It would be much more difficult to find a plant which does *not* turn towards the sun, though its movement might be slower than is fabled. While these confess the sweetness and the potency of the solar presence, that sullen troglodyte, the *Lathrœa squamaria*, or toothwort, of our woods, where the botanist obtains it only by excavating among earth and dead leaves, shows in its skeleton-like configuration and cadaverous hue, that life in the dark is but a compromise with death. When the trees and shrubs, beneath the shade of which it usually secretes itself, are cut away, so as to expose the plant to the full action of the light, like a morose and unsocial man made to laugh against his will, it enlivens into a beautiful pink purple. Superabundance of light, on the other hand, elicits the most beautiful displays, both as to perfection of form, and height of color. Tschudi, in his picturesque "Sketches of Nature in the Alps," tells us that the flowers there have a wonderfully vivid coloring. "The most brilliant blues and reds, with a rich brown, shading to black, are observable amidst the white and yellow flowers of the lower districts, both kinds assuming in the higher regions a yet more pure and dazzling hue." A similar richness of coloring is reported of the vegetation of Polar countries, where the hues not only become more fiery, but undergo a complete alteration under the influence of the constant summer light and the rays of the midnight sun, white and violet being often deepened into glowing purple. This happens not alone with the flowers. Within the arctic circle, the lichens and mosses shine in hues of gold and purple quite unknown to them in lower latitudes. The balsamic fragrance of the Alpine plants, likewise caused by the brilliant light, is, according to Tschudi, no less remarkable and characteristic. From the auricula down to the violet-scented moss (*Byssus colithes*), this strong aromatic property is widely prevalent, and far more so in the high Alps than in the lowlands. The strict physiological reason of the ill development of plants when deprived of the proper amount of light, at least of all *green* plants, is that plant-life, as regards personal nutrition, is spent in the decomposition of carbonic acid, water, and ammonia, from the proceeds of which are manufactured the tissues and their contents; such decomposition bearing a constant ratio, *cæteris paribus*, to the amount of light enjoyed. To certain kinds of sea-weeds, it is proper to remark, light seems, by a curious exception, to be unfriendly and distasteful. This is the case with many of the Rhodospermeæ, as Delesseria sanguinea, D. ruscifolia, and Rhodomenia laciniata, which instead of growing in the open parts of the sea-coast, select obscure hollows, shadowed by overhanging cliffs, and in such dark spots alone attain their highest beauty. Some of this tribe will not grow at all in shallow water, or where there is a full stream of solar light; and such as can bear to be so placed, usually show the incongeniality of their location by degeneracy of form and loss of brilliancy of tint. Delesseria sanguinea, made mock of in a glass vase, speedily loses its lovely crimson, and becomes a mere white membrane. Fondness of seclusion from the full sunlight is remarkable also in many ferns. Under the shade of trees, or upon sheltered hedgebanks, they alone reach their maximum of luxuriance.

23. The value and importance of light to Animal life, though the immediate connection is not so obvious, all experience shows it impossible to over-estimate. There is something more than a metaphor in speaking of the "light of life." Light, in poetic language, *is* life. When Iphigenia in Euripides is reconciling herself to the death so happily averted, she exclaims, χαῖρε μοι, φίλον φάος, "Farewell,

beloved Light!"* Digestion, assimilation, circulation, the functions also of the brain and of the nerves, proceed in a more orderly and agreeable manner when we exclude ourselves as little as possible from the light of heaven. No dwellings are so pleasant, because so healthful, as those which have a southerly aspect: people who live in houses looking chiefly to the North and East, suffer seriously, if not sensibly, from the imperfect sunning of the air; the unkindliness of the aspect imparts itself to the occupants; that the heart should look southwards, our windows should do so. No one can say how much sickness and debility, how much ill-temper and moroseness are not owing to self-imprisonment in dark streets, and dull counting-houses, and back parlors, into which a sunbeam never enters: "Truly the light is sweet, and a pleasant thing it is for the eyes to behold the sun." School-rooms, most of all, should be on the sunny side of the house; no sensible school-master ever places them anywhere else. The curious exception to love of light which occurs in the pink sea-weeds, again occurs in marine Animal life. Almost all the animals which inhabit the sea-side are more numerous under the shelter of rocks than where the coast is open. Compared with such localities, shadowless sands and beaches are untenanted. The colours also of marine animals, like those of the algæ, are often brighter when they dwell in comparative shade, as well exemplified in the prawn. It is only in the gloom of deep holes and rocky pools that the fine zebra-like hues of this pretty creature become fully developed. Fishes, especially those of the sea, are well known to be fonder of night than of day, probably because of darkness being more congenial; and

---

* Iphigenia in Aulis, 1519. See in reference to the passage, The Hieroglyphica of Pierius Valerianus, p. 490, *de Lucerna;* and various citations from the Latin poets in Alciati's Emblemata, p. 720.

the same is probably the reason of many animals being most active in the winter. Here again we have a parallel with the vegetable world; it is when the days are darkest and shortest that the Christmas-rose expands its flowers. Sunshine has a wonderful influence even upon *external form*, as we might anticipate indeed from the improvement it causes in plants. Humboldt ascribes the frequency of deformity among certain nations which clothe but scantily, more to the free action of light upon their bodies, than to any peculiarities in mode of life. Those exquisite shapes which Art has immortalized in marble, doubtless owed not a little to the full and free exposure of the body to the light and air, so agreeable in the fine climate of ancient Greece.

24. We may but read of what Light does for life, but we *feel* what is the agency of Heat. Reduce the supply of heat, and development is checked. Remove it wholly, and the organism, whether animal or vegetable, (except in some few very low forms,) is frozen to death. Hence the instinctive avoidance of the impending evil by the tender, migratory birds and animals; and the behaviour and condition during winter of the hybernating species. It is principally through lack of heat that the frigid zones are nearly bare of vegetation; and that through the increase of temperature, as the equator is approached, the eye is delighted at every step, by a richer luxuriance. "To the natives of the north," says Humboldt, "many vegetable forms, including more especially the most beautiful productions of the earth, (palms, tree-ferns, bananas, arborescent grasses, and delicately-branched mimosas,) remain for ever unknown; for the puny plants pent up in our hot-houses, give but a faint idea of the majestic vegetation of the tropics." The operation of heat in the earliest periods of organic existence, is alone sufficient to indicate how important this agent is to life. In the incubation of birds, the warmth communicated by the

parent to the egg, during her long and patient fidelity to her nest, elicits that response on the part of the germ, which leads on to the hatching of the chick. The seeds of plants stand in similar need of the solar warmth in order to germinate, and acknowledge it as promptly. So, indeed, with the gestation of viviparous animals, as woman. The embryo, embedded in the womb, amplifies into a fully-formed child, not more through the contributions made to its substance by the nutrient apparatus provided for the purpose, than through the agency of the genial warmth which flows into it from all sides, and without which neither limbs nor organs could be moulded.

25. What may be the precise way in which Electricity assists in maintaining life, is as yet a profound secret. From what has been observed, however, there cannot be a doubt that it performs a part fully as energetic as either light or heat, and this whether we take animals or plants. As regards the former, its peculiar relation appears to lie with "nerve-force." Nerve-force is excitable by electricity, and electricity may be produced by the exercise of nerve-force, as exemplified in those remarkable creatures, the Torpedo and the Gymnotus. Our personal sensations, which are an unfailing index to the truth in such inquiries, tell us how exhilarating is an atmosphere well charged with this magical element, and how life languishes when it is deficient or rendered inoperative. Plants receive a corresponding benefit. The evolution of new tissue is greatly accelerated by a plentiful supply of the electric fluid, manifesting itself in rapid and lively growth. For particulars respecting its agency, also concerning the relation of heat, light, and electricity, generally, to Organic life, we must refer the reader to treatises the scope of which allows more room than can be afforded here; giving what space remains to a notice of the grand discovery, so ably set forth by Mr. Grove, that in-

stead of being *three* things, Light, Heat, and Electricity are only *one*, variously set forth, and mutually convertible, the doctrine in short of the "Correlation of the Physical Forces." It is important briefly to consider this doctrine, seeing that it provides, in the estimation of some of the most eminent physiologists of our day, a solution of the great problem of organic life. "That Light and Heat," says Carpenter, "become *transformed into Vital Force,* is shown by the same kind of evidence that we possess of the conversion of Heat into Electricity by acting on a certain combination of metals; of Electricity into Magnetism by being passed round a bar of iron; and of Heat and Electricity into motion when the self-repulsive action separates the particles from each other. For just as Heat, Light, Chemical affinity, &c., are transformed into vital force, so is vital force capable of manifesting itself in the production of Light, Heat, Electricity, Chemical affinity, or mechanical motion; thus completing the proof of that mutual relationship or 'correlation' which has been shown to exist among the physical and chemical forces themselves."* That without heat and electricity, life cannot for one instant be sustained, is indisputable; and that without them, the changes and phenomena which disclose its presence can never occur. Equally true is it that (as specially observable in the Cerealia above-mentioned) there is a definite relation between the degree of vital activity and the amount of heat, light, &c. supplied to the organism. Curious and truly wonderful too is the concord between these "forces" and the vital energy, as regards their *restorative* powers; the warmth of the hand restores the perishing fly, and the voltaic current reanimates the half-drowned man. To say, however, that they are *trans-*

---

* "Principles of Human Physiology," p. 123. 1853. See also the "Projet d'un Essai sur la Vitalité," of Andral, p. 35. Paris, 1835.

formable into a spiritual essence—for if life be derived from God, vital force can be nothing else—seems to savor strongly of such a perfect contentedness with the material as surely does not consist with a pure and devout philosophy. The dependence of life, proximately, upon physical causes, is not questioned; life is no miracle, in the special sense; and it is our plain and bounden duty, as investigators of nature, to attempt to give to this dependence a clear and definite expression. But we are not to talk of "vital force" as if it were a thing of merely terrestrial origin, heat and electricity sublimed and transmuted. "According to this doctrine of correlation"* (*i. e.*, of the physical forces with vital force,) observes an author of no common sagacity, "according to this doctrine, heat has only to pass through a cell-germ to be converted into vitality. This doctrine ends, therefore, in *fire-worshipping;* for it makes the light and heat of the material sun, the fountains of the force of organization; and deems that these pass through vegetables, and become vegetable life; through animals, and become animal life; through brains, and become mind, and so forth. Therefore, a fine day, poured into its vessel, man, becomes transmogrified into virtues; dark nights are converted into felonies; dull November days into suicides; and hot suns into love. This is materialism with spiritualism in its pocket. There is no convertibility of forces between life and nature; there are no cells by which heat can be filtered into vitality."†

* On the general subject of the Correlation of Forces see Mr. Grove's admirable work bearing that title, and an excellent article on the "Phasis of Force" in the National Review for April, 1857.

† "The Human Body, and its connection with Man," by J. J. Garth Wilkinson, p. 389. 1851.

CHAPTER IV.

FOOD.

26. WHEREVER provided with instruments of action, life requires for its maintenance unbroken supplies of food. No organized being can dispense with food altogether, though some, from peculiarity of constitution—as reptiles, the carnivorous mammalia, certain hybernating creatures, and trees—can fast for surprisingly long periods. Plants feed in order that they may enlarge their fabric, and renew, periodically, their foliage and blossoms; animals feed because the exercise of their various organs is attended by decomposition of their very substance, which consequently needs to be repaired to the same extent. While the lungs, the heart, the liver, the muscles, the nerves, perform faithfully the several duties assigned to or demanded of them, it is at the expense of the material they are composed of; and were the loss not speedily compensated, life would soon be necessitated to depart, as it actually does in cases of starvation. For life, in animals, is not merely *living*—it consists not alone in the activity and vigorous exercise of the bodily organs. In order to its energetic playing forth, there is needed a nice balance and alternation of death and renewal in every tissue concerned in the vital processes; and only where exchange of new for old is regularly and actively going on, can life be truly said to reign. We cannot live, in a word, as to our total organism, unless we are always dying as to our atoms; nor is there an instant in which death

is not somewhere taking place. Every effort and every movement kills some portion of the muscles employed; every thought, even, involves the death of some particle of the brain. As fast as devitalized, the atoms are cast out—some through the lungs, others through the skin, &c.; every pore and passage of the body supplying means of exit. So general and incessant is the decomposition, and along with it the rebuilding, that a few weeks probably suffice for the dissolving and reconstruction of the entire structure; certainly it does not occupy many years. In the course of a life-time, "every individual wears out many suits of bodies, as he does many suits of clothes; the successive structures which we occupy bear the same name, and exhibit the same external aspect; but our frames of to-day are no more identical with the frames of our early youth than with those of our progenitors." In this wonderful flux and replacement of the atoms of the body, quite as much consists its admirable adaptation to the purposes of life as in its exquisite mechanism and variety of organs. It is so perfect an instrument of life, because composed of millions of delicate pieces, so slenderly cohering that any one of them can be discarded and replaced without difficulty. Hence, in the aged and the diseased, in whom the tissues are hardened and consolidated, in whom the renewal is slow, difficult, and irregular, we see life proportionately feeble; where, upon the other hand, they are soft and delicate, and renewal rapid, it is in the same ratio strong and beautiful. Historically viewed, the periodical renewal, of the human body at least, is one of the most venerable ideas in physiology. Long before Cuvier's fine comparison of the human fabric to a whirlpool, and Leibnitz's simile of a river, it had been likened to the famous ship of Theseus, which was always the same ship, though from being so often repaired, not a single piece of the original was left. Plato adverts to it both in the Banquet and in the Timæus. Mark, for future use, the grand and inevitable sequence that the essentiality of the body is certainly not to be looked for in the *matter* of which it is built, but must needs consist in a noble, imponderable, invisible something, which the changing physical frame simply encloses and overlies. Mark, too, and alike for future use, the fine analogy between the death and renewal of the constituent elements of the individual human being, and the death and renewal of the atoms of the human race.

27. The use of food, accordingly, is to meet this incessant waste. A corresponding and continuous importation of new material from without, available for the restoration of the several organs, becomes, in consequence of the waste, rigororously indispensable. That such new material may be procured, the loss of the old is signalled in the vehement longing we call hunger: this leads to consumption of it in a crude form; digestion and assimilation then come into play, promptly turning what is consumed into blood, or liquid, circulating flesh, and by the fixation of this wherever wear and tear have been undergone, the process of reparation is completed. Incessantly coursing through the body, the blood, as it arrives at the various parts, gives itself up to the *genius loci:* where muscle is out of repair, muscle is renewed from it; where bone is wanted, bone is renewed; cartilage, brain, nerves, alike suck from this noble fluid their restoration, as originally, from the same beautiful and overflowing cornucopia, their birth and substance. The proximate object of food is thus to nourish the blood.* It is because the *blood* hungers and thirsts, that we feel impelled to eat and drink;

* That the formation of blood is the use of food, appears to have been a very early conclusion. "The gods," says Homer, "neither eat food nor drink the purple wine, *wherefore they are bloodless.*"—Iliad, v. 341

the hunger of the stomach is only the voice with which it clamors. Itself the most wonderful substance in nature—for the sake of the blood, everything else in nature subsists. Light, heat, and electricity, animals, plants, and minerals, all in some way subsidize and minister to it. Man is man only by virtue of his blood, and nature is chiefly admirable as supplying its ingredients. Wherever in the human body there is most blood, there is greatest vital energy, and *vice versâ;* and in exact proportion to the decline from the standard quantity and quality required in it, is the departure from the body of health and vigor.

28. Besides integrity of substance, a certain degree of *temperature* must be kept up in the body, otherwise the muscles would lose their power of contracting, and the nerves their power of conveying impressions to and from the brain. This is partly provided for by the ingress of heat from without, as noticed in the preceding chapter; partly by arrangements for the evolution of heat chemically, within,—such arrangements, like those for rebuilding, being immediately dependent upon supplies of proper food. Hence in the raw material of nutrition, along with the substance suitable for masonry, must be included substance that shall be serviceable as fuel; and organic chemistry seems to prove that it is precisely such material which we instinctively select for our diet. Human food, according to the researches of Liebig, is always either nitrogenous or carbonaceous, or both,—the first element serving to furnish flesh, the second the means of warmth; and it would further appear that it is for the sake of procuring these two in sufficient quantity and proportion, that we almost invariably *compound* our food, mixing vegetables with meat, butter with bread. What seems to be luxury, is simple instinct, acting through the palate. During the period of growth, or in childhood and adolescence, an important additional source of demand for

food is the *increase* which the various tissues are then undergoing. The sphere of the activity of the constructive powers exceeds the actual dimensions of the body, which extends itself, under their impulse, in every direction; and induces, while thus enlarging, a corresponding voraciousness. The demand for food during this period is sill further promoted by the circumstance of the tissues having not acquired the degree of consolidation which they hold in adults, and being therefore more readily susceptible of decomposition. Considered as a local affection of the body, hunger is referable to the nerves of the stomach. No affection is more intimately connected with the nervous system, or more powerfully influenced by nervous states and emotions. Sudden grief, anger, and fright, will often remove it instantaneously, and even change it into loathing. In plants, it is important to observe, there is no decay of the ultimate or elementary tissues, such as occurs in animal organisms, and which it is the design of the nutritive processes in animals to compensate. Instead of this, in the vegetable all is *growth*, till the organ which the growth produces, having fulfilled its destiny, ceases to act, and dies bodily. In plants, therefore, there is no such thing, strictly speaking, as *nutrition*, the true idea of this process being, as above described, reparation of molecular waste.

29. The form, sources, and composition of the food of the two great classes of organized beings, involve varied and most interesting considerations. Here it is unnecessary to do more than indicate a few leading ideas upon the several themes. The *composition* of food must necessarily always be the same as that of the organism which lives upon it,—that is, the crude material of food must needs contain ingredients convertible respectively into blood and sap, and thence into flesh, in its various forms, also bones, and in the plant what are called the vegetable tissues. If such ingredients be not

present, the material cannot be called food. It follows that those foods will be the most serviceable and nutritious which contain in a given bulk the largest proportion of parts capable of being easily assimilated into the body of the eater. More or less nutritious as it may be, the action of the digestive organs always separates from our food precisely the same elements. Eat what we will, the composition of the body does not alter,—explaining the celebrated aphorism of Hippocrates, that there is only *one* food, though there exist many *forms* of food. With all the higher animals, and probably throughout the entire range of animal life, it is precisely the same.

30. Next as to the form of food. The more complex the structure of the organism, and the higher its powers, the more complex must be the aliment on which it lives, and also the more varied in its shape. Man needs a more complex food than the brute races do, and animals in general a more complex one than serves for vegetables. Animals, again, need both solid and liquid aliment, while vegetables take the whole of their food in fluid forms. Although thirst is a violent desire, drink, however, appears by no means indispensable to animal life; for several kinds of creatures, as quails, parrots, and mice, do not drink at all; and individuals of our own species have lived in perfect health and strength, scarcely ever tasting liquids. The Sloth, Waterton tells us, "feeds on leaves, and scarcely ever drinks." The doctrine, originally started by Mirbel, that animals live upon organic matter only, and vegetables upon *in*organic, and which is often thought to carry with it a valid distinction between them, is defective; plants, though they absorb the greater part of their nutriment from the atmosphere, and though they take up solutions of many purely mineral matters, also consume dead organic substances; the difference between their habits in this respect, compared with

the custom of animals, being that the latter eat those substances in the bulk, while plants need that they shall first be disintegrated and dissolved,—that they shall have already undergone, in fact, the very process which it is the first office of the animal stomach to effect. Parasites, such as the mistletoe and Orobanche, so far from feeding on purely inorganic substances, or even on dead or decomposing matter, subsist on the living, circulating juices of the trees and plants on which they fix themselves. An exacter distinction is that animals destroy what is actually in possession of life, in order that they may support themselves; while plants, with rare exceptions, are innocent of such deeds. The exceptions occur in the singular plants called fly-catchers; botanically *Drosera,* and *Dionœa,* inhabitants of bogs and morasses, the former abundantly in England. Their leaves are so constructed as to entrap midges and other little flies; the juices of whose bodies, or the gases yielded by their decay, appear salutary and agreeable to them. Thus it is, however, that everything in the world gets eaten sometime; the ceaseless activity of nature is conversion of what is lower into what is higher,—"above the lowest nature each thing is eaten and eater, end and beginning in succession."

31. The *particular* diet, both of animals and of plants, is a subject of inexhaustible interest. That of plants is the leading idea of the new science of "Agricultural Chemistry." Doubtless, the mechanical character of the soil has its influence; but it can hardly be from this circumstance alone that we find the golden cistus, the vervain, and many delicate grasses in perfection only when their roots can shoot in calcareous earth; that some plants thrive best on sandstone, others upon clay; and that the sea-shore alone is found possessed of the salsola, the sea-convolvulus, and the lovely but formidable Eryngo, the blue touch-me-not of the sand hills. Wheat and other cereals require silex; the oak is

reputed to love a soil with iron in it. Generally speaking, however, there is a great uniformity in the tastes of plants, as proved by their intermixture in the fields. Taking one with another, two substances alone seem to suffice them—water and carbonic acid. Widely different is it with animals. Here almost every species has an especial liking, though all tastes may be classed under some few general heads. Gregarious animals live mostly upon the fruits of the earth; solitary ones upon the flesh of other animals. Among the latter, or the carnivora, there are feeders on fish, flesh, and fowl respectively; among the herbivorous, some feed on leaves, some on roots, some pick out the seeds, others take the whole plant, the bees love only the honey. This various choice, together with the selection of different *species* of plants and animals by certain creatures, and the rejection of others, allows of all finding a plentiful supply of what is salutary, and this without interfering with the wants of others. Linnæus tells us, that after a careful course of trials with the domesticated animals, and about five hundred species of the ordinary plants of the fields, the horse was found to eat two hundred and sixty-two, the cow two hundred and seventy-six, the sheep three hundred and eighty-seven. To this, says that observant old naturalist, Benjamin Stillingfleet, is to be referred that capital economy which knows that when eight cows have been in a pasture, and can no longer get nourishment, two horses will do very well there for some days; and when the horses have taken all they care for, four sheep will still find supplies. There are few things more curious in rural life than to watch a cow while grazing, and see how she will push aside the buttercups. Some animals care only for what is harsh, as the camel, whose greatest relish is an oasis of tough, prickly bushes, such as the ass itself would turn away from. Thus consumed, by one animal or other, it follows, that no plant is absolutely uneatable, no plant, indeed, absolutely *poisonous*, but only poisonous to particular creatures. Probably there is not a single species of the vegetable kingdom but is eaten, or partly eaten, by a creature appointed to it, however distasteful and even deleterious it may be to others. The horse gives up the water-hemlock to the goat; the goat leaves the monkshood for the horse; if man eats of either plant, he dies. Slugs eat that very poisonous toadstool, the *Agaricus muscarius;* also the *Agaricus phalloides*, a species still more terrible from the rapidity of its deadly effect. Though the leaves of the laurel are so obnoxious to insects in general as to be the readiest poison for them with the entomologist, the caterpillar of one kind, the *Orgyia antiqua*, finds them wholesome. When driven by famine, it would seem, nevertheless, that there are no creatures but what will eat of other kinds of food than they ordinarily select, and which they are fitted for by nature. Spallanzani made a pigeon live on flesh, and an eagle on bread. Animals domesticated by man, and thus leading a semi-artificial life, will, apart from necessity, also curiously change their habits as to food. In some parts of Persia, according to Fraser, "the cattle have but little pasture; . . . the chief article of their food is dried fish, which, with pounded date-stones, is all they get to eat for a considerable portion of the year." Every one is acquainted with the extraordinary eating powers of *insects*. With these creatures, eating seems ordained less for the preservation of the individual than for the destruction of effete organic matter, a fact peculiarly observable in the Diptera and the Coleoptera. Some kinds seem created chiefly to overpower other insects. Were it not for the carnivorous lady-birds, the fat, green, vegetarian aphides which infest the stalks of so many of our sweetest flowers, would be a thousand times more troublesome.

"Exactly what browsing flocks and herds of deer are to the quadruped of prey, the tribes of aphides are to the lady-birds, and some two or three allies of the Coccinella race; save for which destroyers, not a lover of sweet posies could gather a rose or a honeysuckle undefiled." To the execution of these offices by the insect tribe, the almost incalculable number of their species, the extremely rapid multiplication of many, the unparalleled voracity of others, and the quickness with which digestion is carried in their very short intestinal canal, all tend to contribute. Fishes, and marine animals in general, perform the same offices for the sea that insects subserve upon the land; incessantly destroying and devouring, they contribute immensely to the preservation of its purity; some, as crabs, consuming indiscriminately both dead and living prey, and in their cruel and greedy habits reiterating those of the hyena and the wolf. The stomachs of these creatures, like those of many fishes, not infrequently contain abundance of beautiful little shells, principally microscopic, gathered up during their travels in the country of the mermaids.

32. Man, in a limited sense, is *omnivorous;* not absolutely; he cannot eat many things which to inferior creatures are pleasant, as bones, and the leaves of trees. Whether, as to first intent, he is an herbivorous or a carnivorous animal, is a question only for enthusiasts. His anatomical structure supplies an equal argument for either side, Helvetius and others deeming that it proves a carnivorous nature; and the modern school of vegetarians, an herbivorous one. Rousseau ingeniously urges, in support of the latter view, that woman is a uniparous animal, and provided with no more than two breasts, circumstances predominant among the females of the brute herbivora; while in the females of the brute carnivora, the number is in both cases considerably

higher.* Man is not intended to live upon either kind of food by itself. Inhabiting every variety of climate, he would have been ill provided for, if so restricted; as it is, he can dwell in countries which afford only animal food, or only vegetable food. There are nations who have little within reach besides dates, yams, and the ivory-nut; in the extreme north, there is nothing to be had but flesh. Probably enough, the number of human beings who subsist on fruits and farinaceous roots is preponderant. Though animal food is so largely consumed in cold countries, the inhabitants of the sunnier and warmer parts of the earth derive their chief nourishment from trees and plants. This, however, is no proof of its superior adaptedness; there can be little doubt that human aliments prepared from the flesh of animals, are, generally speaking, both more nutritious and more digestible. The herbivorous creatures killed for the table having already converted the nutrient substances of the vegetable world into animal matter, our own digestive organs are saved the labor. The cow, the sheep, the deer, are natural bridges between the grass of the field and the human body.

33. Not less interesting than the variety of the food of different animals is the variety in the organs by which are accomplished the two preliminary processes of nutrition, or prehension and mastication. So rigidly, moreover, are they modeled according to the character of the food upon which the animal subsists, that we may infer what it eats by merely observing its extremities and mouth. Feet, for instance, of the kind called hoofs, are incapable of seizing living prey; so that all creatures which possess them are necessarily herbivorous. Indeed, there is scarcely an organ of the animal

* *Sur l'Origine de l'inégalité parmi les hommes.* Note 6. *Œuvres,* tome iii., pp. 193—195, very curious and amusing.

frame but serves a more or less direct purpose in regard to feeding, the wing, the fin, the claw, all are bestowed towards this end; so likewise is that amazing quickness of the senses which makes the sight, the hearing, the smell of many predaceous quadrupeds and birds so vastly superior to that of man.* The organ peculiarly identified with the feeding of animals, and which is commonly allowed to be a distinctive characteristic when compared with plants, namely, the *stomach*, is given them because of their powers of locomotion. Vegetables, fixed in the soil, and feeding by their leaves and spongioles on the matter which envelopes them, do not require a special organ of digestion, into which food can be received in bulk. Animals, on the other hand, are obliged to take their food at intervals not so much suited to their wants as to their opportunities of obtaining it. Between the feeding of brutes and mankind, the only essential difference is, that while the former consume their food in the state in which it is yielded by nature, man, even in his rudest condition, subjects it, for the most part, to some kind of cookery. Man, it has been said humorously, is "the cooking animal."

34. The mere knowledge of the waste of the tissues, and of the organic need for food thence arising, would not be a sufficient provocative to eat. Absorbed in darling occupations, many men would never think of taking food, did not hunger at last impel them. As a physical agent, hunger is thus of an importance impossible to over-rate: and its moral value is necessarily commensurate. It is the chief source of social order; for if mankind could do without food, they would be out of reach of rule and control, and necessary

---

* See for illustration in detail, Sir T. C. Morgan's "Sketches of the Philosophy of Life," chap. iii., "The Combination of Organs and Functions."

subordination would not exist. "Hunger," says Bray, "has been the chief source of man's progression, seeing that it constitutes, principally, that necessity which is the mother of invention. We might, perhaps, have been made to do without eating and drinking; but instead of this being a blessing, we should thereby be destitute of the most potent stimulus of the mental powers, upon the action of which powers happiness wholly depends. The privilege of requiring no bread would not be equal to the advantages man derives from the law of nature which compels him to earn it by the sweat of his brow; for nature has imposed no more labor than is pleasurable and necessary to health—unjust laws and regulations with respect to the distribution of the products of human labor, compel the majority to toil more than is consistent with health and happiness—but more fatal than unjust laws would it be to the well-being of society, if all necessity for exertion were abrogated.* No one need think ill of eating, or of any of its associations, except the abuse. Good, substantial, wholesome food, properly cooked, and neatly served up, is one of the highest proofs and privileges of civilization; it is a criterion of every well-conducted household, and of every true and clever wife; while the legitimate enjoyment of it is one of the most honest and innocent of pleasures. All sensible and good-natured people are fond of eating; and one of the pleasantest things it is possible either to feel in one's self or to witness in another, is a healthy and natural readiness for the bounties of the table. To satisfy nature without surfeiting it, is one of the foremost of the "good works" we are required to enact. Thankful enjoyment of our daily bread is no small part of Christianity. If "lying lips" "be an abomination to the Lord," so is the ingratitude of asceti-

* "Philosophy of Necessity." Vol. I.

cism; and infinitely more so, the dyspepsia which disables the intemperate from the great, universal duty of all mankind to *have a good appetite.* While all possible forms of intemperance and excess are denounced both in the Old Testament and New, the substantial viands gathered from the fields and the vineyards, the firstlings of the flocks and herds, the fig, the olive, and the pure juice of the grape, are promised, over and over again, as the rewards of virtuous toil, and catalogued with the blessings to be received in this lower world. "I have no patience," says a wise writer, "with those who pretend not to care for their dinner, or the ludicrous assumption that 'spiritual' negations imply superior souls. A man who is careless about his dinner, is generally one of flaccid body and feeble mind. As old Samuel Johnson authoritatively said—'Sir, a man seldom thinks of anything with more earnestness than he thinks of his dinner; and if he cannot get *that* well dressed, *he may be suspected of inaccuracy in other things.*' When a man is not basely insensible to hunger of soul, the keen intellectual voracities and emotional desires, he is all the healthier, all the stronger, all the better for a noble capacity for food—a capacity which becomes noble when it ministers to a fine, and not merely to a gluttonous nature."* Even a *plain* diet is but half-good. It cannot be doubted that, on the whole, refinement, in board as well as lodging—being a fruit of intelligence—is favorable alike to health and longevity. There are advantages we little think of in those culinary ingenuities which, not significantly adding to the cost of our food—in fact, reducing it, by subserving to diminish waste—at once modify and neutralize ill flavours, and so greatly augment its pleasant sapidity. The pleasure of meal-times is one of the prerogatives of human nature.

* "Sea-side Studies." *Blackwood's Magazine*, September, 1856.

The lower mammalia—the only other animals who appear to enjoy the flavour of their food—are insensible to *haut-gout.* Granivorous birds and most kind of fishes not only have cartilaginous tongues, which prevent them from tasting, but swallow their food whole, guided probably to the choice of it by sight rather than taste or smell. Fishes seem to depend entirely on the eye, if we may judge from the readiness with which they swallow artificial bait. Man's palate, in short, was not given him for nothing; but to procure pleasures for him commensurate with his patrician rank.

35. The benefits which accrue to the body from supplying it with a sufficiency of wholesome food, show in the strongest light the evils which result from *in*sufficiency. Disease is one of the first. Many diseases are induced by it, many are aggravated. Sanitary movements having reference to the poor, cannot possibly effect any lasting amelioration of their condition so long as they go short of proper aliment. It is worthy the attention of philanthropists, that epidemic and pestilential diseases in particular are far more widely fatal in their ravages among the ill-fed than among the well-fed. Certainly there are several such diseases which assail rich and poor alike—small-pox, measles, and scarlet-fever, for example; but even these are much more destructive when they attack persons who have been forced to subsist on poor or too scanty nourishment. Legislators, no less than the charitable, may find in this fact, a vitally important principle of action. Insufficiency overprolonged induces the slow and miserable death of starvation, and no physical calamity can be conceived of as more terrible. Yet starvation—actual, killing starvation—is perhaps the least part of the injury to the human race which comes of privation of needful sustenance. Actual death from hunger is only an occasional thing. The evils which accrue from the debilitating effects of *customary* stint, life still drag-

ging on, are incalculably more extended and severe. Even the physical disease which they engender is a slight evil compared with the impeded *mental* action which must needs follow. A miserable, starving dietary, while it weakens the body, half-paralyzes the soul, and not seldom leads direct to insanity itself. When we remember how entirely the brain depends for its nourishment upon the blood, and that if this sovereign pabulum of life and nervous energy be either diminished in quantity or deteriorated in quality, no organ of the body can possibly work well, how easy it is to see that between insufficient, innutritious diet, and prostration of mind, there is little less than an inevitable connection. Every man has experienced the feeling of debility which attends hunger but a little longer unsatisfied than usual, and how swift and lively is the revival of every function of the mind as well as body which follows its proper gratification. The difficulty of awakening the intelligence of a poorly-fed child compared with that of the well-nourished one, is known to every observant teacher in town Sunday-schools. Intellectual productions which are born, not as literature should always and only be, of the soul's going to it as the hart to the water-brooks, but of the howling of the dogs of hunger, betray no less plainly their miserable origin. Thinking, like acting, requires a good substratum of physical nourishment. Genius, though it has sometimes turned to vegetarianism, is rarely found adhering to it; all its greatest works have been achieved on a basis of generous diet. This is not all. Where the body is debilitated by hunger, the affections also are necessarily dull, and little excitable to anything better than sensualities. Any man who has been compelled to undergo the hardships of fasting, whether by poverty, or the exigencies of travel in remote places, knows the gradual inroad of cross-grained views, indolence, and recklessness on an empty stomach. The crowning and deadly evil which comes of insufficient nourishment is, accordingly, the vitiation of man's *moral* nature; and what a lesson is there in this for the Home Missionaries of Christianity and their patrons! It is no less vain than aggravating to preach faith and loving-kindness where father and mother and children lie huddled together in the pains and apathy of hunger. To the starving, religion may well appear folly and hypocrisy; nor is it any marvel that it should fail to interest them. So long as the gospel is proffered *without* its proper preface of ministry to man's physical necessities, the poor must not only be expected to decline it, but they are not altogether unjustified in so doing, for God requires no man to take sermons and benedictions as a substitute for the bread which the body needs. Every one knows how unamiable even the best-fed are liable to become if kept too long waiting for their meals—how inaccessible they are at such times to appeals which *after dinner* meet most gracious response.* Is it surprising, then, that religious truth should find more indifference than welcome among the hungry and half-nourished? It is difficult for a famished man to believe that there is a Father in heaven till he feels that he has brothers on earth. If there be one farce more wretched than another, it is the building a "Ragged Church" and holding "special religious services" as the first thing indispensable to the bettering the condition of the poor.†

---

* Voltaire knew this well when he told place-seekers—"Il faut toujours prendre *mollia fandi tempora.* Il y a une grande analogie entre les intestines et nos passions, notre manière de penser, notre conduite."

† See for illustrative details on the general subject, "An Inquiry into the Morbid Effects of Deficiency of Food, chiefly with reference to their occurrence among the Destitute Poor." By R. B. Howard, M. D. London and Manchester, 1839.

36. Too *much* food is as bad as too little. To sacrifice to the stomach that nervous energy which ought to be devoted to the brain, the organ of our most ennobling and most pleasurable faculties, is, in fact, so far as regards the retention of genuine manliness, little better than to commit suicide outright. Disease, though probably a third part of all that there is in the world is attributable to this cause, is, as in a former instance, the least of the evils that have to be affiliated on ill-regulated eating: infinitely more dire are the peevishness and ill-humor which it engenders, the gloomy, hypochondriacal and dissatisfied tempers which generally overtake the intemperate eater and drinker, and make him a pest both to himself and to society. Many a man's fall and ruin have come of the overloaded and thence disordered stomach of another; as many a man's rise and prosperity of another's temperance and cheerful health. No less destructive is intemperance to the intellectual energies. The intellects which lie sunk in sluggishness through overloading the stomach, are incomparably more numerous than those which are slow and stupid by nature. The authors themselves of their condition, the cross and imbecile through over-feeding, do not belong to society proper; they are not human, yet neither are they brutes, for no brute is intemperate; no longer men, gluttons and drunkards form an outside class by themselves, the nobleness of their nature to be estimated, as in all other cases, by the quality and end of their delights. It is worthy of remark, that nothing is more speedily and certainly destructive also of the beauty of the countenance. Diet and regimen are the best of cosmetics; to preserve a fair and bright complexion, the digestive organs need primary attention.

37. It is a striking and highly-suggestive fact in human economy, and one here deserving to be noticed, that the two physical powers which have most intimate relation with life,

the one, to its maintenance in the individual, the other to its communication to new beings, should be precisely those which, while they fill it with energy by right exercise, and confer the keenest of sensuous pleasures, are contrariwise the very powers through which may be inflicted, by abuse, the deepest injuries it is susceptible of. Eating and drinking, attended to as nature directs, are the essential origin of every animal pleasure, and the basis of moral and intellectual happiness; similarly, the initiative of the sweet privilege of offspring invigorates both body and mind,* and is the foundation of home and its smiling circle, with all the dearest and most beautiful affections of humanity. The punishments, on the other hand, which fall upon abuse of the first, are paralleled exactly in the intellectual dulness, the melancholy, the pusillanimity and weariness of life which form the inevitable retribution of excess in the other. By Hunger and Love is the world held together and sweetened; by Hunger and Love is it disgraced and made wretched. These are the two poles of the little world of human nature, round which everything else revolves; the very structure of the body in its relation to them corresponding with and resulting from the polar idea. It may be added, that where one of these great institutions is honored, there also, for the most part, is the other; where either is profaned, the profanation extends to both. Though temperance and purity may sometimes not coëxist in nice balance, no two things are ever more frequently in company than gluttony, overdrinking, and immodesty. It is in the intimate relation which they bear to life that the reason exists why in all

---

* See on the latter points, Feuchsterleben's "Principles of Medical Psychology," (Sydenham Society's vol., 1847,) sect. 67, p. 181. The author cites an extraordinary instance in "Casanova, who at such moments solved the most difficult mathematical problems."

ages there has been an intuitive reverence in rightly-ordered minds for the seal of sexual love; and why a species of sanctity has from the earliest days of history attached to eating and drinking, which in ancient times entered largely into religious ceremonies, as they do now and will for ever in the most sacred rite of Christianity. "Eating and drinking," says Feuerbach, "are themselves religious acts, or at least *ought* to be so. With every mouthful, we should think of the God who gave it." It is but an amplification of the custom, which commences every procedure of interest or importance with a plentiful spread upon the table. It may not be suspected, and is often dishonored, but the origin of the practice at least was a devout one. Friendship pursues the same course; because, as life is the most precious of possessions, the highest act of goodness that generous sentiment can perform is to provide means for its maintenance and prolongation. To offer food is symbolical of sincerely wishing health and longevity. How beautiful are affection and the gift of nourishment united in the first tenderness of the mother towards her babe! She loves and she feeds. Even the plant, when it opens its seed-pods and lets its offspring fall to the earth, bestows upon each little embryo an imitative bosom in the milk-like farina which encloses it, and which suckles it during germination.

CHAPTER V.

THE ATMOSPHERE IN ITS RELATION TO LIFE.

38. By the Air—in repose the atmosphere, in movement the wind—"we live, and move, and have our being." So with all other living creatures. The very word "animal," signifies "breather." "Animated nature" means breathing nature; "inanimate" that which does not breathe. The corresponding Greek terms *ζωὸς* and *ζῶον* are similarly derived, through *ζάω*, to live, from *ἄεω*, to breathe, and the intensitive prefix *ζὰ*. Grateful for these expressive figures, the poetic Greeks reflected them on to their source, calling the summer breezes the *zephyrs*, literally the "life-bringers." Zephyrus was emphatically the west wind, and deified, was said to produce flowers and fruit by the sweetness of his breath, charmingly alluded to by Homer in his description of the gardens of Alcinous.* *Ζεὺς* or Jupiter

* Odyssey vii. 119. Compare Virgil—

"——— Zephyris cum læta vocantibus æstas;"
"When gay summer comes, invited by the zephyrs."
Georgic iii. 322.

See also Lib. ii. 330. Modern poets have freely taken up the idea, and often with great elegance and success, as in the "Paradiso" of Dante,—

In quella parte, ove surge ad aprire
Zeffiro dolce le novelle fronde
Di che si vede Europa rivestire.—Canto xii. 46–48.

"In that clime where rises the sweet zephyr to unfold the new leaves wherein Europe sees herself fresh clothed."

himself was originally only a personification of the air whence it is that in the poets his names are not uncommonly used in the place of *aer* and *aura*, as in the *malus Jupiter*, *sub Jove frigido*, &c., of Horace, and when Theocritus says that Ζεὺς "is one while indeed fair, but at another time he rains." Aratus styles the air Ζεὺς φυσικὸς, the physical God. Æschylus gives it the epithet "divine." Virgil describes it as *omnipotens pater Æther*. "But can air," says Cicero, "which hath no form, be God? For the Deity must necessarily be not only of some form, but the most beautiful." The mediate source of life to every occupant of earth, Hare describes it beautifully as the "unfathomable ether, that emblem of Omnipresent Deity, which everywhere enfolding and supporting man, yet baffles his senses, and is unperceived, except when he looks upwards and contemplates it above him."

39. The air is the great physician of the world. Health confides in it as its most faithful friend. The weak it invigorates, the weary it refreshes. What is more grateful than to go from a close room into the pure, blowing breath of heaven, even if it be but on a barren highway! What more animating and delicious than to exchange the hot, perspiring streets for the breezes of the hills or of the sea! It ministers largely even to our *moral* well-being. Children at boarding-schools are always better disposed to be diligent and well-behaved when the day has been commenced with a walk in the fresh air. Under its genial stimulus we forget our vexations and disappointments, we become cheerful and vivacious, and thence—what without cheerfulness is impossible—more willing "to refuse the evil and choose the good." No wonder that the poets seem never in happier mood than when the wind is perceived wafting through their verses—

This castle hath a pleasant seat; the air
Nimbly and sweetly recommends itself
Unto our gentle senses.

This guest of summer,
The temple haunting martlet, doth approve
By his lov'd mansionry, that the heavens' breath
Smells wooingly here.

Far more intimate than we suppose is the relation of the atmosphere to the spiritual and intellectual. Nothing so powerfully stimulates intellectual productiveness, where the slightest capacity for it is present, as a walk in a gently-blowing wind. To the brilliant purity of the atmosphere of Athens, and of Greece in general, and the happy temperature of the gales which fanned its hills, so favorite a topic with the panegyrists of that lovely country, are justly ascribed "the preëminence in learning, taste, literature, and the arts, in all that constituted *σοφὶα* in its widest acceptation, which distinguished Athens among the nations of the civilized world."* Æschylus enumerates among the blessings of a highly-favored land, "the gales of the winds blowing with clear sunshine." Pindar gives the same to the Islands of the Blest, "where shine the golden flowers."

40. At all times and seasons, with all forms and conditions of beings, it is no less the function of the Air to *embellish*. Who so rosy in the cheek as they who oftenest seek the pure country air! How does the plainest face improve, as it blushes under the courtship of the summer breezes! Virgil, with the true poetic instinct, makes Æneas owe his beauty to the heavenly breath of Venus—

---

* Consult, upon the connection of the Greek and Italian atmosphere with their sculpture, Winckelman's "History of Art among the Ancient Greeks," Part 1, section 3.

Namque ipsa decoram
Cæsariem nato genitrix, lumenque juventæ
Purpureum, et lætos oculis *afflârat* honores.

"For Venus herself had adorned her son with graceful locks, flushed him with the radiant bloom of youth, and breathed a sprightly lustre on his eyes."

The wind is necessary even to the vitalizing of the aspects of insensate nature. Scenes dull and uninviting in its absence, become pleasant when we visit them under the inspiration of a breeze; the loveliest lose in charm if the winds be asleep, though viewed by the light of summer. For this is not merely because the zephyrs temper the too fervent heat of the sunbeams, and by their physical action on the lungs and system generally give buoyancy and elasticity to the limbs, and thus enlarge our capacity for enjoyment. Nature never shows so lovely when *still* as when in *movement;* and it is by the wind that all her charms of motion are produced, whether of the clouds, or the trees, or the corn-fields, or the delicate stalks of the harebells. The grandeur of the unceasing roll of the sea, though partly owing to another cause, proves in itself how mighty an ally to whatever is competent to become beautiful or sublime, is this viewless and marvelous visitant. Motion embellishes nature thus largely, because it is an emblem and characteristic of *life,* to contemplate which, is one of the soul's highest pleasures, by reason of its own vitality. It loves to behold its immortality pictured in the outward world, be it ever so faintly; and if it meet no reflex in its surveys, feels defrauded and unsatisfied. The correspondence of the *forms* of nature with the particular elements of our spiritual being, encourages this secret love of movement so strong within the soul; for the soul not only sees in external nature the counterparts of its elements and qualities, but reflections likewise of its activities and deeds. The swaying of the trees, the bending of the flowers, the waving of the corn, severally picture occurrences in the inner life—the one kind promoted by the wind of nature, the other by the Spirit of God.

41. We depend upon the atmosphere for the effectuation of the powers of *sense*. Eyes, ears, nose, mouth, skin or seat of touch, would all be impotent without it. Our physical power of seeing, for example, depends on our inhabiting an atmosphere competent to receive and diffuse the light transmitted from the sun; and our power of feeling in its equal adaptedness to receive and diffuse the solar heat. There is no feeling where there is no warmth; what greater antagonism than between cold and sensation? No *sound* would exist in nature, if there were not an atmosphere sensible to vibrations; here is its needfulness to *hearing*. So with odors and flavors, which it is only by inhalation we distinguish and enjoy—here are smell and taste. If we want to avoid the bitterness of physic, we hold the breath; if to feast on some rich bounty to the palate, we inspire. How beautiful, again, is the imagery here disclosed! As the atmosphere gives ability to see and hear physically, so does the divine life, as it flows into man's soul, fill him with power to exercise Intellect and Affection, which are spiritual sight and feeling. Love, or the will-principle, has from the beginning been "warmth," and Intelligence, or the mental eye, "light." Doubtless, man may *pervert* these inestimable gifts; just as the earth, which keeps fashion and pace with him in everything, applies the pure, sacred sunshine to the production of thorns and nettles as well as flowers. But he has no intellectual or affectional *power* within him, but what is communicated from God; just as he has no power of seeing or of feeling but what he owes momentarily and continuously to the sun or its derivatives. All that man *receives*

is heavenly; only what he prepares in and of himself, is bad. The atmosphere brings day-light though the sun be obscured. However overcast the skies, there is yet produced sufficient illumination by the refracting properties of the atmosphere to constitute day. Here is shown, that however thick the clouds which rise up to interpose between God and our hearts, he himself is ever shining steadily beyond them, and in his benevolence transmits to us sufficient for our needs. God never deserts any one, not even the most wicked; "He is kind even to the unthankful and the evil;" and though man, like the earth sending up its dense vapors, may shut out the direct sunbeams which descend towards him, he is still provided with a diffused light of refreshing, energizing succor, brought by the all-pervading, all-penetrating Spirit. "Whither shall I go from thy Spirit, or whither shall I flee from thy presence?" From the same circumstance, *i. e.* the refracting properties of the atmosphere, we enjoy the solar light for a long time before the sun actually rises above the horizon, and for as long a period after its setting. In the evening, when by the rotation of the earth the sun itself is made to disappear, beams of light are still passed into the higher regions of the air, and thence diffused downwards to the surface of the earth, so that for a while we are unconscious of the loss. Except for this beautiful provision, the evening sun would in a moment set, and the earth be shrouded in sudden darkness. In the morning, by a similar process of irradiation, the atmosphere receives and sheds abroad beams which are not yet visible.

42. The eye and the ear, or sight and hearing, are the types and continents of the senses generally. So, in the conveyance by the atmosphere of light and sound, is summed up, representatively, all that it is the function of the Divine life to communicate. For sound, when its tones

are agreeable and harmonious, is *music*, and music is objective or visible nature reiterated in a vocal form—the audible counterpart of whatever is lovely and perfect to the eye. Hence the wonderful and enchanting variety in the sounds of nature; a variety sufficient, as we have elsewhere seen, to furnish the foundations of all language.* The dashing of waterfalls, the roar of the sea, the voices of the trees in their different kinds, each intoning to the wind in a new mode, together with the multitudinous diversities of utterance proper to the animate part of creation, are not mere accidental results of physical conformation, nor are they meaningless or arbitrary gifts. Every one of them is inseparably identified with the object that utters it, because of an original and immutable agreement in quality. Music, in its essential nature, is an expression of the Creator as truly as his objective works. Expressed in *forms*, the air presents him to the eye—the organ preëminently of the intellect: expressed in *sounds*, it presents him to the ear—the organ sacred to the affections. When we listen to a beautiful melody or "*air*," it is surveying a charming and varied landscape, vivid with life, and adorned with innumerable elegances, only addressed to another sense—heard instead of seen. It is not only a sublime fact that God thus doubly places himself before us—it is a necessary result of his very nature; for music stirs the soul so deeply because of its primitive relation to his goodness, and thus to everything connected with our emotional life; objective nature, on the other hand, so largely delights the intellect (having only a secondary influence on the heart), because it is fashioned after the ideas of his wisdom. Each, moreover, assumes its loveliest when the other is in company, because in Him

---

* "Figurative Language: its Origin and Constitution," chapters 7 and 8.

their prototypes are married. Never is nature so beautiful as when we view it in the hearing of true music; in no place does music sound so sweet as amid her responsive and tranquil retreats.

> Why should we go in?
> My friend Stephàno, signify, I pray you,
> Within the house, your mistress is at hand,
> And bring your music forth into the air.
> Here will we sit, and let the sounds of music
> Creep in our ears.

Echo, due like other sounds to the agency of the atmosphere, exemplifies the same fine truths. The sympathy we feel with the objective forms of nature is the equivalent of the agreeable answers with which she acknowledges our voice. Echo, in her beautiful and undelayed replies, is the image and emblem of the responses in which the emotions of man's spirit, when he addresses himself to God, are immediately reflected back upon himself, coming invisibly, he knows not whence, but with a magical and most sweet power. No wonder that the poets have in all ages given Echo a fond and grateful mention.*

43. Let us pass on to the consideration of the air in its immediate bearing upon the maintenance of organic life.

---

* What can be more beautiful than the following, in the "Persians" of Æschylus (ἐπεί γε μέντοι κ. τ. λ. 386–391)—"When Day, drawn by white steeds, had overspread the earth, resplendent to behold, first of all a shout from the Greeks greeted Echo like a song, and Echo from the island rock in the same moment shouted back an inspiring cry." Moschus, in his elegy on Bion, and Bion, in his own sweet poem upon the death of Adonis, represent Echo as sharing in their lamentations, as does Milton, bewailing Lycidas. Other elegant allusions occur in Horace, Odes 1, 20; Tasso, Gerusalemme xi. 11; Euripides, Shakspere, Camoens, Shelley, and Byron, particularly one in Manfred.

Grand as are the capacities of the vital stimuli, or heat, light, and electricity, and invaluable as are the uses subserved by feeding, it remains incontestably true that without continuous supplies of fresh air, Life cannot go on. We are forever referred back to Respiration as the prime characteristic of a healthy, living creature. The assimilation of food may be suspended for a time; darkness and severe cold may be endured, the former even for years; but respiration must be steady, or the creature dies. Every living thing breathes more or less; only the lowest forms of animal life can bear intermissions of breathing for any considerable period; even the foul parasites called *Entozoa* cannot live without air, though secluded by their position from direct contact with the atmosphere. Entophytal fungi, or those which are found in the interior of other plants, and sometimes in the bodies of animals, are for the most part only the mycelia of species which the imperfect supply of air prevents from developing into the perfect form.

44. Not only is life, as a whole, inseparable from respiration, but every variety in the *manifestation* of life. Where respiration is vigorous, as in the feathered tribes, life is energetic; where it is feeble, as in the reptile, life is slow. Similar phenomena pertain to the various epochs of life. "The restlessness of the child, and the activity of the boy, correspond with the vigor of their breathing: the calmness and power of the man are combined with a usually tranquil respiration, capable of being increased to the utmost as occasion calls for the higher energies of life; in the old man, deliberate in his movements, respiration is limited, and usually slow." Breathing varies even with the condition of the body, and its employments. We breathe differently in sickness and in health; differently asleep and awake; differently in the performance of every action of our animal organs. We breathe in one mode when we walk, in another when we run. Breath-

8

ing, accordingly, is not only a physiological but a *representative* phenomenon. In the respiratory breast dwell, along with its health, magnanimity and heroic courage; where the breathing is languid, we look but for timorousness and debility. In our own species, the face itself, the silent echo of the heart, is not a more faithful index to our states, either of body or mind, than is our breathing. As the emotions manifest themselves in the play of the muscles and the light of the eyes, as they are shown, too, in the tone of voice, in the harshness, the tremor, the asperity or the sweetness of the uttered sound, and are interpreted thereby, so is it with the attendant breathing. Let us but hear how a person is breathing, and though he be out of sight we may infer to a certain extent, how he is employed, and judge of his general tranquility or the reverse. See what testimony to it there is in Language! To be "animated," to be "spirited," or "full of spirits," is to have breath in plenty. To be "out of spirits," "spiritless," or "dispirited," is to be destitute of breath; *literally* in every case; for all agreeable, lively, or "life-like" emotions, tend to raise and quicken the breath, while depressing ones tend to lower and deaden it. Eagerness pants; despondency sighs; weariness yawns; extreme fear makes us breathless or "aghast."*

45. The *object* of respiration is closely allied to that of Feeding; nay, it is no other than that of feeding. Consisting of an infinite number of little stomachs, closely associated and connected, but feeding upon aërial and gaseous food instead of terrestrial and solid, such as is received into the cavity of the stomach proper, the Lungs are no less immediately concerned in the maintenance of the health and

---

* See for an admirable development of the whole subject, Garth Wilkinson's banquet-like chapter of the Lungs, in "The Human Body, and its connexion with Man."

vigor of the blood than the great, proper stomach itself. Not only does the blood require to be nourished with the products of digestion, but to be freely and regularly aërated, not to have air *directly* admitted to it, but to be brought into that peculiar proximity to the air which is effected by the process of natural breathing. This, in the mammalia, takes place, as we are all aware, in the lungs. Immediately the blood enters these organs, in the process of circulation, the fact is signalled by certain nerves to the *medulla oblongata.** In an instant, obedient to an imperious order sent back through certain other nerves, the diaphragm and muscles of the ribs expand the chest, and thus enlarge its cavity. A vacuum would now be caused, but the air, rushing down from without, fills every corner, and in so doing, aërates the awaiting blood, feeding it with oxygen, and receiving carbon in exchange. Then the various muscles renew their play; but this time so as to contract, instead of expand the chest, the lungs *ex*spire, instead of *in*spiring, the carbon is ejected by the mouth and nostrils, and the series of actions constituting a respiration is complete. Renewed by the oxygen thus communicated, the blood now moves on again to the heart, whence it was first propelled, and whence it is again transmitted to the body, again to be carbonized and weakened, and in due course to be returned into the lungs for refreshment as before. Thus is the history of the lungs inseparable from that of the heart. Complementary to one another, these two noble organs, the heart and the lungs, and their functions, circulation and respiration, form a beautiful duality in unity, representing in the body the

* *Medulla oblongata* is the name given by anatomists to a peculiar organ contained within the skull, yet no part of the brain properly so called, but intermediate between this and the spinal cord, upon the summit of which it stands.

understanding and the affections, and their coöperative play in every action of the soul. The latter, as we have seen above, represent in turn the all-supporting wisdom and goodness of God—the infinite, Divine essences which, expressed as life, conserve the universe. They fall, accordingly, under those two sublime, reciprocal principles of creation which in their most externalized physical embodiment we term Male and Female; and whose noblest presentation, or Man and Woman, are the lungs and the heart of the world. As man and woman, by reciprocity and coöperation, instrumentally keep the human race alive; so, by harmonious, conjugal action and re-action, the lungs and the heart instrumentally keep the human body alive. If either fail to perform its office, the other sinks powerless, and the fabric dies. Let the heart be as well-disposed to live as it may, unless its desires be recognized and responded to by the lungs, all is in vain; for though there is no life where there is no blood, there is no proper, life-sustaining blood where there is no air: conversely, the lungs are efficient for their part, as stewards of life, only in so far as the heart coöperates with them; so grand and universal is the eternal fiat that nothing shall exist for itself alone, but only as the husband or the wife of some other thing; that the unions of each pair shall be followed by the development and sustentation of some form or mode of life; that celibacy shall be infertility, and estrangement a gateway for death. Until the two organs are conjoined in complementary action, by the lungs drawing breath, the grand drama of existence, as we well know, does not commence. In the womb, life exists only in potency. Marriage is everywhere the real beginning; and there are no real beginnings without it.*

---

* See the beautiful description of the marriage of the Heart and Lungs, in Swedenborg's "Animal Kingdom," i. 398.

46. It is not to be imagined that the heart and lungs do the whole work of life. Just as marriage, which has for its physical end the sustentation of the human race, requires for its effectuation a variety of subsidiary and contributive conditions, so the maintenance of the life of the body by the heart and lungs, which is a representative of marriage and its object, demands (intermediately through the nervous centres) the contributive functions of the stomach, the skin, the liver, and other organs. And more than this: if the action of any one of them become deranged, neither heart nor lungs can do their work for them; just as with complex machinery, where, if a single wheel be thrown "out of gear," the coördination of actions is so interfered with that the whole apparatus comes to a stand. Every organ of the body is in league with every other organ. Every one of them has its own peculiar province and vocation, but is in treaty at the same moment, offensive and defensive, with every other. Nothing is proper to any member in this unique and truly royal society that does not go forth in turn for the interest and advantage of that society. Local benefits immediately become public ones; what injures in one part, is a calamity to the whole. "The cardinal life of every organ," says Swedenborg—"the excellency of its life over other organs—consists in the fact, that whatever it has of its own, still in a wider sense belongs to the community; and whatever afterwards results from the community to the organ, is the only individual property which the latter claims." It is not that the heart and lungs are all, but that life is preëminently effectuated through them; the cessation of their activity, or of the activity of either of them, being also, as we shall see presently, the most usual and imminent cause of death. So far from any one organ, or set of organs, being autocratic, there is nothing in the whole scope of the natural history of the human body more wonderful than

the sympathy and concurrent energy of its various parts, unless it be the fine illustrative analogy afforded in the relations of the *senses*, as intimated to our daily consciousness. Not one of the senses can be exercised without suggesting to the mind acts and objects which belong to one or more of their colleagues; and the highest pleasures we enjoy through their medium, are those which result from our being able to use some two or three of them at once. The waterfall, we love not only to see, but to hear; and not only to hear, but to see; the eye helps the palate to the higher enjoyments of food, and the nose to be more gratified with the smell of flowers; who ever looks on the smooth cheek of a little child, without seeking an enhanced pleasure in patting it! True science is never science only. On the same principle commences all true investigation. To know any single and individual thing thoroughly, it needs that we gather instruction concerning it from *all* things. To learn the true nature of a primrose, we must inquire of firs and palm-trees, and every other plant that springs forth from the earth's bosom. From the same facts, brought to bear in yet another direction, may we learn how it is that undue indulgence in any sensuality enslaves the whole being, and gradually chains a man's every thought and wish to the adopted habit of the sense given way to.

47. In the full sense of the term, Respiration is a far grander performance than the mere inhalation of fresh air through the air-passages. Essentially, it is concurrent and coëxtensive with the circulation, so that its seat is the entire fabric. Numbers of animals have no lungs, commonly so called; many have no special respiratory organs whatever. They breathe, nevertheless. Such, for example, are jelly-fishes, and the lowest forms of crustacea. In these, respiration takes place through the medium of the *skin*. Not that this is a new arrangement for the purpose of breathing,

now for the first time met with. Animals possessing a special apparatus, have cutaneous respiration; man has it, in a slight degree. Here, however, it is only auxiliary; whereas in the jelly-fishes it stands in lieu of the pulmonary kind, and the creature depends upon it alone. The mechanism of respiration in animals possessing lungs, is to be regarded merely as the *highest development* of a respiratory apparatus. It holds the first place because it is the mechanism by which the greatest quantity of oxygen can be taken into the system. There is no difference in *principle* between the two kinds; it is a difference simply of vigor and completeness, the oxygen being admitted over an infinitely larger surface in lungs than when it has to make its way through the integuments. The *position* of the respiratory apparatus, which, like its form, is most curiously diversified in different creatures, is, generally speaking, regulated by the medium in which the animal is intended to live—on land, or in water. Terrestrial animals, breathing air in its gasiform condition, have *internal* breathing apparatus; aquatic animals, collecting it from the water, have the apparatus in or near the surface. By virtue of these arrangements, neither class of animal can endure exchange of natural location. The bird and the mammal drown if submerged in water; the fish drowns if exposed to the atmosphere. This is, in the former case, because water cannot furnish an adequate supply of atmospheric air; in the latter, because the respiratory organs, from their external position, rapidly become dry by evaporation. Aquatic animals which have them partially covered, live longer out of water than those which have them exposed. The activity of life, in aquatic as well as in terrestrial animals, is universally in the ratio of the development of their respiratory apparatus. The energetic habits of fishes, and the higher crustacea, such as crabs and lobsters, correspond with the higher development of their breathing organs; the comparatively sluggish life of the mollusca, the annelida, and the branchial amphibia, corresponds with the accompanying lower development. A creature possessing both pulmonary and cutaneous respiration, but able to live by cutaneous respiration only, if prevented from breathing through the lungs, sinks into the sluggishness and inactivity which characterize the animals it is then leveled with in regard to qualification for breathing.*

48. By respiration, accordingly, in the complete idea of the process, and however effectuated, whether by lungs or other apparatus, or cutaneously, oxygen is introduced to every part, and carbon removed from every part. The chemical process which goes on during the formation of the carbonic acid in which the carbon is carried away, is attended by the extrication of "animal heat." Here, then, are three purposes served: renovation of the blood, purification of it, and sustentation of temperature. Not that "animal heat," even as commonly so understood, comes exclusively of the combustion concurrent with respiration. The evolution of animal heat is largely dependent on the *nervous energy*. The lower the nervous energy of an animal, the lower is its temperature; the higher the nervous energy, the higher is its temperature. It is not the larger or smaller nervous *system* which is thus operative, but the higher or lower nervous *energy*. Dr. Carpenter, in his large work on Comparative Physiology, gives every kind of proof and illustration. Mr. Newport's papers on the Temperature and Respiration of Insects, published in the Philosophical Transactions for 1835 and 1837, may also be usefully con-

* See for illustrations, an excellent paper on Respiration, by Dr. Sibson, in the Transactions of the Provincial Medical and Surgical Association, vol. xvii., 1850.

sulted. "Animal heat," in the popular use of the phrase, is not animal heat after all. What is so termed by the physiologists is as purely "mineral" heat as any that radiates from inanimate fire or candle. Animal heat, properly so called, is the zeal which urges the creature to the active exercise of its powers. There could not be a particle in the body of what is commonly but erroneously so designated, if the Divine Life did not already warm it with this, the true animal heat. That which the mere combustion of oxygen and carbon introduces is but supplementary and contingent. Under all phenomena lies a profounder cause than chemistry or anatomy can point out. The Divine Life everywhere takes the initiative; the apparent causes are secondary, and are operative only as resting on it as a substratum. It should be noted, too, that the lower we descend in the scale of being, the more do these apparent, scientific causes seem disused. While, for instance, the higher animals have their blood propelled by the muscular engine we call the heart, in many of the lower kinds, and in plants, there is no such engine; the circulation goes on nevertheless. Besides the quasi-chemical use of the air in respiration, there is a use in the mechanical act of breathing it. There is no life where there is no motion, and there is no vital motion but where Air is passing to and fro, or indirectly actuating. The lungs are the first to move under its impulse; the heart beats time to them; the brain falls as often as we inspire, and rises with every expiration. In a child under two years old, the latter may be felt as plainly as the pulse. Place your hand low down on the body, and there too is found constant and consentaneous movement with the lungs. Respiration, in a word, keeps everything on the move, and as soon as it ceases, comes the stagnation of death.

19. Respiration does more yet than bring in oxygen and carry away carbon, and subserve the maintenance of vital

warmth. It is itself a positive feeder of the body, with good aliment or with bad, according to the kind of atmosphere we inhale. The air is no mere compound of oxygen, nitrogen, and carbon, *as such*. "It is a product elaborated from all the kingdoms of nature; the seasons are its education; it is passed through the fingers of every herb and tree. Whoever looks upon it as one universal thing, is like a dreamer playing with the words animal kingdom, vegetable kingdom, and so forth, and forgetting that each comprises many genera, innumerable species, and individuals many times innumerable. The air is a cellarage of aërial wines, the heaven of the spirits of the plants and flowers, which are safely kept there till called for by the lungs and skin. The assumption that the oxygen is the all, is ungrateful for the inhabitant of any land whose fields are fresh services of fragrance from county to county and from year to year." All the virtues of the ground and of vegetation are in the atmosphere by exhalation; it is a kind of solution of some of everything that the world contains, and from it, as from a fountain, all come into the lungs and circulation. Not only does man live in the world, but the world, as to its essences, is contained within itself, literally as well as correspondentially. Thus is our assertion not a meaningless one, that all nature subsidizes and ministers to the blood. The ruins of the air, when chemistry has pulverized it, may be no more than what a brief formula of Roman letters will express; but its influence on us, while unmolested, comes of a compositeness that no art can emulate. "Change of air" is something more to the sick man than change of oxygen, and on the other side of the picture are the dark, sad mysteries of air-conveyed infections, and the endless evils produced by confined, ill-ventilated abiding places. Dirty air is the source of incomparably greater evils than dirty water. Many complaints we are least apt to attribute to it, take their rise, without doubt, in shut-up bed-rooms, and other domestic stagnant air-pools, the contents of which, were they but visible, would fill us with horror and disgust. The body is not the only sufferer from impure air. Though vice and impure air may be found in company, virtue and foul air are incompatible. The temper of a public meeting is often influenced by the condition of the air which it is breathing; to talk of a "moral atmosphere" is not altogether a figure of speech. To the extreme and disgusting foulness of the air which they commonly breathe is, probably, to be referred much of the indulgence of the poor in strong drink, especially ardent spirits. They take it as a necessity, claimed by nature as a kind of counterpoise to the offensive and pernicious actions of bad smells. The best temperance agent that can be got is a clean and well ventilated home. No training, however skilfully conducted, no dieting or teetotalism, however rigid or prolonged, can bring a man into good condition, either of body or mind, so long as he is condemned to breathe an impure atmosphere. Sanitary associations do well in teaching that the life is the blood, and that without pure air, healthy blood is but a name.

50. The particular mode in which the air ministers to *plant*-life is found in the history of the growth or development of the vegetable structure. The great mass of the vegetable fabric is derived, not from the soil, but from the air which bathes the leaves. The strictly "mineral" part of its food, as lime, silica, and potash, it undoubtedly sucks from the earth, whence the value of manures, and the difference produced by "good" and "bad" soils, but it is at the cost of the carbonic acid, water, and ammonia of the atmosphere, that it essentially lives. (p. 63.) Much, indeed, of what it proximately procures from under ground is virtually atmospheric, because previously carried thither by the rain. Thousands of plants have no connection whatever with the

earth, but grow upon the surface of other plants. Such are the beautiful aërial flowers called Orchideæ, which in their wild state, live from first to last on the trees of their native forests, and demand an imitative location when brought into our hot houses and conservatories. They are not like the misletoe, *parasites*—thieves of the substance of the tree they perch upon, but simply "epiphytes"—bird-like lodgers among the branches. Dendrobium, Epidendrum, Dendrolirion, are names ingeniously descriptive of their nature. Essentially, without doubt, they feed as terrestrial plants do—indebted largely to the various decaying organic matters which accumulate round about them, both of animal origin and vegetable. Lifted, however, as they are, so far above the surface of the earth, they show, in the most beautiful manner, how independently of direct connection with it vegetable existence may be maintained, and how thoroughly at home it may be in the atmosphere. Two species of Orchideæ, called Air-plants, find in it their entire nourishment.* What epiphytes are in the air, Algæ are in the water, drawing from it their chief supplies; for their roots, so called, are little more than organs of adhesion. Not wholly so, since many show a decided preference for certain kinds of rocks, and for the branches of certain other Algæ, seated upon which, they attain higher perfection. Under the influence of light, the leaves, both of terrestrial and aërial plants, become the seats at once of respiration and assimilation. If leaves be not developed, as in the cactus, their place is supplied by the tender green skin of the general surface, which is then so modified as to perform the fo-

* The trunks and branches of the trees in tropical Brazil, Mr. Gardner tells us, abound not only with Orchideæ, but with Bromeliaceæ, Tillandsias, Ferns, and various climbing species of Begonia, all of course dependent upon the Atmosphere.

liar functions. Carbon, ammonia, and water are taken up, and oxygen is set free. Hence the leaves are well styled the "lungs" of plants; the lungs, for their part, being animal trees clothed with innumerable foliage. The leafless plants may be compared with the animals whose respiration is wholly cutaneous. To enable respiration to take place, the cuticle of every leaf is pierced with innumerable pores well called by the vegetable anatomist, *stomates,* since mouths they are, both in form and office. The most ordinary microscope will bring them into view, and show a wonderful variety in their figure.

51. Absorbing carbon, and liberating oxygen, which is the reverse of the animal process of respiration, plants are the great purifiers of the atmosphere as regards animals. The only exception to their use in this respect occurs in the fungi—plants which, unlike the purifying tribes, are never of a *green* color. What animal respiration exhales, vegetable respiration consumes, and *vice versa.* There is, however, always some small amount of carbonic acid in the course of *disengagement* from plants, especially at night, when also they absorb oxygen. On this is founded the popular notion, so immensely exaggerated, that plants kept in a bed-room are injurious to the sleeper. Plants, by their assimilation, purify the air much more than by their respiration they vitiate it. They are breathers at once for their own interests, and for those of animals. Plants live by animals, and animals by plants. The girdling and encircling air, their common property, is that which truly makes the whole world kin. "The carbonic acid with which our breathing fills the air, to-morrow will be spreading north and south, and striving to make the tour of the world. The date trees that grow round the fountains of the Nile will drink it in by their leaves; the cedars of Lebanon will take of it to add to their stature; the cocoa-nuts of Tahiti will grow richer on

it; the lotus plants will change it into flowers. Contrariwise, the oxygen we are taking in was distilled for us, some little time ago, by the magnolias of the Susquehanna, and the great trees that skirt the Orinoco and the Amazon. The rhododendrons of the Himalayahs contribute to it, the roses and myrtles of Cashmere, the cinnamon and the clove trees of the Spice islands." In recognizing this fine use of plants in the economy of the world, we must be careful not to *over*-estimate it. The primary use of plants is to *supply food;* the purification of the air is but a subordinate use. For every kindness they do to the lungs of animals there are a thousand done to their stomachs.

52. In the fact that vegetation purifies the air by absorbing from it what is deleterious, resides a capital argument against intra-mural interments. There cannot be a doubt that the beautiful, time-honored, and world-wide practice of sheltering graves with trees, and adorning them with flowers, is attended by valuable sanitary results, such as are wholly precluded when burials are made amid streets and houses. While the sight of evergreen trees, and of flowers in their season, soothes and consoles the mind, by virtue of their associations and emblematic teachings, the atmosphere is improved and renovated. So true it is that whatever is practically wise is always in keeping with what is poetically beautiful, and an exemplification of it. Many of the trees which poetical intuition has pronounced appropriate to the side of the sepulchre, by reason of their evergreen or other symbolical characters, are precisely such as scientific design would approve. Witness the arbor-vitæ, the Oriental cypress, and certain kinds of coniferæ; all of them more or less narrow and conical in form, neither covering a large space with their branches, nor casting too much shade when the sun shines, and freely admitting the air and light. The beauty of the cypress-planted cemeteries of the Turks is well known.

At Constantinople the chief promenade for Europeans is the cemetery of Pera, delightfully placed on a hill-side, and abounding with this handsome tree. "At Scutari," Miss Pardoe tells us, "preferred by the Turks to all other burial-places, because of certain comfortable superstitions connected with it, a forest of the finest cypress extends over an immense space, clothing hill and valley, and seen far off at sea,—an object at once striking and magnificent." In the cemetery appropriated to the Armenians, instead of the cypress, the *Acacia* is the prevailing tree. Marble is good, but waving boughs are better. It will be one of the most certain indications of progress in real, practical science, when town burial-grounds shall be abolished for the sake of rural cemeteries like gardens. Wherever such have been formed, they have been regarded with satisfaction, and their general establishment would unquestionably lead to a marked diminution of average mortality, by removing a deadly evil.

CHAPTER VI.

MOTION THE UNIVERSAL SIGN OF LIFE.

53. Reviewing these various and wonderful processes, we cannot fail to observe how, in its every phase and expression, the great sign and certificate of life is Motion. Usefully, then, may we pause upon the consideration of it as a kind of summary and continent of vital phenomena. Nothing exists independently of motion as its cause; by reason, likewise, of motion, all things hold together and preserve their form. "Passive life," sometimes spoken of, is a contradiction in terms; certain states of being may be relatively passive, but there is no such thing as absolute passivity. In no case a state *ipso facto*, passivity is everywhere an incident of motion, consequently to be referred to motion, and to be explained by motion. Doubtless there is great diversity in the degree and amount of motion; also in its manifestation to the eye. We must not confound it with *moving about*. Motion, ordinarily so called, implying visible change of place and position, and furnishing us with ideas of time, does not comprise the All of motion. There is motion which no eye can perceive, motion which we are made aware of only by witnessing its results. Of this kind, indeed, is the chief part; the most wonderful and efficient movements in the world are those which proceed in secrecy and silence.*

* Robert Boyle has an essay, well known to the curious, "On the great effects of Languid and Unheeded Motion." See in particular, chapters viii. and ix.

The feebler and briefer the exhibition of motion, especially the latter, the lower is the expression of life; the more energetic and continuous it is, the higher is the life—so that apart from structure, motion is a criterion of vital excellence, of course under the reservation that the quality of life depends primarily and essentially upon its End; else would the sea be more living than a plant; and a watch, or other piece of self-acting mechanism, commend itself as of nobler nature than many animals. Inanimate as it is, the watch, by reason of these relations, excites agreeable ideas of life, at least in the minds of the intelligent; while by the child and the savage, unacquainted with its construction, it is unhesitatingly pronounced "alive!" Experience rectifies the error, but vindicates the principle upon which the mistaken judgment was entertained.

54. Animals, as holding the highest offices in the economy of creation, therefore the noblest forms, and the highest degrees of life, present in their various history the completest examples of vital motion. Their movements are both internal and external. The great internal movement is the circulation of the blood, and its familiar token, the beating of the heart. This is the circumstance on which the very name of Life is founded; its proximate root, the Anglo-Saxon *lybban*, "to live," being ultimately assignable to the Arabic *lub*, the heart, or the congenerous Hebrew name for that organ, *leb*. Literally, therefore, "life" means "the heart;" a fact beautifully in unison with the great fundamental truth, alike of religion and philosophy, that Life is Love. It is for etymologists to determine how far the law of transposition of letters may or may not show "lub" and "life" in the Greek word *φιλ-εω*, "I love." The ancient Egyptians used a heart, placed in the midst of a censer of flame, for the hieroglyph of heaven, the source to the world, as the heart is to the body, of all activity and life. Nothing

is easier than to verify that the life of the body consists in its internal movements. How painful to sit perfectly still, even for a few minutes, as when having one's likeness taken by photography! The performers in *tableaux vivans* and *poses plastiques* find that to play at statues is the hardest trial of human nature. Dependent on the circulation, and less admired only because of its deep privacy, is that wonderful and incessant flux of the ultimate atoms of the body which has been described above, and which led the genius of Cuvier to compare it to a whirlpool, an intense and unceasing stream, into which new matter is for ever flowing, and from which the old is as steadily moving out.

55. External movement culminates in the grand prerogative of *loco*motion, the highest terrene presentation of the great omnipresent law of Attraction,—the law which, under the formula and name of chemical affinity, brings together the atoms of the pebble; and which, at the other extreme of creation, under the formula and name of Love, impels all creatures towards what they have need of or desire. Where there is the greatest capacity for locomotion, there also is Ingenuity at its maximum. The animals which possess least of the constructive instinct are the slow-paced reptiles; the expertest artisans in the world, are the birds and flying insects—man, of course, excepted, who has more capacity than either; not, indeed, of the same nature, nor corporeal at all, but derived from the very instruments which prove his ingenuity also the highest, his railways and his ships.

56. As in the animal kingdom, so in the vegetable. Plants, quiescent as they appear, depend for their existence on the motion of the juices contained within their substance; the force with which the sap flows onwards when the plant is in full vigor, is like the rush of a little river; even in winter, when visible vitality is suspended, motion is still going on, though languidly; the process of development is never

entirely arrested; in the season of deepest torpidity, a slight enlargement of the buds, in preparation for the spring, is still to be observed. Were we endowed with eyesight adequately fine, and were the integuments and tissues of plants made transparent, we should see in every twig and leaf of every plant the most energetic and persevering activity; as by means of a glass hive we may watch at our leisure the working of its indefatigable little townsfolk. One class of internal movements in plants does actually allow of observation, just as in certain reptiles, as the frog, it is possible to observe the circulation of the blood-corpuscles. When a small portion of the cuticle of the Vallisneria is submitted to a sufficient magnifying power, in the interior of every one of its delicate cells there is seen a beautiful swimming procession of little globules, round and round, sometimes faster, sometimes slower, till the vitality of the fragment is exhausted. A similar motion has been noticed in many other plants, terrestrial as well as aquatic, and probably it is general. Even the *external* movement of plants, induced by the excitation of the wind, notwithstanding its purely extraneous origin, is a highly important circumstance of their economy. It is evident that the boughs of trees are so arranged, and the leaves of plants in general so distributed and poised, as to admit of the swaying and fluttering which the wind promotes; and that benefit results from such movement, corresponding, as it does, to the exercise of their limbs by animals, it seems unreasonable to doubt. How different the condition of the captives in our green-houses and conservatories, debarred from every opportunity of movement, compared with that of the glad, free trees, waving throughout the year in the breezes of the open country! As exercise gives strength and solidity to the animal fabric, so do the vegetable denizens of the fields and hills wax sturdy through the agitation of their branches. When Homer would indicate unusual strength and toughness in his heroes' spear-shafts, he calls them ἀνεμοτρεφής, "wind-nurtured," or "wind-hardened." "Pine-trees," says the prince of arborists, "in thick woods, where the high winds have not free access to shake them, grow tall and slender, but not strong; while others, placed in open fields, and frequently shaken by strong blasts, have not only thick and sturdy stems, but strike deep root, and raise beautiful and spreading branches."*

57. Astronomy, chemistry, meteorology, though their subjects belong to an entirely different province of being, find, like physiology, that all their phenomena commence in motion. Not only has it been placed beyond a doubt that the group of worlds which includes our own is advancing through the heavens, but it has been determined in what direction it moves, and within certain limits, what is the velocity of its motion. If true of one system of sun and planets, it must be true of all. Every star that we espy is unquestionably rolling onwards, and carrying with it the spheres to which it is the local orb of day, the immeasurable altitude alone preventing the eye from pursuing; as when from the brow of a lofty cliff by the sea we discern far-distant ships that we know by their spread canvas to be sailing, but which the extreme remoteness make appear to be at anchor. "If we imagine," says Humboldt, "as in a vision of the fancy, the acuteness of our senses preternaturally sharpened, even to the extreme limits of telescopic vision, and incidents which are separated by vast intervals of time, compressed into a day, or an hour, everything like *rest* in special existence will forthwith disappear. We shall find the innumerable hosts of the fixed stars commoved in groups in different directions; nebulæ drawing hither and thither,

---

* Evelyn. *Sylva*, Book 2d, chap. 8.

like cosmic clouds; the milky-way breaking up in particular parts, and its veil rent; motion in every part of the vault of heaven." It is the motion of our own little planet which chiefly adorns the sky with its varied splendors, as sunrise and sunset, and the shining and stately march of the constellations. Of the agitation of its enveloping atmosphere come the winds for health of body, and the magnificent scenery of cloud-land for delight of soul; the rain, the tempest, the Aurora, meteors, and those strange "fiery tears of the sky" which we term falling stars, announce over again that the realms of aërial space, all still and passive as they seem, are yet realms of unresting life. The very *substance* of the earth is ever-moving; the interior is incessantly inducing changes upon the exterior; waves of motion are continually passing through, indicated by the sinking of the land in some parts of the globe, and its rising in others, so that old beaches are left inland, and old high-water marks sunk far out at sea; hot springs, volcanoes, earthquakes, attest more vehemently still what agitation there is below. "Could we obtain daily news of the state of the whole of the earth's crust," continues the author of KOSMOS, "we should in all probability become convinced that some point or other of its surface is constantly shaken." Yet all these greater movements of the earth's substance are but stupendous analogues of movements as incessantly going on among its elements—visible, acknowledged movements. What life is there in crystallization! What energy in combustion! What vivacity in effervescence! True, some of them are of brief duration, if we look only at a particular scene of their display; but taking the total of the world, they are unremitting. Even in a given spot, they may be indefinitely prolonged, like the ever-burning fire of the Vestal Virgins, provided sufficient supply of their needful fuel be kept up. Animal movement itself could not be continued were supplies of what it depends on to be withheld. Collectively, these movements express, as we have before styled it, the Life of inorganic nature. Under the impulse of the sustaining and influencing energy of the Creator, every atom of matter is full of moving life; the history of every particle is a history of change, and that of the world an ever-beginning, never-concluding metamorphosis.

58. The moving of *water* is peculiarly like life. Hence the continual application to streams and fountains, by elegant minds, of the terms which pertain primarily to their own nature. The basins at the Crystal Palace, it is announced, are to be "*alive* with fountains and jets;" the river here, says the author of Coningsby, was "clear but for the dark sky it reflected, narrow and winding, but *full of life*." Corinne's delight was in "the fount of Trevi, whose abundant cascade falls in the centre of Rome, and seems the life of that tranquil scene." Virgil has *flumine vivo,* "in the living current;" Ovid, *e vivis fontibus,* "from the gushing fountains." Oersted devotes an entire chapter to the Life of the Fountain, a chapter as elegant in narrative as the principle arrived at is important. He shows us that while motion is the beginning of life, it is likewise the first principle of Beauty. "What a rich variety of inward activity we beheld," he concludes, "in that fountain! Were this to be separated from it, all besides would leave but a faint impression. That which is full of life arouses it in ourselves, and this feeling of life appertains to the complete enjoyment of beauty. An attempt to represent it in painting, if it were executed in a masterly manner, might in some degree please the eye; but the enjoyment which arises from the peculiar nature of the object would be much diminished, because motion, lustre, and the play of light can never be represented in a picture. I have several times seen pictures of fountains, but the impression they produced upon me was poor." To give in

painting a sufficient idea of the ocean, to paint even rain or falling snow, is well known to be an equally fruitless effort, while nothing is easier than to sketch a still expanse of flooded fields, which, for the same reason, are unattractive and uninteresting, and incapable of exciting ideas of beauty. These, as so lucidly set forth by the accomplished Dane, we can realize only when movement is either present or forcibly implied, and thus only where the idea of *life* is secretly placed before the soul, which loves it, and hungers for it, and is depressed when there is none to be seen, because of its own innate, burning activity. How beautiful the waving of the trees, and the quiver of the leaves before the wind!* With what delight do we watch the gliding of the clouds across the sky, the heaving of the sea,

> The river rushing o'er its pebbled bed.

Why are we never tired of looking upon the ocean? From land-scenery, however charming, after a while, the eye turns away, deliberately and content; the Sea, on the other hand, holds the whole soul in immortal fascination. The meadows and ferny lanes, even the woodland glades of perfect Spring, sheeted with the wild blue hyacinth, and sparkling with the crimson lychnis, even at that earlier sweet season, when the trees, though they have leaves upon them, give no shade to the chaste anemones, we can quit satisfied; but the beach, though it offer nothing but high-water mark of withered wrack, we never turn away from without reluctance. As in a glass we see our features reflected, so in the movement of the waves, and their sound, we recognize an image of our

---

* How largely the movement of trees contributes to their picturesque, may be seen in Gilpin, who indicates more than once the fulness, as well as the nicety of his appreciation of its value. *Forest Scenery.*

life. So with the movements, though silent, of the clouds, as, massively dark or softly brilliant, their swelling mountains change, unite, separate, and unite again, unveiling infinite depths of calm, sweet azure, or if it be sunset, fields of clear, burning brightness that seem to reach into heaven itself. Looking at the clouds merely as aqueducts, we miss the chief part of their beautiful ministry, which is to fill the sky with the idea of Life. Rhymesters and parlor naturalists would have us believe the skies, to be perfectly beautiful, must be "cloudless." It is not only not true, but it would be contrary to the nature of things for it to be true. The skies even of Italy are not cloudless, except as in our own country, at certain periods, and derive their charm from their transparency rather than from cloudlessness. Clouds are to the heavens what human beings are to the earth. They dwell in them, and move about them, various in their aspect and their missions as men and women; and as of the latter come all the true dignity and grace of earth, so of the former comes every splendor that glorifies the sky.

59. Things even which are incapable of visible motion mainly acquire what beauty they may present from in some way referring us to it. We are so pleased, for instance, with the undulating outline of distant hills, because they unroll before the imagination the rising and falling of the waves, and thus transport us into the very presence of life's grandest emblem. There is no pleasure derived from the view of a mere flat extended plain, unless relieved by waving corn or the movement of animals. These being absent, everything seems to have subsided into stagnancy, and the pictured idea is death rather than life. We call it, without a libel, "a *dead* level." Even the shadows in still water, depending, as they do, on the most exquisite placidity of surface, are no exception, for they seldom so powerfully appeal as when the objects they depict are gently agitated by the

breeze. Feeling how important it is that life should thus be presented to the mind even in scenes of the profoundest repose, the poets rarely delineate such without introducing some delicate allusion that shall suggest it.

> Homines, volucresque ferasque
> Solverat alta quies: nullo cum murmure sepes
> Immotæque silent frondes; silet humidus aër;
> *Sidera sola micant.*—(OVID, *Met.*, vii. 185–188.)

"Men, birds, and animals lie dissolved in deep repose; the murmur of the woods is hushed; the leaves are motionless; the humid air is still; *the stars alone twinkle.*"

Not that motion is sufficient to excite ideas of beauty; everywhere in nature there must be a combination of two separate ideas, complementary to each other, before we can realize satisfaction in the beholding; the second, in the present instance, being the idea of Repose, as we may easily perceive by considering the movements of animals, and more particularly, those of man. Swimming, flying, walking, are graceful, and therefore pleasing, only when we gather from them ideas of Rest, such as are conveyed by that aspect of ease and security, resulting from a perfectly-felt balance, which characterizes them when unlaborious and unaffected. Attitudes, on the same principle, which commend themselves as peculiarly beautiful and graceful, though they seem to depend for their effect upon the exquisite arrangement of the body and limbs, derive the half of it from their flowing, motion-hinting curves.

60. Repose is needful not only to physical beauty; it belongs as largely to the finest attitudes of the spiritual life, and is the state in which the imagination is most exquisitely unfolded. All true genius recognizes this. Shakspere would not let the players "tear a passion to tatters." He directs them, "in the very torrent, tempest, and as I may say,

whirlwind of your passion, you must acquire and beget a temperance that will give it smoothness." "The turmoil, the battle, the tumult of the Iliad is accompanied by the repose of studied measure. Amid the carnage of men we see the gods tranquil spectators, and when *they* are in the conflict, Achilles rests." So in Art. The same beautiful combination of action and repose in nature which reflects from the verses of the poet, is the foremost quality of the best efforts of the painter and the sculptor. The noblest and loveliest statues are those whose pure white marble is consecrated not more to life's emotions than to Repose.

CHAPTER VII.

DEATH.

61. THE cessation of the vital activities is Death, which, though commonly spoken of as an actual existence, is simply another name for discontinuance. All forms recipient of life die some time. Some few may be privileged to survive the rest, even for thousands of years, as happens with certain trees, but the same death which in regard to the children of men, while it surprises many, skips not one, at last overpowers the most tenacious. "Come like shadows, so depart," is the law of the entire material creation, in fact, as great a law as that it *lives*. For death is no accident of nature, neither is it in the least degree punitive. It is an essential and benevolent part of the very idea of material existence, bound up with the original scheme and method of creation as completely as gravitation is. Things die, not because they have been sentenced to, judicially, the sentence being effectuated, as often supposed, by a change superinduced upon their original constitution; but because without death, nature could not endure. Birth, growth, and arriving at maturity, as completely imply decay and death as the source of a river implies the termination of it, or as spring and summer imply corn-fields and reaping. Hence, whatever the vigor and the powers of repair that may pertain to any given structure, whatever resistance it may offer to the shocks of Ages, Time, sooner or later, dissolves it; careful, however, to renew whatever it takes away, and to convert,

invariably, every end into a new beginning. There is not a grave in the whole circuit of nature that is not at the same moment a cradle.

62. That death was brought into the world by Adam, we by no means intend to deny. Nothing is more true. Let us rightly understand, however, what *kind* of death it was. For death is no unitary thing; there are as many ways of dying as of living. Death commonly so called it certainly was not. Scripture, the supposed authority for the popular belief, rarely speaks of *physical* death. It uses the language of the material world, but intends spiritual ideas. Concerning itself primarily and essentially with the soul of man, what it has to say about his body is but casual. Only in purely biographical notices, as when it is said of Joseph that "he died an hundred and ten years old," and in some few such texts as "it is appointed unto all men once to die," is physical death ever alluded to, or even compatible with a just and practical interpretation. "In the day that thou eatest thereof thou shalt surely die," was not a threat that *corporeal* death should be inflicted; it signified that, breaking the commandment, he who had it given him, should lose the high, lovely life which is union with God, and sink into irreligiousness, which is infelicity and disquiet. He died to the true life of the spirit the moment that he tasted; but as to his material body, he continued as he was before. "He begat sons and daughters, and lived nine hundred and thirty years." Equally unscriptural and groundless is the notion that physical death was even an appendix to the "punishment." Adam would have died had he never fallen, and so would all of his posterity, though none, perhaps, would have died of *disease*. Death probably would have resembled sinking into an easy and gentle slumber, such as overtakes us when agreeably fatigued; it would have been that *euthanasia* to all men which Augustus Cæsar used so passionately

to desire, and which is so beautifully predicated of the Christian in a well-known and lovely hymn:—

> So fades a summer cloud away,
> So sinks the gale, when storms are o'er,
> So gently shuts the eye of day,
> So dies a wave along the shore.

If the Fall bore in *any* way on physical death, it was in leading to the sensualities which often hurry it on with pain; and to the violations of the laws of peace and order which make so much of it unhappy and untimely. It is absolutely needful that man should die as to his material body, in order that he may rise into his eternal dwelling. He has faculties which cannot possibly be developed here, and which can only expand in heaven, or under purely spiritual conditions, so that it is only by dying that he can become truly himself.

63. What Scripture really tells us, is that physical death was *not* brought into the world by Adam; and the testimony of the inspired volume is supported by the incontestable evidence of science. Geology proves that the world had been familiar with death for ages before mankind was placed upon it; every fossil in the museums of palæontology is a voucher that mortality and human sin neither had nor possibly could have the least connection; to suppose otherwise, is to place the effect before the cause. It is a simple evasion to say, in order to reconcile the geological teaching, that it was only *man* who became subject to death through his moral defection; and that geology does not object to this doctrine. Geology knows but of a single law of life and death.* Assuming, however, that no geological discoveries

---

* See for the arguments set forth by upholders of the notion here repudiated, the *Quarterly Journal of Prophecy*, vol. 4, p. 317. July, 1852.

had ever been made; assuming that no fossil shell or skeleton had ever been dug up, and that the pre-Adamic condition of the globe were still a secret; the very history of the creation of animals and plants, in the gateway of the Bible, is sufficient to show that physical death is proper and congenital to nature. The command given both to animals and man to "be fruitful and multiply," implies the removal of successive races by death; otherwise the world would long since have been overstocked; plants, for their part, are described as created "yielding seed," which carries with it the same inevitable consequence. The produce of so minute a creature as a fly would, if unchecked, soon darken the air, and render whole regions desolate; the number of seeds ripened by a single poppy, were they all to grow and be fruitful in their turn, would in a few years suffice to clothe a continent. Of course it is easy to object, as done by a certain class of reasoners, that this might have been corrected by a supplementary "miracle," but to evade fair philosophical deductions by inventing and ascribing miracles where none are spoken of and none are wanted, is as weak as it is irreverent. God does not perform his work so imperfectly or short-sightedly as to be obliged to interpose with miracles to set it right; nor are we at liberty to speculate on the possibility of something supernatural in order to escape our difficulties, when to industry and patience nature itself is sufficient. Death, if not an absolutely necessary and inalienable counterpart to procreation, or being fruitful and multiplying; is at least a concomitant of every scene of procreation that the world contains, whether animal or vegetable: there is not the slightest reason to suppose that the animals and plants now existing are dissimilar to the first individuals of their respective species, but every reason to believe that they resemble in all points, and thus in the power of procreating their like: hence may we be assured that with the creation of organized beings came also the limitation of their life. Mankind could be no exception to the rule, as Eve was created before the Fall, and the nuptial benediction pronounced upon herself and consort.

64. The supposition that physical death was introduced by human sin, requires our first parents to have been *invulnerable.* No moral state, however exalted, could possibly exempt a race of organized beings such as man, however few in number, and though inhabiting the fairest and safest of material worlds, from the casual injuries of which organization, from its very delicacy, is susceptible. The same fire by which Adam "unfallen," must be supposed able to have warmed himself, would have burned him had he approached too near. Had he fallen from a tree, he was in no less danger of a broken limb than ourselves; had he struck his foot against a stone, he would have been no less easily bruised or cut. From such injuries, he would probably have recovered with an ease and rapidity which our present vitiated state of body debars us from conceiving, though faintly memorialized in the ready cure of the child and the temperate man compared with the tedious and uncertain one of the drunkard; but that he was not liable to them cannot for an instant be supposed, and if liable to them at all, of course he was susceptible of injuries terrible enough to kill. The more exquisite the capacity for life, always the readier is the liability to injury, as the eye, which holds the highest office in the empire of sense, is the organ most easily hurt and lost.

65. Death has its *proximate* causes, and its *remote* causes. The remote causes are thousand-fold; they are connected, directly and indirectly, with every solid and fluid in the body, and will only be determined, therefore, when pathology shall have become a perfect science. Every organ, and member, and tissue, is a possible threshold of death, and there is not one by which it may not enter unawares.

Our life contains a thousand springs,
And ends if one start wrong;
Strange that a harp of thousand strings
Should keep in tune so long!

The proximate causes, on the other hand, are few, and easily understood, being resolvable into the negation of these grand fundamental processes of life which have been described in the preceding chapters. Reduced to their smallest denomination, we saw that the processes in question are the Assimilation of food, and the Respiration of atmospheric air. The former we found to have for its main object, the nourishment of the blood, the organ with which that fluid is pre-eminently identified being the *heart*. Respiration we also found concerned with the blood, but identified peculiarly with the *lungs*. To facts, accordingly, connected with one or other of these two organs, death, like life, is in all cases proximately referable. We die, *proximately*, either because the blood has lost energy and volume, or because atmospheric air is insufficiently admitted to it. Popularly regarded, death consists simply in *loss of breath;* and founded as the common idea is, upon external appearances, it is not improper thus to speak of it. It always has been, and always will be right to speak of things in our common converse *as they appear to the senses.* We should always seek to *think* with the philosopher—to understand what is the *genuine* truth—but in our ordinary intercourse with one another in daily life, it is proper and expedient to speak of things as they *seem;* to say, for example, of the sun, that it "rises." So in the case of the dying. Here, to appearance, the breath only is concerned. The breath, accordingly, do we alone take note of, and further, in truth, we need not look. Whatever terrible disease may be ravaging the frame; whatever paralysis may hold the organs of sense and locomotion in deadly torpor—if there be

Breathing, we know that all is not over yet. "While there is life, there is hope," is only a paraphrase of—while there is breath, there is life. The primary cause of death may date from years before; it may baffle all physicians and physiology to determine; but in the final one there is no enigma.

'Tis the cessation of breath;
Silent and motionless we lie,
And no one knoweth more than this.
I saw our little Gertrude die;
She left off breathing, and no more
I smooth'd the pillow beneath her head.
She was more beautiful than before.
Like violets faded were her eyes,
By this we knew she was dead.
Through the open window looked the skies
Into the chamber where she lay,
And the wind was like the sound of wings,
As if angels came to bear her away.

Wedded to pictures and external shows of things, and inapt to rise from the merely symbolical representations to the holy presence of the thing signified, Pagan antiquity deemed that the breath was the very life itself. So persuaded were they of the identity, that they even thought that by inhaling the last sighs of their dying friends, to suck the fleeting spirit into their own bodies. Many beautiful allusions to this occur in the poets: Anna, lamenting over Dido, exclaims as she expires, "And ah! let me catch it with my mouth, if there be yet any stray breath about her lips!" A collection of the references may be seen in Kirchman, who, in his little book, *De Funeribus Romanorum*, devotes a chapter to the superstitions this people connected with the breath of the dying. The elegy of Bion on Adonis contains one of such far higher beauty than any of the Roman poets afford, that it is surprising he makes no mention of it,

"Rouse thee a little, Adonis, and again this last time kiss me! Kiss me just so far as there is life in thy kiss; till from thy heart thy spirit shall have ebbed into my lips and my soul, and I shall have drained thy sweet love-potion, and drunk out thy love; and I will treasure this kiss, even as it were Adonis himself."

66. While legitimate to speak of death as "ceasing to breathe," we must remember, therefore, that breathlessness is only a *part* of the idea of death. Ordinarily the circulation goes on a little longer, requiring, if death is to be affiliated on a single event, that it be referred to the heart rather than to the lungs. Slowly and sadly does the blood consent to death; like the tenderness of woman, its ministration is first and last in the history of life; that which was our safety, and stronghold, and delight in our noon-day vigor, in our sunset is still sedulous and faithful.

O my love! my wife!
Death, that hath suck'd the honey of thy breath,
Upon thy beauty yet hath had no power:
Thou art not conquer'd; beauty's ensign yet
Is crimson in thy lips and in thy cheeks,
And death's pale flag is not advancèd there.

Both ideas are right in their own province and connection. It is true that the heart is the last to die; it is true that the ceasing to breathe is death. The question to be answered is simply, how is death most truly *signified*, and in what formula of words is it most accurately described. Here, we have already seen, there is no mystery. That which in death arrests the attention of the bystander, and tells only too surely that all anxieties and cares are over, is the external, visible circumstance, the ceasing to breathe, not the invisible, secret circumstance of the blood ceasing to move; and thus, though the latter may be last in point of time, the former is death ostensibly; and this is sufficient to vindicate the expressions summed up in "the breath of life," the synonym in all ages of vitality. A true idea of the cause of death will of course include both circumstances; whichever occurs first, the other is sure to follow almost immediately, just as they are themselves inevitably brought on, though less rapidly and directly, by the stoppage of any other of the vital functions.

67. Essentially, then, death is the devitalizing and disorganizing of the Blood. We showed, when speaking of food, that it is from the blood that every tissue and organ of the body is constructed and repaired; and that as these are continually wasting away, there is a proportionate demand made upon the fountain from which alone they are renewable. It is obvious that if the needful supply of food for the blood be withheld, the blood itself must diminish and lose in virtue. It becomes too much reduced to circulate vigorously, and to meet the demands of the wasted tissues, and the body gradually withers away. This is most obviously shown in the lingering and miserable death induced by starvation. But it is common also as the result of certain diseases, which prevent the digestive organs from assimilating a sufficient amount of food to maintain the required quantity and quality of the vital fluid. To deficiencies of this nature may be referred an endless variety of morbid affections, one disease springing from another, as sickness from drinking of poisoned wells. So with death proximately connected with the *oxygenation* of the blood. If the natural power of breathing be so affected, whether by disease of the respiratory organs, or by mechanical hindrance, as to prevent the inspiration of air in sufficient quantity to supply the needful oxygen, the balance of action between the heart and lungs is upset, and death ensues as surely as in the former case. In cholera, according to one theory of this direful malady, although the blood circulates freely, and the patient breathes as in health; from some unknown cause connected with the nervous system, the blood fails to

become aërated. The discoloration of the body is attributed to its super-carbonized condition.* Not without reason then, has the blood always been famous, and regarded as the very seat of life. Blood and the life have in all ages been convertible terms, and justly. In Hades, says Homer, "the shades can neither speak, nor recognize the living, except they first drink blood." But it does not appear ever to have been used as a *name* for life. This has been the prerogative of the Air, just as the human race, though born of woman, and nourished by her, is proudly called Man. The only approach to such use is in such phrases as to "shed blood," meaning to kill; and calling death by the name of "the sword." An oath with the ancient Scythians was "by wind and sword," meaning "by life and death." The dignity which has in all ages been connected with Red, as a color, probably owes its ascription, in part at least, to the sanctity of that of which blood is the chief sign and emblem.

68. Violent deaths similarly come either of arrested circulation, as in the case of bleeding to death, and death by lightning; or of arrested respiration, as in strangulation, stifling, and suffocation by drowning, or by inhaling noxious vapors, such as the fumes of charcoal. A violent blow on the head, affecting the brain; or upon the stomach, affecting the ganglionic centres, although unattended by fracture, kills by the shock to the nervous system, which is instantaneously followed by stoppage both of the circulation and the breathing. Both of these great functions of course require that the nervous system shall be in good order, and

* Cholera, say others, appears to kill by separating the serum and the crassamentum of the blood. The former runs off by the bowels; the latter clogs the minute vessels, and causes the discoloration. Assuming this to be the true theory, it is a no less beautiful illustration that death is induced by the rupture of a complementary dualism.

thus, in tracing death to its profounder causes, we find that we cannot stop till in the presence of that mighty sphynx, the Brain, the fountain of nervous energy to the whole body. What the lungs and heart are to the blood, the lungs and brain are to the nervous fluid, which circulates through the nerves as the blood does through the veins, coëxistent and coëxtensive with it. Any irregularity in the stream, however it may be caused, is attended of course by analogous evils to the system. Denied by some, the existence of this fluid admits nevertheless of demonstration, both from analogy, and by inductions founded on experience. It exists and acts according to laws similar to those which regulate the existence and action of the blood, of which it may be regarded as a higher and more exquisite species.

The following table of the proximate causes of death is kindly furnished me by my friend, Dr. Henry Browne, of the Manchester Royal School of Medicine. It will be seen that he at once recognizes the great division that has been adverted to; and in the spirit of true philosophy, reconciles what in different authors appear to be conflicting views, though essentially the same.

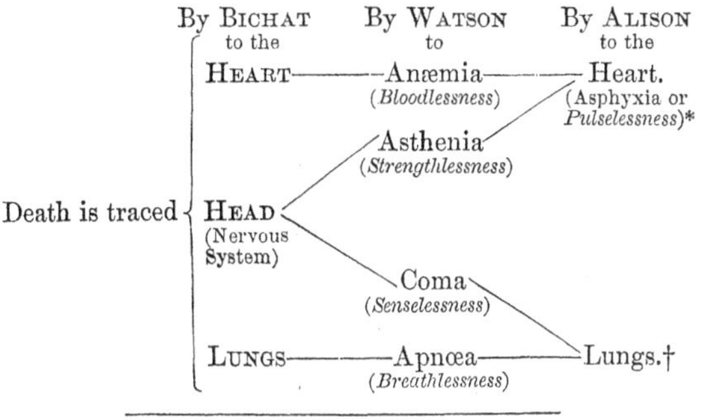

* The term *asphyxia* is often misapplied to breathlessness. Properly, it denotes nothing more than the cessation of the pulse, σφύξις.

† See on the proximate causes of death, and its phenomena, as

69. Among the inferior animals death is referable to analogous, if not identical hindrances to the due performance of the vital functions. Deprivation of food and air, violent shocks to the nervous system, especially where a brain is present, exposure to severe cold, are among the more frequent causes; one circumstance or another being more quickly and imminently fatal, according to the idiosyncracy of the species. As we travel towards the outermost circles of animal life, conditions which would speedily destroy a human being, a quadruped, or a bird, are borne, however, with astonishing indifference. It has often been observed of desperately wounded soldiers, who have nevertheless recovered, that while in most cases nothing is so soon destroyed as human life, in others there is nothing harder to dislodge. Applied to many of the smaller races of the animal world this almost becomes a rule. To say nothing of those extraordinary animalcules which, according to the experiments of Spallanzani,* may be dried into mummies, kept indefinitely in that state, and then revived; creatures even so large as insects† are in many cases nearly proof against the ordinary agents of vital overthrow. Several extraordinary instances of this may be read in that amusing work "Episodes of Insect Life," vol. ii., pp. 162–

above briefly set forth, the excellent Outlines of Physiology and Pathology of Dr. Alison. Edinburgh, 1833.

* Tracts upon the Nature of Animals, vol. 1, p. xxxvi., &c.

† Insects are commonly cited to express ideas of *smallness*. But to innumerable creatures they are what whales and elephants are to ourselves. The animal which holds the middle place in the scale of size, reckoning from the *Monas crepusculum*, the minutest to which our microscopes have yet reached, is the common house-fly. That is, there are as many degrees of size between the house-fly and the Monas, reckoning *downwards*, as, reckoning upwards, there are between the house-fly and the whale.

167, &c. It is worthy of note that these latter creatures, like reptiles, can better endure intense heat than intense cold, of which they always stand in dread. Tenacity of life is wonderfully exhibited also in the tortoise family, and in toads, which appear to be capable of living in a state of torpidity for very considerable periods. The stories however, so common in newspapers, of their leaping out of stones when suddenly broken in two, and out of timber when being sawn, seem to be none of them sufficiently authenticated. Many naturalists positively deny that it ever occurs. Experiments made by Dr. Buckland led him to the conclusion that when totally secluded from the access of atmospheric air, these creatures cannot live a year, and that they cannot survive beyond two years if entirely prevented from obtaining food.

70. Death purely from *old age*, whether in man or the inferior animals, is of course not to be confounded with such as comes of accident or disease. Here it is induced by the gradual closing up of delicate vessels; the hardening and ossification of tissues; the languid and imperfect action of important organs. These changes promote others; by and bye some principal part becomes affected, and lastly, where present, the great dualism of heart and lungs. No creature can exist without these changes taking place in it, and superinducing, sooner or later, senility and dissolution. Agerasia belongs only to the soul; this alone lives in perpetuity of youth.

71. In the Vegetable Kingdom, as in the Animal, death is the stoppage of the process which maintains life. Starvation, drought, exposure to intense frost, or to an atmosphere infected with acids and other obnoxious chimney-products, will arrest the functions of plant-life as effectually as the opposite conditions encourage them. Plants suffer the more sorely from such influences through their inability to move

away from the place of danger. To compensate this, they are endowed with a tenacity of life far exceeding that of animals, or at least, of animals of equal rank. The stricken quadruped falls never to rise again; the stricken plant buds anew in calm endurance. "There is hope of a tree, if it be cut down, that it will sprout again, and that the tender branch of it will not cease. Though the root thereof wax old in the earth, and the stock thereof die in the ground;—yet through the scent of water it will bud, and bring forth boughs like a plant."

72. In the mineral world, death is simply Decomposition. All bodies resolve into their elements at the time of death; but whereas in plants and animals this occurs only as the result and supplement of death, in minerals death and decomposition are the same. Life, we must remember, is expressed in the mineral simply as chemical affinity;—no *functions* take place in it; death accordingly, consists simply in the setting aside of that affinity. Some stronger affinity coming into operation from without, one or more of the constituent elements is drawn away, and the substance ceases to exist. No mere melting, or crushing, or pulverizing, or modelling by the hands of Art, affects the life of a mineral. Though a piece of marble be ground into impalpable powder, the atoms are living marble still; every fragment is still animated by the life which holds together its component lime and carbonic acid; the minutest particle as completely represents and embodies the nature of the original mass as a drop of spray from the advancing wave does that of the sea. Such at least is it to the eye of the *chemist*. To the unversed in his magical science, demolition is annihilation, and in a limited sense, it is not erroneous thus to regard it. Put side by side, the compact and solid stone naturally speaks more of life than the mere heap of scattering dust; the one preserves the chiselled writing of forty centuries, the

other disappears with the first curl of wind. Hence it is that in Scripture, dust is the common name for what is unvitalized or dead; while Stone or Rock, which give the highest possible idea of solidity and permanence, characters the very opposite to those of dust, are the equally common appellations of the Fountain of Life. Mr. Ruskin explains these beautiful metaphors on the principle that with consolidation we naturally connect the idea of purity, and with disintegration that of foulness. "The purity of the rock," says he, "contrasted with the foulness of dust or mould, is expressed by the epithet 'living,' very singularly given to the rock in almost all languages." Doubtless there is a truth in this, for life and purity, both in the physical and the moral world, are correlative, but as Mr. Ruskin himself acknowledges in the next sentence, the deeper reason is the coherence of the particles in the stone, and their utter disunion in the case of the dust. The page is well worth turning to, not merely for the philosophic views on the general subject of inorganic life, but for the admirable commentary on the text that "pureness is made to us so desirable because expressive of the constant presence and energizing action of the Deity in matter, through which all things live, and move, and have their being; and that foulness is painful as the accompaniment of disorder and decay, and always indicative of the withdrawal of Divine support."* Neither consolidation nor purity are at all times intended in this remarkable epithet. In Virgil, for example:—

> Fronte sub adversa scopulis pendentibus antrum;
> Intus aquæ dulces, *vivoque sedilia saxo*.
> Nympharum domus.—(*Æneid* i. 16–18.)

"Opposite is a cave, the retreat of the wood-nymphs, formed by over-hanging rocks; inside are limpid waters, and *seats of living stone*."

* Modern Painters, vol. ii., pp. 73–75.

What then shall be the meaning here? At first sight there is none. But when we bethink ourselves that the cool, humid atmosphere of such sweet natural summer-houses and grottoes as the poet describes, causes every surface upon which the light can fall to clothe itself with green and most delicate moss, in an instant the words become animated and picturesque, we hear the trickling waters, and feel ourselves sheltering from the fervid noonday sun, each great stone a living cushion for our repose. The characteristic of true poetry is, that by single words thus artlessly introduced, it awakens all the most beautiful memories and associations of the heart.

73. Hitherto we have spoken of inorganic *compounds.* The life of the *simple* substances, the fifty or sixty primitive elements, or as-yet-undecompounded bodies, is much less precarious. When, under chemical agency, a compound is broken up, though the mass ceases to be, the constituents are in no wise affected. As in the crowding together of a multitude of men for some great social or political object, though it is the assemblage which attracts our attention, every member of it has an interior, unnoticed life of his own, so is it with the several elements which in combination form the acid or the salt. The compound has one life, the elements have another; and as the individuals which compose the meeting live on, though the meeting itself dissolves and dies with the conclusion of the business that brought it together, so do the simple elements of destroyed compounds; they separate, not to perish, but to enter upon new activities. Though several even of the most solid of the simple substances may, under the influence of heat, be volatilized and altogether dissipated, zinc and potassium for instance among the metals, no one can say that any one of these substances is destructible *absolutely.* No one can assert that like iodine vaporized and condensed in a Florence flask, or

like camphor in a glass jar (which evaporates only to descend again in glittering frost-work), they do not consolidate afresh. That they would do so we should certainly expect, though it is quite as likely that when so attenuated, new changes and decompositions come into process, causing them to return to the eyes of men in the form of some *other* "primitive element;" for, as we saw in our second chapter, it is not only possible, but extremely probable, that all the so-called primitive elements are but different presentations of two fundamental ones, their respective atoms being variously associated, and giving us oxygen, gold, silex, &c., in turn, according to the nature of the union. For anything we can tell, the identical oxygen, gold, silex, &c., of the primæval world, are still in being, though in the course of ages they may have undergone innumerable vicissitudes. For aught we know, on the other hand, the primæval gold, silver, &c., may in great measure have perished, and as many reproductions have occurred in the secret but mighty laboratory of inorganic nature, as there have been procreations of plants and animals in its organic realm.

CHAPTER VIII.

THE VARIOUS LEASES OF LIFE.

74. Though death is the universal end, nothing is more curiously varied than the Lease of existence. The present chapter will be devoted to the consideration of what is certainly one of the most interesting mysteries in the economy of life—the question, why do things live for determinate periods? We do not mean, why do certain *individuals* die earlier than others of their kind, as when infants and young people are removed by death; but why does the ordinary maximum of age vary so immensely in regard to the different *species* of things; why do some come to maturity and perish in less than a year, while others endure for three, four, ten, twenty, a hundred, even for thousands of years? For that the duration of the different species of animals and plants is thus determinate, is certain; every one of them has a lease of life peculiar to itself, though true that in the greater part the exact term remains yet to be ascertained. Did we know the minute history of horse and lion, thrush and pelican, antelope and red-breast; were we intimately acquainted with the natural constitution of each brute and bird, the duration of the different species of the organized creation would unquestionably allow of being tabulated as exactly as the daily rising and setting of the sun. We might anticipate such a fixity of duration from the determinate character of everything else which concerns living beings. Every species of animal and plant has its deter-

minate form, size, and organization; the period of gestation, though it differs widely in the aggregate of the animal kingdom, is invariably the same in the same species; similarly, the growing of seeds, which is vegetable incubation, and the period of the flowering of plants, are in any given species uniformly the same; it is but reasonable then to expect that there are definite leases of existence, and observation proves the opinion to be well-founded. Under hostile conditions, the allotted periods of duration may doubtless be greatly shortened, as experience shows us every day, while under favorable ones they may sometimes be surprisingly extended. As in the human species, mortality cuts down myriads before puberty, while now and then we are called to wonder at an Old Parr, so in all other tribes of being, though the unusual longevity is perhaps never so great in proportion. Making all allowance for such exceptions, and giving everything fair judgment, it still comes true that there is a fixed lease which the mass of the healthy individuals of the species attain, and beyond which the life of the mass is seldom prolonged. Whether all or any living things at present reach, even in exceptional cases, the *full* term of life originally allotted to their race, it is impossible to know—the probability would seem that few, perhaps none, reach their intended maximum, except an individual here and there. That individuals do sometimes prodigiously outlive their generation, certainly does not seem explicable on any supposition but that in the longævals the native capacity is fully realized. We ought perhaps to consider enormous ages less as exceptions to the rule than as revelations of the lease with which the species is potentially gifted by the Almighty. Thus, if a certain percentage of mankind live to a hundred and fifty, and a certain percentage of horses to sixty, are not these ages to be esteemed the terms respectively prescribed in the beginning? Very little is yet known with certainty as to the periods of life *ordinarily* attained. Beyond some broad, general peculiarities in the larger classes of living things, and tolerably correct statistics respecting the animals man is most familiar with, and the shortest and longest lived plants, scarcely anything precise has yet been arrived at. The literature of natural history is almost barren upon the subject; physiologists generally dismiss it in a paragraph. Buffon is the most copious in detached observations; the best summary, brief though it be, is contained perhaps in the admirable and celebrated little treatise of Hufeland.* The recently published work of the eminent Parisian *savant* Flourens,† to which attention has been so largely attracted in intelligent circles, sets forth a masterly doctrine on the relation between the period of attaining maturity and the duration of life, amending the well-known theory of Buffon, and placing it on a sound physiological basis; but in other respects it has little really new. The whole subject is thus in its infancy. The profounder and more interesting question, or part of the question, namely, *why* the divine lease of life varies so widely; why, for example, the rabbit is ordained to live for only eight years, while the dog is allowed to run on to twenty-four; why the wheat-plant fruits and dies in a few months, while the cedar is appointed to watch the lapse of centuries; this appears wholly untouched, probably from its involving a spiritual idea, usually the last to be considered, though the first in importance and illuminating power. That there is a reason for the various duration of life, we may be sure; there can be nothing acci-

---

* The Art of Prolonging Life, excellently edited, in one volume, by Erasmus Wilson, 1853.

† On Human Longevity, and the amount of Life upon the Globe. From the French, by Charles Martel, 1855.

dental or capricious about it; what that reason may be, is a magnificent problem for Christian philosophy.

75. The question applies of course only to *organized* beings, at least in its fulness. In minerals, for reasons already amply stated, duration is altogether irregular and indeterminate. Ruled wholly by contingencies, no scale of existence can be drawn up with regard either to simple or to compound bodies. It cannot be said that the diamond averages so many years; gold so many more; flint so many less. The same with any composite substance, as a lump of marble, or a mass of common salt; it lives as long as it is not assailed by the particular chemical agencies which would decompose it, and which nothing in the substance itself can repel: it is liable to them from the first moment of its existence, and may thus be extinguished in an hour, or enjoy a kind of immortality, conditional on its seclusion from them. How vast the antiquity of many a little pebble, yet how slender the tenure of its existence, which a few drops of acid would overthrow in as few minutes! It is to be observed, however, that, as if in prefiguration of the higher kingdoms of nature—a beautiful subject, hereafter to be illustrated at length—in the more exquisite and delicate developments of the mineral world, or crystals, there are species that actually seem subject to a kind of natural and organic dissolution. After arriving at what may be esteemed a kind of maturity, certain crystals decompose, (of course under the influence of new conditions at variance with those under which they were formed,) and decaying, give curious skeletons of what they were in the bloom of their existence. Such relics are found in mines, often with crystals of different composition forming amid the ruins of the extinct one, just as on the shoulders of an ancient oak we may sometimes see sapling trees of other species, the products of seeds carried thither by some bird or wafting wind, and which have fat-

tened on its decaying heart. Vary the text-word to suit the especial theme, and there is no part of creation to which those fine philosophic verses of Pope's will not apply:—

> See dying vegetables life sustain,
> And life dissolving, vegetate again;
> All forms that perish, other forms supply;
> By turns we catch the vital breath, and die.

There is no *essential* difference between the violent death of the crystal in the laboratory of the chemist, and the quasi-natural in the mine; only in the latter the idea of determinate duration seems first to reveal itself.

76. To obtain clear and comprehensive ideas respecting the duration of life, it is requisite that a tolerable acquaintance should be formed with the particular circumstances and phenomena of vital action, also with a fair number of the *species* of things. No true advance can be made in any department of the philosophy of nature while we rest in such generalities as beasts, birds, and fishes; we must learn *species* minutely and accurately, watching them from season to season, and from year to year, and penetrating, as far as possible, into their anatomy. None are better for this purpose, or so good, as our own common native plants, and wild animals, winged and wingless, with which we can so readily become familiar, and ignorant of which no one can pretend to the name of naturalist. With such knowledge in hand, the further steps can be taken pleasantly and safely, but not before. We shall consider, primarily, the phenomena connected with the duration of life in the Vegetable Kingdom, seeing that this is essentially the outline and prefigurement of the Animal, and thus the natural starting-point of all high physiological inquiry.

77. No one has entered Nature through its "gate Beautiful," the world of plants, without soon discovering that the

duration of life is here of three general denominations. Some species are annual, or rather semi-annual, living from spring only to the close of the autumn of the same year; others are biennial, living to the close of the second autumn, but never beyond it; the greater part are perennial, or competent to live for a long series of years. Annuals include many of the commoner garden flowers and culinary vegetables, as marigolds and lupines, peas and beans, which require accordingly to be freshly raised from seed every season: biennials are likewise common in gardens: perennials comprise all those plants which form the staple vegetation of a country, withering to a certain extent in the winter, and even dying down to the roots, but sprouting afresh with the return of spring; also the countless varieties of trees and shrubs, whether deciduous or ever-green. The perennials exhibit as great diversity in lease of life as the different species of animals. Some decay in as few as four or five years; others, often remarkable for their odoriferous and balsamic qualities, as sage, balm, and lavender, endure for ten or more; next come the larger and robuster kinds of shrubs, as rhododendrons and azaleas; then such trees as are of rapid growth, and the substance of which is soft, as the poplar and willow; and lastly, those mighty, slow-growing, solid-wooded pillars of the forest, as the cedar and oak, at whose feet whole nations rise and fall.*

"Non hiemes illam, non flabra, neque imbres
Convellunt; immota manet, multosque per annos
Multa virum volvens durando secula vincit!"

---

* There are olive-trees in the supposed garden of Gethsemane which have been estimated at two thousand years; but these are probably mere descendants of those which are connected with the narratives of the Gospels, put forth originally as suckers from their roots, and thus to be regarded rather as restorations than as identically the same.

How vast are the periods of life allotted to the longæval trees may be judged from the following list of ages known to have been reached by patriarchs of the respective kinds:—

Cercis	300 years.	Walnut	900 years.
Elm	335 "	Oriental Plane	1000 "
Ivy	450 "	Lime	1100 "
Maple	516 "	Spruce	1200 "
Larch	576 "	Oak	1500 "
Orange	630 "	Cedar	2000 "
Cypress	800 "	Schubertia	3000 "
Olive	800† "	Yew	3200 "

Four and five thousand years are assigned to the Taxodium and the Adansonia, and Von Martius describes Locust-trees in the South American forests which he believes to have begun their quasi-immortality in the days of Homer. Whether or no, it may safely be asserted that the world possesses at this moment *living* memorials of antiquity at least as old as the most ancient monuments of human art. How grand and solemn is even the thought of a tree coeval with the pyramids of Egypt and the sculptures of Nineveh, yet still putting forth leaves, and inviting the birds to come and "sing among the branches!" Well might the old preacher of Alexandria discern in a tree the terrestrial image of heavenly truth.

78. The way in which the ages of these vegetable Nestors have been ascertained leaves no doubt of their correctness. In some few cases the data have been furnished by historical records, and by tradition; but the botanical archæologist has a resource independent of either, and when carefully used, infallible. The whole subject of the signs and testimonies of particular age is interesting, and deserves to be here dealt with, but unfortunately scarcely anything is yet known about it. The deficiency is much to be regretted,

seeing that it is often of serious importance to the interests of society that means should be possessed for determining the exact period of a given life. The most important of all, the data whereby the age of one of our own species may be determined, are as yet altogether undiscovered. Though long habits of social intercourse may enable us to guess pretty nearly, by the altered form of the features, wrinkles where once was smoothness, changes in the color and luxuriance of the hair, also in the gait and general physical exterior, still it is only a guess; we cannot be sure until we have consulted the register or the family Bible. With the lower animals it is a little easier; the age of the horse, for instance, to about eight or nine years old, may be told by its teeth; the horns of certain quadrupeds similarly announce their ages up to a given epoch; in birds the age may sometimes be deduced from the wear and altered form of the bill; in the whale it is known by the size and number of the laminæ of "whale-bone," which increase yearly, and seem to indicate a maximum of three or four hundred years to this creature; the age of fishes appears to be marked on their scales, as seen under a microscope; and that of molluscous animals, such as the oyster, in the strata of their shells; still, there is no certain and connected knowledge in reference to any but the first-named, and even this applies only to the youth of the animal. Of all the forms of nature, TREES alone disclose their ages candidly and freely. In the stems of all trees which have branches, that is to say, in all "Exogens," the increase takes place by means of an annual deposit of wood, spread in an even layer upon the surface of the preceding one. The deposits commence the first summer of the tree's existence, and continue as long as it survives; hence, upon taking a horizontal section of the stem, a set of beautiful concentric circles becomes visible, each circle indicating an annual deposit, and thus marking a year in the biography of the general mass. So much for the felled tree; in the living and standing one of course the circles are concealed from view; to learn their number here, therefore, some ingenuity is required. The simplest and most certain method is to burrow into the trunk with an instrument like an immense cheese-taster, which intersects every layer, and draws out a morsel of each, sufficiently distinct for enumeration. Where this is not convenient, the age may be estimated by ascertaining, as nearly as possible, the annual rate of increase, then taking the diameter of the trunk at about a yard from the ground, and calculating by "rule of three." Thus, if in the space of an inch there be an average of five annual layers, a hundred inches will announce five hundred years of life. The latter method requires to be used, however, with extreme caution, because of the varying rate of growth, both in individual trees, and in their different species. In the earlier periods of life, trees increase much faster than when adult; the oak, for instance, grows most rapidly between its twentieth and thirtieth years; and when old, the annual deposits considerably diminish, so that the strata are thinner, and the rings proportionately closer. Some trees slacken in rate of growth at a very early period of life; the layers of the oak become thinner after forty, those of the elm after fifty, those of the yew after sixty. Unless allowance be made for this, and also for the irregular thickness of the layers, which vary both with seasons and with the position of the tree in regard to the sun, errors are inevitable. The concentric circles are not equally distinct in the different kinds of trees; the best examples occur perhaps in the cone-bearers, as the fir, cedar, and pine. The opinion not infrequently held, that the trees of cold and temperate countries show them better than those of the tropics, is, however, a mistaken one. Certainly there are equinoctial woods in which they are less decidedly marked than in particular European species, but in others again they are plainer. Indistinctness and emphasis in the rings are phenomena independent of climate, being characteristic, in fact, of particular species, genera, and even families. There are trees which are altogether destitute of rings. These belong to the class called "Endogens," of which the noblest and typical form is the Palm. Here the sign of age is furnished by the scars or stumps of the fallen leaves, which are of enormous size, few in number, and produced only upon the summit of the lofty, slender, branchless trunk. A certain number of new leaves expand every year, and about an equal number of the oldest decay, so that by taking the total of the scars, and dividing it by the average annual development of new leaves, a tolerable approximation may be come to. But it can rarely be relied upon; it is a method indeed by no means universally practicable, the scars of the fallen leaves being very variable in their degree of permanence in different species. The fan-leaved palms preserve their scars only at the lowest part of the stem; they lose them as they increase in age and height, so that from the middle to the top it is nearly bare. Sternberg says that the fossil *Lepidodendra* are the only plants in which the scars remain perfect throughout the entire length. Wood-sections, neatly cut and polished, so as to display the concentric circles, are highly ornamental objects, independently of their scientific instructiveness. A collection of specimens from the lopped boughs of the hedgerows and plantations, and from the timber-yard of the furniture-maker, where many rich exotics may be procured, rivals in beauty a cabinet of shells or fossils, and quite as abundantly rewards intelligent employment of the leisure hour.

79. Of the *potential* longevity of a tree or plant, a pretty fair estimate may be arrived at from a variety of circumstances. For example, there are relations between the

duration of life and the quality of the *fruit* which plants produce. Those which give tender and juicy fruit, or at all events such trees as do this, are in general shorter-lived than those which yield hard and dry, and these are shorter-lived than such as produce only little seeds. The apple and the pear live shorter lives than nut-trees, which are out-lived in turn by the birch and the elm, as these are by the major part of the Coniferæ, in which long-lived family there is probably not a species that does not flourish for at least a hundred years. The Alpine firs and larches frequently attain five centuries, and even the common red pine and the Scotch fir reach three to four. With a few exceptions, the seeds of the whole family are noticeably small, though the containing cones may be of considerable size. One of the greatest trees in the world, the *Wellingtonia gigantea* of California, a member of this tribe, with an estimated maximum age of two thousand years, has a beautifully-formed but remarkably small cone, and seeds in proportion. Such trees as the birch, the elm, and the conifers, are useful to man for their timber, a service rarely rendered by the fruit-bearers. Trees again, that yield pleasant fruit, fit for human food, ordinarily live for shorter periods than those of which the produce is bitter and austere, and unserviceable to him as an edible. Most, if not all of the plants on which man in his civilized state depends for food, are exceedingly short-lived. The Cerealia or corn-producing plants, as wheat, rice, barley, and oats, are annuals without exception; so are nearly all kinds of pulse. The large classes of esculent vegetables represented by the turnip, carrot, and cabbage, are also either annual or biennial. How much man has benefitted by this wise arrangement it is impossible to estimate. Did his daily bread grow on longæval trees, like acorns, asking no care and toil, the most efficient means to his development would have been wanting, as is still evidenced in the lands of the cocoa-nut and banana; but depending, as he has been so largely obliged to do, on *annual* plants, demanding incessant care, they may be gratefully regarded as the prime instrument of his rise in intelligence and morals.

80. The form or configuration of plants has most important relations with their lease of life. Those trees usually live to the greatest age which attain the least vertical height in proportion to the diameter of their trunks, and the lateral spread of their branches. Size and substance have also to be taken note of. Small and attenuate plants almost always live for shorter periods than bulky ones, and tender and delicate species than the stout and hard-grained. The latter owe their longer lives, in a physiological point of view, to the abundance of firm, fibrous matter which enters into their composition, and without which it appears indeed impossible that any considerable age can be arrived at, though there are instances where hard and durable wood is found in trees of briefer life than some that are soft-wooded. The lime-tree has softer wood than the walnut, beech, and pear, yet lives longer than either of them; and the Baobab of Senegal, which undoubtedly lives to a great age, though some of the accounts of it are probably exaggerated, is said to be so soft that it may be sliced with a knife. That bulk should be accompanied by long duration, it is easy to understand. The larger a plant or tree, the greater is the surface which it exposes to the atmosphere; and as it feeds by every leaf, the scope and opportunity for the exercise of the vital functions is proportionately extended. The more leaves a tree can put forth, and maintain in healthy action, the firmer is its hold upon the future. Viewed in regard to their annual rejuvenescence, trees may be regarded as little worlds in themselves,—solid masses from which a multitude of separate and perfect plants is vernally put forth, every new

shoot and twig being exactly analogous to an annual that has risen from a seed. As the successive generations of plants fill the earth more and more with the seeds of life, and thus both maintain its actual richness in verdure and blossom, and enlarge its potential, in reference to years to come, so the annual crops of twigs and leaves that clothe the tree, by their re-action tend to consolidate and strengthen it. The more exuberant its fertility, the more does it augment in energy of life,—picturing therein, one of the finest truths in our spiritual history; the soul energizes as it works. But extent of leafy surface will not of itself induce longevity. There are many annuals that develope an immense amount of leaf, as the gourd and the melon. In such plants, it is counteracted by their exceedingly rapid growth, and consequent want of solidity; for while too great a degree of solidification of the tissues, whether in plants or animals, hinders their proper vital activity, especially those great processes on which life so eminently depends, namely, the free movement of the juices,—the other extreme, or a too lax and succulent texture, is no less surely fatal to stability and endurance. Such texture is almost always found in the short-lived plants, coming, as in the gourd, of their rapid extension, while firm, dense, and compact texture is fully as characteristic of the longævals. Compare the wood of the yew and the box-tree with that of the soft, sappy black poplar, and the willows that "spring by the water-courses." Fungi, mushrooms, and toadstools, which, as regards their superterraneous portion, are the most rapid in development of any plants, often reaching their full size in the course of a night, are also the loosest in texture, and the soonest and speediest to dissolve. Some decay in a few hours; while none, perhaps, last longer than from seven to fifteen days, excepting the perennial Polypori and their congeners, the life of which extends to several years. Beautiful specimens of these last, of a rich and glossy brown, have been sent to me from New Brunswick, where they grow upon the birch and maple trees.

81. The distinction of annual, biennial, and perennial, in regard to the duration of plants, is liable to be affected by certain accidents, but the changes are never so great or so deeply-seated as for the principle of a fixed lease of life to be abnegated by them. An inhospitable climate will shorten the life of perennials to a single season, as happens with mignonette, which in Barbary is shrub-like, and with the Palma-Christi, which in India is a stately tree, though in England neither survives a year in the open air; on the other hand, unsuitable food, excess of wet, or any other circumstance by which the flowering of the plant is retarded, will induce unaccustomed longevity. This brings us to the consideration of one of the greatest truths in the philosophy of nature, namely, that all living things exist, and feed, and grow, and gather strength, in order that they may propagate their race. Doubtless, things universally have their social uses to subserve, and to perform which they were originally created, and are sustained in their respective places by the Almighty; but all these uses have reference, essentially, to the great ultimate use of preserving the race extant upon the earth, and multiplying it indefinitely, seeing that in the maintenance and multiplication without end of receptacles of His Life, consists the highest glory of God. This is the end and design not only of the physical, but even of the moral and intellectual uses performed by mankind towards one another, all of them tending, more or less directly, to promote and adorn it. However unconscious we may be of their influence and private agency, and however little we may feel ourselves to be personally identified with the result, the perpetuation of the race is at once the beginning and the end of all the feelings incident to our nature. What

ever we may seem to ourselves to be working for, the secret aspiration of the heart is always Home and one's own fire-side, bright and sweet with filial conjugal affection; every virtue, desire, and passion, that stirs the soul, may finally be referred hither; in a word, whatever is friendly to humanity, in any of its needs, whatever gives life and solidity to existence, is a collateral means to reproduction, and was purposely introduced to aid it, and without such aid reproduction would languish and at last fail. *Why* reproduction is the great end of physical existence, is found in its needfulness as the counterpoise of Death. As the destiny of all things is to die, were there no means established for their replacement, the earth would soon become a desolate void; but through the magnificent law of procreation, nothing is ever extinguished, nor a gap ever caused that is not instantly filled up. Though Time slays and devours every individual in turn, whether animal or plant; by procreation the species is preserved perfect and immortal, the whole of nature unchanged and ever young.

States fall, Arts fade, but Nature doth not die!

By the continual succession of beings, all exactly resembling one another, and their parents and ancestors, the existence of any one of them is virtually maintained in perpetuity; the balance and the relations of the different parts of nature are kept intact, and to philosophic view, Time itself, rather than the temporal, is the slain one. Thus looked at, with the eyes of a large philosophic generalization, all the individuals of any given species that have ever existed, and all that have yet to come into existence, form but one great Whole; the process of reproduction whereby they follow one another in the stream that unites the living representatives to the primæval Adam of the race, being only Nutrition on a grand and perennial scale. Every individual, so long as it lives its little life, is the species in miniature, reproducing all its tissues as fast as they decay, through vital action and reaction, or marriage in its simplest form; conversely, the aggregate of the individuals, or the race, is as it were a single one, diffused over an immense area of time and country, and nourishing and regenerating itself by means of that highest and most complicated play of the marriage-principle which the word marriage popularly denotes. Every man, for example, and every woman, considered physiologically, is the human race in little, everything that belongs to the race being enacted, essentially and daily, in their individual bodies; at the same moment every man and every woman is but as a molecule of one great Homo, now some six thousand years of age, and spread over the whole surface of the earth.

82. Feeding, growing, all the vital functions and phenomena of the earlier stages of life are to be regarded accordingly, as Nature's preliminaries to Reproduction. Every part of organic creation illustrates this, but in the plant it is seen in chief perfection, excepting only the butterfly, in whose little life the history is epitomized. In the first or grub state, it is a creeping cormorant; the alimentary organs greatly predominate, and growth is rapid. In the last or winged state, on the other hand, though it sips from a thousand blossoms, it takes little or no sustenance, the excess of intestinal canal has given way to the generative organs, which now assume the mastery, and up to the time of its early death, influence almost exclusively its habits. Many kinds of butterflies cannot eat indeed, if they would, for they have *no mouths*. Adorned in their bridal vestments, love and pleasure, as they flirt their painted fans, form the brief and brilliant pastime with which they close their days. The winged state of the butterfly is what the period of flowering is to plants, and the reason why longer life is

occasioned to plants by delay in flowering, as above alluded to, is that in the flowers are contained their organs of procreation. Hence until they have bloomed they must needs remain childless, or with the consummation of life unrealized and unattained. Procreation, or the production of seed, is made to actuate plants with a vital impulse so wonderful and so like the instinct of animals towards the same end, that no other name conveys an adequate idea of it; they prepare for the effectuation of it from the first moment of existence, and until they have accomplished their purpose, unless killed by intense cold, or sudden and absolute deprivation of nourishment, will keep their hold on life with a tenacity almost invincible. It may be taken as an axiom in vegetable physiology, that *cæteris paribus*, no plant dies a natural death till it has ripened seeds. If its life be endangered, by penury of food or mutilation, the entire vital energy of the plant concentrates itself in the production of a flower, it ceases to put forth leaves, and expends its whole force in efforts to secure progeny. This is strikingly exemplified in hot, dry gardens, and by summer waysides, where, as if conscious of the impending danger, plants ordinarily of considerable stature, begin to propagate while scarcely an inch high. Delay in flowering, attended by prolonged life, is usually the result of *excess* of nourishment. Thus, if a plant grow in too luxurious, or too watery a soil, causing it to become unduly succulent, or if it be subjected to an atmosphere too warm for it, and thus unnaturally stimulated, instead of producing flowers, it "runs to leaf;" it passes into the condition of an over-fattened or pampered animal, and is similarly unfitted for the reproductive function; and like the animal again, to re-enter upon it, must become depletheric. No plant can suffer from phyllomania and be fruitful at the same moment. Diclinous plants, when growing in wet localities, are remarkable for the excess of male flowers over female. Delay in flowering and consequent prolongation of life beyond the usual limit, also occur through insufficiency of nourishment, and want of kindly climatic aid. Many plants live longer in our gardens than in their native countries simply for want of the encouragement to blossom which they are accustomed to at home. In Mexico the great American Aloe comes into bloom when four or five years old, and then dies, while in England it drags a kind of semi-torpid existence for so long before the flowers appear, that it is a proverb for a hundred years' preparation. Some plants may have their lives prolonged a little while by nipping off the flowers as soon as they begin to fade. Here, however, so much of the vital energy has been expended in the production of the floral organs, that they never properly recover themselves. When the flowers of a plant, under cultivation, become double; that is, when they have their reproductive organs changed into petals, and are thereby prevented from seeding, their life is considerably prolonged; annuals even become perennial; Tropœolum minus, when double, has endured for twelve years. The life of annuals may also be prolonged by grafting them upon perennials. Many annual Solanaceæ will live for years when grafted on ligneous species of the same genus, as the annual kinds of Tobacco, when grafted on the Nicotiana glauca, that beautiful woody species which grows to a greater height than a man. A similar extension of life may be given to some of the annual species of Dianthus. Lastly, as regards the relation of procreation to the lease of life, it is a universal law, both in animals and plants, that the earlier the puberty, the earlier is the death. Annuals, which flower when only a few weeks old, die in a few months; those plants only live long which do not blossom till their fifth or sixth year; the highest ages invariably pertain to those which are the slowest to celebrate their nuptials. Very young forest trees are never found in flower.

83. Many of the conditions which affect the duration of vegetable life, are thus results or accompaniments of Cultivation. The object of cultivation is, for the most part, greater *fruitfulness;* few plants are cultivated merely for the sake of their wood or foliage; the aim is to procure either more flowers to delight us with their beauty, or more seeds to make use of as food. In either case, the stimulation which they receive at the hands of the gardener tends to hasten them on towards maturity, and to excite the reproductive energy to the utmost. The consequence is that the conservative power is reduced, and the organism prematurely exhausted. Cultivation, therefore, as a rule, may be regarded as a shortener of plant-life. Of course it is only the life of the *individual* that is abbreviated; the absolute lease of life in the *species* is unaltered and unalterable, and is completed wherever the individuals enjoy their existence unmolested.

84. The result of *one* of the arts of culture makes it seem as if there were no such thing as a fixed lease of life in plants, viz., the art of propagation by slips and cuttings, which, when, carefully detached and placed in the soil, will grow into counterparts of the original, and (they themselves being extensible after the same manner) effect for it a kind of perpetuity. Vines of the time of the Roman empire, have been thus transmitted to the present day, gifted as it were, by man with a longevity unknown to their state of nature. Many herbaceous perennials, especially in gardens, possess in this aptitude such ample and efficient means of propagation as to incline to the belief that their flowers and seeds are of quite secondary importance, dedicated rather to the heart and appetite of man. The lily of the valley, for example, and the strawberry.

85. To see how this curious phenomenon harmonizes with the indubitable law of specific lease, we have to consider the peculiar structure or organic composition of plants, and, as flowing from this latter, the nature and amount of their individuality. The organic composition of a plant is very different from that of an animal. In all except the very lowest forms of animals, there is but one of each kind of organ, or of each set of organs, as the case may be, as one heart, one mouth, one set of limbs, one system of bones. Every organ is more or less in connection with every other, and not one of those which are preëminently "vital" can be removed without causing instant death to the whole fabric. The animal, in a word, is an absolute Unity, every part being reciprocally dependent upon every other part, and the springs of its life *centralized.* In the tree, on the other hand, there is *no* centralization; no organ occurs only once; everything is a thousand times recapitulated; there are as many lungs as there are leaves, as many procreant parts as flowers. Like an arborescent zoophyte, a Sertularia, for example, a tree is a vast congeries of distinct organisms, every one of them as independent of the others as one sheep is independent of the remainder of the flock, only that all are organically united, and contribute, by their union, to the general welfare, and to the building up of a magnificent social edifice. Every separate twig is a little plant in itself; consociated with the others, but still independent of them, it feeds, grows, and procreates in its own person. A tree, therefore (and any plant old enough to have thrown out buds and shoots), is at once an Individual and a Community. It is an Individual in respect of its presentation of the physiognomy and characters of the species, the form, the altitude, and the gracefulness or robust dignity; also as standing alone, and dying at the expiration of an allotted term; it is a Community in respect of its consist-

ing of innumerable minor trees. So long as the constituent twigs remain seated on the bough, they are subject to the laws and vicissitudes of the general mass, sharing its life, and dying when it dies; detached from it, every one of them is competent to strike root, and by degrees become the pillar of another such edifice. A fuchsia may be multiplied into a hundred, in the course of a single season, without destroying the original stem; and every one of these hundred may, three years afterwards, be multiplied into as many more. Such division of one organism into many is possible only where the fountains of life are not centralized—where there are neither brain nor heart, the means and tokens of concentration; hence it is practicable as regards the animal kingdom only in those humble tribes from which these organs appear to be absent, and the nature of which approximates to that of plants. The analogy, we may add, between trees and the arborescent zoophytes is in various other ways most curious and attractive. Here we cannot do more than advert to their wonderful correspondence in respect to the longevity of the general mass. Ehrenberg judges that certain enormous corals which he saw in the Red Sea, and parts of which are still tenanted by working polyps, were alive in the time of the Pharaohs, and have been growing and enlarging ever since. Others, of equally vast age, have been observed in the waters of tropical America.

86. Dr. Harvey, in his most ingenious little book on "Trees and their Nature," revives the hypothesis originally propounded by De La Hire, and subsequently held by Darwin, Mirbel, Du Petit Thouars, Gaudichaud, and others, that a tree is merely a mechanical and passive structure, as regards the trunk and woody portions, these serving simply to support the annual twigs, and to allow the passage of fluids to and from the latter, by exosmose and other physi-

cal and chemical laws. The tree, in its totality, he views, with these authors, simply as a collection of living yet perfectly distinct annual tree-plants, the produce of the year, and of the dead remains of a still larger number, the produce of preceding years; the living plants evolved from buds, and growing as parasites on the organic remains of the dead plants. According to this view, the stem has no intrinsic vitality; and all plants whatever are *annuals*, those commonly so called differing from such as grow on trees merely by having their connection *directly* with the soil, instead of indirectly through a woody pillar. A corollary is that there is no natural limit either to the life of trees, or to their size. Schleiden holds similar opinions. After citing examples of old trees, he observes:—"These examples are quite sufficient to prove the probability of a compound plant living on without end. These plants die ordinarily in consequence of mechanical injuries. A storm breaks off a branch; the broken surface is exposed to the action of rain-water; decay takes place; the firmness of the heart-wood becomes affected; a new storm casts the whole tree to the ground, separates the trunk from the roots, and it perishes of hunger." ("Principles of Scientific Botany," p. 538.) Let us see how this consists with facts. Every species of tree, like every species of animal, has its definite configuration and physiognomy, by which we recognize it whether covered with leaves or in the bareness of winter, and attains, under fair circumstances, a certain maximum size and height. Neither of these would be the case were the tree gifted with indefinite powers of life. The period of the culmination of the life of a tree is that when it shows its perfect and characteristic outline; and this being acquired, though for awhile there may be little change in aspect, and though crops of new twigs may be annually produced for some years, declension as inevitably follows as with a man after he has reached his meridian.

87. Thus independent—actually as regards themselves, potentially as regards the tree—healthy cuttings are equivalent to *seedlings*. Strictly without doubt, the new individuals procured by taking slips from a given plant, are but portions of it, since those plants alone can legitimately be called new which come from seed. There are no absolute beginnings anywhere in nature except as the direct produce of sexuality. To view them, however, with Mr. Knight, as portions of a whole, disconnected merely, and involved in a common destiny, is quite incorrect. This eminent man went so far as to account for the extinction of certain varieties of apples and other fruits, on the hypothesis that when the original tree died, the extensions of it raised from cuttings, though firmly rooted, and grown into large trees would die likewise. According to this hypothesis, an individual can exist in many places at once; the willow, for example, which shades the first tomb of Napoleon at St. Helena, is the same as that which at Ermenonville weeps over the ashes of Rousseau. The original and the derivatives form a whole only in a historical point of view. In regard to the lease of life, a vigorous cutting is in the same position as a seed, and the tree raised from it enjoys a complete and independent term of being. It has nothing to do with the lease of its predecessor, but commences life *de novo*, and attains the age proper to the species. Probably enough, a cutting taken from an old and enfeebled tree, past its climacteric, may be unable to develop itself luxuriantly, and may die almost as soon; but taken from a young and healthy one, its lease runs to the full term. Plants, it should be observed, are not equally capable of propagation in the way described. As regards trees, those of which the wood is light and white succeed the best, the willow, for ex-

ample; while with pines, oaks, and trees in general that have dense and resinous wood, the reluctance is extreme. Reviewing the whole matter, it will appear that so far from the principle of a fixed lease of life being invalidated by the facts of horticulture, it is verified with new illustrations.

88. Sea-weeds, like terrestrial plants, are annual, biennial, or perennial. The common green Ulva is an example of an annual; the great black fuci which hide the rocks on many coasts with their curious bladdered drapery, are perennial; the biennial include, among others, the Rhodomenia palmata, or dulse, and the Delessaria sanguinea, that lovely translucent plant which carries the palm with no less justice in the gardens of the sea, than the rose, which it emulates in color, in those of the land.

CHAPTER IX.

DURATION OF LIFE IN ANIMALS.

89. In Animals, the lease of life is comparatively short. Though many species live longer than the generality of plants, none attain to ages so prodigious as occur among the patriarchs of the forest; neither are so many species longæval in proportion to the whole number. The elephant and the swan outlive myriads of shrubs and flowers; but when they have themselves waned into senility, the leafy pride of many trees has scarcely begun. Few of any tribe of animals live more than forty years; whereas trees, almost without exception, endure for at least a century.

90. The physiological or proximate reason of this disparity is, that in the animal kingdom, taken as a whole, life is present in a higher degree of concentration. This involves a more elaborate and complex organization, and a greater intensity of vital action; sustained, moreover, in unbroken continuity, and in every portion of the fabric at once—the very conditions which, as illustrated in the machines constructed by human art, are identified with fragility and early exhaustion. In plants, without doubt, the organization is exquisitely fine, and the vital functions are various and wonderful. The microscopist well knows how beautiful is the system of cells, and tubes, and spiral vessels, constituting the internal substance of a plant; and the physiologist, how admirable and profound is that vital economy which enables it to grow, to put forth leaves and blossoms in their proper

season, and to prepare sugar, oil, farina, and the thousand other products which render the vegetable kingdom so invaluable to man; still, it is not such an organization as pertains to Animal life, which demands both new varieties of tissue and new forms of organic apparatus. For while the animal is the completion of the design so marvellously shadowed forth and prefigured in the plant, it is not merely the plant more nobly and curiously developed. It is a *reconstruction* of the plant, effected, certainly, with the same crude materials, but wrought into forms more rare and composite, and with an entirely new set of ideas superadded. It is a mistake to suppose, as some have done, that plant and animal exactly agree, even in a single circumstance of their respective natures. There are organs of digestion, respiration, reproduction, and so forth, in both; and there is a general correspondence between the functions which these organs severally fulfill; but they are never the *same* organs, nor the *same* functions, in the strict and proper meaning of the word. The animal dwells on a higher platform, and all the phenomena of its history are in keeping.

91. The intenser life of the animal gives it a completer *individuality*, and to this, as the end for which it is gifted with intenser life, is properly to be ascribed its shorter lease when compared with the durability of the plant. The end for which a thing is designed is always the noblest feature of its being, and therefore the most useful as well as philosophical to keep uppermost in view. It is for the sake of sustaining its individuality that the organization of an animal is so complex and elaborate; it is for the same reason that the vital functions are so varied, ceaseless, and interwoven; and further, that they are so universal as to the theatre of their performance. For they are not exercised only at certain periods, or in certain portions of the organism, but unceasingly, from birth to dissolution, and as vigo-

rously in one part as another. Certain great duties are assigned to special organs as head-quarters, it is true; but practically and in effect, every organ is diffused throughout the body, and every function is everywhere performed. The heart is wherever there is blood; the brain wherever there is feeling. The great characteristic of concentrated life, or of Individuality in high perfection, is this vivid, ceaseless, omnipresent Activity. In all the forms of nature which are endowed with it—that is, in all animals of any complexity of organization, as we saw when considering the subject of food—there is a continual drawing-in of nutrient matter from without, and conversion of it into living tissue, and as continual a decomposition of what has previously been assimilated, and concurrent expulsion of the fragments. Every moment, in the life of an animal, witnesses a new receiving, appropriation, and giving back; old age and rejuvenescence revolving upon each other; death destroying over again, and creation beginning afresh. On the *excreting* part of the process, the maintenance of the vital condition is more closely and immediately dependent than it is even upon the supply of new aliment. Feeding may be suspended for a considerable period without causing anything more than debility: but the removal of the effete particles generated by the decomposition of the tissues, cannot be checked even for a few minutes, at least in the warm-blooded animals, without inducing a fatal result. For every act of respiration is in effect one of excretion, and to stay the breathing, as we all know, is to quench the life.

92. In trees and plants, on the other hand, where the concentration of life is slight, the individuality faint, and the organization comparatively simple, so simple that no part of the organism is absolutely dependent upon another part, where there are no consecrated vital centres, no heart, lungs, brain, or digestive cavity, existence no longer depends upon

incessant and total change of the very substance of the fabric, and the vital activity is proportionately low. The bulk of the tree, that is, all the consolidated or woody portion, and every other part which has been finally shaped and hardened, instead of living by perpetual decomposition and reconstruction, and depending on these processes as the very condition of existence, remains fixed and unalterable till the lease of the entire organism has run out. Those parts only which are immediately employed in the vital processes, as the flowers, and leaves, and the extreme ends of the rootlets, in which parts there is also more concentration of life, are subject to such decay as takes place in the body of an animal. In these it occurs in close and striking correspondence, along with as complete a renovation. What the tissues are to the animal, the foliage is to plant and tree; every perennial plant, like every animal, dies innumerable molecular or leafy deaths prior to its total, somatic death; and, as the years roll by, is reinstated in as many molecular or leafy lives. Autumn and spring are to the tree, by correspondence, what every day of its existence is to a living animal; all that is concerned in keeping it alive withers away, but all is rapidly renewed. The difference as to the *time* that elapses between the respective deaths and renovations, *i. e.*, of the molecules of the animal frame, and the leafy atoms of the tree, in no wise robs the phenomena of their essential unity. That which is most concentrated is always most vivacious, as the mountain-rivulet runs faster than the broad river of the plain. It was no mere play of fancy that led the ancients to call man *arbor inversa.* Man is not only man; he is all things, every part of the universe in turn, according to the point of view from which we look. The fable of Proteus is but a description of human nature: "First indeed he became a lion with noble mane, and then a dragon, and a leopard, and a great bear; and he became liquid water, and a lofty-leaved tree." Flesh and blood to our first or anatomical ideas, under the alchemy of the imagination, the human body transmutes into tree, fountain, temple, and all things in succession that are beautiful and glorious. Things are intelligible in fact, and truly seen, only in the degree that we discern *ourselves* in them, and read them through the lens of human nature. "To describe any scene well," says Richter, "the poet must make the bosom of a man his camera obscura, and look at it through *this;*" similarly, to enter into the full, philosophic understanding even of the simplest objects and phenomena of the world, we must take that "choice optic glass," the human body and its life.

93. On a general survey of the ages reached by animals, when not shortened by violence or disease, the area of time which they cover is found but small compared with that of plants. With a few exceptions, forty, as before said, is about the maximum age, and three or four about the minimum. No such exact division can be made among them as that of annuals, biennials, and perennials, among plants, unless certain insects correspond to the first named. It is to be observed, however, that there is an ordinary maximum age, and an *extra*-ordinary. Every known lease of life, at least in the vertebrate animals, appears capable of renewal, or rather of extension, even to the doubling of the ordinary period; that is, while every creature has its customary or natural term, it appears competent to live, under certain favorable circumstances, for an extraordinary or additional term of the same, or nearly the same, extent. Thus, while the ordinary life of man is three score and ten, he is capable of an extraordinary life of seventy years more; the ordinary life of the camel is forty or fifty, but individuals sometimes last out the century. Query, then, which is the actual and original lease? And if the longer one be the original (as

all the probabilities favor the belief of its being), why is it cut short by one-half in all but a few memorable cases?

94. The longest-living Mammal, after the whale, already mentioned, appears to be that affectionate, docile, and sagacious creature, the elephant. Nothing is known positively as to its lease, but the estimate of one hundred and fifty years is certainly not beyond the mark.* The rhinoceros and the hippopotamus are reputed to come next, a maximum of seventy or eighty being assigned to each of these huge brutes; then, it is said, follows the camel, a meagre, dry, active, exceedingly hardy animal, whose useful life extends not infrequently to fifty. The period, reckoning by decrements, between fifty and thirty, is reached by few. The stag, longæval only in romance, dies at thirty-five or thereabouts; the leopard, bear, and tiger, fail fully ten years earlier; twenty-five or thirty is the ordinary maximum of the horse and ass, though the severe treatment of man rarely allows them to reach even this. The mule, it is worthy of notice, is stronger-lived and becomes older, a circumstance anticipated in plants, where hybrids frequently live longer than their parents. The cause is probably the same in both, and to be found in their infertility, whereby their whole vigor is left at liberty for self-maintenance, instead of being expended in two directions. Many leases expire between twenty and ten. The former seems to be the ordinary maximum of the lion, as reached in menageries, though when unconfined it evidently lives longer, for it has sometimes been found without teeth. Twenty is the limit also with the bull, despite his great strength, size, and solidity; the dog and the wolf seldom pass eighteen; the sheep, the goat, and

* An elephant aged one hundred and twenty years was put to death in London, in July, 1855.—*Times*, July 23d.

the fox, rarely live more than twelve. The maximum of the domestic cat is said to be ten; that of the rabbit, hare, and guinea-pig, seven or eight; that of the mouse, five or six, and of other such little animals about the same. As to the leases of the remainder of the four-footed creatures of our planet, excepting a dozen or so, zoology is entirely uninformed, and until they shall have been ascertained, of course nothing like a proper list can be constructed. The animals which have been mentioned are certainly among the chief, and indicate the scope and limits which a table of ages, when completed, will exhibit; but so far, the list is only like a boy's first map, unfurnished except with the names of the seas, the metropolis, and his native town. One thing is plain, that Man, regarded as a member of the animal kingdom, has no occasion to murmur at the shortness of his lease of life, but should rather congratulate himself, seeing that he enjoys a considerably longer term, even in his ordinary duration, than the great mass of his physiological fraternity, while it is pretty certain that there is not an animal of his own size that does not return to dust before half as old.

95. The scale of ages attained by Birds is much about the same as that of mammals; but taking one with another, they probably live longer in proportion to their bulk. No creatures are better adapted for longevity; they are peculiarly well clothed, for no covering can be more complete, or better calculated to preserve warmth, than their soft, close-lying feathers; and as these are renewed periodically, they are maintained in the best possible condition. Many birds also cast their bills, and acquire new ones, a most advantageous exchange for them, since they are thereby rendered so much the better able to feed themselves. Besides these peculiarities, birds live almost entirely in the fresh air, and their habits are cheerful and sportive, conditions emi-

nently conducive to long life. As to the particular terms of life which obtain among them, Flourens says he knows "nothing certain." There is plenty of evidence, nevertheless, that such birds as the eagle, the vulture, the falcon, and the swan, far surpass all others in longevity, and attain ages so remarkable as often to exceed very considerably that of man. Even the crow is reputed to live a hundred years, and the raven no less than ninety. There have been instances of the parrot living for sixty years a prisoner, and its age, when captured, would have to be added. Pelicans and herons are said to reach forty to fifty years; hawks, thirty to forty; peacocks, goldfinches, and blackbirds, about twenty; pheasants and pigeons, about the same; nightingales, fifteen; the robin, a little less; domestic fowls, about ten; thrushes, eight or nine; wrens, two to three.

96. Concerning the ages of Fishes, even less is known than about birds. It is vaguely believed of them that they are longæval. The reasons for this opinion are, that the element in which they live is more uniform in its condition than the atmosphere, and that they are less subject in consequence to those injurious influences which tend to shorten the lives of terrestrial creatures; and secondly, that their bones, being of a more cartilaginous nature than those of land animals, admit of almost indefinite extension, so that the frame is longer in growing to maturity. Gesner gives an instance of a carp, in Germany, which was known to be a hundred years old; other writers assign to this fish as much as a hundred and fifty, and to the pike a longevity even greater. Hufeland remarks that natural death occurs among fishes more rarely than in any other part of the animal kingdom. "The law of the transition of one into another, according to the right of the strongest, prevails here far more generally than elsewhere. One devours another,—the stronger the weaker. This regulation," he

continues, "is a proof of divine and exalted wisdom. If the innumerable millions of the inhabitants of the waters were to remain when they died a single day unentombed, they would speedily diffuse abroad the most dreadful pestilential evaporation. But passing, while scarcely dead, into the substance of another living being, death exists less in the water than on land,—the putrefaction takes place in the stomachs of the stronger."

97. Reptiles attain surprising ages. The tortoise, which is so slow in growing that in twenty years an increase of a few inches is all that can be detected, has lived even in captivity above a century. One placed in the garden of Lambeth Palace, in the time of Archbishop Laud, lived there till the year 1753; and its death was then induced seemingly through misfortune rather than old age. The enormous creatures of this kind, natives of the Galapagos, undoubtedly live twice or thrice as long as the common species; an individual possessed some years back by the London Zoological Society, had every appearance of being at least a hundred and seventy-five. Even these immense ages were probably far exceeded by the great fossil testudinata of the Himalayahs. It is easy to see the cause of such longevity. The same law which obtains in the mechanics of inanimate matter, operates in the organisms of vitalized matter, namely, that what is gained in time must be lost in power. The active habits which in shorter-lived animals accelerate the vital processes, and bring the lease to an early close, here are no longer found. The tortoises have no excitable nervous system to wear out the durable materials encased in their impenetrable armor; they spend the greater part of their lives in inactivity, and exist rather than live. By analogy, it may be inferred that the loricate and ophidian reptiles reach an age fully as advanced as the tortoises.

The crocodile, large, strong, vigorous, enclosed in a hard coat of mail, and incredibly voracious, is, without doubt, exceedingly long-lived. The larger serpents, also slow in growth, and passing a considerable portion of their lives in semi-torpor, are also unquestionably longæval. Feeding voraciously, at long intervals, so familiar in the case of serpents, seems invariably associated with prolonged life. As regards the Amphibia, Smellie refers to a toad known to have been at least thirty-six. The frog, which, by reason of its slow growth, in this climate at least, is incapable of producing young till its fourth year, reaches, however, what in proportion to this late puberty is the very inconsiderable age of no more than from twelve to about sixteen.

98. Insects, for the most part, are short-lived, especially after their last transformation. Some, after acquiring their wings, live only for the remainder of the day. In calculating the ages of insects, of course they must be reckoned from the hatching of the egg. Different species exist two, three, and even four years in the grub state; then a considerable time in the chrysalis; the winged state being merely that of completed maturity. That which especially marks the latter is the fitness of the creature for propagation; and this, as the period of its bloom, is also the briefest. The Ephemeræ, in their winged state, are not even creatures of a day. Scarcely a single gnat, as such, survives a week; not half the beetles, nor any of the grasshoppers nor Tipulæ, those long-legged dancers of the autumn, enters on a second month; a fortnight sees the death of almost every kind of butterfly and moth. One of the longest-living insects is that brilliant beetle, the *Scarabæus auratus*, or Rose-chaffer, the only one that feeds upon the flower from which it takes its English name. After four years spent as a grub, and a fortnight as a chrysalis, it has lived in captivity from two to

three years more.* That curious but treacherous and cruel creature, the *Mantis religiosa*, or Praying cricket, which holds up the foremost pair of its long, desiccated, skeleton legs, as if in the act of prayer, is said to attain a full octave.

99. Whatever errors there may be in the particular figures above quoted, the general principles which they illustrate are indisputable. Whatever class of organisms we may take, the ground of longer or shorter life lies universally in the structure, the temperament, and the less or greater vital energy. We have seen how this is manifested in regard to the aggregate of organic nature; also how it is verified in respect to plants; it obtains with animals, in their several tribes and species, after precisely the same manner, only that the phenomena are played forth in greater variety, and in costumes appropriate to the nobler stage. All the diversities in the duration of animal life may be referred perhaps to the two general heads—of Size, as regards the substance of the creature, and Energy, as regards its vital powers. Other circumstances are but adjuncts, though inseparably connected with and conditional on them. All the longæval creatures, like all the longæval trees, are considerable in their bulk; at all events they are the largest forms of their respective tribes, the swan, for example, among birds,† and the crocodile among reptiles; the smallest forms, on the other hand, are always the shortest-lived. The reason consists in the ampler command which they possess over the world around them. As the colossal tree owes its longevity to its immense feeding-surface of

---

* See for an entertaining account of the keeping this beautiful insect as a pet, "Episodes of Insect Life," vol. ii., p. 76.

† The ostrich, as the largest of birds, is undoubtedly the longest liver, but nothing is known with certainty as to its lease.

green leaf, so the largely-developed animal lives longer than the little one, because it possesses more vital capacity, more contact with external nature, more scope and opportunity for acquiring strength of every kind; there is also greater power of resisting what is inimical to life, as intense cold, though marvelous examples of the latter property occur among those living riddles, the animalcules. Great size, however, does not carry long life with it necessarily. More intimately connected with longevity even than bulk, is the greater or less intensity of the vital action; in proportion to the rapidity with which an animal lives, is invariably the brevity of its lease. That is, of two animals, alike in regard to bulk, that one will have the shortest duration which lives the fastest, and that one the longest which lives slowest. The expression "fast living," now so commonly applied to extravagant expenditure of the resources, involving premature stoppage and decay, is not a mere phrase of gay society; it denotes a condition of things which in nature is sometimes normal. The two great kingdoms of organized nature are physiologically characterized in fact, by this very thing. It is because trees live so slowly that they endure for centuries, and because animals live so fast that few of them reach fifty. All the longæval animals have a relatively lower vital energy; all the short-lived (or at least such as attain any considerable bulk) possess it in excess. As a result of this condition, we usually find the longæval creatures deliberate and stately in their movements, and leading calm and placid lives, as the elephant, the giraffe, and the swan; while the short-lived ones are as remarkable for their sportive restlessness, as they course about the fields, or sail through the sky or water. Creatures that run much are rarely, if ever, long-lived. In the vegetable kingdom it is the same; the longæval tree is like the elephant it shades, tranquil and august; the gourd that dies with the close of summer is rampant and wanton. In the whole compass of nature, perhaps there is nothing more full of quiet grandeur than the sacred, ever-verdant cedar of twenty centuries.

100. The circumstances of animal life which bear intimate relation to its lease, though not immediately promotive or preventive of longevity, are chiefly, as in plants, those connected with Reproduction. Early puberty, which in plants forebodes an early death, similarly announces it in animals, for it shows that maturity will soon be reached, and we scarcely need the proverb* to learn what happens next. Contrariwise, those creatures live the longest which are latest in acquiring ability to procreate. The long life of man, for example, follows as a natural sequence upon his protracted infancy. Other animals of his size begin to propagate after a much earlier anniversary of birth than *he* does; they attain their puberty in a few years, or even months; waiting for it the seventh part of a century, man is compensated at the end. The period occupied in *gestation* is remarkably correlative with the term of life. The longer time an animal requires for its formation in its mother's womb, the more extended is its life; the shorter the period between conception and birth, the less is the lease extended. The duration of gestation is of course largely determined by the creature's size and organization in general. The bulky elephant goes with young no less than twenty months, and lives a century and a half; the puny rabbit requires only thirty days, and dies in eight years. What is reputed concerning the long life of the swan becomes credible when tested by this law; for incubation in birds corresponds to gestation in mammals, and no bird, unless the ostrich, is so slow in hatching its eggs. The law, like all others, belongs

---

* *Quod citò fit, citò perit.* "That which is quickly formed, quickly perishes." Vulgarly, "Soon ripe, soon rotten."

as much to plants, wherein the gestation of animals is prefigured in the ripening of the fruit. The longæval trees are among the first to open their flowers (the instruments of vegetable coition), yet their seeds are the latest to become ripe, the whole season, from early spring to the close of autumn, being required for their proper maturation. Thus, though the yew blossoms in March, or several weeks before the apple, its berries are not ripe till the end of October; the box-tree opens its flowers at the same time, but is scarcely parturient till winter. Many kinds of pine-trees, also the cedar, and several oaks, as Quercus Cerris, suber, and rubra, all of them long-lived, require two seasons to bring their fruits to perfection. On the other hand, the short-lived perennials, and annuals universally, complete the whole process of reproduction, from the opening of the flowers to the ripening of the seed, in the course of some six or seven weeks. In the mistletoe occurs a curious exception. Like the yew and the box, it blossoms early in the spring, and ripens its berries certainly no sooner, perhaps not till near Christmas, yet it is by no means a longæval plant. How are we to account for this? May it be referable to the parasitic nature of the plant, being dependent on plunder for its sustenance?

101. The *number of young* produced at a birth is again correlative with the duration of life. The longest-living animals produce the fewest, while the shortest-lived are also the most prolific. The female elephant, rhinoceros, hippopotamus, and camel, never have more than one at a birth; the horse, the ox, the stag, one, and occasionally two; the goat and the sheep have from one to three or four; the leopard and tiger, four or five; the dog, the fox, and the cat, three to six; the rabbit, four to eight; the guinea-pig, the most prolific of the mammalia, four to twelve. In the human race, where the lease of life is considerable in propor-

tion to the size of the body, twins come only once in every seventy or eighty births; triplets only once in seven thousand.* About fifteen seems the highest number of young ever produced at one birth among the warm-blooded animals; in fact, a larger number would be incompatible with the economy of utero-gestation, and subsequently with that of the maternal nourishment, the fountains of which are usually about double the number of the young produced at a birth. It would be incompatible, also, with the fair sharing of the earth's surface, and thus with the fine balance, harmony, and proportions of nature. The economy of incubation puts a similar limit to the number of eggs that a bird hatches at once, which is seldom less than two or three, and never above sixteen. The most astonishing cases of fecundity occur among fishes and insects. In the genus Cyprinus among the former, comprising the carp, the barbel, the tench, the bream, &c., hundreds of thousands of ova have been counted; and in the common cod, several millions. Crustaceous animals often produce many thousands; and the Batrachians, some hundreds at the least. Like the preceding, this great principle is exemplified also in plants. The number of seeds produced by annuals and short-lived plants is infinitely greater than trees usually yield; for though in the aggregate of their crops of fruit trees are so fertile, in the strict physiological sense they are few-seeded, and not infrequently only one-seeded. In comparing plants and animals as to their productiveness, we must remember that a tree is a nation, every bough a province, every branch a large district; we have to consider, therefore, not the sum total of the produce of the entire

* This proportion is not universal, varying with different nations. The Greenland women scarcely ever have twins; whereas among the people of Chili they are remarkably common.

number of flowers—the total, for instance, of the acorns upon an oak—but how many seeds are produced by each separate and independent flower, which is the real equivalent of the animal, the tree itself being equivalent to a whole herd of quadrupeds, or a whole city-full of mankind. Thus, the flowers of the oak-tree, which lives above a thousand years, produce, like the elephant, only one at a birth; the flowers of the apple-tree, about ten; those of the strawberry-plant (a perennial), more than a hundred; those of the poppy (an annual), eight thousand. That there is an exact ratio between the productiveness of a plant and the period to which it lives, is by no means asserted. There are plenty of few-seeded annuals, and of many-seeded perennials; but, as a rule, the former are more fecund. Puff-balls and parasitic fungi, the most ephemeral of plants, cast their seeds into the atmosphere like impalpable dust, agreeing in their fecundity with fishes. The quantity of fruit produced by the entire tree or plant, corresponding as it does to the population of a country, has its own laws of increase and fluctuation, and is a different matter altogether from fertility of the species, as correlative with lease of life. When we find longævals very fecund, it is probably because their produce is an important food to some creature of superior rank. How few acorns ever become oaks.

102. What may be the lease of HUMAN life, is a question for which the Psalmist is almost universally acknowledged to have provided a final answer: "The days of our years are three score years and ten, and if by reason of strength they be four score years, yet is their strength labor and sorrow, for it is soon cut off, and we flee away." There are plenty of examples, however, of longevity far exceeding even the higher figures, accompanied by retention of all the faculties and powers the exercise of which forms the true life of man. Arguing from these, it has been thought that, by using proper means,

an age of no less than two centuries may be attained; less ambitious minds have been content to hope for a century and a half; in Genesis itself one hundred and twenty years are fixed. (vi. 3.) Buffon considered that the maximum need never be under ninety or a hundred, which "the man," says he, "who does not die of accidental causes, everywhere reaches." Flourens, the latest writer upon the subject, concurs in the opinion of his famous countryman: A hundred years of life is what Providence intended for man; it is true that few reach this great term, but *how few do what is necessary to attain it!* With our customs, our passions, our miseries, man does not die—he kills himself. If we observe men, we shall see that almost all lead a nervous and contentious life, and that most of them die of disappointment. How few, comparatively, number even the three score and ten! The weakness of infancy, the intemperance of the adult period, the violence of diseases, the fatality of accidents, and other circumstances similarly inimical to long life, prevent more than about seventy persons in every thousand attaining natural old age. There is great solace, nevertheless, in the thought of what *may* be reached. Haller, who has collected a great number of examples of long life, reckons up more than a thousand instances of individuals having attained the age of one hundred to one hundred and ten, sixty of one hundred and ten to one hundred and twenty, twenty-nine of one hundred and twenty to one hundred and thirty, fifteen of one hundred and thirty to one hundred and forty, six of one hundred and forty to one hundred and fifty, and one of one hundred and sixty-nine. Curtis, but without the credibility of Haller, cites one hundred and seventy-two, one hundred and eighty-five, and two hundred and seven. As regards the life of the Antediluvians, before the question is examined physiologically, it may be well for those who are curious about it to be sure what the inspired narrative really means. When the belief that the names of the patriarchs denote communities rather than individuals, shall be shown to be more at variance with the spirit and the object of the sacred records than the popular opinion is, it will be time to take it up as a matter of science. A noted living theologian suggests from out of one of the darkest caves of literalism, that our first parents did actually eat of the Tree of Life, and that its virtue was transmitted through several successive generations, till at last it became dissipated and lost, and man was reduced to a miserable tithe of his first possession.*

103. Flourens fixes a hundred as the normal life of man on the principle that there is an exact ratio between the period occupied in growing to maturity and the full term or lease of existence, a principle which he shows pretty conclusively to prevail throughout the whole of the mammalia. Aristotle was the first to enunciate this great doctrine; Buffon the first to throw it into coherent shape. As set forth by the latter, it teaches that every animal lives, or at least is competent to live, from six to seven times as many years as it consumes in growing. The stag, he tells us, is five or six years in growing, and lives thirty-five or forty in all; the horse is about four, and lives to be twenty-five or thirty. "One thing only," says Flourens, "was unknown to Buffon, namely, the sign that marks the term of growth." This is the essential point; it is by having determined the sign that Flourens has vitalized the doctrine, which, so long as it lay undiscovered, was little better than a speculation. There might be no hesitation in conceding the theory; but until the basis of the calculation could be indisputably shown, there could

* See, on the non-literal character of the statements respecting the ages of the Antediluvians, Rev. E. D. Rendell's "Antediluvian History," chapter xviii., (1850), also the "Prospective Review," vol. ii., p. 251.

be no security felt in the conclusions. Still, it was a grand idea—one of those fine truths in outline which nature seems to delight in sketching on the thoughts of imaginative men, and filling up gradually and at leisure. The maturity of the body in general of course consists in the maturity of all its parts, but the period of such maturity differs almost as much as the parts themselves. The muscles, the composition of the vocal apparatus, even the eye-brows, have their respective periods of perfect development, and were we minutely acquainted with every particular of the body, each would probably furnish the sign required. Flourens finds it in the BONES. The bones are the basis of the whole system; they are the first principle, so to speak, of its configuration; they support, defend, and contain the nobler organs. To fulfill these functions, they uniformly require to be possessed of the three mechanical properties of firmness, lightness, and tenacity, and in order to these it is needful that they be exquisitely organized. We are apt to suppose, from the hardness and durability of bones, that even in the living body they are scarcely vital; that they should be subjects of gradual and delicate growth, seems almost impossible to conceive. But minute anatomy, the most pleasing and rewarding part of the science of the human fabric, shows bones to be as full of life, in their degree, as any of the softer parts, and that the organization is inferior to none. In order that they shall possess the three properties alluded to, bones are formed of two principal ingredients, an animal matter and an earthy matter, intimately interblended. In the bones of the infant the quantity of earthy matter is comparatively small, and the animal substance itself is softer than at later periods. As it grows, however, the proportions change; the animal matter becomes firmer; earthy particles are deposited in it abundantly, and the bone gradually assumes its proper density. The total of the process constitutes "ossification." The proportion of earthy to animal matter is not the same in the different bones. The maximum occurs in those of the head; the long bones of the limbs have the next largest quantity, those of the upper limbs exceeding the lower; and last of all come the bones of the trunk. Thus, the

	Earthy matter.	Animal matter.
Temporal bone contains.........	63·50	36·50
Humerus "	63·02	36·98
Femur "	62·49	37·51

The earthy matter is not deposited in every part at once; it spreads, so to speak, from ossific centres, gradually diffusing itself throughout the mass. This is of the utmost importance to observe, for it is upon this apparently trifling circumstance that the whole of the conclusions are primarily founded. In all the long bones, as those of the legs and arms, there are portions at the extremities which, at first, or in the child, are united to the intermediate portion only by the cartilage or animal matter of which the bone then principally consists. These end-portions of the bone (called its *epiphyses*) are ossific centres—points at which the deposition of earthy matter commences, and from which it gradually extends. As growth proceeds, ossification progresses from the middle part of the bone towards the epiphyses, and from the epiphyses towards the middle part, till at last they are joined into one continuous mass of hard, completed bone. As soon as the junction is effected, and the bone consolidated, growth is completed, and the sign of maturity established. "As long," says Flourens, "as the bones are not united to their epiphyses, the animal grows; when once the bones and their epiphyses are united, the animal grows no more." Not that growth is completed and maturity established, in that strict sense of the words which would imply an absolutely stationary condition thenceforwards, or at least of the whole body. There is no period when the system is absolutely stationary; it is always either advancing to a state of perfection, or receding from that state. The skeleton alone remains fixed. "It is true that at the adult age, the determinate height and figure, the settled features, and in man, the marked moral and mental character, naturally gave rise to the supposition that a fixed point has been attained; but a little inquiry soon teaches us that the individual is still the subject of progressive changes. The capability of powerful and prolonged muscular exertion increases for some years; there must consequently be a change in the muscular tissue. The intellectual faculties have not attained their maximum, although we do not hesitate to consider them mature; we must therefore infer that there is a corresponding development in the substance of the brain." In the camel, Flourens goes on to say, the union of the epiphyses to the bones is completed at eight years old, in the horse at five, in the ox at four, in the cat at eighteen months, in the rabbit at twelve months, and in every case the duration of life is five times, or pretty nearly, the age of the creature when this process is accomplished. Flourens does not differ essentially from Buffon in saying five times instead of six or seven times the period of maturity, because Buffon fixed maturity at earlier epochs. It is the same thing in the end to say seven times five with Buffon, or five times seven with Flourens. In man, the union of the epiphyses to the bones takes place at twenty years of age, and as observation appears to establish five as the legitimate number by which to multiply in regard to the remainder of the mammalia, the conclusion is that five times twenty, or a hundred, is the normal lease in our own species. If the principle be sound—and there is no reason for distrust—to determine the lease of life in animals where it will apply, will be, for the future, a comparatively easy matter. A few careful examinations of the bones in growing individuals will enable the period of maturity to be learned with certainty, and five times this period may be inferred to be the lease.*

104. Numerous facts of a miscellaneous character invite our notice in regard to the duration of human life. *Cœteris paribus*, large men are said to live longer than little ones; married men longer than bachelors. Celibacy as well as marriage has its advocates in this respect, the fact probably being that there is plenty of illustration of both opinions, though on the whole, matrimony certainly has the advantage. We may reconcile the different views by considering that in the one case there is less wear and tear of the vital energy; and that in the other the weakened frame is restored and replenished by the tender offices of affection. "If two lie together then they have heat, but how can one be warm alone?" As a rule, longevity is greater in women than in men. Childbirth and its antecedents occasion indeed a considerable loss of life; the age of puberty carries off eight per cent. more maidens than youths; the proportion of deaths in parturition is one in one hundred and eight; the difference, however, which these losses would seem to produce disappears in the general average. Either sex may calculate their *probability of life* by reckoning the difference between the age already attained and ninety.

* For a variety of other and curious details on the subject of the duration of life, both in man and the lower animals, such as it is unnecessary here to introduce, the student may refer to the works of Flourens, Hufeland, and Buffon, above cited, and on the particular subject of maturity, to the article "Age," in Todd's Cyclopædia of Physiology. See also the reviews of Flourens in Blackwood for May, 1855, and Colburn for July of the same year.

Half that difference is what the assurance offices would call their "expectation." For example, a man of forty years old has fifty between his age and ninety; half of that fifty is twenty-five; and provided he is free from any undermining disease, he may trust that for those twenty-five years he will continue, with God's blessing, to enjoy the honor and privilege of existence. One thing it is important to remember—the period of maturity is the only one that admits of prolongation. Infancy, childhood, and youth, have certain limits, which are seldom come short of or exceeded. The same in old age—it cannot endure beyond a certain length of time, and when once it begins, it speedily leads to the grave. In other words, neither childhood nor old age can be arrested; middle life alone can be stretched out. Of the three conditions of life we cannot possibly alter the first and third, for they are out of our control; the middle one we may abbreviate or prolong, since it is left for us to deal with as we choose. The influence of *pursuits and occupations* on the duration of life has often been illustrated. The average is said to be with clergymen sixty-five years; with merchants sixty-two; farmers sixty-one; military men fifty-nine; lawyers fifty-eight; artists fifty-seven, and so on. Poverty and destitution tend to shorten life; comfort and happiness to prolong it.

CHAPTER X

GROUNDS OF THE VARIOUS LEASE OF LIFE. SPIRITUAL BASIS OF NATURE.

105. THE primary, essential reasons of the diversity in the duration of life (as distinct from the proximate or physiological), are comprised in the law of CORRESPONDENCE, and the law of USE, the two great principles which furnish the whole rationale of existence. CORRESPONDENCE unfolds the relation of the material world to the spiritual, and shows the first Causes of visible nature; USE instructs us as to the particular Ends for which the various objects of creation have been designed, and the necessity there is for every one of them. Springing out of these laws, and dependent on them, is the condition of FORM, by which term is to be understood not merely the configuration of a thing, but the total of the circumstances which establish its identity, such as the size, organization, and vital economy; and according to these last, according to the peculiarities of the Form, is eventually determined the duration of the life. The inmost, original causes of the diversity in the lease of life we thus discover in spiritual philosophy, the last, concluding ones, in the philosophy of nature. We should accustom ourselves thus to trace things to their first beginnings, whatever may be the subject of investigation. Our mental progress is immensely contingent upon it; desire to discover, and success in finding them, are the surest signs of enlarging intellectual empire. For the true philosophy

of cause and effect does not consist in the simple determination of immediate antecedents, nor is it satisfied to remain in them. Every cause is itself only the effect of a still finer cause, which again results from a yet finer, no longer physical, necessarily, and the whole chain, from beginning to end, must be considered, if we would acquire a just notion of the last effect. Nowhere is it more needful to investigate these successive causes than in regard to the duration of life. To see the reasons of longer and shorter life purely in its organic apparatus, is to see the cause of Language in the movements of the lips and tongue. It is a truth, but not the whole, nor the vital truth. Every physical fact is the last issue and expression of something spiritual, which must be sought before the former can become properly intelligible, and to which reason will direct its steps, though half-reason may stand indifferent and mocking.

106. With Correspondence, accordingly, or the relations of the material world with the Spiritual, lies our first concern. To enter successfully upon the consideration of it, obviously requires that we should hold clear ideas of what the material and the spiritual respectively *are*. Concerning these we must therefore primarily inquire, and especially concerning the *spiritual* world. Strictly, the consideration of the spiritual expression of Life should precede that of the spiritual World. The obligation to take the latter before its time comes of the fact that all great truths have many points of contact, whereby it becomes impossible to treat intelligibly of any one of them without approaching and anticipating others. The truth, however, of the general system which comprises them is declared by it, since in order to the harmony of a whole, every part must be in alliance, and the insulation of any one part impracticable. The spiritual world is no mere abstraction. Viewed *theologically*, it is the place in which we shall consciously reside after the

death of our material bodies, enjoying its sunshine, or walking wretched in its gloom, according as we have adapted ourselves during our time-life;—viewed *philosophically*, it is the same old beautiful world of God with which we are familiar under the name of earth and sky, only on a higher plane of creation, and prior to it. When we would think accurately of "Nature," we must not confine ourselves to the visible world. "Nature," in the full sense of the word, denotes whatever exists externally to the Creator, not having been planned by human contrivance, or executed by human labor, thus not only earth and sky, but the heavenly mansions also. The one is physical nature; the other, spiritual nature; and the former presupposes the latter. The world, say rather the *worlds*,—those sparkling spheres we call the planets and the stars,—are not independent and original creations. Every one of them is derived and representative, a sequence and disclosure of some anterior sphere in the spiritual world. Every object they contain is of similar history and origin, a figure demonstrating the spiritual, and supported by it. Not that the physical world is destitute of Reality. By no means the mere illusion of the mind which certain metaphysicians would have us believe,—for there are no quintessential metaphysics that can gainsay common sense,—the material world is emphatically a Real one. On the other hand, it is quite as wrong and unphilosophical to think of it, as many do, as primitive, independent, self-supporting. When we look on a beautiful landscape, we see mountains, trees, rivers, real and substantial as regards the material universe; nevertheless, only images of forms originally existing in a world which we do *not* see, and from which they are derived;—forms that are neither comprised within material space, nor related to terrestrial time,—forms which are as real, therefore, as the material; yea, infinitely *more* so, since the material is local and temporary, whereas the spiritual is unlimited, and the home of immortality. Nothing exists except by reason of the spiritual world; whatever pertains to the material is purely and simply Effect;—a fact in itself commending the spiritual to our philosophic curiosity and affection, since,—as all well know who are ever so little in the habit of meditating upon things not present to the bodily sight,—it is only by thinking of the invisible productive *powers*, in connection with the resulting *products*, that the latter acquire true being, life, beauty, and physiognomical expression. Seeing how the material world changes, yet how permanent it is, we cannot persuade ourselves but that there must be an indestructible and vigorous *something* which underlies and from time to time refashions it,—something which is the same yesterday, to-day, and forever. Whatever *shape* a material organism may possess, nothing but spirit, we are well assured, can *act*. Only by virtue of force communicated from something spiritual, is matter, under any circumstances, consolidated and configured. In itself matter is unable to effect anything; it passes indifferently from mould to mould without retaining the shape of any. That invisible, potent something cannot be a mere Energy either. A Cause, that is to say, an active, productive force, cannot be efficient unless it operate from and through a *substance*. If there be a spiritual world at all, it must be like the material world, *substantial*. Substance must not be confounded with *matter*. Substance is a generic term; matter is one of the species which it includes. Substance is that which is indispensable to the being of a thing, as the continent of its sustaining life. For, *to be* is the same as *to be alive*, which is to be a recipient of life; and wherever life is received, whether in the material world or the spiritual, there must needs be a substance to receive it. Granted, the substance of the spiritual world cannot be detected or defined scientifically. But that there *is* such a substance may nevertheless be affirmed, just as reasonably as when we hear Echo, we may affirm an echo-producing instrument. Spiritual substances are none the less real because out of the reach of chemistry or edge-tools, or because they are inappreciable by the organs of sense. Indeed it is only the grosser expressions of matter which can be so treated, and which the senses can apprehend. Heat and electricity are as truly material as flint and granite, yet man can neither cut, nor weigh, nor measure them; while the most familiar and abundant expression of all, the Air which we breathe, can neither be seen nor felt till put in motion. As for invisibility, which to the vulgar is the proof of non-existence, no warning is so incessantly addressed to us, from every department of creation, as not to commit the mistake of disbelieving simply because we cannot see. When we reflect how many things there are which cannot be measured and comprehended even by Thought, which nevertheless are true, visibility to the material eye, as the test of reality, sinks to the least and lowest value. Each class of substances is real in relation to the world it belongs to;—material substances in the material world; spiritual substances in the spiritual world; and each kind has to be judged of according to its place of abode. Distance in nature from the material no more disproves the existence of the spiritual, than distance in space disproves the existence of the bottom of the sea. The common notion of spirit is that of an attenuate form of *matter;* that it is what matter would become were it rarified into a perfectly free, fluent, unfixed, unbounded condition; and conversely, that matter is congealed or concreted spirit, bearing to it something of the same relation that ice does to steam, or a pastile to the fragrance into which it burns. Spirit and matter are utterly and incommensurably distinct; under no circumstances are they transformable or convertible.* To *deny* the existence of spiritual substance, is to assert that heaven is an empty void, whereas St. John represents it as a plenitude of objects and scenery, of the most substantial kind. It is to depopulate it also of its angels, who if they be real enough to be *persons*, must assuredly be real enough to consist of substance. Unless always upon the wing, they must likewise have a substantial surface whereon to stand.

107. Lying thus, at the back of the visible and sensible, the spiritual world is the universal fountain. Therein are contained "the invisible things of God," which are "clearly seen by the things that are made." Therein, likewise, are contained the "patterns" which were shown to Bezaleel in the mount. That history of Bezaleel has wonderful instruction in it. What the spiritual world is to the spontaneous, objective forms of nature, it is also, we may gather from it, to Art, which like those forms, is not an ornament placed upon the surface of the world from without, or purely by man, but an outbirth from the unseen universe within; just as the verdure of the fields is not a carpet laid down and spread over them, but an outvegetation of hidden seeds. All the men who have been greatest in Art have been distinguished by their consciousness that they were merely revelators of spiritual facts. "Appeal to an artist, and ask him why he so painted any given heroic head, without any old "family portrait" to guide him. If he be a true artist, a race not numerous, he will say, "I could not do otherwise. That man had such a temper, such a life, in him. I, therefore, mastering the inward spirit of the man, found his

---

* See, on the grossness of the popular error, its prevalence, and its evil tendencies, Barclay's "Inquiry into the Opinions, Ancient and Modern, concerning Life and Organization," chap. iii., sec. 11. (1822.)

fashion and his features created for me and given to me." Because such is the ultimate origin of the products of true art, of such, that is, as are something more than mere servile, tradesmen's copies of familiar physical objects, there is a Natural Theology of Art. For Art, rightly understood, is a portion of nature, and genuine Natural Theology cannot take either part without the other.* Briefly, as the Soul is the essential Human Body, so is that grand, invisible, imperishable fabric we call the spiritual, the essential World. The spiritual world is the total of Essential nature; this visible, material world is a portion of Representative nature, a portion only, because the little planet we call our own is the covering of a very minute part indeed of the infinite spiritual realm which is its parent. *Here* we have but a few detached sketches of the panorama which belongs *there*, and what few we have, albeit they are so lovely, we see but "as through a glass, darkly." It will not be so always. The spiritual world known to philosophy is no other, as said before, than the spiritual world of the hopeful Christian—the very same which we shall consciously inhabit when by death we cease to be conscious of the present. Our introduction in this life to mineral, vegetable, and animal, to air, and sky, and sun, is the beginning of a friendship that will never be dissolved, only that hereafter we shall view things as they really are, instead of their effigies and pictures. In this world we do not so much live as *prepare* to live, nor enjoy nature's sweet amenities so much as *prepare* to enjoy them. We shall leave it, but we shall not lose its beauty; we shall learn rather how most thoroughly to delight in it, often turning in pleased remembrance to those

* Excellently set forth in an article in the North American Review for July, 1854, "On the moral significance of the Crystal Palace."

early days which now we reckon as our "life-time," and to that little sphere which was our birth-place and education.

108. Philo Judæus calls upon us to observe that the derivation of the physical world from an anterior spiritual world is expressly taught in the book of Genesis: "These are the generations of the heavens and the earth, . . . and of every plant of the field *before it was in the earth*, and of every herb of the field *before it grew;*" which words, says Philo, "do manifestly teach that before the earth was green, verdure already existed; that before the grass sprang in the field, there was grass, though it was not visible. The same must we understand from Moses in the case of everything else which is perceived by the external senses; there were elder forms and motions already existing, according to which the others were fashioned and measured out. The things which he has mentioned are examples of the nature of all."*

109. The *evidence* that there is a spiritual world underlying the material, is quite as ready and plentiful as of the material world itself, if men will but look for it in the right place, and consent to receive it, for spectacles are less needed than willingness. It is rarely that incapacity hinders the reception of truth; rather is it want of cordiality to give it welcome. We speak now, of course it will be understood, of the spiritual world as a truth of Philosophy, *i. e.*, as the basis, as to first principles, of terrestrial nature. Most men believe in it under the name of "Heaven," or as a country which they will enter *after death.* Few, however, think of it in its *relation to existing nature;* yet so to regard it is little less important to enlarged and encouraging views of Life, for it brings heaven into our daily thoughts, as a living, familiar, and practical Reality, a thought for the *present*, for the fields and the woods, for the hills and the valleys, instead

* On the Creation, Chap. xliv.

of only for the future, at church on Sundays, and nothing so fills the soul with bright ideas. How differently the minds of men are constituted with regard to particular kinds of truth, we are perfectly aware. Some are made to superstition, some to enthusiasm, others are inapt for either; so that what in many cases men fancy to be contest for "truth," is simply comparison of their mental tastes, just as they compare their physical likings over the dining-table, and fancy they are contending for what is best. Oftentimes, without question, this will account for their insolicitude. "Inductive minds," says Whewell, "those which have been able to discover laws of nature, have also commonly been ready to believe in an Intelligent Author of nature; while deductive minds, those which have employed themselves in tracing the consequences of laws discovered by others, have been willing to rest in laws without looking beyond to an Author of laws." So with the views men take of the material world, its substance, derivation, and life. Deductive minds are content with the study of matter; inductive minds feel themselves invited to look further. But it is still a question of *willingness*, since nothing is ever sought except from the heart. There is something more even than willingness wanted. Before we can thoroughly recognize and approve a truth superior to the region of the senses, our moral character must have risen into harmony with it. It follows that the spiritual world is not a thing to be *argued* about. We should never argue with a man about things which require for their understanding a higher plane than he has risen to; until he has lifted himself into the requisite soul, he cannot be expected to see with similar eyes. Show him how and where to learn, but do not argue with him till he is on a level with your own vision. Hence, too, the utter worthlessness of the usual objection to the doctrine of the spiritual world, that it has no place in popular systems of philosophy. Some men reject it unconditionally—they simply "do not believe." It is very convenient to conceal incuriousness and ignorance under the name of *scepticism*, and thus invite the community to suppose that superior acuteness has detected unsoundness in what actually has never been even looked at.

110. Certainly, the proofs of spiritual things are not of the same *kind* as those of material ones. A man must not expect the same species of proof that there are angels, as of the existence of a railway or a tree. What visible, sensuous proof is to the material, philosophical induction is to the spiritual, and when this is assisted and borne out by Revelation, it is not merely as good a kind of proof, but an incomparably better and more cogent one. Not from the substance, time, and space of the material world, is the spiritual world to be judged of. Like the soul, which is a dweller in it, it must be thought of purely *from* the soul. This is the indispensable course in every inquiry that seeks to end in something better than grossest materialism. It is because people will persist in carrying their material ideas with them, wherever they go, that the soul itself has become a mere tradition, and the idea of immortality profaned into a supposed rebuilding of the rotten carcase of flesh and blood. While we should unceasingly strive to be men of sense, we should remember that this is not to be simply creatures of the *senses*. The external senses are among man's richest inheritances, still are they only the

> Fine steps whereby the Queenly Soul
> Comes down from her bright throne to view the mass
> She hath dominion over.

The man who attends only to what his senses inform him of, imprisons and kills the better half of his nature. He may acquire tolerable knowledge of outlines, weights. and colors, but a philosopher he can never be. With the diagrams he may become conversant, but not with that sublime geometry and universal arithmetic, the constructions of which form the real history of nature. The philosophy which the outer senses teach, dwells where *they* do, on the surface of nature. *Their* business is simply with effects. Causes, and spiritual things are seen by the internal, poetic, seventh sense—that divine faculty which men call the Imagination, the clear-seeing spiritual eye whereby the loftier and inmost truths of the universe, whether they be scientific, or religious, or philosophical, can alone be discerned. We are apt to suppose that to acquaint ourselves with nature, diligent observation and experiment will suffice. Not so. Nature has secrets which Imagination only can penetrate. So grievously has the imagination been perverted—so widely has the fancy been mistaken for it—so bad, in consequence, is its current repute as to its relation to Truth, that the mere mention of it, in connection with the subject in hand, will probably provoke many a smile, and in the charitable awaken compassion. It will be found, nevertheless, that all the greatest minds the world has produced, in any department of inquiry or of wisdom, have been so by virtue of their imagination. The imagination is not, as many suppose, *hostile* to truth. "So far from being an enemy to truth, the imagination," says Madame de Staël, "helps it forward more than any other faculty of the mind." Of course there are such things as diseased and prostituted imaginations, but the abuse of the faculty is neither its quality or design. Imagination rightly so called, presupposes an enlarged and tranquil mind, which having in its command a wide property in living nature and its laws, steps to undiscovered things from the standard of the known. "That," says Goethe, "is no true imagination which goes into the vague, and devises things that do not exist." Reason, or to use a preciser term, common sense, the very arbiter of Truth, and imagination, rightly regarded, are each other's *complement.* To esteem them as *contrary* comes of the very same mistake as that which asserts reason and faith to be foes. As the perfection of human nature is, in the body, the union of strength and beauty, so in the intellect is it the union of common sense and imagination. Again deceiving themselves, many suppose that the imagination is constantly needing a check. Say rather that it constantly needs the spur. Especially is this the case in Science and Religion, which instead of having suffered, as it has been taught, from excess of imagination, suffer rather from not being as hospitable to it as they ought. What is idolatry, but inaptitude to rise, on the pinions of the imagination, from the symbol to the thing symbolized? What other than imagination is the soul and centre of the very highest act of religion, or faith? To science, to philosophy also, imagination is nothing less than *pioneer.* The Columbus of the human mind, imagination opens the way for observation and experiment, which left to themselves, know not in what direction to proceed, and find their way, if at all, slowly and by accident; it provides us with the clue to what we seek, and enables us to anticipate the answer we shall receive. Every true investigation is the working out of some noble idea of the imagination; no great discovery was ever made without employing it. It is the vital characteristic of the Davys, the Owens, the Faradays, the Herschels—of all to whom the world is indebted for its highest scientific wealth. Genius itself might be defined as imagination well directed and well regulated. With all his science, so called, the *un*-imaginative man gives us only the osteology of the rainbow; it is the imaginative or poetic one who delineates its life and beauty. Like prisms, the men of imagination convert colorless light into exquisite hues; in their hands does the merest matter of prosaic detail become lustrous and glorified. Witness Garth Wilkinson's noble book on the Human Body, which, were it re-written in verse, would be the finest poem in the world. Like its subject, it is matter and spirit united, and "common sense" from beginning to end.

111. To attempt, therefore, to *prove* that there is a spiritual world, *i. e.*, in the way that a material or physical thing is proved, is, after all, superfluous. Those to whom it is interesting are conscious of it of themselves; and the opposite class logic would make no wiser. In a certain sense it is above and beyond proof; yet not strangely and peculiarly so. Not one of the greatest truths admits of proof commonly so called. We *feel* them. The highest of all, or the consciousness of God, we ascend into intuitively from our consciousness of self. That God exists, and that it was he who created the world, and who sustains it, we can neither "prove" to another, nor have "proved" to ourselves; and the same with the soul, and the spiritual world, and the life to come. For what, in fact, is it "to prove," but to trace a subordinate proposition up to a higher, or rather, to a primary truth? The nearer that proposition is to God and heaven, the further is it away from what is proveable. Were we, in short, to refuse to receive anything until "proved," we should remain strangers for ever to the noblest and most animating subjects of contemplation. Proof, rigid, mathematical proof, belongs only to inferior truths, and it is only inferior minds that make it the condition of their acceptance. If such minds be often characterized by their credulity, they are still oftener marked by their *in*credulity. "Ignorance is always incredulous; the amplest knowledge has the largest faith." It is right, without doubt, to *desire* proof; it is a man's *duty* to desire it; but then he must remember that many things are *un*proveable, or rather, that things are proveable in different ways. The heart and imagination have their eyes as

well as the head and the understanding. Great minds, or those in which the capacity for reading truth is quickest and highest, are not simply "intellectual" minds. They know what they have to believe on the showing of the feelings and the imagination, and of such things they never demand "proof." Not he is the wise man who cunningly thinks to take nothing on the word of the imagination, but he who takes what nature intends he should. The proof, the essential and best proof of the divine origin of Christianity and the Bible, does not consist in those weary piles denominated the Evidences, historical, archæological, and so forth, which commend themselves only to low and unenviable schools of thought, but in its *felt* adaptation to the needs and aspirations of the soul.

112. Scientific considerations may be adduced notwithstanding, both in proof of the Spiritual world, and of its causative action into the physical. Why have many animals, especially the saurians, the power of reproducing amputated members? How is it that when the foot or the tail of a lizard is torn off, a new one sprouts in its place? One of two things, either "nature performs a miracle," which is an indolent hypothesis; or else, which is a sufficient and reasonable explanation, material substances mould themselves universally upon preëxistent spiritual forms, as upon a model, and wait upon them as servitors. The reason usually assigned, namely, that the lower we descend in the scale of organization, the more is life diffused throughout the organism, is correct to a certain point, but it leaves the enigma where it was. It is not enough to be told that in the lower animals the vital mass which appears as brain in the higher kinds, is dispersed throughout the body; and that it is owing to this dispersion of the great centre of life into many small, separate centres, that the tentacula of polyps, the rays of the star-fish, the entire head of the snail, will

grow again if cut off. The question still remains—*why?* Life, like any human constructive power, cannot work without a pattern; nervous centres are but instrumental.* Why the wonderful privilege of replacing lost members of the body is enjoyed only by the lower tribes of animals, and not by the higher, is that the latter are enabled to make themselves amends for such losses in other ways. The office of one limb or member, to an extent sufficient to the necessities of life, can, in effect, be executed by another; while man, for his part, has the resources of mechanical contrivance in addition. The more helpless a creature is, the more amply is it always befriended with compensating gifts.

113. So with plants. Why does the acorn always produce an oak, and never an elm or an apple-tree; why the bulb of the hyacinth always the verisimilitude of its fragrant cluster, and never a cowslip or fleur-de-lis? Simply because in the acorn the spiritual substratum of the oak already in effect exists; and in the bulb, in like manner, the spiritual form or vegetable soul of the flower. Hence the multiformity of the beautiful pictures in wood and field, and their return to us, year by year. Every wild flower comes back in its perfect lineaments; in the early spring the golden celandine and the coltsfoot; then the Mayflower and the woodruff, then the forget-me-not, bathing its feet at the water-side; and so onwards till the purple crocus of October. True, they unfold themselves from roots and seeds, lying concentrated as it were till their proper season; but wanting a spiritual form to clothe with stem and leaf, a seed could

---

* The power of reproducing lost parts which made that beautiful little creature the *Hydra* such a miracle to first observers, and suggested its zoological name, appears to exist in scarcely inferior degree in the *Actinias* or Sea-anemones. On its prevalence in the Star-fishes consult Forbes.

no more grow than a grain of sand. The real reason of the flowers is that every line of beauty in nature is the expression of a divine thought, and inherits the immortality of its first development in the spiritual world. It is in spiritual philosophy, and in this only, that we have an answer also to the puzzling question, why it is that the mules, or hybrids, both animal and vegetable, cannot permanently produce themselves; why also the graft will only consort with a tree of the same species as itself. *Material* forms may be coupled, and a cross be procured for a brief period, but it is impossible in the same way to establish *spiritual* forms, and without these, as their prototypes, material forms cannot be propagated. The best introduction to knowledge of what constitutes a "species," either in Zoology or Botany, is to be sought in the philosophy of spirit, and its relation to matter.

114. So even with inorganic forms. Why do salts and metals always crystallize in determinate shapes, their proportions and angles invariably the same? Let a number of different salts be dissolved in water, and they will sort themselves out, unassisted, and re-adjust and re-crystallize their particles in the precise polyhedra they originally possessed. Clearly, as in the former case, this is because there are underlying spiritual forms, sustained by the Divine life, and which, by virtue of that life, draw the particles together, each to its own body. The terms chemical affinity, chemical attraction, power, property, agency, *vis formatrix*, &c., currently used when speaking of the consolidation of inorganic matter, denote nothing more than the action of the Divine life, under different methods, through the medium of spiritul creations in the first place.

115. On the dim and half-traditional perception that organic forms repose upon an interior spiritual form, was built the Alchemists' beautiful doctrine of the *palingenesis*, or resuscitation by art, of the spirits of plants and flowers.

"Never," says the historian of the Curiosities of Literature, "was a philosophical imagination more beautiful than that exquisite *palingenesis* of the admirable school of Borelli, Gaffarel, and Digby." The way in which the resuscitation was supposed to be brought about, was to burn a flower to ashes, and place them in a phial; then to add a certain chemical mixture, and warm it; when there would slowly rise a delicate apparition of stalk, and leaf, and blossom, successively, faithful as the lovely transcripts of scenery in still water, "the phantastical plant" disappearing into nothingness as the heat gradually declined. Southey, in the second volume of the "Omniana," gives a full account both of the doctrine and of the manipulation requisite to produce these curious phantoms. That they were actually exhibited by the alchemists, there would seem to be no doubt; having been produced, it is not unlikely, by tracing the figures of the plants and flowers on the glass reputed to contain their spirits, with chloride of cobalt, drawings made with which salt are invisible till brought near the fire. So firmly was the doctrine held by the honest, that it was adduced as an argument for the resurrection of man.* Perhaps the Hamadryads of ancient poetry, nymphs who were born with trees when they rose out of the ground, who lived in them, and who died when *they* died, were but their spiritual forms, separated and personified by fancy. "Trees,"

---

* Disraeli's account of the Palingenesis is under the head "Dreams at the Dawn of Philosophy." On the practical part of it, see Boyle's Philosophical Works, abridged, vol. i., p. 69, "Surprising things performable by Chemistry," and the Philosophical Transactions for 1674, vol. ix., p. 175. Palingenesis, as a word, is simply the Greek for resurrection, learnedly illustrated by Mr. Trench in his New Testament Synonymes. Theodore de Rycke applies it to the revival of letters, "Oratio de palingenesis Literarum in Terris nostris." Leyden, 1672.

says a lively Frenchman, "are animated; they have their enjoyments, their grief, their sleep, and their loves. The ancients placed a nymph under their rind. To be sure she is there! Life is a very pretty nymph; we ought to love her wherever she is found." How beautifully does another of the same country allude to his love of trees, and their influence on his imagination, regretting that there are no longer any Dryads, or it would have been among these that he would have formed an attachment in which his heart should find its home.*

116. In fine, recognition of the spiritual world, as the foundation of the material one, and in connection with it, of the momentary influx of the Divine life into every object and atom of creation, the spiritual world receiving that life primarily, and the material world by derivation from it, is the beginning of all genuine philosophy. Unperceiving these two great, fundamental truths, the whole kingdom of truth is beclouded: only as men learn to appreciate and to apply them, does their knowledge begin to live. "What but apparitions," says Coleridge, "can belong to a philosophy which satisfies itself when it can explain nature *mechanically*, that is, by the laws of Death, and brands with the name of Mysticism every solution grounded in Life?" "As Nature," says Dr. Braun, "without man, presents externally only the image of a labyrinth without a clue, scientific examination which denies the internal, spiritual foundations of nature, leads only to a chaos of unknown matters and forces. From this dark chaos no bright path leads up." Yet, ordinarily, it is precisely the live facts from which men of science turn away! "Nothing is more evident," says one of the shrewdest writers of our day, "than that the men of facts are afraid of a large number of

* Rosseau. Confessions, book ix.

important facts. All the spiritual facts about us, of which there are plenty, are denounced as superstition. Not only are they not received by that courtesy which takes off its grave hat to a new beetle or a fresh vegetable alkaloid, but they are treated by it worse than our vermin." We do not seek to disparage the efforts of the non-spiritual. Whoever faithfully explains one of "the things that do appear," assists in explaining the hidden and invisible ones which are *not* seen, and deserves approbation and gratitude accordingly. Let him, with equal courtesy, not undervalue the efforts of the "spiritual;" falling into the error of those "fools" and "blind" of old, who knew not whether was greater, the gold of the temple, or the temple that sanctified the gold. The "spiritualist" may seem mad to the materialist,—and mad he is, if *merely* a spiritualist; but how much more sane is the mere man of science, who seeking the living among the dead, values the tabernacle more than the occupying spirit?

CHAPTER XI

GROUNDS OF THE VARIOUS LEASE OF LIFE—Continued.
CORRESPONDENCE OF NATURE AND MIND.

117. CORRESPONDENCE, or the science of the relation of the two worlds, *i. e.*, of the objects and phenomena of the material, to the typical forms and *noumena* of the spiritual, is the key and Open Sesame! to every species of human knowledge. With correspondence for our guide, perhaps nothing is absolutely unintelligible; without it, the commonest things are clouded. To right conceptions of the unseen it is indispensable at the very outset. Most of the metaphysical difficulties which surround revealed theology, really originate in neglecting the light which Correspondence is fitted to throw upon them; the phenomena of the senses find in it their only true solution. Vast as nature itself, of course it can here be only commended to minds zealous in pursuit of genuine wisdom, except in so far as relates to the lease of life.

118. To this end it will suffice that we consider the *particular* correspondence, derived from the general, which nature holds with the faculties and emotions of the Soul, that wonderful and delicious concord whereby the sunshine, the sea, everything in nature is so companionable, and which gives to the soul a kind of omnipresence. The ground of this concord is that man, as to first principles, is a synthesis of the spiritual world, and thus of the material world which clothes and represents it. As a concave mirror contains

pictures in little of all the thousand objects of a beautiful landscape, so in the soul of man is contained an epitome of all the forces and principles that underlie the works of God, whether visible or invisible. The poets and philosophers call him a *microcosm*, or "little world;" "the kingdom of heaven," says holy writ, "is *within* you." External nature is not the independent thing, having no connection with man, which we are apt to suppose. It is at once a second *logos*, and a second *homo*. It is so varied, so lovely, so exquisitely organized, because of the variety, the loveliness, the exquisite composition, primarily of the spiritual world, secondly of the human soul. The sun, the stars, trees, flowers, the sea, rivers, animals, exist, not irrespectively and independently of man, but *because* of him. In him are all of these, along with spring, summer, autumn, and winter, light and darkness, heat and cold, all natural objects and phenomena whatever, only after another manner, felt instead of seen, as sentiments and emotions, instead of physical incarnations. Were they *not* in him, there would be none of them anywhere else. "Had I not had the world in my soul from the beginning," says Goethe, "I must ever have remained blind with my seeing eyes, and all experience and observation would have been dead and unproductive. The light is there, and the colors surround us, but if we bore nothing corresponding in our own eyes, the outward apparition would not avail." When, therefore, we admire nature, when we love it, it is virtually admiration of the spiritual and immortal, and this is why the love of nature is so powerful a help towards loving God. Hence also the concurrence of Science and Metaphysics, which are concerned with things essentially the same, only presented under different aspects and conditions. So intimate is the correspondence even between the body of man, and the faculties of the soul, that Klencke has built upon it an entire system of organic psychology, incited perhaps by the hint of Lord Bacon, when he says that "unto all this knowledge of the concordances between the mind and the body, that part of the inquiry is the most necessary which considereth of the seats and domiciles which the several faculties do take and occupy." We little think how near, by correspondence, the body is like the soul, and the soul like the spiritual world. Novalis says truly that "we touch heaven when we lay our hand on a human body." Think how the face is the epitome of the body, repeating in little its every organ and every function, and we see why the face is of all natural mysteries the very grandest. That plants and animals were created, and light and darkness ordained *prior* to the creation of man, is no objection to their being effects or results of him, because although the last to be actually moulded, he was the first in conception and plan, all the works of Almighty wisdom being prefigurative of His own image and likness.

119. It is no new doctrine that such a concord or correspondence exists between nature and the soul of man; it is no new discovery; neither is it a deduction from any new or narrow circle of experiences. "The world at large is the school that believes in it, and daily life, in all its immense detail, is the theatre of its exemplification." Language rests entirely upon the sublime fact that the universe is a hieroglyph and metaphor of human nature; there is no poetry that has not sprung from the deep feeling of it, and that does not owe to it all its eloquence and graces; all philosophy implies and unconsciously proclaims it; the magic, idolatry, and mythology of the primævals; the "language of flowers," emblems, fable, allegory, the rites and ceremonies of religion, are all founded upon it, and are alone explicable by it. It is no less the ground of our most living enjoyments. The sweetness of a kind look, the solace

of a loving smile, come purely of the correspondence of the features with the soul within; the pleasure we derive from music, scenery, flowers, comes of our feeling, when in their presence, the "sweet sense of kindred." The light of the soul, like the light of the sun, makes everything beautiful on which it shines, but it is by being *reflected* from it. As we can only give to others what they can take, so can we only be affected by what is congenerous to ourselves—the secret of all loves, friendships, and social unions. The inmost spring of our attachments to one another is our Correspondence. Hence, too, that beautiful innate image in the heart of the beings we most deeply and permanently love, which gives to our first sight of them almost a sense of recognition.

> Some are never strangers,
> But soon as seen, the soul as if by instinct
> Springs towards them with resistless force, and owns
> Congenial sympathy.

120. Save for the unity of the mind with the inmost, spiritual essence of the world, nature would not only be incomprehensible to man—not only be no object of his intelligence, but not even an object of his consciousness. Only by virtue of our correspondence with nature do we become familiar with it. There can be no reciprocation where there is no similarity. Were it not a mirror, it would be a void, as to the brutes it really is, since they see it not, and feel it not. Not that there is any of our proper *life* in the things of nature. They are instinct with spiritual vitality, but only in man is spiritual vitality exalted into spiritual Life, since he alone is intelligent of God. Doubtless there is great diversity in men's estimate and appreciation of natural objects, and thence in the pleasure derived from them, but this so much the more substantiates the principle. Why

some minds are most delighted by flowers, others by birds, others by mountains, others by trees, even by particular species of living things, as when one loves above all other birds the industrious, sociable rooks, it is that the correspondent spiritual principles are in those minds preëminently developed. The whole of nature is in every mind, but some one part of it more actively than the remainder; while all men are joint heritors of the total of the world, every man has a little piece of it to himself. Every man has a secret affinity, a secret love, a secret pleasure, known in its fullness and rewards, like his conscience, only to himself and to his Maker.' Were we wise, this great principle would be made the basis of Education, which should never fail to respect the correspondences of individual minds, and cannot be expected to be efficient till it is recognized. The efficacy of correspondence is truly wonderful. While new feelings are awakened, old, familiar ones are heightened and improved by the presence of the natural object that represents them. Beneath the still skies of night we become more reverent; looking at the green leaves of spring, more young in hope. Why do the tenderly-attached find such happy hours in sweet, sequestered, rural pathways, where the wild flowers blow, and the clear streams ripple, if it be not that nature mirrors and echoes their affections, and enriches them with a new enthusiasm? Hence it is also that those who love tenderly always feel peculiarly endeared to one another while participating in the admiration of works of Art, which, fulfilling the highest end of Art, namely, to excite emotions, and not merely awaken recollection, speak to the soul by their true grandeur. A chief reason why so much originally good feeling becomes chilled and debased, is that we do not oftener quit the world that man has made, for the company of our kindred in the world that God made. Immuring ourselves in the narrow boundary of our parlors, we cannot properly expand; "in the presence of nature we feel great and free, like that which we have before our eyes." Things again, which away from their correspondent imagery seem weak and trifling, in its presence become beautiful and noble. "Love-scenes," says an amiable writer, "such as in a parlor look foolish and absurd, assume a very different aspect when seen amid the soft hush and spiritual beauties of an evening river-side, or in the light of an autumn moon. We feel then that the beautiful picture has received its proper setting. Who has forgotten the moonlight scene in the Merchant of Venice, or the interview of Waverley and Flora near the waterfall?" Lastly, it is in the convergence towards him of all its nature and attributes, that the thoughtful man finds the *dignity* of the world consist. "He reads the mystery of human existence in the relations of the forms which encompass him; and discovers the solution of nature's problems in his own physical and mental activities." He sees that it is the same life which connects events and phenomena, whether in him or without him, and with the change from terrestrial to human, finds it glorify.

121. External nature being then what we find it, by virtue of previous ideas and affections in the world of spirit, and of its synthesis, the human soul, the phenomena, changes, and vicissitudes which take place in it, will be so many correspondences and translations of what occurs *there.* Here, accordingly is the first solution of the problem of the lease of life. Why the oak and the elephant live so long; why the gourd and the insect die so soon, is that the principles, sentiments, and emotions in the human soul to which these things severally correspond, are of the same relative constitution and capacity of endurance. How many are the emotions which we feel, year by year, growing and strengthening within us, like noble trees; how many others do we feel spring up, blossom, and pass away like the day-lily!

The whole matter of the "growth of the mind" is translatable into the history of the growth of nature, its changes, decays, and rejuvenescences. What is longæval in the soul, is longæval also in nature; what is ephemeral in the world, is the picture of something ephemeral in ourselves.

122. The law of USE, wherein consists the second grand cause of the diversity in the lease of life, is like Correspondence, vast as creation itself, seeing that subserviency to another's wants and happiness is the purpose for which all things have been designed, and the world framed and methodized so admirably. The greater the amount of the difference between any two or more objects, the stronger is the proof of their necessity as regards the general welfare, and thus of their having some special use in their respective spheres, whether we can perceive the exact nature of it or not. The difference, for example, between an elephant and a rose, and between a rose and a pebble, is the precise measure of their value and importance in the collective economy and constitution of things. Wherein these two qualities consist, of course is a separate matter of inquiry, and falls to the province of the accurate observer of nature.

123. All uses are referable to one or other of three great ends; they were designed for these ends, and they are perpetually promotive of them. The first is the physical welfare of the living organisms of our planet; the second, the instruction and delight of man; the third, which presupposes and ensues upon the other two, is the glory of God who ordained them, and for whose "pleasure" all things were created. Physical uses comprise all those by which things reciprocally sustain one another in health and comeliness, and preserve their respective races extant upon the earth. The soil supports the plant; the plant feeds the animal; both repay all that is rendered them, and with interest; and strengthened by what they have received, succor their own

species. According to the needs of each superior thing is the adaptation of every inferior one that supports it, as regards structure, configuration, and vital economy; every plant and animal, every bird and tree, every mineral even, is so constituted as to enable it to minister to a nobler nature; the term of its life is exactly adequate and proportionate to its office, and concludes when the duties of that office have been fulfilled. The tree that provides timber lives for centuries; the corn required for food is ripe in a summer.

124. Nature ministers to the instruction and delight of man by shadowing intellectual and religious truth; and this great use it most efficiently subserves in the circumstance of its incessant change. Change, at least in the material world, implies death; and death, for its full efficacy and impressiveness as a monitor, needs to be various and wonderful as life. Were there no such thing as external nature, man would be an irremediably ignorant savage; he becomes civilized and intelligent by the just contemplation of its mysteries. Nature is the grand, rich book of symbols which we prove it, not simply in the significance of its *forms*, but in the significance and lessons of the phenomena of its *mortality*. Were all things like the granite mountain-peaks, that have caught the first beams of immemorial morning suns, enduring forever, though we might wonder more, our love and true spiritual activity would be less. The very frailty of things excites a tender interest in them, and when to this is joined an almost endless diversity as to the period of their stay, they become to us store-houses of curious wisdom and satisfaction. Where would be the gladness of the spring if the primroses blossomed throughout the year, or the grandeur of the ancient woods if the trees were but children of the summer? Man is a thousand times happier from the fact of some plants being annuals, others perennials, others longæval trees, than were all to die at a common age.

125. Finally is the use of all things in reference to the glory of their Almighty Framer; and this, as in the preceding case, is exalted by what to a small and narrow view, is their very weakness. Why the mass of organic nature is so brief-lived, why it seems to exist only to die, is that, taking a thousand years together, the amount of enjoyment (or of picturesque on the part of what is not competent to enjoy), shall be greater than were it to survive for the whole period. The larger the number of beings that enter the world, whether by fertility of individuals, or by successive renewals, one generation after another, so much the more scope is there for that happiness and physical beauty which it is the Divine "pleasure" to communicate and sustain. Doubtless, a solitary tree, a single animal of each kind, or of any kind, attests the hand of God as powerfully as a world-full, and a single generation as powerfully as a hundred; but God is essential Love, and the nature of love is to *give;* its satisfaction is to surround itself with receptacles for the blessings which it burns to bestow, and in a finite kingdom such receptacles are best multiplied—perhaps only so—by the magnificent institutions of Death and Renewal, whereby myriads are successively introduced upon the scene, instead of a few antique and venerable ones remaining always. It is infinitely more to the glory of God that ten men should live for seventy years a-piece, one after another, than that there should be only one instead of ten in the same period. It makes ten happy lives instead of only one, for seventy years properly used, are as good as seven hundred. In a word, whatever advantage it is to man's welfare, either physical or moral, that the lease of life should be various, is also a glory to God, beeause all human enlightenment and delight shine back upon the heaven of their origin.

126. A question yet remains in connection with this sub-

ject, namely,—Let the maximum duration of the individuals constituting a species be what it may,—a few months or a thousand years,—does a period arrive in the history of the species when, like a title of nobility without an heir, it absolutely "dies out," every individual becoming extinct? Geology makes it plain that during the infinite past, species of animals and plants now no longer existing, successively occupied the surface of the earth, in considerable variety and amazing numbers; the legitimate conclusion is, therefore, in favor of the affirmative. How long the particular species now alive have been upon the earth, how long they will continue, man can neither know nor surmise; it is sufficient for the principle that they can be shown to have had predecessors, and that those predecessors have wholly disappeared from the ranks of the living. The highest interest attaches to the existing organic population of the world, both as to its beginning and its final destiny. The origin of noxious plants and animals; the descent of the various races from a single individual or a single pair of each kind, or on the other hand, from a plurality; their dispersion over the earth's surface; the extermination of different species by the hand of man; and many similar matters, treated as they deserve, would suffice to fill whole volumes. Here they must be dismissed with the bare mention.

127. The general question as to the lease of life in species being answered, there arise upon the solution other and more curious problems:—What were the leases of those anterior species?—Why have they not continued to the present time? —Under what laws were the new and superseding forms introduced? Geology solves them in part, or as regards the proximate, physical reasons; and no portion of this noble science is more interesting and satisfactory. But Geology of itself is insufficient; we are compelled to fall back, as in everything else, on the spiritual laws of which physical ones

are Effects. Then we find that the same laws which primarily determine the duration of the individuals of a species, determine also the duration of the species as a whole. They are problems no less magnificent than vast, if only from the immensity of time covered by the events and changes they have reference to. Six thousand years, or thereabout, the period we are accustomed to regard as comprising the history of life, and as taking us to the beginning of creation, is in reality but the pathway to a point from which we look forth on an expanse without horizon. Yet not hopelessly, because with all the sublime antiquity in the works of the Almighty, stretching so far back, and upon a scale so grand, there is indissolubly connected the fact of his Unchangeableness, assuring us that he was always employed *as now;* that we shall find all in perfect harmony; that all that exists, as worlds, systems of worlds, contents of worlds, *to-day,* is but a continued exemplification of original and eternal principles; thus that all lies within the reach and compass of our understanding.

128. The spiritual laws alluded to are again those of Correspondence and of Use, which apply to the ante-hominal world no less than to the existing state of things. The pre-Adamite plants and animals, like those which now surround us, were material shows of forms contained in the spiritual world, flowing from them in the same manner, and possessed therefore of similar affinities with principles and affections in the soul of man, which is the spiritual world in little. For though later in production, as to time, man virtually and essentially preceded every Spirifer and Trilobite, every Coralline and Conferva. Prior to all worlds, man is the oldest idea in creation; nothing was ever moulded into form, or vitalized by the Divine breath, that had not a prefigurative reference to something eventually to be exhibited in *him.* The geological history of our planet is the biography

of human nature, told in the imagery of correspondence; all those great phenomena of stratification, disruption, change of surface, and succession of living being, which make the annals of our earth such glorious reading, are to the true reader a narrative in symbol of his own emotional and intellectual development. From the time when darkness was upon the face of the deep, through all the grand sequences of light, land and water, vegetation and animal life, the record is of man's advance from the state of vacant infancy up to that of ripe and opulent maturity. Did we know the particular correspondence of the extinct plants and animals that once lived upon the earth, we should discern in every one of them a picture of something in the mind or heart of childhood; we should comprehend the scheme of sequence in which they successively appeared, the ground of their various duration, why they were of such and such figure, habits, and degree of bulk. The great size of many of the pre-Adamite animals, and their strange and unshapely forms, consist, we may see at a glance, with the wild, ambitious phantasies of early youth, when the Arabian Nights are thought to be solid facts;—the small number of distinct species, relatively to the present numbers, corresponds with its scanty stock of emotional experiences and ideas. Who is there that, wandering through the museums of memory, is not reminded of the time when the plains of his little world were trod by gigantic Mastodons and Dimotheria, and when in place of its now innumerable flowers and fruit-trees, there were only huge Calamites and Sigillarias. Thus will it be that Correspondence, in the ratio that men study this matchless science, will throw light on the history of the fossil fauna and flora of our globe. Its companion law, the great principle of Use, rightly brought to bear, will supply what more is wanting. For all these ancient forms of life had their uses to subserve, and doubtless their respective leases were adapted to them. The plants, for example, whose compacted and bitumenized relics constitute Coal, must have been gifted with a duration and a prolific power commensurate with the use they were destined to in the remote future; and the magazines once filled and covered in they would cease from living occupancy of the soil.

CHAPTER XII.

THE SPIRITUAL EXPRESSION OF LIFE,—NATURE AND SEAT OF THE SOUL.

129. THE spiritual expression of life is the prerogative of MAN. It is the gift which distinguishes him from all other animals; just as the organic life is that which distinguishes those animals, together with plants, and his own material body, from earth and stone. By virtue of his spiritual life, man is an emotional and intellectual being. By virtue of this he thinks, speaks, sings,* worships, loves, pities, weeps,† hopes, laughs, marries; performs, in a word, the innumerable actions, internal and external, which the observation of thousands of years has never once detected in any of the inferior orders of creation, but has established as the noble diagnosis of human nature. This also is the primary ground of his *physical* peculiarities. By virtue of his possessing a Soul, animated with spiritual life, the spine of man has those wonderful curves in it, and that curious pyramidal arrangement of bones, whereby he is enabled to stand erect. The more complicated brain than any other of the mammalia have; the smoothness and nakedness of his skin; the peculiar muscle for the extension of the fore-finger; the capacity for being tickled, and for blushing; smiles and kisses; the

* Birds only whistle; they do not sing.

† The occasional flow of a few tears from the eyes of certain quadrupeds, is not *weeping*, the true idea of which implies intelligent emotion, and strength rather than weakness.

breast of woman, so exquisitely unlike that of any other female animal, both in its shape during the flower of her age, and the longer retention of its normal form after the period of lactation; all these have their essential origin in that inner and regal life which links earth to heaven. Flowing from God cotemporaneously, the spiritual and the organic life are the same *in essence*, the difference between them is simply one of expression. As played forth by the body, it is Organic life; as played forth by the soul, it is Spiritual life. Man, while a resident in the material world, is a recipient, therefore, not merely of one, nor even of two, but of three expressions of the Divine sustaining energy. Chemical affinity, cohesion, molecular attraction, &c., which are its lowest expression, sustain the elemental ingredients of his frame, the carbon, water, lime, and so forth. Organic life arranges and builds up those ingredients into apparatus, and impels the several portions to the due performance of some fixed duty. Spiritual life, which is the highest expression, vitalizes and energizes his soul; impelling it, after the same manner, to the exercise of its intellect and affections. The knowledge of the lowest expression of life constitutes Physics; that of the organic, Physiology; that of the highest or spiritual, Psychology. The latter may be defined as the science of the Life of God in man's soul; physiology as that of the Life of God in his body. And as that life is essentially One, psychology and physiology, in their high, philosophic idea, are connected as soul and body, and each is an exponent of the other. What in relation to physiological life, are called the "functions of the body," or the "functions of organization," re-appear in relation to the spiritual life, as the "intellectual powers," the "operations of the mind," &c., which are the same thing essentially, only expressed after a higher manner, according to the law of discrete degrees. Functions in the body, faculties in the soul; the terms alter as the theatre changes. Doubtless there are broad distinctions in the mode of their procession. The phenomena of which physiology takes cognizance are both simultaneous and successive; those which belong to psychology are successive only. "Physiological phenomena exhibit themselves as an immense number of series bound up together; psychological phenomena as but a single series. Thus, the *continuous* actions of digestion, circulation, respiration, &c., are also *synchronous;* but the actions constituting Thought occur, not simultaneously, but one after another." Taken together, physiology and psychology meet as Philosophy, or the science of the antecedent unity of which the spiritual and the material are the dual development.

130. The spiritual expression of life is a perfectly distinct thing from the *soul;* which is no mere "principle," either of intelligence as regards this world, or of immortality as regards the next; but a definite, substantial entity, as much a part of created nature as a flower or a bird; and so far from being Life, or even possessing any inherent or separate life, depends for existence, no less than the body which encloses it, on continually renewed supplies from the Creator. "The inner man drops into metaphysical dust, as the outer man into physical, unless the parts be kept in coherence by some sustaining life; and that latter is no other than the life of the living God." In itself, the soul is neither immortal nor indestructible. However common such epithets may be in books and sermons, the Bible knows nothing of them; though it unquestionably teaches that God having once created a soul, it pleases him to sustain it with life for ever; and to allow it to exercise that life freely, as if it were its own, just as the free exercise of the organic life is allowed to the body. The possession respectively of *independent* life and of *derived* life, constitutes the grand characteristic by which we distinguish at all times and in all places, between

the CREATOR and the created. If not a generally-received distinction, even among philosophers, that the soul is one thing and its life another is at least the doctrine of the New Testament, where the Divine, vitalizing essence is discriminated as *ζωη*, while the vessel into which it is communicated is called by some such name as *ψυχη*. Thus, *πνεῦμα ζωῆς ἐκ τοῦ Θεοῦ εἰσῆλθεν ἐν αὐτοῖς*, "the spirit of life from God entered into them;" (Rev. xi. 11,) *τὰς ψῦχὰς τῶν πεπελεκισμένων*, "the souls of them that were beheaded." (Rev. xx. 4.) The body is distinguished as *σωμα*, as in Matthew x. 28, "Fear not them which kill *το σωμα*, but are not able to kill *την ψυχην*, but rather fear Him who is able to destroy both *ψυχη* and *σωμα* in hell."

131. Rightly to conceive of the spiritual life, it is needful, accordingly, first to obtain clear ideas of its receptacle, the soul; just as in order to the conception of physiological life, it is needful first to inquire into the composition of the body. If we are to judge by the loose, indefinite notions ordinarily entertained respecting the soul, even by intelligent people, a positive, coherent idea of it is one of the greatest desiderata of the age. How common is it to hear the soul alluded to as a mere abstract intellection; an ethereal, unimaginable, immortal something, located nobody knows where, but surmised to be in the brain, and capable of subsisting, in the trans-sepulchral world, in the most independent and isolated condition, free from any kind of connection with any kind of body. This is not philosophical, to say the least of it. Granted, the nature of the soul is a mystery; a mystery, too, of which all the most grand and sacred part futurity alone can reveal. We shall compass it when, and not before, our "eyes behold the King in his beauty," Him who is "the end of problems and the font of certainties." We should be thankful, indeed, that we feel it to be a mystery, for the mind that repudiates or is insensible to the mysterious, is in-

accessible to the sublime. But to be mysterious is not necessarily to be inscrutable. The prime feature of mystery is that it recedes before wise and calm interrogation. Mystery, therefore, should never be allowed to deter. It ought rather to incite, especially when, as in the present instance, Revelation stands ready to shed its clear and willing light, and assures us that to the earnest disciples of truth "it is given to *know* the mysteries of the kingdom of heaven," of which the Soul is indisputably one of the sublimest. "It is the essential mark of the true philosopher," says Coleridge, "to rest satisfied with no imperfect understanding, so long as the impossibility of attaining a fuller knowledge has not been demonstrated." While we reverently attempt not to be "wise *above* that which is written," one of our highest duties is to strive, and that most studiously, to be wise "*up to* that which is written." The reward is abundant, if we do but discover the nature of the difficulties, and what is within, and what beyond, the scope of our powers.

132. That a most partial and defective interpretation of the mystery is all that purely secular philosophy can achieve, may be as readily conceded as the enigmatical character of the theme itself; and recognizing this, it is no matter of surprise that Pagan antiquity bequeathed to us nothing but a mass of shapeless and contradictory hypotheses. The ancients' ignorance of physiology was likewise a serious, perhaps fatal, impediment.* That a people claiming to be enlightened Christians, in a country like England, should not hold a single fixed and positive opinion on the

---

* Anaximenes taught that the soul was nothing more than *air*. Socrates, in the Phædo, jocosely remarks to the disciples of this doctrine, that surely their souls will be run away with by the wind, when they die, if of no better composition, and warns them against residing in an open and windy country!

nature of the soul, to say nothing of an established doctrine, is, however, truly astonishing, and not a little *reproachful.* An exalted theology, like a sound philosophy, never rests content with general, indefinite ideas. It avails nothing to know the ancients' deficiencies if we are careless about our own. Only by making the detection of their errors the means of true knowledge for ourselves, do we acquire a right to pity the ignorance of our predecessors, and to lay claim to an enlightenment which they had *not.* One would think that though no one else cared to do it, those at least whose entire solicitude is presumed to have reference to the soul, and whose studies and occupation so peculiarly qualify them, namely, the priests and ministers of religion, would never rest till they had enabled themselves to propound something intelligible and satisfactory. So far from it, the pulpit is mute, and its companion literature is barren.* Affirmations of the general fact of immortality are plentiful enough, we are aware. But this is not the question, nor is it a question at all. No one from his heart disputes the general proposition of immortality; and it is notorious that even those who affect to deny it with their lips, confess it in their fears. The belief in immortality is a natural feeling, an adjunct of self-consciousness, rather than a dogma of any particular theology, or of any particular age or country, and is concurrent with the belief in an Infinite, presiding Spirit, which is allowed to be spontaneous and universal. What we want to be instructed in is, not that man is immortal, but what the Soul is; and this not so much as regards our future, as our present existence. This is the

* With the exception of the Rev. J. Clowes' "Letters to a friend on the Human Soul, as being a Form and Substance deriving its life continually from God," 1825, and the excellent little work of the Rev. W. Mason "On the Human Soul."

knowledge with regard to which intelligent curiosity seems dead, and which is so beclouded by error, yet which even the pulpit takes no trouble to purify and correct, and place before the world in its proper, illustrious beauty; as if it were quite unimportant that what is philosophically false can never be theologically true.

133. The soul of man, considered in its true character, namely, the seat and immediate organ of his emotional and intellectual life, is his SPIRITUAL BODY. The body of flesh and blood is only half the human being. Another body underlies it. "There is a natural body," says the Apostle, "and there is a spiritual body." By "spiritual body" he plainly means a body altogether different from the "natural," which is the material, or as Wiclif calls it, the "beestli" body; yet by speaking of both in the present tense—saying of each that it now *is*—he gives us to understand that the two bodies are cotemporaneous and co-existent, so long, that is, as the natural one may endure. By adding that it is to be "raised," he intimates that this "spiritual body" is the immortal portion of our being.* In this glorious revelation

---

* It is scarcely necessary to point out to the intelligent reader that the "it" in the English translation of these verses does not and cannot mean the dead material body, but man as to his personality, or consciousness of himself. He knows himself as "a natural body" while in this world; as "a spiritual body" in the next. This is proved by the word "sown," which refers, not as careless readers suppose, to the interment of one's corpse in the grave, but to the birth of our living into the world. "The time," says Locke, "that man is in this world, affixed to this earth, is his being sown, and not when, being dead, he is put in the grave, as is evident from St. Paul's own words. For dead things are not sown; seeds are sown, being alive, and die not till after they are sown." &c. *Paraphrase and Notes on the Epistles*, Works, vol. 3, p. 207. Ed. 1714. We shall see this more plainly in a future chapter.

is thus furnished the "key to the mystery;" for everything which philosophy asserts to be constitutional to the soul is involved in the idea of a spiritual body, of a nature superior to the material one, and continuing to exist after that body expires; and conversely, everything which is said by the Apostle concerning the spiritual body, is exactly what we should expect from an inspired writer, seeking to communicate a general notion of the soul and its destiny. But so far we have little more than a substitution of one name for another. What *is* this "spiritual body?" Here historical Scripture comes to our aid. It is an admirable characteristic of the Bible that there is not a single doctrine enunciated in its *didactic* portions, but is somewhere illustrated in its *histories;* either in the actual histories, including the biographical notices, or in the *quâsi*-histories, as the parables. Take, for instance, the history of the Transfiguration. During its progress, there were seen by the disciples, *ἄνδρες δυο*, "two *men*, which were Moses and Elias, who appeared in glory." The event in question took place more than eighteen hundred years ago; the bodies, therefore, in which the patriarchs appeared, could not have been the resuscitated and transformed material bodies which it is commonly supposed will be re-attached to the soul at the day of judgment, "when the graves are opened, and the sea gives up her dead." They must, nevertheless, have been real and substantial bodies, or they would not have been identified as Moses and Elias by spectators, who it is expressly stated, were "awake." Elias (or Elijah) certainly is stated, in another place, to have been taken up into heaven by "a chariot and horses of fire;" but to the enlightened reader of the Word of God, it is evident that he did not go as flesh and blood, seeing that these "cannot inherit the kingdom of heaven;" and in any case there is no authority for supposing Moses to have gone in such a form.

So in the parable of Lazarus and the rich man. Here too the several actors are represented as being perfectly well known to one another, and as holding the perfect human form, implied in their possessing the customary corporeal organs. The time of this parable is laid, it will be remembered, as prior to the "day of judgment" and the "resurrection of the body," as popularly thought of (suggesting, by the way, an enormous discrepancy between the popular notions and the doctrine of the parable), the rich man's father and brethren being still alive upon the earth. Here again, therefore, there is no material body present; nothing but the *soul;* yet all the circumstances of the narrative imply bodies no less real, and no less truly organized and sensitive. What, then, is the inference to be drawn from these facts and divine teachings? Clearly this; that what is popularly called the "soul" is what the Apostle terms the "spiritual body;" and that the latter is a substantial, organized form, exactly correspondent with the external, physical frame; that it presents a precisely similar assemblage of parts and features; and that when disengaged from it at death, it still holds intact both the human configuration, and every lineament on which personal identity depends, and by which individuals are recognized and distinguished from one another. Thus that the soul is no "will-o'-th'-wisp in the swamps of the cerebrum," but an *internal man;* a body within a body; "a life," as Aretæus says of the womb, "within a life;" in the material body as God is in the universe—everywhere and nowhere; everywhere for the enlightened intellect, nowhere for the physical view; no more in the brain than in the toes, but the spiritual "double" of the entire fabric. All the organs of the material body have soul in them, and serve the soul, each one according to its capacity, yet is the soul itself independent of them all, because made of another substance. "And though it fill the whole body, yet it taketh up no room in the body; and if the body decrease, if any member be cut off or wither, the soul is not diminished, only ceaseth to be in that member it was before, and that without any hurt or blemish to itself."* A beautiful image of their interconnection is supplied in the structure of *bones*, which consist of inanimate earthy matter, and living gelatine, so intimately incorporated that although the parts are really *two*, the seeming is of only *one*, atom answering to atom so completely that the whole of the earthy matter may be dissolved away by acid, or the whole of the gelatinous matter be burned by calcination, and yet the form of the bone remain entire. The inner, spiritual body is represented in the gelatine; the outer, material one in the earthy matter.

134. It may assist us to form an idea of the spiritual body, if we consider the various parts and systems of organs of which the outer or material body is constructed. Man is in reality a series of human forms, one wrapped within the other, and successively more perfect and complete as we approach the seat of his highest powers. Begin with the skeleton. In this we have the rude image of a man, correct as far as it goes, showing his bulk, his stature, his general outline. It is a skeleton, we may remark in passing, distinctly and absolutely human. No single bone of it exactly agrees with a bone of any other animal whatever. Next take the muscles. Separate these, and we again have a man, more perfect and substantial than the former, but still only an approach to the true idea, wanting the fullness of contour. Then take the veins. Here is a human figure again; a drawing of the venous and arterial system includes the whole area of the body. Taking, however, lastly, the brain and nerves, we have a much closer resemblance. If every

---

* *Psychosophia*, by N. Mosley, p. 18. 1653.

nervous thread could be extracted and exhibited in its natural position, the perfect human outline would be delineated. These several elementary structures, the skeleton, the muscles, the veins, the nerves, woven and interlaced together, form in their total the material body, the skeleton being least like the total, the nervous system the most like it. The Spiritual body lies within again, but higher and more exquisite in every circumstance and particular; formed, not of material substance, but of spiritual; invisible therefore, and intangible, except to organs formed of substance similar to its own. What the skeleton is to the muscles, what the muscles are to the veins, what the veins are to the nerves, what all these together are to the man in his full physical integrity, as the continent of the whole, such is the material body in its totality to the spiritual. Hence, if we want to see what the soul is *like*, instead of taking a microscope, or an Essay on Immortality, all we have to do is to contemplate the living and moving beauty of a human figure in its ripeness and perfection. The true εἰκὼν βασιλική is the human body.

135. That the soul or spiritual body is a form in exact correspondence with the external, material body; that it presents a similar assemblage of parts and features; and that it undergoes no change in these respects when it casts off the material envelope, and enters the eternal world—unless to acquire infinite access of beauty or distortion, according to its governing principle of conduct, good or evil—is involved in *ghost-belief;* a belief which, *when rightly directed*, has infinitely more truth in it than the dogmatic nonsense which describes the soul as a mere "principle." How often do we find men's actual, secret faith, ahead of their spoken Creeds and Articles! The former comes of the truth-telling intuitions of the heart; the latter are the manufacture of the less trustworthy head. Every one knows that there is

such a thing as *feeling* a proposition to be true, though the understanding may be unable to master it. The feelings, it has been well remarked, are famous for "hitting the nail on the head." Unlike the conclusions of the intellect, which are shaped more or less by education and country, their voice is no solitary sound, but the utterance of essential and universal human nature. It is to our *feeling* rather than to our *thinking*, that all the sublimest arguments in the universe are primarily addressed. Where logic works out one truth, the heart has already realized twenty; because love, which is the heart's activity, is the profoundest and nimblest of philosophers. All things that live and are loveliest are born of the heart. This is why the ancients regarded the heart as the seat of wisdom—not of *knowledge*, but of that primary, intuitive wisdom to which knowledge is only an appendix. Hence then the value of the fact that in all ages and nations there has existed an intuitional conviction that the spirit of the dead *immediately* enters the eternal world, carrying with it an unmistakable corporeal personality; and that it can re-appear, under certain circumstances, to the survivors.* It is obvious that the reappearance of the dead requires, as a necessary condition, that there shall be

---

* "'That the dead are seen no more," said Imlac, "I will not undertake to maintain, against the concurrent and unvaried testimony of all ages, and of all nations. * * * This opinion, which prevails so far as human nature is diffused, could become universal only by its truth."—*Rasselas.*

"From what remote source universal tradition may have derived this idea, would be a curious inquiry, and might be rendered important. It is a pleasing subject, and imbued with that tender melancholy which peculiarly befits it for a mind of sensibility and fine taste. Its universality, independently of the testimony afforded it by revealed religion, is no small presumption of its being founded in fact."—Dr. Good, *Book of Nature*, Series iii., Lect. 1.

a spiritual body, perfect in form and feature, as in the case of Moses and Elias. Unfortunately, the actual, solemn truth of the matter has had so much that is false and foolish heaped upon it, as to be in itself well-nigh smothered. Rightly understood, ghosts are no mere offspring of vulgar, ignorant superstition and creduilty. Our prejudices and education may dispose us to think otherwise, but we should be slow in chiding opinions which have been embraced by any considerable portion of our fellow-men; since the fact that a given doctrine has been widely accepted, and earnestly contended for, is a presumption that it contains a truth, or an aspect of a truth, essential to the complete rational life of man. Most opinions are right up to a certain point, but with few men do they go far enough, or straight enough, to reflect the *whole* truth. All human beings are at this very moment ghosts; but they do not so appear to you and me; nor do you and I, who are also ghosts, so appear to our neighbors and companions, because we are all similarly wrapped up in flesh and blood, and seen only as to our material coverings.* Literally and true, the ghost of a man is his soul or spiritual body; and in order that this may be seen, it must be looked at with adequate organs of sight, namely, the eyes of a spiritual body

* "Could anything be more miraculous than an actual, authentic ghost? The English Johnson longed all his life to see one, but could not, though he went to Cock-lane, and thence to the church-vaults, and tapped on coffins. Foolish Doctor! Did he never, with the mind's eye, as well as the body's, look round him into that full tide of human life he so loved—did he never so much as look into himself? The good Doctor was a ghost, as actual and authentic as heart could wish; well-nigh a million of ghosts were traveling the streets by his side. What else was he, what else are we? * * It is no metaphor; it is a simple scientific fact."—Carlyle, *Sartor Resartus*, Book 3d, chap. 8th.

like itself. We *have* such eyes, every one of us; but during our time-life, they are buried deep in flesh and blood, and thus it is only when specially opened by the Almighty, for purposes of his providence, that it is possible for a ghost or spiritual body to be beheld. Much as our material eyes enable us to see, they *prevent* our seeing inconceivably more. "The sight of man," says Lord Bacon, "carrieth a resemblance with the sun, which openeth and revealeth the terrestrial globe, but covereth and concealeth the stars and celestial globe. So doth the eye discover natural things, but darken and shut up divine." Such an opening of the spiritual sight took place at the Transfiguration, when the ghosts or spiritual bodies of Moses and Elias were seen. Such also takes place when the ghosts or spiritual bodies of the dead are *now* seen, and without it, it is impossible they can be viewed. Material eyes to material substances; spiritual eyes to spiritual ones. Hence it is that in accounts of spiritual appearances, both Scriptural and secular, however many persons may be present, it is rarely that more than one perceives the figure. The narrative in 2 Kings vi. 14—17, is a remarkable instance:—"And Elisha prayed and said, Lord, I pray thee, open his eyes that he may see. And the Lord opened the eyes of the young man, and he saw"—what previously was visible only to the prophet. So in Daniel x. 7:—"And I, Daniel, alone saw the vision, for the men that were with me saw not the vision." Tasso introduces the vision of Michael and his warrior angels to Godfrey only. Shakspere represents the spirit of Banquo as unseen by any one at the supper table except Macbeth. The popular or vulgar notion, that before a spirit can be seen it must assume our material nature, so far, at least, as to reflect the light of this world, is exactly the reverse of the truth; which is that the change must be made in *ourselves, i. e.,* by opening our spiritual sight.

136. Ghosts, therefore, so far from being mere phantoms or apparitions, the terrifying illusions of a heated imagination, are far more real than our bodies of flesh and blood. *They* endure forever, whereas the latter are but temporary consolidations of a little atmosphere, with a few pounds of phosphate of lime. The invisible world is populated by them just as the visible one is occupied by material things; and as that world is all round about us, so are they too closely present.

> Millions of spiritual creatures walk the earth,
> Unseen, both when we wake and when we sleep.

They have their similitude in those glorified and imperishable languages which we are accustomed to account and speak of as "dead." True, they have ceased to be alive in the vulgar sense, or as spoken languages; yet are they living and immortal, to man's intelligence; and one of our greatest privileges is to be sensible of their presence and their influence on us. Would men but ascend to this high, and true, and most sacred understanding of the inhabitants of the unseen world, there would be no more *fear* of ghosts, nor would ghost-belief lay itself open to the ridicule which now it too often deserves. They would be relieved, too, of the embarrassment which, when scepticism stands mocking, often seduces to an insincere denial. Ghost-belief, in a word, notwithstanding its bad reputation, is coincident with belief in spirits and angels, who are themselves the risen souls or spiritual bodies of mankind; and to know that there are angels, and to have so beautiful and salutary a subject of meditation, is one of the chief privileges and blessings of the Christian. Pity but it were dwelt upon more frequently. "There have been times, we know, when men thought *too much* of the dead. Such is not among the faults of the *present* age." It is quite likely that many supposed spiritual appearances may be explained on strictly physical principles, as shown by Drs. Ferriar and Hibbert;* and especially in some kinds of disease it is likely that men fancy they see ghosts. But whoever is disposed to laugh at and repudiate the general proposition, should first read Mrs. Crow's "Night-side of Nature," applying to its narratives the principles we have laid down.† When spiritual bodies are really allowed to mortal view, it is probably not to the diseased, but to the healthy mind; and coming under the providence of God, as they always must, they may furthermore be considered as vouchsafed, like the miracles of the New Testament, and all the spiritual appearances therein recorded, not to the immoral or the unbeliever, "because of their unbelief," but only to those who are prepared to receive and appreciate intelligently.

137. POETRY witnesses that "there is a spiritual body." Poetry is not, as some deem it, mere "privileged lying;" neither is it, in its essential nature, the simple embodiment of elegant but illogical fancies. The tales which the poet tells, as wilful and deliberate, may be, and doubtless are for the most part, fables. But the sayings and phraseology in which those tales are told, flowing half-unconsciously from the poet's heart, and altogether beside the mere Art of poetry, take place with the eternal verities of the universe. As regards scientific matters, and the minutiæ of Natural His-

---

* An Essay towards a Theory of Apparitions, by John Ferriar, M. D. London, 1813.

Sketches of the Philosophy of Apparitions, or an Attempt to trace such illusions to their physical causes, by Samuel Hibbert, M. D. Edinburgh, 1824.

† See also a Review of Mrs. Crowe's work in Ainsworth's Magazine for February, 1848, wherein the claims of this department of knowledge are mildly and intelligently enforced.

tory, doubtless there are errors in poetry as well as in prose. But the truth of poetry is independent of blunders in learning; no less than of the imperfect science of its era. The supposition equally common, that poets must be dreamers, because there is often much dreaminess in poetry, is, again, purely gratuitous. "Vulgarly considered deficient in the reasoning faculty, the poets are remarkable rather for having it in excess. They jump the middle terms of their syllogisms, it is true: and assume premises to which the world has not yet arrived; but Time stamps their conclusions as invincible." Especially is the true and great poet a profound metaphysician; a far profounder one, in general, than the metaphysicians by profession. "I have found more philosophic knowledge," says Dr. Millingen, "in the productions of our poets, than in all the metaphysical disquisitions of the learned." The only difference between the poet's reasoning and that of other men, is that it is a reasoning more from feeling than from induction. Therefore is it that to those who approximate, and thus understand him, the true and great poet is not only a musical singer and a painter of beautiful pictures, but a speaker of Wisdom and Truth. To such, his utterances commend themselves as an apocalypse of human nature. Take, for instance, the lines in Twelfth Night, where Viola asks Sebastian if he is "a spirit:"—

> "*A spirit* I am indeed,
> But am in that dimension grossly clad,
> Which from the womb I did participate."

Here, whatever may be attributed to the poet's imagination, we have at least the calm conclusion of the philosopher, for the character of Sebastian is one which fully justifies the belief that of two possible answers Shakspere would assign to him the one which he himself considered the more sensible.* Coleridge, Wordsworth, Bailey, (in "Festus,") all our best English poets, unite in teaching the same truth to the understanding that can rise to it. Shelley has an exquisite passage:—

"Sudden arose
Ianthe's soul! It stood
All beautiful in naked purity,
The perfect semblance of its bodily frame,
Instinct with inexpressible beauty and grace.
Each stain of earthliness
Had passed away; it re-assumed
Its native dignity, and stood
Immortal amid ruin."

How finely the self-disengagement of the soul at death, in the form of the body it leaves behind, is spoken of by the ancient poets, the scholar is well aware. When, for example, in the 11th Æneid, Camilla is described as extricating herself from her corpse, after the spear of Aruns has brought her exploits to an end:—

Tum frigida toto
Paulatim exsolvit se corpore; lentaque colla,
Et captum letho posuit caput, &c.

"Then of vital heat bereft, she disengages herself from the whole body by degrees, and reclines her drooping neck and head, captivated by death."

It is not simply her life, or her "principle of volition," that goes, but *se*, herself. The souls of the dead, as ferried by Charon across the Styx, Virgil elsewhere designates *corpora*, "bodies."

---

* See an "Essay on the Ghost-belief of Shakspere, by Alfred Roffe," (Hope, London, 1851,) in which admirable performance, says one of his reviewers, "we have the first beginning of a study of Shakspere according to facts and nature."

138. The facts before us are borne out also by LANGUAGE, which is a form of Poetry. "It is good," says an able writer, "to look to the ordinary language of mankind, not only for the attestation of natural truths, but for their suggestions; because common sense transfers itself naturally into language; and common sense, in every age, is the ground of the truths which can possibly be revealed. If we set our ideas before the glass of language, they receive, to say the least, a cordial welcome." By language we do not mean the mere art of speaking and writing according to some specific, arbitrary mode, which though intelligible in one country, is unintelligible in another. We mean that beautiful and inevitable flowering forth in speech of the inner living intellect of man, which, older and more excellent than all prosody and spelling, is an integral work of nature; and which, were it possible for the accidental forms which it may hold at any given epoch, as English and French, Latin and Greek, to be suddenly and totally abolished, would in itself be unaffected, and speedily incarnate afresh, unchanged save in the extrinsic circumstances of costume. Looking into Language, we find accordingly, that whatever is vitally and essentially human, whatever distinguishes man from the brutes, it attributes, in all ages and countries, to "the soul" or "the spirit." It recognises the latter, not as a mere abstract principle, which is impotent, but as a living, active, substantial entity, such as alone can effect the deeds ascribed to it. It is "the spirit" that moves, prompts, withholds, and inclines us; that is grieved and troubled; that is elated and depressed. David exclaims, "Why art thou cast down, O my soul, and why art thou disquieted within me?" We speak also of the rejoicing, triumphing, and despondency of the spirit; of having no spirit for a thing, and of being dispirited. Also of a poor spirit, a mean spirit, and a great spirit; a good soul, a kind

soul, and a willing soul. Every one of these affections or qualities, as they are ordinarily termed, is a disposition for the time being, of the true, immortal, spiritual man, who, underlying the material body, is the real thinker and the real emotionist. Call the expressions "figures of speech" if you will. But take care first to understand what *are* figures of speech, in their proper, essential nature; whence they arise; and why they are the same with all people, in all parts of the globe, independent of any instruction or compact. Men who seek to escape from a truth which presses inconveniently by beginning to talk about "figures of speech," only betray their ignorance of the first principles of language. Figures of speech, rightly so called, are the profoundest texts philosophy can start from.

CHAPTER XIII.

SOUL—SPIRIT—GHOST.

139. Not a little of the confusion prevailing in the popular mind with regard to the Soul, may unquestionably be referred to the fact of our having three distinct words for it, a proof at the same time of the inestimable value of an enlarged and accurate appreciation of the nature of Language in the determination and establishment of Truth, and of the evils that arise from inattention to it. Ordinarily, the "soul" of man, his "spirit," and his "ghost," are imagined to be three separate and distinct things. Directly we look to the inherent meaning of the several words, we find them, however, synonymous and convertible, and originally of a single signification and a single application. The soul of man is his spirit, and his spirit is his ghost; neither word meaning more or less than the Spiritual body. Undoubtedly a conventional distinction has been made between the three terms, and a very proper and useful one it is, but unfortunately it is not observed. "Soul" is well applied to the spiritual body during our residence in the flesh: "spirit," by metonymy, to that deep, interior, intellectual and emotional consciousness which is evidence to us of our spiritual life: "ghost" to the spiritual body when, casting off its material vesture, it becomes an inhabitant exclusively of the spiritual world, and if pure, an angel. Were they always thus limited and applied, the words would carry meaning. As matters stand, they carry *none,* since no two writers use

them alike. That psychologists should have been content to go on discussing about the soul, year after year, and yet have allowed the sense of their text-word to go irreclaimably adrift, certainly is no credit to them; nor is it surprising that they have made so little way. Till a man is prepared to state the exact significance which he attaches to his terms, and till he has learned to be consistent in the use of them, it is better both for himself and for the world that he should fling away his pen.

140. Together with the equivalent words in Hebrew, Greek, Latin, Sanscrit, and other languages, soul, spirit, and ghost literally denote Air or Breath. The metaphor is eminently just and beautiful, seeing that the air is the physical image and representative of Life; and that it is in the invisible, spiritual part of man that Life is supremely throned. It is a truth alike of Scripture, philosophy, physiology, and poetry, that the Breath is the representative of Life. It stands in the first place as symbol of the organic life; secondly, and in superior degree, as symbol of the spiritual life. What language, by its intuitional usages, broadly asserts, the expositors of truth ratify and substantiate. Language indeed, or Philology, in its highest sense, is only another name for Philosophy. We have seen above how intimately the air is connected with organic life; that Respiration is the beginning, and ceasing to breathe, the end. Because of this connection, all the primitive names applied to organic life were simply transfers of the current appellations of the wind; subsequently, by virtue of the correspondence of the organic with the spiritual, the same names were extended upwards to the soul. Every one of these names denotes accordingly, in addition to air or wind, the life of the body, and is thus possessed not merely of a two-fold, but of a triple meaning. There is nothing singular in this. It exemplifies a general principle. No word either

does or can denote a spiritual thing without at the same time denoting both a physiological or organic, and a physical or inorganic thing. The reason is, that language rests universally upon objective Nature, and that objective Nature, in turn, is universally representative of spiritual things, proximately in its organic forms, remotely in its inorganic ones. The spiritual universally carries with it the physiological, and the physiological the physical, just as the capital of a column involves the shaft, and the shaft the pedestal. The physical and physiological meanings of words denoting spiritual things may be *obsolete,* but they are there, nevertheless, palpable and instructive to the philosophic eye, to which nothing that has ever had a meaning for mankind, ever absolutely dies.

141. To place these great principles in the clear light supplied by facts, let us briefly examine the etymologies of the several words. If it serve only to give an agreeable variety to the general subject, the time will not be spent in vain. "Soul," as the most celebrated and familiar, naturally comes first. Soul, (Anglo-Saxon *sawle,* German *seele,*) is coincident with the Latin *hal*itus, breath, derived from *hal*are, to breathe, a root familiar in the words ex*hale,* in*hale,* and itself only an enlarged form, (like *σαος, salus,*) of the earlier word *αἔω* or *ἀω*, a beautiful onomatopœia, expressive in its long, open vowels, of the very act which it designates. Permutation of initial sounds, as in *halitus* and soul, a sibilant taking the place of an aspirate, a dental of a labial, &c., is one of the most common phenomena of spoken language. Colloquially, and in miscellaneous literature, soul is not now used in the sense of "breath;" but in the authorized version of the Scriptures, or the English language of 1611, it often has this meaning. In 1 Kings xvii., for instance, "There was no *breath* left in him; . . . . . . and the Lord heard the voice of Elijah, and the *soul* of the child

came into him again, and he revived." The second or physiological sense is also exhibited in the Bible, but more frequently in secular authors, as when they term the life of brutes the "animal soul." "There are," says Mr. Blakey, "in a certain sense, two souls in man. We give the name, first, to that physical life and organic power which we possess in common with the animal and vegetable creation; secondly, to the principle of sensibility and thought, the soul which thinks, feels, reasons, and judges, and exists only in man." (Vol. 1, p. 61.) In the original, physical sense of the word soul, all creatures whatever have souls, inasmuch as they live by inhalation or breathing; so that to be "a living soul" is nothing peculiar to man, if we judge by the words alone, without exploring their philosophy. Many people, naturally ambitious, and unwilling to observe so many agreements as there are between themselves and the lower forms of creation, make it a matter of pride that our first parents were formed, as they suppose, in a manner different from the parents of other animals. "God," they remind us, "breathed into man's nostrils the breath of life, and he became *a living soul*," a circumstance not mentioned of the progenitors of any other species of creature. But neither is it mentioned of the first species of any other creature that they were created "male and female." This, however, can well afford to be let pass, when compared with the fact that the distinction apparently established by the words "living soul," presents itself only in the translation. There is no such distinction in the Hebrew, which in this instance applies identically the same terms to man and to brute. Each was made נפש חיה (*nephesh chayah,*) "a living soul;" only our translators have rendered the references to the brute creation (Gen. i. 21, 24,) "living *creature*." Either word might legitimately be substituted for the other. It is amusing that while many have entrenched themselves in this phrase of "living soul," and found in it man's inalienable characteristic, the exactly opposite conclusion has been arrived at by some of those whose curiosity had led them to the original. Both brutes and man being called "living creatures," or "living souls," some have inferred that brutes are as immortal as man; others that man is mortal as brutes. Man differs from the brutes not in respect of his being a "living soul," which is simply to be a "breather," such as they are; but in respect of his being so constituted as to be recipient of the knowledge of God, and of power to love him. Shakspere accredits the word soul with its full, final meaning, namely, the spiritual body when set free from flesh and blood:—

> Where souls do couch on flowers, we'll hand in hand,
> And with our sprightly port make the ghosts gaze.

142. Ghost, (Anglo-Saxon *gast*, German *geist*,) shows its physical meaning in the cognate word "gust," as "a gust of wind;" also in the term used to designate the aëriform substance called "gas." In Old German, the grand-parent of English, *geisten* signified to blow. In a German Bible of the year 1483, "the breath of life" is translated "der *geist* des lebens." To "give up the ghost" is literally, to surrender the breath; the "Holy Ghost" is literally the breath of the Lord, as implied in his own words, when "He breathed on his disciples, and said, Receive ye the Holy Ghost." Where the English version of the Scriptures has "ghost" and "spirit," the Anglo-Saxon reads "*gast.*" Wiclif, in his New Testament, spells "the holi *goost.*" The "gist" of a subject, like the "spirit" of a book, or the *animus* of an action, signifies its soul or inmost principle. In German, *geist* continues to be used in many of the meanings which, with ourselves, are conveyed by "spirit." Thus—

Was der *Geist* versprecht leistet die Natur.—*Schiller*.
"What the Spirit promises, Nature performs."

143. Spirit, (Latin *spiritus*,) takes us to the very origin of words, resting on the beautiful lisp or whisper with which the breezes quiver the leaves. All words, we may observe, are expansions of a few hundred primitive onomatopœias, more or less obviously preserved in them, and which, like the *sp* in spirit, constitute their ultimate "roots."

Fresh gales and gentle airs
Whisper'd it to the woods.—*Paradise Lost*.

And there is heard the ever-moving air
Whisp'ring from tree to tree.—*Shelley*.

In solitudes
Her voice came to me through the *whisp'ring* woods.—*Ib*.

Virgil shows the etymology at a glance, for who that knows aught of the sweet music of nature does not perceive that the bare idea of *blowing* is the least part of his *auras spirantes?* The Greek form of the word, *ψιθύρισμα*, is one of the most beautiful onomatopœias extant in any language. "*Αδύ*, sings Theocritus—

"Αδύ τι τὸ ψιθύρισμα καὶ ά πίτυς."
"Sweet is the whisper of the wind among the fir-trees!"

Whoever wrote that little gem of the Orphica, the hymn to the Zephyrs,

αὖραι ποντογενεῖς Ζεφυρίτιδες, ἠεροφοῖτοι,
ἡδύπνοοι, ψιθυραὶ, κ.τ.λ.,

the introduction of this one word is enough to announce him Poet. Now-a-days a man can adopt epithets from a thousand predecessors; the Greek had only nature, and his own apt, living, luxuriant heart. Virgil not only illustrates the origin of the word spirit, but its severai applications.

Thus, as given to the breath, in that charming description where Iris, mingling with the exiled Trojan ladies as they walk mourning by the sea, though she has laid aside her goddess' vestments, and personates a decrepid old woman, is still unable to conceal herself:

> Non Beroë vobis, non hæc Rhœteia, matres
> Est Dorycli conjux: divini signa decoris,
> Ardentesque notate oculos: qui *spiritus* illi,
> Qui vultus, vocisve sonus, vel gressus eunti.

"Matrons, this is not Beroë who stands before you, not the wife of Doryclus. Mark here the characters of divine beauty! See how bright her eyes! What fragrance in her breath! What majesty in her looks! Or mark the music of her voice, and the graceful mien with which she moves!"

It denotes Life where Æneas is heard protesting fidelity to the too-confiding, ill-requited Dido:

> Nec me meminisse pigebit Elisæ
> Dum memor ipse mei, dum *spiritus* hos reget artus!

"Never shall I be slow to think of Dido, while I retain any recollection of myself, or life to actuate these limbs!"

144. In connection with the word spirit, it is interesting to note the cognate term "spiral," seeing that it involves the same idea. Similarly derived from *spiro* to blow, its fundamental allusion is to the well-known phenomenon of the spiral movement of the wind. Now this peculiar movement, the spiral, delineates a Form, which form thus becomes an emblem or pictorial representative of the wind, and thence of what the wind itself represents, namely, Life. All forms are representative, and their significance is the science of sciences. There are lower, higher, and highest forms. Forms made up of straight lines, and thus angular, with flat surfaces, as crystals, are of the lowest degree, and accord with what is inorganic, inanimate, and basal gene-

rally. Next comes the form of which the sphere and the circle are the type—a form derived from the extension of the primitive point in all directions, and which is essentially connected with the organic and animate. Whatever in the universe exhibits a totality, is always a solid circle or sphere. Portions of circles, or curves, conjoined with the straight line and angle, give that innumerable variety of profiles and configurations which we see among animals and plants. Rarely is the curve found in the inorganic department of creation. Only perhaps in the spherules of quicksilver, on the convex side of drops of water and other liquids, in bubbles, and in some few minerals. In the degree that crystals multiply their surfaces, and thus lose their great angles and facets, they approach the spherical or organic form. The dodecahedron, for example, approaches the sphere more nearly than the octohedron; the octohedron more nearly than the cube. Highest of all is the Spiral form, which in its own highest kind, or as produced by winding a thread round a cylinder, is the circle infinitely continued. The circle returns into itself, ending where it began; but the possible beginning and ending of a spiral the imagination cannot conceive. The spiral, therefore, rather than the circle, is the true symbol of eternity. The spiral form is identified with no department of creation in particular, because an emblem of the omnipresent principle which equally sustains all. It shows itself most remarkably in the Vegetable kingdom, where it is the law of the arrangement of the leaves, and thus of the buds and flowers. Almost all the wonderful diversities in the contour of plants come of their spirals of development being more or less stretched or contracted. Thus, alternate leaves become opposite by a slight contraction; opposite ones become verticillate by a greater. Flowers universally are produced by the contraction of the spiral into a series of concentric rings, the highest part of the spiral becoming the centre, and its lowest part the circumference. Certain fruits, as fir-cones, show the spiral in the most beautiful manner. Internally, plants abound with a delicate kind of veins known as "spiral vessels." Stems, again, which are too slender to stand upright, lift themselves into the air by twining spirally round a stronger neighbor. As respects the animal kingdom, the spiral is a frequent and beautiful feature in univalve shells; where also, as in plants, much of the wonderful variety comes of the spiral being more or less contracted. In the lovely genera Cerithium, Pleurostoma, Fusus, Turritella, &c., one extreme is shown; in Cypræa, Conus, Strombus, &c., the other. The beautiful spiral by which the Vorticellæ extend and retract themselves gives to the movements of these little creatures an elegance and sprightliness unsurpassed. In human organization the spiral is less observable, except that it adorns the head with curls and ringlets. Human *life*, on the other hand, is one unbroken, endless spiral, and here we realize the greatness and amplitude of the significance of the spiral Form. Life winds its little circles, hour by hour, day by day, year by year, faithfully concluding each before another is begun, but never failing to commence afresh where it left off, and so goes on everlastingly, ring rising upon ring, every circle covering and reiterating its predecessors, on a higher level, nearer and nearer to the heavens. The material body drops away, like dead leaves, but Life goes on, in beautiful and ceaseless aspiration. Nowhere in nature is there a more charming emblem of Life than the common scarlet or twining bean of our gardens, while rising to its maturity.

145. *Animus*, the usual Latin word for the soul, shortened in French into *âme*, is the same word as *anima*, the wind, in Greek ἄνεμος, whence the pretty name *anemone*, or wind-flower The subordinate senses are preserved, like

those of *spiritus*, in the Latin authors. Thus, "aurarumque leves *animæ*," "the light breezes of the winds;" (Lucretius v. 237.) "Ah miseram Eurydicen, *animâ* fugiente, vocabat," "Ah, unfortunate Eurydice, he cries with his fast-fleeting breath." (Georgic iv. 526.) The earlier etymological history is found in the Sanscrit language, in which breath is called *ânas* and *ânilas*, the root being *an*. Though essentially the same word, a useful practical distinction is made in Latin between the two forms anim*a* and anim*us;* the former being restricted, in its figurative ascent, to the organic life, whence it is usually translated "life," "vital principle," or "animal soul;" while to the latter is allowed the higher meaning of spiritual life, whence it is generally translated "rational soul:"—

Mundi
Principio indulsit communis conditor illis
Tantùm *animas*, nobis *animum* quoque, &c.
Juvenal, Sat. xv. 147.

"In the beginning of the world, the Creator vouchsafed to brutes only the principle of vitality; to us he gave souls also, that an instinct of affection, reciprocally felt, might urge us to seek, and to give, assistance."

146. *Ψυχὴ*, the Greek word generally understood to mean "soul," comes from *ψυχω* to blow, and would seem to be of kindred onomatopœtic origin with *spiritus*. *Καιροὶ ἀναψύξεως*, "the times of refreshing," (Acts iii. 19) is literally "the times of the blowing of the cool wind." There is a good deal of misconception as to this famous word. What it ordinarily intends in Greek literature, both sacred and secular, is not the spiritual, immortal part of man, but his animal or time-life. "Take no thought for your life"—*μὴ μεριμνᾶτε τῆς ψυχῶν ὑμῶν*, with the context, well illustrates its ordinary New Testament significance. In Rev. xvi. 3, *fishes* are called *ψυχας*. Conformably with these

usages, "the natural body," *i. e.*, the material body, endowed with organic, animal life only, and belonging exclusively to the temporal world, is termed by St. Paul, *σῶμα ψυχικὸν*, while the spiritual, immortal body he calls *σῶμα πνευματικόν*. Undoubtedly, "soul" in its high, metaphysical and theological senses, is occasionally intended by *ψυχη;* but its most useful signification is simply the life which animates the temporary, material body. Many of the ancients attributed to the latter all that is psychological as well as physiological in our nature. With these, accordingly, *ψυχη* includes both "life" and "mind," or *anima* and *animus*, and is their collective appellation.*

147. What is generally intended in to-day's English by "soul," *i. e.*, the immortal, thinking part of man, is in Greek mostly called *πνεῦμα*. Translators render it "spirit." The primary or physical sense is illustrated by St. John—"the *wind* bloweth where it listeth;" and the secondary or physiological one by St. Matthew—"Jesus yielded up the *ghost*," (xxvii. 50,) *πνεῦμα* being the Greek word in both cases. When in the New Testament *ψυχη* and *πνεῦμα* occur in juxtaposition, the sense is tantamount to the colloquial phrase "life and soul." But they are translated soul and spirit," as in Heb. iv. 12, fostering the popular mistake that the soul (theologically so called) and the spirit are distinct things. Nothing can exceed the confusion into which even intelligent people are often unconsciously drawn, through the want of a clear understanding of the great truth, so sublime in its simplicity, "that there is a natural body, and there is a spiritual body,"—not there *will be*, but there *is*, and that this spiritual body is the ever-living soul or spirit. If any doubt the existence of such confusion, let them read

* On Homer's use of the word, see a learned paper from the German of Voelcker, in the Classical Museum for 1845.

Wesley's 41st hymn—"And am I born to die?" and see if they can shut the book with the least glimmering of comprehension of what it means. "Spirit, soul, and body," as in 1 Thess. v. 23, is a Scriptural periphrase for the whole man, as he exists during his time-life; "spirit" denoting the life of the intellect and affections, or of the internal man; "soul" the life of the body, as exercised in the appetites and animal instincts; "body" the sacred instrument with which those lives are enabled to be played forth into the world. Soul and body, or ψυχὴ and σῶμα, have reference to this world only; spirit, or πνεῦμα, belongs also to the world to come. Consentaneously with this, man is Scripturally called "flesh" when his mortality is the subject of discourse; "soul" when his animal propensities are chiefly alluded to; "spirit" when his intellectual or emotional nature or the internal man, is the theme. The ghosts, or disengaged spiritual bodies of the dead, are called πνευματα, or "spirits," by the inspired writers, on a principle already set forth.

148. The Hebrew words corresponding with soul, &c., offer precisely similar histories. רוח (*ruahh*) denotes the wind in Gen. viii. 1; breath, frequently; temporal life, in the history of Samson—"when he had drank, his spirit came again;" spiritual life, and life in the general sense, or the all-sustaining energy of the Creator, also very often. נפש (*nephesh*) and נשמה (*neshamah*) are equivalents in every way. A minute exposition of the application of these words, constitutes, along with relevant matter, an invaluable little book by the Rev. George Bush, Professor of Hebrew at New York—"Soul, or an Inquiry into Scriptural Psychology." New York, 1845.

149. Comparing these various facts, the conclusion we come to is, that while on the one hand, the soul is no mere appendage to human nature, shapeless and incomprehensible, or at best, "life;" on the other hand, that wondrous

spiritual body in which we find it, is the veritable, essential MAN—*ipse*—"*the* man *in* the man." Rightly regarded, it is not the *soul* that is the appendage, but the *body*. *As* a material body, it is admirable and incomparable; but placed beside that which alone gives dignity and glory to the idea of man, it confesses itself no more than a piece of mechanism, spread over him for awhile, in order that during his retention of it, he may act on the material world and its inhabitants, and fashion his intellect and moral character. It is the strong right arm with which he is impowered to enforce his arbitrations. Man is created for heaven, not for earth; therefore he is fundamentally a spiritual, and only provisionally a material being. The *εἶδος* of his nature is the spiritual body; the material is only its *εἴδωλον*.* The *εἴδωλον* is first to mortal eyes and understanding; but the spiritual *εἶδος* is the first to fact and truth; just as the uttered word is the first to the listener, but the invisible, underlying thought the first to the speaker. Truly and beautifully has man been called a "word" of the Creator. The spiritual body is the seat of all thought, all emotion, all volition; excepting, of course, such purely animal volition as belongs to the organic life, and is participated in by the brutes. The material body does no more than fulfill the instincts of its own proper organic or brute life, save when the spiritual body gives forth a mandate. Intimately combined with its envelope till the latter wears out, or falls sick, and dies, the spiritual body then renounces all connection with it; throws it back into its native dust, as

* The difference between *εἶδος* and *εἴδωλον* is not generally discriminated by the lexicons as it deserves;—*εἶδος* denotes the true, essential form of a thing; *εἴδωλον*, on the contrary, the apparent, painted, or external: *εἴδωλον* is the diminutive of *εἶδος* not in reference to extent or bulk, but in respect of perfection and essence.

— the snake casts his enamell'd skin:

or as

The grasshoppers of the summer lay down their worn-out dresses,*

and becomes conscious of the Better Land. Its own life goes on as before. At least there is not the slightest reason to suppose, either on Scriptural or philosophical grounds, that its vital activity is for one instant suspended. The notion that the soul falls into a kind of sleep or lethargy, on the death of the body, though a very common one, is indeed utterly at variance both with the deductions of philosophy and the intimations of Holy Writ, which plainly informs us that the spirit rises immediately after death, as in the parable of Lazarus and the rich man, and in the address of our Saviour to the crucified thief, "*This day* shalt thou be with me in Paradise;" a prophecy, moreover, impossible on any other understanding than that of a spiritual body. Just what the soul *is*, when it shakes off the material envelope, it *continues to be*, retaining all its loves, desires, and inclinations, be they good or evil, pure or impure; and upon these it goes on expending its life, the only difference being in the immediate results to the individual, seeing that the sphere wherein those loves, &c. are now played forth, is absolutely spiritual, and governed by laws and conditions of its own. Of the origin of the notion of the soul's sinking into a state of torpor after death, there can be no doubt. Like most other falsities in psychology, and like many in theology, it comes of false physiology, and is directly traceable to the materialist's figment that life is a function of organization, the corollary of which is, that as there is no visible organi-

---

* ut olim
Cum veteres ponunt tunicas æstate cicadæ.
LUCRETIUS, Lib. iv. 55–56.

zation but that of matter, therefore matter is essential to man's existence; and thus, that when denuded of it at death, his soul collapses into an insensate, motionless, incompetent nothing, so to remain till reclothed with flesh and blood. But this, as we have seen, is altogether fallacious. Man is a thinking, feeling, immortal creature, not by virtue of his material body, but by virtue of his spiritual body. From the first moment of his existence, he is an inhabitant both of the material and of the spiritual world. He dwells consciously in the one, unconsciously in the other; and the change induced on him by "death" is simply that this state of matters is reversed. That is, he then dwells *consciously* in the spiritual world, but is no longer a percipient of the material one. Why, during his first state, he sees and knows nothing, consciously, of the spiritual world, is that he is blindfolded by the "muddy vesture of decay." Why he is afterwards unconscious of the material world, is that in order to realize it, he must possess an appropriate material organism. We live in the spiritual world, all of us, as persons blind from birth live in the present material one, *i. e.*, *in* it, but not seeing it; and the death of the material body (which involves the permanent opening of the spiritual sight) is like the couching of the eyes of such persons by an oculist, and enabling them to see what surrounds them. In our chapter on the Future State, this will receive its due meed of illustration.

150. That there are many and great difficulties in conceiving of the mystery of the spiritual body, that is, of the Soul, has already been amply conceded. He who would affect to deny them would only betray his ignorance both of himself and his subject. Embedded as we are in the material, the mind needs first to *assume* the doctrine, and then gradually ascend to the verification. Following a clue, and knowing what we are looking for, the evidence is found.

We act no differently, day by day, when we enter on the study of any new and comprehensive subject in physical or physiological science. Not that *this* is a new doctrine, but only an unfamiliar one. "It is a venerable creed, like a dawn on the peaks of thought, reddening their snows from the light of another sun, the substance of immemorial religions, the comfort of brave simplicity, though the doubt of to-day, and the abyss of terrified science." It is hard, for instance, to think at first of spiritual *form*, because all our ordinary experience of form presses upon us the idea of material solidity. It is hard, likewise, to think how the spiritual body is circumstanced with regard to what in the material world are called Time and Space. Accustomed as we are to regard space and the spiritual as antithetical, we are at first quite indisposed to admit that a spiritual being can be bounded by space. It is true, nevertheless. Nothing but Deity can be everywhere at once. There must be portions even of the spiritual world where a given spirit is not. Therefore the spiritual body is subject to a condition at all events *answering* to space. Again, it is hard, nay, it is impossible, to conceive of what may be called the procreation and birth of the spiritual body, and in what mode and respect these are concurrent with the procreation and birth of the material body. We can satisfy ourselves of nothing more than that God creates the soul when needed, and not before.* The *organization* of the spiritual body is equally

---

* For opinions on the subject, see Dickinson's *Physica Vetus et Vera*, cap. 11; Blakey's History of the Philosophy of the Mind, vol. 1, p. 197; and Clowes' Fourth Letter on the Human Soul. The famous doctrine of the "pre-existence" of the soul, it is beside our present purpose to discuss. See, for an enthusiastic defence of it, "*Lux Orientalis*, or an Enquiry into the opinions of the Eastern Sages, concerning the pre-existence of the Soul." 12mo., 1662.

beyond the range of man's present powers. There can be little doubt, however, that instead of a simple homogeneity, as commonly supposed, the soul is eminently composite. "There are some things in Paul's description of the spiritual body," says Dr. Hitchcock, "which make it quite probable that its organization will be" (or rather *is*) "much more exquisite than anything in existence on earth. He represents the spiritual body as far transcending the material body both in glory and power; and since the latter is 'fearfully and wonderfully made,' nothing but the most exquisite organization can give the spiritual body such a superiority over the natural." (Religion of Geology, Lect. xiv.) Then there is the nature of the *sex* of the spiritual body, which is as immortal as itself, albeit that in heaven "there is neither marrying nor giving in marriage." Sex, in its true idea, belongs to the soul, not to the body, in which it is only representatively and temporally present. This fine subject the reader may see treated with admirable delicacy and philosophy in Haughton's "Sex in the Future State."

151. Because of such difficulties, and because too intensely accustomed to the material to welcome such propositions as have been set forth, some will not improbably receive them with a laugh, and tax us at least with superstition.* Good. If superstition it be to hold such views, it is a superstition far more valuable and fertilizing to the mind than all that some men esteem the truth. Putting faith before charity in all they do, and deceiving themselves by substituting nar-

---

* It is scarcely necessary to repeat that the vulgar notion respecting ghosts, including "haunted houses," "spirit-rapping," white sheets, &c., &c., is altogether apart from the doctrine of the spiritual body. The latter is Scriptural and philosophical, whereas the former is neither, but utterly contemptible, and does not even call for the disclaimer which would asknowledge it to deserve one.

row and exclusive notions for a comprehensive and benign belief, many men's "truth" is nothing but traditional, barren error. We ask no one to accept uninquiringly, and should be sorry for any one who did. "What a man takes upon trust," remarks Locke, "is but shreds, which however well they may look in the whole piece, make no considerable addition to his stock who gathers them. So much only as we ourselves consider and comprehend of truth and reason, so much only do we possess of real and true knowledge. The floating of other men's opinions in our brains, makes us not one jot the more knowing, though they happen to be true. Like fairy money, they turn to dust when they come to be used." On the other hand, let no one too hastily *reject*. Disbelieve *after* inquiry, if you see cause to; but never *begin* with disbelief. Premature condemnation is the fool's function. It goes for nothing to say that the evidence of the truth of a proposition does not appear. Do you see the evidence of its *falsity?* Before you reject a proposition or series of propositions, for what you suppose to be their error, take care that you apprehend all their *truth;* or as Carlyle shrewdly advises, "Be sure that you *see*, before you assume to *over*see." Indeed, till the truth of a theme be appreciated, its error, if any, cannot be detected. Such doctrines as this of the spiritual body it is impossible to grasp on the instant. They must be *thought out*, from the data which Scripture supplies, and philosophy illustrates. Hypothetical though they may be, in certain points, this again is no valid objection, since without hypothesis it is impossible to advance a single step. "Philosophy proceeds upon a system of credit; and if she never advanced beyond her tangible capital, her wealth would not be so enormous as it is."* Difficulty in finding interpretation of anomalies and perplexities "is no

* Rev. W. Thomson, "Outlines of the Laws of Thought"

argument," as Baden Powell truly observes, "against the *general truth* of a proposition; nor need it lead us into extravagant and gratuitous speculations to bring about a precise explanation where the circumstances do not furnish sufficient data. Having once grasped firmly a great principle, we should be satisfied to leave minor difficulties to *wait their solution*, assured that time will clear them up, as it has done before with others." The fact is, all great and sacred truths, and there are none grander and more sacred than this of the spiritual body, come to us at first, "like the gods in Homer, enveloped in blinding mist." But to him whom their descent to earth concerns,—to him who stands most in need of their help, and who can most gratefully appreciate, and best apply the privilege, "the cloud becomes luminous and fragrant, and discloses the divinity within." The eye that in the beginning was so dim, presently feels itself sparkle and dilate, and what the intellect fails to read, the quick heart interprets.

> As when the moon hath comforted the night,
> And set the world in silver of her light.

152. It may be interesting to conclude the argument that the soul is a spiritual body with a few citations of authors by whom the doctrine has been treated or approved. Among the Fathers there does not appear to have been one who regarded the soul as most modern authors do. They seem rather to have been unanimous as to its corporeity, though on the nature of this corporeity they widely differed. Tertullian argues not only that the soul is a body, and that it holds the human form, but that God himself is a body, for that what is bodiless is nothing.* Augustin, though he finds

* *De Anima*, near the beginning, *Opera*, p. 307; and *Adversus Praxeam*, ib. p. 637. (Ed. Paris, 1641.)

fault with Tertullian, from the mistaken notion that his views involve materialism, by no means rejects them.* Theodotus is very explicit; ἀλλὰ καὶ ἡ ψυχὴ σῶμα κ. τ. λ., "the soul also is a body, for the apostle says, It is sown;" &c.† Methodius, also, in his treatise on the resurrection; "The souls," says he, "created by the Creator and Father of all, are σῶματα νοερά, intellectual bodies, and adorned as they are, with members which are perceived by reason, ... are said to have a tongue, finger, and other parts, as in the case of Lazarus and the rich man.‡ Macarius, the celebrated homilist, observes—"Each one, according to his nature, is a body, whether angel or soul. For although these bodies are attenuate, nevertheless they are in substance, character, and figure, according to the respective subtleties of their nature, subtle bodies; in like manner as the body we now possess in one that is παχυς, dense."§ Suicer, in his great theological cyclopædia, the *Thesaurus Ecclesiasticus*, article ψυχη, may be consulted for more of the same kind. Passing on to later times, we find the doctrine upheld by Lord Bacon:—"And this spirit whereof we speak," says he, "is not from virtue, or energy, or act, or a trifle, but plainly a body, rare and invisible, notwithstanding circumscribed by place, quantitative, real."|| Andrew Bax-

---

* See the vindication of Tertullian in Dr. Edward Burton's "Bampton Lectures," Appendix, note 59, 1829.

† Clemens Alex. *Opera*, p. 791. (Ed. Paris, 1629.)

‡ The curious student will find this treatise well worth attention, or at least the excerpta given in that inestimable treasure-house of Elegant Extracts, the *Myriobiblion* of Photious, pp. 907–932. (Ed. Rouen, 1653.)

§ Homily iv. Works, p. 21. (Ed. Paris, 1722.)

|| History of Life and Death. Works. Vol. xiv., p. 410.

ter, in his Enquiry into the Nature of the Human Soul, confesses that a difference between the soul after the death of the material body, and a spiritual body, is a difference he cannot comprehend. Sennertus adopts the doctrine in his *Epitomes Physicæ.** Cudworth, likewise, though with some diffident reservations, in the True Intellectual System:—"Even here, in this life, our body is, as it were, twofold, interior and exterior; we having, besides the grossly tangible bulk of our outward body, another interior, spiritual body, ... which latter is not put into the grave with the other." (Page 806.) The introductory chapter of one of the first metaphysical works in the English language, Butler's Analogy of Religion, though it does not speak of the doctrine by name, in argument fully acknowledges it. From recent writers may be selected as follows:—Monck Mason, in his Creation by the Immediate Agency of God, written in reply to the Vestiges, after describing the incessant atomic change of the material body, observes in reference to the preservation of its identity.—"There *must* be a permanent representative within, which is not material, —which is the Soul." Dr. Moore, in the Preface to his work on the Power of the Soul over the Body, defines the former as "a spiritual being, resident in the body." "The being," he continues, "that now feels, thinks, acts, and agitates the vital frame-work, will forever be subjected to affections and emotions, wherever it may dwell." Geoffroy de St. Hilaire expresses similar opinions in a communication to the Royal Academy of Sciences at Paris, published in their Reports for 1837. Morell, in his Elements of Psychology, is disposed to call the mind "a spiritual organism." "The real man consists in the abiding power which the body contains to assimilate everything to a given form and idea."

---

* Lib. viii., cap. 1. *Opera*, vol. ii., p. 81.

The doctrine is set forth in all its excellence and plenitude in J. J. Garth Wilkinson's masterly work, "The Human Body, and its connection with Man;" also in the "Anastasis" of Professor Bush, and in the Rev. E. D. Rendell's truly excellent "Treatise on the Peculiarities of the Bible."

CHAPTER XIV.

TRUE IDEA OF YOUTH AND AGE.

153. THE phenomena of the spiritual expression of life are the operations of the Intellect and Affections, or what phrenologists term the Intellectual and the Affective faculties. Everything which belongs to man as a reasoning and emotional being, is included in these two great divisions, and the language of nature calls them, in its most ancient as well as in its most modern tongues, the Head and the Heart. The distinction is the Scriptural one, though philosophy is only beginning to recognize it.* It is the Intellect and Affections, accordingly, which essentially express *human* life; for the life of the body is but the life of an animal, and little more than that of a tree. All things eat, and drink, and sleep, and propagate, but only man can think

---

* "Metaphysicians," says Cory, "have at length approximated to a truth which in the metaphysics of Christianity, is laid down with as much perspicuity and decision as the immortality of the soul, or any other of those points which have been so continually agitated among philosophers, modern as well as ancient. The distinction between the Intellect and the Emotions or Affections, to which, simple as it may appear, such laborious approaches have been made, through the thorny paths of metaphysics, is clearly drawn in the Scriptures, and the respective seats of them assigned, figuratively, but most naturally, to the Head and Heart, and to the heart the Scriptures most constantly appeal."—*Metaphysical Inquiries*, p. 200. (1833.)

and love. Everything which brings genuine delight and dignity to human existence—everything implied in hope and faith, in wisdom and affection, comes of this heavenly boon. Introducing man firstly to the loveliness of the material creation, which to the brute is invisible; afterwards it introduces him to the immortal splendors of the spiritual creation, and to the company of the angels. The veritable golden chain let down from heaven, which old Homer saw dimly, the life of the Intellect and Affections is that by which man is allowed to become sensible how near and enduring is his relation to his Creator, for it is by these alone he is approachable. Essentially expressing human life, the acquirements of these two great spiritual faculties, or Ideas and Emotions, are man's only genuine Property. We have nothing else that we can either call or make absolutely our own; we *need* nothing besides, for these comprise all things worth possession. They are the cup of ambrosia presented to immortalized Psyche.

154. With such a destiny attached to it, how inestimable a prerogative is human life! And what ingratitude to misuse it. Life may be *mis*used without being *ab*used. It is misused if it be not so employed as to be enjoyed, *i. e.*, by making the most of its opportunities; in other words, devoting it to honorable deeds, affectional as well as intellectual. The more strenuously we enact such deeds, the more genuine, because practical, is our acknowledgment of the Divine goodness in bestowing life, and the keener becomes our aptitude for sucking the honey of existence. Work or activity, of whatever kind it be, uprightly and earnestly pursued, is a living hymn of praise. It is truest obedience also, for it is God's great law that whatever powers and aptitudes he has given us, shall be honorably and zealously employed. The energy of life, when fairly brought out, is immense; immense beyond what any one

who has not tried it can imagine. Too often neglected, and allowed to lapse into weakness; trained and exercised, it will quicken into grandeur. It is better to wear out than to rust out, says a homely proverb, with more meaning than people commonly suppose. Rust consumes faster than use. To "wear out" implies life and its pleasures; to "rust," the stagnation of death. Life, rightly realized, is embosomed in light and beauty. The world is not necessarily a "vale of tears." God never intended it to be so to any one. All his arrangements are with an opposite design, and to be fulfilled, only need man's response and coöperation. True, in his all-wise providence, he sends troubles upon men, and grievous ones; but they are never so great as those they bring upon themselves, and willingly suffer. What shall be our experience of life rests mainly with ourselves. The world may render us unfortunate, but it cannot make us miserable; if we are so, the fault lies in our own bosoms. It is not only the great who order their own circumstances. On the wide, wild sea of human life, as on that where go the ships, the winds and the waves are always on the side of the clever sailor. Though one breast prove unfaithful, there are plenty of others that do not. It is still our own to rejoice in the belief of the good and beautiful, and to weave out of this belief a perennial happiness. If we take precautions to form and preserve a sound estimate of what is past, the joyful experience and the sorrowful alike, we rarely have cause for regret, and always abundance for hope and thankfulness; for that which spoils life is seldom so much the *occurrence* of certain events, as the *perverted recollection* of them, and of this, happy events no less than unhappy ones may be the subject. Even if a man make no effort of himself—if he be so neglectful as not to realize the brilliant opportunities permitted to him, so fully as he may, still is life crowded with pleasures. When there is shadow, it is because there is sunshine not far off. Its weeds and thorns are known by contrast with surrounding flowers, and though upon many even of the latter there may be rain-drops, those that are without are yet more abounding. There are more smiles in the world than there are tears; there is more love than hate, more constancy than forsaking: those that murmur the contrary, choose not for thy companions. When the mist rolls away from the mountains, and thé landscape stands suddenly revealed, we find that Nature always has Beauty for her end. However long and dreary may be the winter, we are always indemnified by the spring—not merely by the enjoyment of it when it comes, but by the anticipation. So with the mists and wintry days of life; while they last they are painful, but their clearing away is glorious, and we find that they are only veils and forerunners of something bright. Nature never forgets her æstivalia, nor Divine love its compensations. The common course of things, says Paley, is uniformly in favor of happiness. Happiness is the rule, misery the exception. Else would our attention be called to examples of wealth and comfort, instead of disease and want.

155. Giving full, fair play to the intellect and affections, we not only discover what it is to live, and how easy to live happily; but the period of our existence upon earth ceases to be short, and becomes immensely long. It is only the life of the body which is short, or need be so. Real, human life, is immeasurable, if we will have it so. Each day, remarks Goethe in his autobiography, is a vessel into which a great deal may be poured, if we will actually *fill it up;* that is, with thoughts and feelings, and their expression into deeds, as elevated and amiable as we can reach to. It needs little reflection to perceive that life truly consists only in such exercises. "The mere lapse of years is not life. To eat, and drink, and sleep, to be exposed to the darkness and

the light, to pace round the mill of habit, and turn the wheel of wealth; to make reason our book-keeper, and convert thought into an implement of trade; this is not life. In all this but a poor fraction of the consciousness of humanity is awakened, and the sanctities still slumber which make it most worth while to be. Knowledge, truth, love, beauty, goodness, faith, alone give vitality to the mechanism of existence."*

Grandly expressed in "Festus."

> Life's more than breath, and the quick round of blood;
> 'Tis a great spirit and a busy heart.
> We live in deeds, not years; in thoughts, not breaths;
> In feelings, not in figures on a dial.
> We should count time by heart-throbs. He most lives
> Who thinks most, feels the noblest, acts the best.

To measure life by years is, to the true liver, to measure it rather by ages. If we do not feel its immensity, it is to confess to inactivity and slumber. When we would ask ourselves how old we are, we should find that we must cast up, not anniversaries, but days and hours; and to satisfy ourselves how long our life has already been, should reflect, not on the mere animal adjuncts of life, but on the books we have read, the agreeable objects we have had before our eyes, the pleasant places we have visited, the intercourses of friendship by which our hearts have been made glad; together with the aspirations which have ennobled, and the hopes which have cheered us. We should "taste in thought again" the sweet hours spent by the sea, in the green fields, and in the woods, and the shining, balmy, fragrant moments, each in itself a little summer, brought by the tones, the smiles, the touch, of our Beloved. These are the things that make Life.

---

* Martineau, "Endeavors after the Christian Life."

The study even of a single science adds many years to one's biography. For he who busies himself with chemistry, or botany, or geology, enjoys a thousand pleasant thoughts in the same space of clock-time wherein the indolent and incurious know but one; and every onward step in discovery becomes a new *elixir vitæ.* The invention of logarithms, says Laplace, has "lengthened the life of the astronomer." As truly may it be said that the invention of the microscope has lengthened the life of the physiologist. Age, accordingly, or, as it would be better to call it, *oldness,* in its highest idea, is no mere matter of birth-days. The oldest man, truly so called, is he who, giving a free and cheerful recognition to life, in its depth, variety, and majesty, has enjoyed the largest number of agreeable spiritual experiences, and retains them vividly before his mind.

156. "Old," in the popular sense of aged and decrepid as to body, denotes a state of things which pertains to man only in his animal, temporal relations. This kind of oldness goes along with eating, drinking, and so forth; the idea of it, therefore, should be wholly detached from the mind when we would think of man in his highest or spiritual reality. The soul that is in right order concerns itself little about physical age, no more than about death; for youth and life preöccupy its interest. Neither does it feel old age to be an evil. Physical old age, like mortality, is afflictive in proportion to the want of inward strength to fall back upon. "It is painful," says one who has proved the value of such strength, "it is painful to grow old, to lose by degrees the suppleness, strength, and activity of the body; to perceive each day our organs becoming weaker; but when we feel that the soul, constantly exercised, becomes daily more reflective, more mistress of herself, more skilful to avoid, more strong to sustain, without yielding to the shock of accidents, gaining on the one hand what we lose upon the

other, then we are no longer sensible of growing old." If the soul be not young, youth as to birth-days has no advantage over senility. To men who have no resource in themselves for being happy, every age is burdensome; and were those who complain of the shortness of life as bringing them so soon to the weakness and torpidity of old age, to live for seven hundred years instead of seventy, they would be none the better off. People past their bodily prime are often heard complaining of the decline and degeneracy of things. Since *they* were young, they say, the world has lost its old simplicities, beauty is tarnished, and novelty at an end. What does it amount to? Simply, that "they who utter these dismal ditties have not cared to keep alive the sympathies which carry a man along with his age; that they have not cultivated a habit of genial observation, but have shut themselves up in self and sophistication, under the delusion that the pleasures of youth belong only to the young in years. Foolish and lamentable error. If men have little or no pleasure in their experience of the changes which are brought by increase of years, it is because they are not good and wise enough to find and contemplate the past in the present, and thus induce a sweet and meditative continuity of earliest life." Dullness is not in lapse of years, but in the unskilful use of them; the tedium of a long journey is not in the miles, but in the complainer; if time be tiresome, it is because we do not spin amusement out of ourselves, as silkworms spin their silk. With the man who has really lived, the time is never past for sublime pleasures. Though many he enjoyed in his youth may no longer be accessible, by reason of his failing muscles, his capacity for the attainable is free and buoyant to the last.

My heart leaps up when I behold
  The rainbow in the sky!

So was it when I was a boy;
So is it now I am a man;
So be it when I shall grow old,
Or let me die!

157. While true old age is that honorable and happy state of soul which intellectual and emotional activities induce, there is thus another oldness which comes of those activities being checked in their very start, or turned astray from the course wherein alone are youth and life. How many are there who have scarcely run a score of birth-days, yet are already sere in spirit! How many are there, again, who, though the snow may have long whitened the mountain tops, are green with all the spring freshness of thought and feeling, and who dispel, by their manner, all idea of their being "old." Time, necessarily, nowhere implies youth: Time, necessarily, makes no one old. Those who are old at sixty or seventy are not made old by lapse of years; they have been old ever since they were twenty or thirty. Doubtless, here and there, men are made old by the attrition of care and distress on account of others,—and none are more to be sympathized with than these; but in the majority of cases, the oldness we are speaking of comes of sloth or weakness, the result probably of crushing injuries in early years—bad school discipline taking the first place,—or it comes of indifference to religious principle, and thus of giving way to "envy, hatred and malice;" since nothing sooner cankers and shrivels the spirit than uncharitable, ungenerous, and selfish habits of will. That which makes old, in the sense of loss of youth of spirit, is not Time, but the consuming action of evil passions, or neglecting to nourish the mind with wisdom. Youth, under right culture, may be preserved to the very last. Is it not promised to the obedient, that "the child shall die an hundred years old?" "Age," well observes Mr. Dendy, in his nice little book, The

Pilgrimage of Thought, "is a mere relative term, and ought not to be employed *quoad* time, but *quoad* condition. A thousand disturbing causes may reduce to apathy or imbecility the opening intellect of youth; and repose, or management, or habits of devotion, may render it perennial and energetic to the very close of life." How many and splendid are the examples of the latter! Mason, on his seventy-second birth-day, wrote one of the most beautiful sonnets in our language. Jussieu employed himself, between his eighty-third and eighty-eighth year, in dictating a new edition of his Introduction to Botany; and this not in his mother tongue, but in choice Latin. Goethe was four-score when he completed the second part of Faust. The late Marquis Wellesley was nearly or quite eighty-two when he produced those extraordinary verses,—

O Fons Salutis! Vita! Fides mea!

158. Youth, in fact, viewed as to its essential qualities, is not a state into which we are born, and which we grow out of, and leave behind, but a state to which we gradually advance. We are born *old*, not young. We enter the world blind, deaf, senseless, emotionless, passionless, ignorant; all which conditions are characteristic of oldness, and are representatively expressed in the bald head, the toothless gums, the tottering gait, and the dozen other physical infirmities and negations which belong alike to senility and infancy. By degrees only do we become young, learning in succession to observe, to wish, to will, to think, to love, to hope. If the expanding intellect and affections be affixed, under kindly guidance, to what is truthful and good, youth spreads its wings, and goes on growing in everlasting life; if they be affixed, under vicious or repressing influences, to what is base or ignoble, the beautiful progression is arrested, and the spirit relapses into its original, vacant old age. How it

is that "the angels are for ever growing younger," we may readily understand by noting the history of the soul which earnestly and prayerfully seeks and strives to be angelic; for this is a history of forsaking the evil and choosing the good, bringing youth as its result, and foretelling on earth the law of heaven.

159. Now to attain to this happy state of youth, and thus virtually to lengthen life, requires but that the spiritual energies of our nature should be allowed full, fair play. Giving them their due, old age itself, called dark and feeble, may yet be rendered lovely. It is not only the "mind" or understanding that must be cultivated; the heart must be attended to no less carefully. Nothing is more importaat to remember in reference to self-culture, than that intellectual pursuits call forth only *half* our nature. True, they infuse a wonderful duration into life as exercises of the attention, the memory, and the agreeable power of investigating the relations of things. But in order to the full realization of life, there is needed also the play of the affections. We must love, as well as think, in order truly to live. Bad as is intellectual sloth, to neglect the cultivation of the feelings is worse. There is no idleness so ruinous as that of the heart. By the affections, as already said, is not meant love towards certain of our fellow-creatures only, and preëminently towards One; though this, next to love of the Father of all, is their most excellent activity. The affections are the dispositions of the Will, love to one's wife, and child, and neighbor, forming a part of them. The dispositions of the Will give quality and intensity to a man's life in a much higher degree than do the perceptions of the understanding. "Sho,w me what thou truly lovest," says Fichte, in that beautiful book, The Way to the Blessed Life, "show me what thou truly lovest, show me what thou seekest and strivest for with thy whole heart, when thou hopest to attain

to true enjoyment, and thou hast hereby shown me thy life. What thou lovest, is that thou livest. This very love is thy life, the root, the seat, the central point of thy being." Nothing is *attainable* unless we *love* it. "We can sometimes love that which we do not understand, but it is impossible clearly to understand what we do not love." Learn to love *well* is therefore the first and golden rule of wisdom. Our true birth-day is when we begin consciously to love the good and comely, and our true birth-place the scene of that love's arising. Eve, rather than Adam, was called "Life," though our first father, considered physically, was equally if not more deserving of the name, because in woman the Affections predominate, as in man the intellectual powers. Loss of the power of loving is loss of life. Directly we cease to love a thing, it no longer has any of the beauty of life for us, nor, though the hands may still possess it, can we any longer call it *our own*. Affection, therefore, alone makes possession sacred. No man can *avoid* loving, nor can he avoid loving that which God gave him for his affections' chief delight. Hence it was that the monks, when they made their vow of celibacy, and refused to love woman in her proper person, still were unable to escape loving her in the ideal, and took her image in the Virgin, able to dispense so much the more easily with the genuine, the more ardently they attached themselves to the imaginary. To love the Virgin may be pious, abstractedly, and may bring many pleasant thoughts; but real, practical piety, as well as wisdom, is to get a terrestrial wife, and love *her*. You have the advantage, to say the least, of her society. As Adolphe Karr says, in "A Tour round my Garden," talking of the Hamadryads, "I love women *under* trees, not *in* them." True reason and religion have an eye for the earth as well as for heaven. Like the cedar of Lebanon, they have their branches turned to the sky, and soaring beautifully, but they have their roots in the soil beneath. Hence then the great and impregnable axiom that Life is Love. Commonly restricted to the play of the amative and philoprogenitive feelings, Love properly denotes the energy, in a happy and beautiful direction, of the entire spiritual nature. It is in this high, impartial, unsensual sense of the word, of course, that we are to be understood as using it. In a derivative sense, it denotes also the *ruling desire* of a man; that disposition of the will which is predominant with him, and which may or may not be in concord with the intellect. Every man has such a desire. It is ever secretly present to him, and, though he may be immediately occupied with something else, unconsciously governs all his actions.

160. Every one proves that life is love:—that we live only when in union with what we love. Do we not feel it daily? Absence from what we love is not life, but only dull, uninteresting time. "It is but a little part of our life that we live," says an ancient poet; "the whole space of it is not life, but time only."* Many are the sayings which record how wide-spread has been this experience:—*Vitâ in exilio vitalis non est.*† *Nec voluptas sine vita, nec vita sine voluptate.* Life away from that which makes the enjoyment of life, the Greeks called βίος ἄβιος, "lifeless life." When others of the ancients shouted, "O King, live forever!" it was but a metaphorical way of saying, "O King! so long as you live, may you be prosperous and happy!" Life and

---

* Menander, in a fragment preserved by Stobæus, *Sententiæ*, Tom. 2, Tit. 108.

† Thus Romeo,—

> There is no world without Verona's walls,
> But purgatory, torture, hell itself.
> Hence banished is banish'd from the world,
> And world's exile is death.

well-being are in their briefest definition, union with the object of our love; death and ill-being are the reverse. The poet addresses his beloved as —"My life! my soul!" but what does he in this beyond clothing in speech what all men utter silently? Whatever be the object of our leading affection, where the heart is, there too is our life; and as we are beings directly constituted for sympathy and intimate communion with one of complementary sex, life is real to us in the degree that there is least absolute separation from the chosen. They only can be truly said to live who have a faithful heart to receive and reciprocate the outpouring of their own. It is because all life, whether physical, physiological or spiritual, is a state of marriage, or the union of two complementary forces, acting and reacting; and because all marriage, rightfully so called, is life; that the bitterest of privations is prolonged severance from one's other self, and the sweetest of delights, reunion and companionship with her. The presence of those we love is a *double* life. Hence also the enthusiasm of the lover, emphatically so called, when in the society of his beloved; and his pining loneliness when away from her;—*her own* enthusiasm, *her own* solitude, no less. "Five days," says Clemanthe,—

> "Five days,
> Five melancholy days I have not seen him."

To the genuinely fond and faithful, the world has in it two places only—that where she *is*, and that where she is *not*. Yet has the lover his gay as well as his lonely hours, since the love which is his life beguiles the mind into one long unbroken thought of the beloved, and since into every thought and affection of human nature enter both summer and winter. The summer of his absence is whenever he sees what is beautiful, whether in nature or art, for the Beautiful is ever the likeness of her he loves. He goes into the still country, and while other men see flowers, and clear streams, and golden and purple sunsets, *he* only sees the features of the wished-for. Who that has read *Eloisa* cannot but remember St. Preux in the Valais?

> Te loquor absentum: te vox mea nominat unam!
> Nulla venit sine te nox mihi, nulla dies!
> (Ovid. *Tristia*, Lib. iii. El. iii.)

"Thee, beloved consort, I talk to, far away; thee alone does my voice name; no night, no day, comes to me uncheered by thy sweet vision."

161. But the brilliant charms of sexal love, and the richly glad life which it fashions, are not the lot of all. That many of both sexes should remain celibate all their lives is something more than an accident. It is an arrangement of Providence for great and benevolent uses which it is not difficult to estimate. Moreover, of no one of youthful years can it be affirmed that they shall unquestionably enjoy the life which comes of sexal love. Therefore is it wisdom to encourage those other loves which, though they may not cast upon our pilgrimage an equal radiance, are solid, substantial, enduring, independent of time and place. These are, first, the love of the performance of good uses, in the lecture-room, the Sunday-school, the domestic circle, wherever, in a word, there may be opportunity of sharing with others what Providence has blessed us with, each one according to his aptitude and ability; secondly, the love of nature. Cultivating these loves, the intellect itself expands and grows wealthier. If the love of these things can be enjoyed along with the love that has its root in sexal difference, it is a joy untold. "Life," says Schiller, writing to his friend Körner, "life at the side of a beloved wife is a different thing from what it is to one who is alone—even in summer. Now, for the first time, I can thoroughly enjoy

Nature, and in her, myself too." A wife should be chosen for "her own sweet sake alone," but if the choice be true, we secure at the same moment, an enlarged aptitude for all minor loves. All minor loves indeed, after some mode or other, enter into and become a part of true, fond conjugal love, which thus procures to its possessors a summary or compend of all the riches of the world. "With persons whom we love," says one of the most charming of authors, "sentiment fortifies the mind as well as the heart; and they who are thus attached, have little need to search for ideas elsewhere."—(J. J. Rousseau. Confessions, Part ii., Book 2.)

CHAPTER XV.

THE AFFECTIONS IN RELATION TO LIFE. LOVE OF NATURE.

162. FIRST then, as to good uses. No man is happier than he who loves and fulfills that particular work for the world which falls to his share. Even though the full understanding of his work, and of its ultimate value, may not be present with him; if he but *love* it,—always assuming that his conscience approves,—it brings an abounding satisfaction. Indeed, we none of us fully comprehend our office, nor the issue we are working for. To man is entrusted the *nature* of his actions, not the result of them. This, God keeps out of our sight. The most trivial act doubtless goes to the promotion of a multitude of ends, distant it may be from us, but only as the leaves of a tree are distant from their supplying rootlets. And therefore does it behoove us to be diligent in our several spheres. We should work like the bees, sedulous to collect all the honey within our reach, but leaving to Providence to order what shall come of it. The good which our exertions effect, may rarely or never become visible. In teaching, which is the readiest of good uses, how often does all exertion seem in vain. Our duty is nevertheless to go on, and strive to do all we can. "Every man," says Fichte, in the beautiful book already quoted, "every man should go on working, never debating within himself, nor wavering in doubt, whether it *may* succeed, but labor as if of necessity it *must* succeed." Between the result of single

efforts and the end we have in view, and the magnitude of the obstacles to be overcome, there may often appear a large and painful disproportion; but we must not allow ourselves to be discouraged by *seemings;* warm, hearty, sunny endeavor will unfailingly meet with its reward. Good uses are never without result. Once enacted, they become a part of the moral world; they give to it new enrichment and beauty, and the whole universe partakes of their influence. They may not return in the shape wherein played forth, but likelier after the manner of seeds, which never forget to turn to flowers. "Philosophers tell us that since the creation of the world, not one particle of matter has been lost. It may have passed into new shapes, it may have combined with other elements, it may have floated away in vapor; but it comes back some time, in the dew-drop or the rain, helping the leaf to grow, and the fruit to swell; through all its wanderings and transformations Providence watches over and directs it. So is it with every generous and self-denying effort. It may escape our observation, and be utterly forgotten; it may seem to have been utterly in vain, but it has painted itself on the eternal world, and is never effaced." Nothing that has the ideas and principles of heaven in it can die or be fruitless.

Talk not of wasted affection; affection never was wasted;
If it enrich not the heart of another, its waters, returning
Back to their spring, like the rain, shall fill it full of refreshment;
That which the fountain sends forth, returns again to the fountain.*

Carlyle, in that extraordinary book, *Sartor Resartus,* shows us that it is from our work we gain most of our *self-knowledge,*—one of the most important desiderata of life. "Our

* See a beautiful theory of the Fine Arts, founded on these great truths, in Mrs. Child's Letters from New York.

works," he says, "are the mirror within which the spirit first sees its natural lineaments. 'Know thyself' is an impossible precept till it be translated into this partially possible one, Know what thou canst work at." Work is obedience, and self-knowledge is invaluable, and thus is proved over again that duty and interest are but two names for one fact.

163. Secondly, as to the "love of nature." This is not to be understood technically. People who by its exercise carry their youth along with them, may not prove to be botanists or geologists. Quite as likely they will *not*. But it will rarely prove that they have not accustomed themselves to an earnest and constant friendship with that of which geology, and botany, and all sciences, barely as such, are only the husks and coverings. They have lived in that which is the spirit and life of all love and all knowledge—the Poetic sentiment. They have lived in the poetry of *common things;* not necessarily in written poetry, but in the love of the omnipresent ingredients of poetry existing throughout creation, and which are the ingredients likewise of all science and philosophy, sacred and moral as well as physical; whereby, in fact, they are true poets, though they may never have written a single verse. They have learned, in a word, to *feel* and to *see;*—arts which, though they may seem native and universal, and which, exercised after the manner of quadrupeds, are common enough, in reality are rarely practiced. Happy the man whose walk, in calm April evenings, is arrested by the odor from the opening buds of the balsam poplar. Happy again, who, when he visits the sea-side, is quick to the

Crimson weeds which spreading flow,
Or lie like pictures on the sand below;
With all those bright red pebbles that the sun
Through the small waves so softly shines upon.

There is no greater mistake than to suppose that a minute knowledge of nature is requisite either to the love or to the enjoyment of it. Every man who in his walks derives pleasure from the common things of creation, who looks to the fields, the woods, the mountains, and the things that are therein, and reflects upon what he sees, has the true spirit of the naturalist within him, and so far is a botanist and geologist; thereby is he proved also to be of poetic temperament, for in these objects is the soul of poetry contained; it is from no other that the poet draws his inspiration, since in nature is the only fund of great ideas. "Persons," says the author of Kathemerina, "who in regard to science may be a whole encyclopædia behind the rest of the world—who do not know where to look for the Bear, or the place of a single star, may yet have as much pleasure in the sight of nature as those who know its secrets; the poetry of common life does not require men to be versed in philosophy; Nature never intended that all her children should be engaged in what are pompously called 'solid studies.'" In these common things of earth lies far more power to delight us than people in general know of. All possess them in some sort, as all possess the atmosphere; but few appreciate them so highly as they deserve, or extract the full value from them. How beautifully is their worth acknowledged in the Song of the Three Children—"O all ye works of the Lord, bless ye the Lord!" Strange to say, the educated classes seem rather to dislike than to favor common things. They seem to prefer the maxim *quæ rara, cara.* Not so the man of genius. *Him* we may almost recognize by his sympathy with the familiar and unpretending. The finest understandings, and the noblest souls, says Charron, are the most universal and free. Accustomed to behold the grand whole of things, to such minds all alike "discourse sweet music." Whether it be the objects of nature, or the hearts of mankind, the simple and plain are as pleasing as the great and lustrous. To him, in fact, who realizes the beauty and the freshness of common things, who looks with love upon nature in *all its developments,* not questioning within himself whether any particular part is more pleasing than another, but attaching himself to the whole, as a great and beautiful power capable of imparting purest joy, there is never any need to *search* for pleasure;

> The meanest floweret of the vale,
> The simplest note that swells the gale,
> The common sun, the air, the skies,
> To him are opening Paradise.

Hence too we find such minds taking fullness of delight in *little children,* their pretty faces, and innocent smiling gestures; glad also to hold intercourse with what are called "common people," who so far from being the "vulgar people" of the world, include no small portion of "nature's aristocracy." The vulgar are not necessarily the ignorant, but the proud and the selfish, whatever their rank in society. The pleasure such minds receive, they shed around. As men of genius have faith and joy in simple minds, so these latter, "timid before the crowd, mute before merely clever people, feel quite at ease in the presence of a man of genius. There is a sympathy of simplicity between them." Beautiful as are the letters of the highly-cultivated, none are so sweet and touching as those that breathe the feelings and sentiments of the simple-minded, especially of the kind-hearted, amiable woman, whose insight and education qualify her to *appreciate* her husband, without ever aspiring to compete with him. "Heaven only knows how many simple letters from simple-minded women, have been kissed, cherished, wept over, by men of far loftier intellect. So will it always be to the end of time. It is a lesson worth learning by those young creatures who seek to allure by their accomplishments, or dazzle with their wit, that though he may admire, no man ever *loves* a woman for these things. He loves her for what is essentially distinct from, though by no means incompatible with them—her woman's nature and her woman's heart, guileless, simple, and unaffected. This is why we so often see a man of high intellectual power passing by the De Stäels and Corinnes to take into his bosom some way-side flower, who has nothing on earth to make her worthy of him, except that she is, what so few of your 'female celebrities' are—a true woman." In fine, whoever teaches us how to enjoy common things, is our greatest benefactor. So to represent familiar objects as to awaken the minds of others to that freshness of feeling concerning them which is the great privilege of genius, is one of the divinest uses human nature can fulfill.

164. It is the very same poetic sentiment which shows itself in the love of good uses; also in genuine sexal love. It is the same, indeed, which forms the mainspring of true intellectual activity. Wherever any spiritual energy is so exercised as to realize to a man the glory and blessedness of Life, it is the Poetic sentiment seeking to express itself. Therefore would it be no misuse of terms to say that, in its genuine realization, life is Poetry; that divine habitude of soul which "lifts the veil from before the hidden beauty of the world, and makes familiar things be as though they were not familiar;" which, discerning the holiness, the loveliness, the bright side of all things, makes joy more joyful and sorrow less sad, gives new comeliness to virtue and religion, and "makes the whole human race grow more noble in our eyes." The very essence of poetry lies in its power to beautify and exalt, and what is this but to lift into a higher realization of life?

We live by admiration, hope, and love;
And even as these are well and wisely fixed,
In dignity of being we ascend.

Therefore also is perennial youth identified with the encouragement and culture, primarily, of the Imagination, one of heaven's most gracious gifts to man, and therefore one of the most practically useful. Concerned not only with science, and the penetration of the secrets of nature, Imagination is a first essential to human happiness. It is by the play of the imagination, unconsciously it may be, that we are strengthened for the common avocations of life, and that they are rendered not only untiresome, but agreeable; it is by the play of the imagination, no less unconsciously it may be, that every emotion of pleasure is vitalized. Knowledge in itself, feeling in itself, is inanimate. How lovely the rose! Where is the man who is indifferent to it? Yet the rose does not please simply because it is red, nor because so fragrant, nor because of its configuration, nor even from the combination of all these properties. It pleases because the imagination connects it with something human and divine, probably the cheek of woman. "Divine," we say, because the imagination is the faculty which preëminently links us to heaven, its proper home; and because whatever is vitally and essentially human is an expression of something contained in Him of whom man is the image and likeness. More nearly than we suppose is imagination connected with morality and religion. So with everything else that men delight in. The senses view one thing, the imagination views another—higher, lovelier, immortal. Whatever *seems* to gratify, by pleasing the senses, owes its charms to the pencil of the incomparable artist within. An "unimaginative man," absolutely so styled, or self-styling, is a non-existence. Some individuals may be more imaginative than others, but absolute unimaginativeness is one of the negations which degrade brutes. Imagination is the very essence of Hope, without which there is no life. Holding fast when all other parts are threatened with destruction, and bidding defiance to the storms of devastation, Hope, the rebuilder and regenerator, fresh, every morning, like the manna from heaven, represents, in the little world of man, the sanatory powers which maintain nature in its total. *Spero*, "I hope," is the same word as *spiro*, "I breathe;" *spes* is only another name for the "breath of life."* He who has no future in prospect, is already dead. Life is one incessant wish to live "in the thick of all we desire, *some day*, and meanwhile we do live there as well as hope and imagination can contrive it."

165. The love of nature, if we would prove how long and beautiful it makes existence, must not be left as a mere amusement that can be taken to at any time. Like the love of virtue, it must be commenced *in youth*. A man may learn a language or a science when he is grown up, but he cannot then learn to love nature. This love he must bring with him from his boyhood, when it germinates in all, though with most dried up in its earliest leaf. How many who have mildewed and rusted amid the mock pleasures of towns, would fain return, when too late, to their first, young love. Doubtless every man carries with him some remnant of his early love for nature, but it is not that deep, animating love which, by its freshness and fullness, keeps the heart green. Vitally to affect us, it must grow with our growth, and strengthen with our strength. Hence the paramount

---

* Our English word "hope" conveys precisely the same idea, being cognate with the word "gape," that is, to open the mouth wide in order to breathe freely. The exchange of *g* and *h* is a very common occurrence; "give" and "have," for instance, are etymologically the same.

value, in the education of youth, of Natural History; or at least of a fostering of the native taste in the human heart for the poetical contemplation of natural objects and phenomena. "Let everything be taught a girl," says one of the most sagacious of educationists, "let everything be taught a girl," and a boy as well, "which forms and exercises the habit of attention, and the power of judging things by the eye. Consequently, Botany, that inexhaustible, tranquil, ever-interesting science, attaching the mind to nature with bonds of flowers. Then Astronomy, not the properly mathematical, but the Lichtenbergian and religious, which with the expansion of the universe, expands the mind."* Especially should these things be taught to the children of the *poor*, whose means of indulgence in costly pleasures are so scanty. There is not a child who does not delight in wild flowers, and whose intelligence cannot be led, if kindly dealt with, to find in Botany a pleasure which of all others requires least outlay of time and money, and is most easily and permanently within reach. To suppose that the poor are less able to learn than the rich, that they have not "minds" for such things, and that they are adapted only for operatives and domestic servants, is most thoughtless. Many a servant girl has as much taste and talent as her mistress and the young ladies.

166. It is the forming and strengthening this *habit of attention* which stamps so much efficiency on natural history, even in its most prosaic pursuit. When Solomon tells us with all our gettings to "get understanding," it is but another way of saying, Learn to observe. One of the chief functions, therefore, of the instructor of youth, if unable to communicate positive knowledge of natural objects, should be so to consolidate the interest of the youthful mind in

---

* J. P. Richter. Levana, or the Doctrine of Education, p. 255

what of its own free will it is never slow to observe, that the country shall continue, what it may be to all, a perennial gladness and solace, not unintelligently, but because thronged with old friends. A human heart can never grow old if it bring with it from its childhood a lively interest in the re-appearance of spring flowers, the habits of birds and insects, the changing tints of the October leaves. The naturalist's poem is the Pleasures of Memory and the Pleasures of Hope both in one. He has always a to-morrow to *his* pleasures, whereas with most there is only a yesterday and to-day. Let the young not neglect or despise these sweet pleasures, and they will find that when old they will not depart from them. Unhappily, children's love of nature is for the most part not only not encouraged, but checked and deadened. How else is it that the mass of mankind—say only of the "educated" and well-to-do—how else is it that they are so indifferent to the works of creation, except in so far as they can be made to subserve some selfish end? Who is to blame? Not He who gave them, for nothing is put in the presence of mankind that the universal human intellect may not appreciate. Neither is it from lack of opportunity or invitation. It is the half-system of teaching which, born of the ruling half-system of theology, loves to dwell with it among the tombs, instead of coming out into the light and pure air of genuine philosophy and genuine Christianity. The poor lad of the streets, to whom the very daisy and buttercup are strange exotics, whose holiday is with marbles down in the dust, is in vital education no worse off than many a little gentleman who gets his prizes for Latin*

---

* No sort of disparagement of Latin is here intended. We know its value too well. But how inordinately and ridiculously the dead languages have been honored, to the almost total exclusion of other branches of knowledge, is sufficiently notorious. See the clever ar-

Drill a boy at mere book-lessons, and the chances are that either he becomes a pedant, or disgusted with learning and books for the whole of his life after; whereas in using natural history as a lever of education, you secure numberless and most happy opportunities for communicating both knowledge and the taste for it, together with just and amiable sentiments. It is one of the best of mental *disciplines.* No mere pastime for the observation and the memory, natural history, pursued seriously and connectedly, calls for the activity of every faculty of the mind. To take a grass or a fern, and determine in succession its family, genus, and species, is an educational exercise little, if at all inferior to the verification of a theorem of Euclid. Let there be a deep, unsophisticated love of nature, and it will even serve in the place of much that is commonly called education. How much grace and dignity does the love of nature give to minds in other respects simple and scantily furnished, especially in females. There may be no learning, there may be no "accomplishments," but if there be a deep, fond love of nature, it compensates for the want of all, and we find a more lively and engaging companionship than in the society of the profoundest scholar who is void of it. People should cultivate this love, and bring up their children in it, if they would but realize the full beauty of the commonest objects of household ornament. Nobody knows how to like shells who has not collected them on the firm wet sand uncovered by the retiring waves. Nobody knows how to like flowers who has not gathered primroses beneath the tender foliage of the spring. Where, moreover, we find this love present, we may take it as a sign of still better things, seeing that its

ticle in the Westminster Review for October, 1853, on Classical Education, its use and abuse; or better still, Mr. Chapman's reprint of it, with the appendix of extracts from cotemporary writers very province is to refine. When, on entering a house, you see a few choice flowers tastefully arranged, you may expect a shelf of wise and good books not far off. And so with the manifestation of the soul.

167. The love of nature requires no peculiar circumstances. Its sphere is wherever the sun is shining, because it addresses itself to what the listless call weeds and stones, finding poetry and delight where the dull cry all is barren. It revels in a glorious landscape, but where the landscape is not, it constructs one in miniature for itself. Nothing in the world is absolutely uninteresting to it, nor can be—what is there indeed that, in any relation, has lost its primal quality of "very good?" What is there that we should not esteem it a privilege to possess, although it be "common?" Is it nothing to have the frost-flowers on the window-panes? Is it nothing to have the blue sky? Is it nothing to have the stars and the rainbow? Oh, what grand and awful things surround us, if we will but look forth upon them! But because they are "without money and without price," we make nought of them; refusing to enjoy, because acceptance and admiration alone are asked. That sublime sense of the wonderful which they excite in us when children, is one of the sentiments we should most anxiously keep alive. When we cease to view with interest the familiar phenomena of nature, its rarest and grandest lose in charm. Why do not preachers speak more of these things? If the office of religious teaching be to amend man's heart, surely the study of the works of God, as well as of his word, deserves some little notice and recommendation. The religious contemplation of nature has more efficacy in this way than mere scholastic theologians suppose. "The moral constitution of man," beautifully observes Dr. Moore, "is so intimately in keeping with the outward *cosmos*, that it is vain to attempt to regulate our faculties and feelings without respect to the

ordinances of God in the material creation."* The pulpit is not the place for lectures on natural history, but neither is it a place for discarding or forgetting it, at least after the manner of the preachers that be. "In recommending the love of God to us, how seldom do they refer to those things in which it is most abundantly and immediately shown! They insist much on his giving of bread, raiment, and health (which he gives to all inferior creatures), but they require us not to thank him for that glory of his works which he has permitted us alone to perceive. They tell us often to meditate in the closet; but they send us not, like Isaac, into the fields at even. They dwell on the duty of self-denial, but they exhibit not the duty of delight." To genuine theology nothing in the world is without significance; nor is it anything unfit for citation in its discourses, when it would seek to interpret the word of God, and enforce its teachings. The test of enlightened preaching is its ability to "consider the lilies," and deduce from their history religious wisdom. The great defect of what is called moral and religious teaching, as ordinarily carried on is, that it continually tells us what we are *not to do*, whereas genuine wisdom begins by giving something *to be done*, and showing how to do it. In its very simplest form, if you would keep a child out of mischief, set him to some interesting employment. "Don't do that," goes for nothing unless followed by "do this." That mankind may become more moral and religious, let those who are anxious for it, administer less reproof, and give in place of it, an interest in life; show how much there is to live for, and how easily procured.

168. The love of nature should be cherished for the sake of the *tranquility* it induces. A man can be of importance to others only when he is himself happy and peaceful, and

* Use of the Body in relation to the Mind. P. 163.

nothing so much tends to make him so as the contemplation of nature. The serenity we find in the fields and the woods, and by clear streams, we imbibe into our own hearts, and thus derive from nature itself the very condition of spirit which is needful to the enjoyment of it. In towns we *may* find diversion, but we cannot find repose; calmness, in which alone can the soul put forth its leaves and blossoms, is for the solitudes of nature alone to give; cheerfulness, which arises only from the peaceful enlightenment of the spirit, finds in the same its sincerest and warmest friend. "I wondered," says Rousseau, describing his first experience of this, "I wondered to find that inanimate beings should over-rule our most violent passions, and despised the impotence of philosophy for having less power over the soul than a succession of lifeless objects." It is not the prerogative of a few. Ask any man who has accustomed himself to commune with nature, and he will testify that apart from the intellectual culture attained by scientific acquaintance with its objects—and apart from the admiration of creative skill and goodness which they excite—there is in nature a nameless and subtle *influence*, analogous to the influence of human beings, and like that, acting upon us silently and secretly, but most powerfully. If any would prove it in his own person, let him go in the refulgent summer to where the warmth and breeze will wrap him round; where he may hear the singing of birds, and the sound of leaves and boughs stirred by the wind, so like the grand, perpetual song of the sea; where he can view without effort, the smooth, green grass, stretching far away, interrupted only by masses of the heavy, sumptuous foliage of the year's glorious centre; water in the distance, its ripples lighted by the sun; let him go alone amid these things, or even a small part of them, and live with them for half an hour, then say seriously, if he can, that he has not felt his spirit breathed on by some unseen Power, and ascend under that breath into a holier life. It is good to leave other people sometimes, even to leave our own thoughts, and to dwell amidst this mysterious, powerful, moulding influence, submitting our whole being to it, passively. If we take calmness *with* us, that calmness transmutes into religion; if we take trouble and disquietude, they melt away. "When the vexations of the world have broken in upon me," says Waterton, "I go away for an hour or two amid the birds of the valley, and seldom fail to return with better feelings than when I set out." Doubtless it is true that nature is "colored by the spirit;" that it dons a festive or a mourning garment according as its master does: that in nature of itself, there is nothing either sad or joyful. But none of this is incompatibly true. What soothes, ameliorates, and ennobles us when in the presence of nature, consists not in the objects we find there, but in the ministrations from the spiritual world, which, by going into that sacred and peaceful presence, we provide with congenial opportunity. For it is one of the sublimest laws of Divine Providence that spiritual gifts (which are influences on the heart), shall always be best conferred in the presence of their material representatives. Hence the institution of the representative bread and wine, of sacrifices on altars, of baptism, and of every other genuine religious rite and ceremonial. Hence likewise the taking of the disciples to the sea-shore, the mountain, and the corn-fields. The spiritual is ever near to us, but it is in the solitudes of nature, when we are face to face with the unmarred works of God, that our hearts are most accessible to his inspirations. *These* it is which refresh us; not the sunshine and the landscape: as in reading the Bible, it is not the reception of the words by the eye which invigorates, but that which during our reading is infused into the soul. Let us not unduly exalt nature. People say God made the country, and man made the town, as if the latter were altogether evil. Both have their sanctities, and both their mighty influence for good. How many are the sweet, endeared and endearing Homes, where the affections, taste, elegance, and holy communings beautifully intermingle, and sustain each other's life. The true place to *live* in is a great city. If vice be there, and turbulence, still it is there only that we get society, stimulus, libraries.

CHAPTER XVI.

THE INTELLECTUAL FACULTIES IN RELATION TO LIFE.

169. MORE readily to apprehend the nature and use of the spiritual faculties, especially those which belong to the Intellectual province of the soul, we may here briefly consider the fine correspondence which they hold with physical Hunger and Thirst, and the means by which the latter are satisfied and allayed. The hunger and thirst of the body represent our spiritual desires and longings; the eating and drinking which appease them are counterparts, respectively, of the solacing of the affections with what they love, and of the acquisition of knowledge by the understanding. *Mutatis mutandis*, all the governing principles, requirements, and activities of the soul and the body with regard to nourishment, are the same. They similarly famish under privation of food, and improve upon generous diet; hunger, which has done so much for man as a physical affection, has scarcely done less as a spiritual one. Figuratively, or in acknowledgment of the correspondence, we speak of feeding our hopes, thirsting for knowledge, listening with avidity, imbibing information. When we acquire that information, we "digest it,—we "read, mark, learn, and *inwardly digest*." How beautiful are the allusions of the poets!

My heart is *thirsty* for that noble pledge!—*Julius Cæsar*, iv. 3.
Urged by a restless longing, the *hunger and thirst* of the spirit.
Evangeline.

In Ion, the pestilence-stricken, dying mother (fearing to communicate the infection,) forbears to give a last embrace to her little child,—

> Stifling the mighty *hunger* of the heart.

What pathos, again, in the unhappy Lady Constance,—

> O Lord, my boy, my Arthur, my fair son!
> My life, my joy, *my food*, my all the world;
> My widow's comfort, and my sorrow's care!

The "hunger of the heart" is not merely the longing for that which is beloved, but far away, or denied to it; it is that beautiful fervency of the affections which makes them yearn for something to call their own, something that shall be the secret joy and solace of their life. Of its very nature, the heart must and *will* have something to love and be kind to; it cannot live without; it never was intended to; whence if precluded from that which it knows of and longs for, but cannot secure, it will half-unconsciously pet even a dog or a bird. In Scripture, the native land and home of all true poetical expression, "eating" denotes the reception in our souls of the love of God; "drinking" the reception of his wisdom; these being the Divine elements by which our spiritual nature is invigorated and sustained, and the gift of which was representatively expressed in the miracles of feeding the hungry. It is because all things come of the Divine Love and Wisdom, and because physical things universally are images of spiritual ones, that the bodies of all living creatures require both food and drink, and are constructed of solids and liquids, and that no vital function ever does or can take place except through their combined instrumentality. Agreeably, thirst is used in the inspired volume to express desire for truth; hunger to express aspiration after love. "Ho! every one that thirsteth, come ye to the waters, come and eat,* yea, come, buy wine and milk without money and without price!" Of this present life it is said, "Blessed are they who hunger and thirst after righteousness;" and in the Apocalypse, of the multitudes of heaven, that "they never more hunger nor thirst," which means that in the Better Land is plenitude of wisdom and delight. Bread, the staff of life, is so often spoken of in the Word of God, because the representative of heavenly good, or Divine love, and because there is not a single condition of life in which we can dispense with that good, although we may not receive it consciously. A man who will not eat must needs die in a little time. Correspondingly, the spiritual life soon becomes extinct, or reduced to its lowest ebb, if the means which can alone support it be not used. Hence we are instructed to pray without ceasing, "Give us this day our daily bread." Ashur, says the promise, which all may realize, "shall always have bread." Elsewhere Jehovah is described as pouring out his spirit on the earth, and saying,—"I will give water to those which are athirst." Water is the emblem of truth, as bread is of good. "Whosoever drinketh of the water I shall give him, shall never thirst." Perceiving the correspondence, in the inmost of our minds, we speak of truth, even colloquially, as flowing from a fountain, also as a sea, and an ocean. "I seem to myself," said Sir Isaac Newton, "to have been picking up a few shells upon the beach, while the great ocean of truth lay all undiscovered before me."

170. Religious or theological truths universally represent themselves in secular things; as the religious life needs the divine "flesh and blood," which "except ye eat, ye can have no life in you," so does the life of temporal intelligence and

---

* "Eat," as applied to drinking, is similarly used by Homer,—"eat the fat sheep and excellent sweet wine."—(Il. xii. 319.)

emotion need its own appropriate aliments, "the food for the mind" so often talked of, and which true Benevolence always remembers to provide, by establishing the means of Education. To urge this latter principle would be no more than to dilate upon one of the oldest texts of common-sense; but it is *not* superfluous to observe that were the simple rules of common-sense which those who have it are so zealous in enforcing upon the body, as zealously enforced upon man's moral and intellectual nature, they would prove the best practical philosophy. That "food for the mind," moreover, must be nutritive and wholesome. "The stalwart and florid components of a masculine life-hood demand the materials of vitalization, not those which conserve squalor. The intellect, as well as the body, demands strong, regular, *solid*, aliment. If the human mind," continues one of the most eloquent preachers of modern times, "grow dwarfish and enfeebled, it is, ordinarily, because left to deal with common-place facts, and never summoned to the effort of taking the span and altitude of broad and lofty disclosures. The understanding will gradually bring itself down to the dimensions of the matters with which alone it is familiarized, till, having long been accustomed to contract its powers, it shall lose, well-nigh, the ability to expand them." Mental *culture* is thus, essentially, mental *nourishment*. We cannot expect to enjoy "*strength* of mind," "*vigor* of mind," "intellectual *power*," or by whatever other name the manly energy of the soul may be designated, unless we furnish it with food such as it can turn into swift, red blood. Neither can we expect to see these things if by training we do not teach the soul *how to be hungry*, which is to be done by demanding of it constant, tasking exercise. The laws of the body are those of the mind. Exercise and excitement strengthen and energize,—though both may be carried to an extreme, and then be hurtful by exhausting—indolence and habits of insensitiveness contract, and debilitate, and at length kill. As a man may always judge of his physical state of health by the quality of appetite with which he sits down to his meals, so may he of his spiritual health by the interest he feels in wisdom. Men who realize and thoroughly enjoy their animal life, do so by virtue of their good Appetite, and by the legitimate satisfaction of it; they who live the higher life of the intellect, do so by virtue of their Curiosity, which is the appetite of the understanding. No man is truly happy who has not a large curiosity as to the beauties and riches of the world in which we dwell; tempered, nevertheless, with prudence as to the time, and method, and extent of his gratifications. Of all the evils man is subject to, assuredly not the least is *in*curiousness; perhaps it should be classed among the greatest. Certainly there is no evil more abounding. How many listen to philosophy, if they can be said to listen at all, only with polite aversion, as though the speaker were discoursing in an unknown tongue; how many are the minds whose appetite is altogether vitiated and depraved, which is tantamount to being lost, turning away from all really substantial food as if it were so much poison. It needs not that a man be *uneducated* to be incurious. It is not so much of Education commonly so called, that curiosity comes; but of quickening the mind with life to educate *itself*. The customary endeavor to instil a large amount of mere dry, unvitalizing knowledge tends to repress curiosity rather than to excite it. Grammars and lexicons, whether of language or of any other form of knowledge, serve oftener to kill than to make alive. Lessons, as such, or in the sense of parrot-knowledge, are only "mind-slaughter." If it be desired to promote a good appetite, whether of mind or body, it is not to be done by confinement and gorging, which soon destroy it utterly; the body must be taken into the play-grounds of nature, and the mind be inspired through the imagination, upon which curiosity itself depends. A child's imagination can hardly be too much encouraged, provided always that it be guided to some resting-place, where it can repose awhile, and in due time, onwards again, but always with an interval. To excite a child's imagination, sets all its best feelings in motion; mere facts are as useless to it as they are dreary; they die upon a child's heart like rotten leaves.* Education, in the popular acceptation of the word, might often be dispensed with to advantage if Inspiration could be communicated in place of it. To that genial stimulus of the best energies of the soul into work on their own behalf, which it is the mark and proud office of a great nature unconsciously to communicate—that stimulus of which all who have stood in the presence of such natures, have been rapturously sensible; and which they look back upon as the Aurora of their spiritual day—to that alone should the sacred name of Education be applied. It was his power of *inspiring* that gave such wonderful success to the late truly eminent Professor Stuart, of Andover. Many a man of celebrity has been heard to say—"I first learned to think under the inspiration of Mr. Stuart; he first taught me how to use my mind; his first words were an epoch in my history." Stuart proved more perhaps than any other man has ever done, that the excellence of a teacher does not consist in lodging his own ideas safely in the remembrance of his pupils, but in arousing their individual powers to independent action, in giving them vitality, hope, fervor, courage, in dispelling their drowsiness, and spurring them onward to self-improve-

---

* See the excellent remarks on this subject in Harriet Martineau's Home Education, chapter xxii.; also the article "Civilization" in Blackwood for January, 1855, p. 26 and onwards.

ment.* It is to such men and their influence that Plato alludes so eloquently; "Inspired by the Muses, they communicate the sacred fire to others, who again pass it on to other minds, and so form whole circles of divine enthusiasts." Longinus also, in that beautiful passage where he speaks of those who, though of themselves they little feel the power of Phœbus, "swell with the inspiring force of those great and exalted spirits."† The notion that we must be *taught* everything is false and destructive. It is better to be taught very little, provided that a noble curiosity be excited, and then the object of education is virtually accomplished. The most extended course of teaching, conducted by the best-informed masters, often fails to take the anticipated effect; it is by that which we acquire for ourselves that we are really elevated, and it is that alone which lifts us above other men. What the world calls "great men" owe their nobility mainly to their self-culture. Great minds, moreover, it will almost always be found, are such as have had this invaluable sentiment of curiosity early awakened and judiciously fostered. The avowed principle of education with the mother and first intellectual guide of Sir William Jones was to "excite his curiosity." With curiosity for its dominant force, the mind becomes open and prepared for everything; and although on many points it may long remain uninformed, it is capable, at a moment's notice, of receiving information. It is the inquiring boy who usually becomes the philosophic man, and the philosopher thus engendered who is most likely to "ripen into the priest," the highest (and seldomest) development of human nature.

---

* See the memoir of this eminent man in Kitto's Journal of Sacred Literature for January, 1853, to which we are indebted for the above.

† Compare Coningsby, Book 3d, chapter 2d.

What the Boy *admires*,
The Youth *endeavors*, and the Man *acquires*.

The incurious man, on the other hand, is *not* thus receptive, and from his very incuriousness, never becomes great.

171. Appetite, after all, must not be mistaken for Acquisition. It is not much *reading* that builds up wisdom and life; a man may injure himself and cancel his true life by careless or ill-timed reading, as readily as he may hurt his body by unseasonable eating and unwholesome foods. It is through not properly discriminating between these two courses and their results, that with many persons there is a kind of suspicion and distrust of the value of learning. But that culture, whether of body or soul, is alone injurious, which has no regard to time, and means, and measure. "Desultory reading is indeed very mischievous, by fostering habits of loose, discontinuous thought, and by relaxing the power of attention, which of all our faculties needs most care, and is most improved by it. On the other hand, a well-regulated course of study will no more weaken the mind than hard exercise will weaken the body; nor will a strong understanding be weighed down by its knowledge, any more than an oak is by its leaves, or than Samson was by his locks. He whose sinews are drained by his hair, must already be a weakling."* What we have to do, in order to be healthy and strong, is not merely to eat, but to *assimilate* what we eat. To read merely for reading's sake is almost as unprofitable as not reading at all. Setting out, in the first place, with a clear idea of what we wish to learn, which is eminently important, we must afterwards, if we would realize what we have read, reperuse it in thought. This only makes it truly our own. Better still is it to *write down*

* Guesses at Truth. 1, 212.

the central ideas, or seek to communicate them in conversation. "All knowledge," says Whipple, "however imposing in appearance, is but superficial knowledge, if it be merely the mind's furniture, and not the mind's nutriment. It must be transmuted into mind, as food into blood, in order to become wisdom and power. Many of the generals opposed to Napoleon understood military science as well as he did, but he beat them on every occasion where victory depended on a wise movement made at a moment's thought, because science had been *transfused* into his mind, while to theirs it was only *attached*."* It does not follow, because we seem to ourselves to possess things, that we veritably possess them. Though a man may have collected a thousand facts in the *ologies* and the *graphys*, he may yet not possess one of them in reality; though he cover himself with feathers, it needs something else that he may fly; it is of no use merely to *see* what is true, unless by assimilating it, we prove its efficacy, and feel it exerting upon us some salutary effect. Accordingly, it is not so much the reading of books, and the manual part of science, and the promenade part of visits to the fields and the sea-side, from which we are to expect spiritual aliment; we are nourished only as these things are incorporated into our inmost thought. Many, especially young persons, make it a matter of pride that they are "great readers." They literally *devour* books, yet what good does it do them? Life, real, enjoyable life, is immensely dependent on intellectual and reading habits, but it never comes of mere gormandizing. "We read to live, not live to read." Mere consumers of books not only derive no true nourishment from what they read, but are total strangers to the higher pleasures of literary taste. Like the

---

* "On Intellectual Health and Disease," in a clever set of Essays on Literature and Life. (American.)

lower animals, they *feed* only, they do not *eat*. To eat, in the true idea of the act, requires a far more scientific use of the mouth than is the case with mere feeding. Epicurism is no mere invention of low sensuality; they who practice it do but carry to an unworthy extreme one of the most excellent and characteristic powers of human nature. No man is wise who is not an epicure within the legitimate limits; none are more foolish and unkind to themselves than those who regard only quantity and speed. So with the mental palate. If we be not deliberate epicures in our reading, half our advantages and privileges are thrown away, and we are only like quadrupeds unintelligently munching grass. Not that we ought to pick out Apician morsels. We are not to read books merely with a view to passages which have reference to ourselves, or for the sake of the more splendid ones, or of such as may support favorite theories. This is to refuse the greater part of their worth, often not to discover it at all, and is the secret of many books being thrown aside as dull and tiresome. Often when a man says he "sees nothing" in a given book, the fact of the matter is simply that he does not see *himself* in it, which, as a clever writer remarks, "if it be not a comedy or a satire, is likely enough." No book should ever be read except with two distinct aims, first, our own improvement; second, the just apprehension of the author, whom we have never properly read, and therefore not benefited by, till we have seen his subject as *he* saw it, whether right or wrong. To this end we must possess ourselves of all the spirit that lies beneath the words, mastering that internal character, sense and design of the work, to which our regard from the first moment should be directed. Hence too the value as well as pleasantness of two persons reading together. Each perceives different beauties, and in each is awakened a train of differently-associated ideas, throwing light from opposite sides upon the arguments and illustrations, so that the author is more thoroughly understood, and as a consequence, more truly enjoyed. Especially should husband and wife associate in their reading, *he* profiting by her feminine or affectional insight, *she* by his logical intelligence.

172. Many read less than they would perhaps, from the seeming difficulty in the *selection* of books. How are we to judge, they say, what books will, and what will not repay perusal? To tell a good book is not really perplexing, any more than to distinguish a wholesome food. A good book, like a great nature, opens out a fine foreground, wherever we may open it, and like the breath of a summer's morning, invites us onward. It may be known by the number of fragmentary, aphoristic sayings which may be gleaned from it, full of grace and pleasing truth, as flowers on that summer morning's walk. Bacon and Shakspere have multitudes of such sayings. The Bible has more than all other books together. Books that soon perish, die because void of them. They make the difference between books of *ideas,* and books of mere *words.* The value of a book consists not in what it will do for our amusement, but in what it will *communicate.* Whether dealing with fancy or with fact, all books in their kind are dictionaries, and those are the best which yield most material for reflection. It is not fine writing, as many suppose, that makes fine books. Books are fine only in so far as they flow from sound and abundant knowledge, a picturesque and unobtrusive presentation of which is their infallible characteristic. It is given, moreover, *compactly.* When an author of any pretensions is found *abridging* everything, the simple fact of the matter is that he *perceives* everything. Diffusiveness is always a sign either of poverty or pride; nothing of *his,* the vain man thinks, can ever be too much. Good books, again, may be known by their rarely containing anything unintelligible to earnest reading,

whatever hardness may appear upon the surface. We should always be glad to find a book invite us further and deeper than we have previously gone; for if it do *not*, it will only leave us where we were. Those writers who never go further into a subject than we can readily accompany them, or than is compatible with making what they say indisputably clear to man, woman, and child, may gratify us, indeed;—by awakening and enlivening our recollections, they may even benefit us;—but they do nothing whatever to increase the vigor of our intellect, for how can we gather strength except by exercise? They may, by virtue of popularity of theme, be the lights of *their own* age; but they certainly will not be the lights of *succeeding* ages; nor though they may please for the hour, can we permanently entertain a high opinion of them, any more than we esteem a river deep when we find that we can readily see the bottom. On the other hand, we should never allow ourselves to be dismayed by seeming hardness, remembering rather that the author has only half the work to do, the reader a duty on his own side; that to apply ourselves closely, in fact, is the way to get the mental strength we find ourselves deficient in. The best writer, it has been said, is he who merely states his premises, and leaves his readers to work out the conclusions for themselves. Still may we be sure that men who are really competent to teach, always so teach that attention may understand. The truly instructive mind, when it plays forth the beautiful abundance of its wisdom, always condescends to be *intelligible*. The lessons of true intelligence are like the rays of the morning sun; the light and magnitude are revealed, but the splendor is reserved, pleasing the more, by dazzling the less. No author can be expected to do all. "Learn to observe" is as needful a maxim in reading as in natural history. It was remarked by the celebrated Haller, that while yawning we are *deaf;* the same act of drowsiness that stretches open our mouths, shuts up our ears. It is much the same in the exercises of the understanding; a lazy half-attention is in effect a mental yawn. "Where a subject that demands thought, has been thoughtfully treated, we must be willing to make similar efforts on our own part, and think with the author, or in vain will the author have thought for us." Another excellent test of a good book is that the opinions of its author do not range with those of any recognized *party*. It will not readily fall in with any particular creed in theology or school in philosophy; librarians do not know what to do with it; and sectarians become angry and abusive. Freedom from sectarian bias by no means implies freedom from religion. So far from this, every great and good book, whatever may be its subject, discloses from beginning to end, a devout and intelligent submission to revealed truth. Books that give no recognition to religion are stones rather than bread. Here we see our way towards learning what to *avoid*,—a difficulty almost as great as that of choice. One golden rule will almost include the whole, namely, Avoid all that class of literature which has a *knowing* tone. "Every truly good book, or piece of book, is full of admiration and awe; it may contain firm assertions or stern satire, but it never sneers coldly, nor asserts haughtily, and it always leads you to reverence and love something with your whole heart." What constitutes an "improper" book, depends chiefly on the intelligence and purity of the reader. To charge unfitness upon a book, unless it be in palpable antagonism with Scripture and good manners, is often only to show that the plane of thought is low and contracted. Detractors and small critics would do well to remember that many kinds of errors are only possible to great souls, and that the very circumstances which in their weak vision render a work "unfit," may certify a most royal nature and descent. The assistance in choice of books furnished by Critics and Reviewers, upon the whole is untrustworthy. They may have *intellect* enough to criticize, but the preëminent quality needed to their vocation is Christian love to the neighbor. The primary office of a critic is not, as many seem to think, to detect imperfections. That is a very shallow mind which seeks to distinguish itself by facility in finding errors, trying to make superior ones appear stupid. "The first duty of the critic is to create happiness where it may be done faithfully, and to shrink from giving pain where it can honestly be avoided." Steadfastly to adhere to this, the highest principle of criticism, requires, however, too noble a nature to be met with frequently. "A true critic," says Addison, "ought to dwell upon excellences rather than defects; to discover the concealed beauties of a writer; and communicate to the world such things as are worth its observation." The rule applies universally. Rightly to comprehend and estimate things, whether in Art, literature or nature, we must train ourselves to admiration of Excellence. The contrary course serves only to blind and darken. He who does not strive to rise *above* nature, will sink below it. Finally, let our favorite subject of study be what it may, we should above all things take care not to restrict our reading too much to particular themes or particular authors. "Preserve *proportion* in your reading," says Dr. Arnold. "Keep your view of men and things extensive, and depend upon it, a mixed knowledge is not a superficial one. As far as it goes, the views it supplies are true; whereas he who reads in one class of writers only, contracts views which are almost sure to be perverted, and which are not only narrow, but false."

173. Solicitude for food, or hunger, and the appeasing it legitimately and discreetly, are thus the inseparable signs and attestations of health and vigor in the life of the spirit as well as in that of the body. Where there is no desire for

food there is no true enjoyment, and he is the happiest man who feels how closely he relies both upon physical food and spiritual food. A constant question in our self-examination should be, what is the disposition of our minds, including both the intellectual and the affectional faculties, towards nature, and towards literature, and preëminently, towards the word of God—in a word, what is our appetite for the "feast of reason?" No man can ever say to himself "enough." As the meals we made in our youth avail nothing to the renewal of our bodies of to-day, so, if we would live spiritually, we must perpetually feed the soul. Irrespectively of *new* truths, how much of what we acquired in years gone by, imperceptibly slides away, and needs to be reclaimed! "The ideas, like the children of our youth," as Locke beautifully observes, "often die before us, and our minds not seldom represent those tombs to which we are approaching, where, though the brass and marble remain, the inscriptions are effaced, and the imagery is mouldered away. The pictures in our minds are drawing in fading colors, and if not sometimes refreshed, vanish and disappear." Hence the importance of surrounding ourselves with what is beautiful, as far as lies in our power, so as to keep those ideas as much as possible from decay. Hazlitt has said somewhere of the portrait of a beautiful female, with a noble countenance, that it seems as if an unhandsome action would be impossible in its presence. Most men of any refinement must have felt the truth and force of this sentiment; it helps us to understand the importance of having beautiful pictures, statues, models, and other works of art, round about us in our daily sitting-rooms, so that correspondent ideas may be continually excited, ideas of opposite nature repulsed, and old thoughts kept alive. As famishing men feed upon what is nearest, so does the hungry soul upon what is close at hand, thus possibly upon *evil* things, if we omit to encircle it with good. Hence, too, we may see the importance of keeping our books within *sight*, instead of in a book-case upstairs.

174. After the correspondence of physical feeding with intellectual feeding, as regards the general principle, it is interesting to note how close is that which subsists between the two principal *species* of spiritual food, or books and objective nature. As there is a "book of nature," so in a good library are there "waving woods and pastures ever new." Books, regarded in their highest and truest light, are as much a part of nature as gardens. Gardens indeed they are. We do not quit nature when from walking in the fields we step into our study; we only enter into another presence of nature. We must not suppose that because in dictionaries nature is the contrary to art, there is nature only where art has not been superadded. As in winter, though the forests be bare and the birds mute, the delights of the true lover of the country are nevertheless not deciduous till the spring; so where there is solid affection for truth and loveliness, no place is empty of nature, but simply filled after another manner. The only difference a soul so animated is conscious of, is that while summer is more peculiarly the time to feel, and winter to think, the fields and the library are their happiest arenas respectively. Books teach us to understand nature; nature, in turn, teaches us how to understand books. So animated, going into rural paths is *reading*. When Goethe's exemplar, Kleist, was asked why so fond of lonely country walks, "I go," said he, "hunting for images." Similarly, when we tread our "dukedom large enough," we find in its immortal voices that benign, medicinal tranquility, without which, Life is a thing we hear of, but never truly feel. For, as said before, we become conscious of Life in the degree that our minds, though at work, are in repose—not unemployed, but at ease and

peaceful. Work and repose are not antagonistic; they are each other's complement. The grandest workings of nature are precisely those which present to us, along with movement, the sublimest pictures of tranquility, as the roll of the sea, the circling of the constellations round the pole. Great workers, or those who most largely realize life, are always at rest. They accomplish so much because they have learned the secret of tranquility. Free from those contentions of spirit which most men allow to distract them from the true ends and prerogatives of life, the tranquil find the time and the opportunity which the mass of mankind so loudly complain that they have *not*. Like the calm-flowing river, they reflect every tree and cloud, while the brawling and troubled stream shows not a single picture. It is the tranquil who truly "inherit the earth."

175. Good books, like nature, at once alleviate care, repress the insurgency of evil passions, and encourage and animate the amiable. "When I come into my library," said Heinsius, "in the very lap of eternity, amidst so many divine souls, I take my seat with so lofty a spirit and such sweet content, that I pity all those great and rich who know not this happiness." "These friends of mine," writes Petrarch, "regard the pleasures of the world as the supreme good. They are ignorant of my resources. I have friends, whose society is delightful to me; persons of all countries and all ages, distinguished in war, in council, and in letters. Easy to live with, always at my command, they come at my call, and return when I desire them; they are never out of humor, and they answer all my questions with readiness. Some present before me, in review, the events of past ages; others reveal to me the secrets of nature; these teach me how to live, and those how to die; these dispel my melancholy by their mirth, and amuse me by their sallies of wit, and some there are who prepare my soul to suffer everything,

to desire nothing, and to become thoroughly acquainted with itself. As a reward of such services, they require only a corner of my little house, where they may be safely sheltered from the depredations of their enemies." But to enjoy such friends, which is to enjoy literature, we must, as in order to love nature permanently, begin *early*. He who would long remain a man, must early begin to be one. Whatever affluence of intellect we may enjoy in riper life, we owe not so much to the acquisitions purely of manhood, as to the successively renewed and re-invigorated impressions of boyhood. Growing up with such dispositions, old age itself lives in serene enthusiasm, and like the old man in Chaucer, who had nothing hoar about him but his locks, is adolescent to the last.

Though I be hoar, I fare as doth a tree
That blosmeth ere the fruit y-woxen be;
The blosmy tree is neither drie ne ded;
I feel me nowhere hoar but on my hed;
Mine harte and all my limmès ben as green
As laurel through the year is for to seen.

To carry, as somewhere remarked by Coleridge, the feelings of childhood into the powers of manhood, to combine the child's sense of wonder and novelty with sights and experiences which every day for perhaps half a century has rendered familiar—and to which achievement wise mental culture alone is needful—is assuredly, after virtue, the greatest triumph of life. We often hear of *fine boys*. The finest of all boys is the fine *old* boy, he who has obeyed the poet's great command, Keep true to the dream of your youth.

CHAPTER XVII.

THE RELIGIOUS ELEMENT OF LIFE.

176. WHILE the axiom that "Life is Love" verifies itself in the manner set forth, there is involved in it another and yet higher truth. Love is a word of many different senses. Lowest is the physical: the middle one is that wherein it denotes the *ruling desire* of a man, the disposition of the will which is predominant with him, and which may or may not be in concord with the intellect: highest is the sense wherein it denotes the energy, in a happy and beautiful direction, of the entire spiritual nature, or the intellect and affections combined. (See page 259.) This last thus applies to and denotes the *religious* state of the soul, which is the blossoming of our humanity, and of which Love is the essential characteristic. The development and marriage of the intellect and affections is at once the great duty and the blessedness of our being, and thus our highest Life. The perfection of human nature is when these two are conjoined, as man and wife, in even and lovely flow. As a happy marriage is the most perfect and beautiful state of existence that can be attained, as regards the social relations of mankind; so the most perfect and beautiful state of the soul is when the affections delight in what the intellect says is right and true; and when the intellect (always referring itself to the Word of God as the standard), commends what the heart inclines to. To be so disposed towards each other, is to live in conjugal amity,

which is pure and unchangeable Love, and thus true and perfect Life. Such a state of things is not only the *perfection* of human nature; it is the only one proper to be designated human nature, and only where it is present is man in his natural state. All lower conditions are *un*natural. It is important to observe this, because people are apt to call the life of savages the natural state of man; a mode of speaking, unless merely intended to signify ignorance of the arts, utterly inconsistent with all reason and analogy. No one would say that a tree was in its natural state when, through adverse circumstances, it was stunted and barren. Nature is Excellence; anything that is *not* excellent is want of, or departure from nature. The natural state of the tree is when it is appareled in all the luxuriance of leaf and opulence of fruit which it is capable of; and the natural state of man is when the intellect and affections unite before the altar of the law of God, which is to engage in pure and faithful love. If either of these great spiritual powers unduly predominate, error, and therefore unhappiness, necessarily ensues. Apart from the tendency there may arise towards moral wrong, if the heart hold too great power, instead of religion there is fanaticism; if the head be too masterful, there is rationalism. Regarded as a being adapted for society, man, it may be added, is in a much more "natural" state when he is living civilized in a town than when ignorantly vegetating in the wilderness. The nearest approach to genuine natural life is in reality that which we mistakenly call "artificial" life.

177. Religion is the feeling and exercise of such love, and the primary purpose of all true religious culture is to induce, or rather to *renew* it; for the spiritual declension which was the loss of Eden was no other than the estrangement of the affections from their affianced partner, and until these become reconciled, the heavenly garden cannot be re-entered.

The end of religious culture is threefold; namely, to reconcile man to God, to reconcile him to nature, to reconcile him to *himself.* The first is the final and crowning object, but the last is its indispensable ground-work. The practical beginning must always be made in man's own bosom, and the sign and certificate of the truthfulness and efficacy of a given system of religious culture, is the degree in which this lovely harmony is reëstablished. There is no religion which can be referred exclusively to the heart, and none which comes solely from the head. There is none which is only Faith, and none which is only Works. However grand and profound the perceptions of the understanding, if the heart be indisposed to carry them out, still there is no religion. Neither is there any if the intellect have nothing to proffer to the affections, or only what is unworthy. For in the one case, instead of love, there is variance; and in the other, though there is a bride, there is no husband; or if the ideas be selfish and sensual, a husband with whom true love cannot grow up. Man cannot be virtuous in his heart, if he do not know in his head what virtue *is;* we cannot love that which we are ignorant of. This takes us to another great truth; namely, that as there is no virtue unconnected with God, or underived from him, or intelligible except by reference to him, a right intellectual conception of God is the very foundation of true religion, and thence of all genuine life. How grateful should we be that no conception is more readily accessible! We have but to think of the examples set by Him "in whom dwelleth *all the fullness of the Godhead,* bodily." Striving to imitate these examples, makes the difference between religion rightly so called, and mere mental acquiescence in a particular scheme of religious doctrine. Religion is to *live* a doctrine, not simply to *believe* in one; and the best doctrine a man can live is the life of Christ. He who most practises this, is the most truly religious. It does not follow that defective knowledge of God, or a *wrong* intellectual conception of him, is a man's destruction. Men are not saved or lost by what they *think*, but by what they *do*. The essence of religion is a God-fearing and devotional spirit, and no man is rejected who acts faithfully and sincerely up to that which he has been taught to believe true. He who can pray, honestly and silently, and feel his prayers answered, is no stranger to the heavenly fold, however imperfect and erroneous may be his ideas. The peculiar characteristic of the intelligent religious man is, that he is continually aspiring after a *larger* knowledge of his God. A true Christian is never satisfied until he knows his Maker and Saviour more accurately than any object of his senses. Unpossessed of religious life, man only half lives. No matter what intelligence, and learning, and love of nature there may be, no matter what health of body, what aptitude for pleasures of sense, what money and opportunity wherewith to procure them; wanting the true, high life of the soul, existence is but sapless and inanimate, and all things no more than what the poet calls the imaginary wife of the bachelor, ψυχρὸν παραγκάλισμα, "a cold armful."* With it, science, literature, love of nature, as we have seen, make our experience long and beautiful, but there are hours when all are vanity, and wretched is he who then has no higher solace to take refuge in. Looking on how much some men *possess*—some in the material world, some in the intellectual —we are often inclined to envy them. Could we look into their hearts, and see how little of their property they *enjoy*, for want of this life, when the sorrows of our mortal pilgrimage come thick and heavy, we should be more disposed to pity them. All wisdom and philosophy resolve into this one simple principle, that the happiness of intelligent crea-

* Lycophron. Cassandra, 113.

tures depends upon the development of their moral and religious nature.

178. These two classes of the religious, namely, those with whom Life or Love is uppermost, and those with whom Belief, are the only real sects or parties of the religious world. Other differences are but superficial and temporal. Every church and denomination has its proportion of them; every man is either an *amo* or a *credo,* and society suffers or prospers according as the *credos* or the *amos* hold most power. In the *amos* chiefly originate measures of social reform and improvement. From the *credos* come most part of the discouragements and obstructions which they meet with; for the *credos* think that their creed is the incarnation and consolidation of all possible truth, and that "reforms" are only disguised attacks upon it. Hence they are prone also to condemn all rival corporations of *credos,* and to work diligently at procuring proselytes to their own. The *amos,* on the other hand, as they make religion to consist in goodness and love, care little to quarrel about dogmas; they try rather to promote peace and happiness. They believe, nevertheless, and quite as reverently and firmly as the *credos* do; the difference is that the *amos* use their belief as a means, while the *credos* stand still in it as a finality. The *credos,* in like manner, also *love,* but for the most part their affection is all "given to heaven," wherein they find excuse for loving nobody on earth. Church and chapel they visit punctually, but the fatherless and the widow they care little to interfere with: these come to the province of the *amos.* Hence, until we know pretty certainly whether a man is an *amo* or a *credo,* in regard to the sect he is identified with, the mere *name* of his sect supplies not the least clue to his religious quality. Unitarians are just as likely to be *amos* as High Churchmen who fight duels, live luxuriously and wantonly, and heap up treasures, not for heaven. Quite as

likely to be merely *credos* are those who rant and stamp, and have spiritual hysterics, proclaiming their conversion, and its day and hour, as if that could be effected in a moment which is coëxtensive and concurrent with one's whole life. From the mere holding of a doctrine, in short, little can be predicated, nor are the names of the doctrines themselves truly descriptive. "Tell me a man's creed and I know where to look for him, but I have still to inquire what are his morals. Tell me, on the other hand, that he is a man of justice, charity, and love, and I have no occasion to ask whether he be religious." The *credo*, as to his mental character, is well described by Morris. "It is possible," he says, "to be delighted with a doctrine, and yet have no just conception of its practical bearings; to revel in the thought of a blessing, and yet not discern its force as a moral motive; to have an intense admiration of the principles of equity and love, and yet be a stranger to both the theory and the practice of them in the varied relations of life and the world." (Religion and Business, p. 6.) The highest idea of the religious man is plainly that which is sought after by the *amos*. A true reverence of divine sanctities proves itself by an equal reverence of human sanctities.

179. Men often suppose, that to rise into the religious life, it is necessary that they shall withdraw from intercourse with the world of secular things. Not so. It is realized better in society than in the hermitage; and the world, instead of being closed as a scene of pleasure, acquires new interest and value; it manifests power even to amend us. "Use the world," is the doctrine of purity. To forsake it, is ungrateful to God and prejudicial to our best interests. The truly religious man cannot see how it is a proof of piety to emasculate his natural instincts. He knows how to be both "merry and wise," and that it is religious to be so. Those who make destruction of the common affections of our

nature the condition of rising to God, confound use with abuse, will with wilfulness. The value and importance of the sensuous life are such as it is almost impossible to overrate. The evil consists in *staying* in it, or rather in neglecting to engraft upon it a higher life. There is nothing in the spirit of religion hostile to cheerful enjoyment of the world. Dissipation and unlawful pleasures unquestionably it prohibits, and also that unlawful degree of attachment to pleasures in themselves pure and innocent which withdraws the attention from the fulfillment of duty. But it never seeks to forbid pleasure, or to demand the renunciation of anything that it is of real advantage to us to possess, however intensely secular. Pleasure in every form, is good in itself. It is the sweet allurement with which God, the all-wise, and the all-good, surrounds useful things and needful acts, in order that we may seek and perform them. It is not pleasure which corrupts men, but men who corrupt pleasure; rightly regarded, it leads men, not *away from* God and religion, but *towards* them; resembling, in this respect, the sun and stars, which never tempted and diverted men to that idolatry we read of, but began to be worshiped only when men were idolaters already. In becoming religious, in fact, so far from losing anything, we gain, and often where least expected. Nature, art, science, poetry, music, shape a very different experience to the religious and to the non-religious. No man can perceive their more excellent beauties unless he give his heart to what is beautiful morally. As light and heat come together in the sunbeam, so, as a law, do elevated intellectual perceptions connect themselves with virtue of desire and deed. *Ubi charitas, ibi claritas.* "Blessed are the pure in heart, for they shall see God," is a promise applying to this world no less than to the next; for to "see" God, is to be sensible of His immediate presence, and this depends on no outward change, no shifting in time and place, but on adaptation of one's heart. So with the glorious promise of the new heaven and the new earth. Whatever kind of cosmological fulfillment it may be intended to have, and whatever deep spiritual meanings may be enclosed in it, it is a promise realized by every man who looks forth upon the universe with the eyes and heart of religion. When in the 65th chapter of Isaiah, our Lord says in reference to his advent to those who seek him,—"I create new heavens and a new earth," he means, as the event proves, not that he literally reconstructs the world and sky, but that by filling the soul with his divine love, it sees everything after a more admirable manner. If, therefore, a man would read creation in its fullness,—if he would thoroughly appreciate what nature and art have to offer, his best preparation is observance of the precepts of faith to God and charity to the neighbor. "To know nature, thou must be true to nature. To be true to nature, thou must live looking forever to the mighty Spirit who presides."* Nature has been well said to have an exhaustless meaning; but it is a meaning to be rightly seen and heard only by him who strives, ceaselessly and prayerfully, to become all that the Divine image and likeness is capable of becoming, which is, in fact, to become human and religious. Human nature is like a microscope; every step in its regeneration is an additional lens, enabling us to see more beautifully and profoundly. "As we become more truly human," says an amiable writer, "the world becomes to us more truly divine. Light from heaven must beam upon the world within, before the outward works of God will appear in the perfection of beauty. It is only when reason has acquired motive to look beyond outward sight, and is enabled to dwell on a brighter futurity, that the present world becomes fully sig-

---

* Panthea, or the Spirit of Nature, by Robert Hunt, p. 24.

nificant."* Religion is the green mountain-slope which commands the incomparable view. Blessed are they who find it. As the light we admire on the discs of the moon and planets is not their own, but the sun's, so the beauty of outward nature is from heaven through humanity. Form can only be duly estimated when we are capable of sympathizing with the spirit: no man can go further than his own measure; the small and weak therefore no further than the small and weak: only from the height of our own nature can we see the height of *others'* nature, or of the world's; some men see no beauty in the Venus. To be a physiognomist therefore, in regard either to the face of nature or the face of man, needs first that we be great-souled; else we cannot possibly compass the greatness of that we contemplate. No bad, conceited, or affected man can ever be a physiognomist; Nature and the soul are things altogether beyond his grasp. The whole matter is contained in the ancient canon that every scripture is to be interpreted by the same spirit which sent it forth;—a canon so essentially fundamental in philosophy, that every fresh acknowledgment seems an unconscious echo of those before. "In order," says Plotinus, "to direct the view aright, it behooves that the beholder shall make himself congenerous and similar to the object beheld. Never could the eye have beheld the sun, had not its own essence been soliform (*i. e.* pre-configured to light by a similarity of essence with that of light); neither can a soul not beautiful attain to an understanding of beauty."† What but an expansion of this, is that delicious little book, The Ministry of the Beautiful?‡ "The thickest night cannot veil the

* The use of the Body in relation to the Mind, by Dr. Moore, p. 162.

† Ennead 1, Book 6, "Of the Beautiful." (Page 57, F G. Ed. Ficini.)

‡ By H. J. Slack. 1852.

beauty and mystery of nature one-tenth part so effectually as a low moral state. Divinest forms in vain present themselves to eyes whose mechanism communicates with no recipient soul. Beauty without is the reflection of love and obedience within. To the true worshiper nature exhibits beauty and sublimity, where to the irreverent is barrenness and vacuity. Two men may live on the same spot, one dwelling in an Eden garden, sparkling with fountains, odorous with the loveliest flowers, full of celestial sounds, while the other is in a desert, the abode of uncleanness and desolation. In proportion as a man developes beauty within, does he find it without." Emerson follows in words of gold:—"The problem," says he, "of restoring to the world original and eternal beauty, is solved by the redemption of the soul. The ruin or the blank that we see in nature is in our own eye. The axis of vision is not coincident with the axis of things, and so they appear not transparent, but opaque. The reason why the world lacks unity is, that man is disunited from himself. A life in harmony with nature, the love of truth and virtue, will purge the eyes to understand her text, so that the world shall be to us an open book, and every form significant of its hidden life and final cause." Thus eloquently and variedly is it testified that in the degree that we become sensible of the charms of virtue, our hearts open to the true seeing of those that are physical; in other words, that a man's opinion of the world is always in proportion to his own comeliness. All who *do* see the world from such a stand-point are Poets. To become virtuous is to open the eyes to poetic sights; and conversely, before a man can be a poet, or at all events, a true and great poet, he must have a loving and religious heart.* An immoral

---

* Almost a truism, from the variety of authors in which this idea may be found expressed; its earliest occurrence appears to be in

genius is no genius, simply a man of talent. Such an one was Lord Byron. Shakspere, on the other hand, was of the highest moral purity, therefore capable of all the functions and rewards of poetry in the completest signification of the word. "The profundity and simplicity of his poetical view of life," as Ulrici finely remarks, "was simply on this account sublime and profound, *because it was Christian*, and Christian also, even because it was sublime and profound."* Not that Poetry and Religion are in any way synonymous or convertible. Delighting "to sit under the boughs of poetry, and to be washed by the surging waves of music," religion still carefully distinguishes itself from them. The one implies faith in a Saviour, the other simply love for a Creator.

180. To realize these things, it is not necessary that a man should be always thinking about what is spiritual and religious, any more than that he should quit the world of sensuous enjoyment. Doing so, he could not properly address himself to the details of his secular duties; but he should always have his mind *governed* by what is religious. Religion does not consist in forever busying one's self with religious ideas, in season and out of season; but in letting our knowledge of what is right, color and ensoul whatever we do. Unhappily, in many minds, it has been made to consist too much in the performance of certain ceremonies, acknowledging God at stated hours, speaking on given subjects in a certain way; to be, in a word, not what in its

---

Strabo, about the middle of his first book. (P. 17, Ed. Cassaubon, 1620.)

* Shakspere's Dramatic Art, and his relation to Calderon and Goethe, p. x. See also p. 118. Those foolish people who are better able to see ignorance and impiety in Shakspere, than wisdom and virtue, are provided in the pages which follow, with the completest explanations to be desired.

purity it really is—a *temper*, but a *pursuit*. The consequence is that to a great extent it is shut up in the church at the close of service, and left there till Sunday comes round again. The *week*-days are the true periods for religious action, which, rightly understood, is doing as we would be done by, and performing acts of Christian usefulness; while Sunday, in the proper idea of it, is a day for receiving and communicating specific instruction in sacred things, and joining with our brethren in the externals of ritual worship. If it be possible to carry pride, selfishness, avarice, cheerfulness, diligence, into the execution of our daily work, it is quite as competent to us to carry into it a religious spirit, without which, in fact, religious action is merely show. Two things are greatly to be distrusted in regard to religion—an inactive profession, and rigor and multitude of ceremonials, which latter, with the truly religious, are nevertheless observed, and even more sedulously, only with this distinction, that they are without advertisement to the world. "True religion," as Charles Lamb tells us, "prescribes a kind of grace, not only before meals, but before setting out for a pleasant walk, for a moonlight ramble, for a pleasant meeting; a grace before reading any author that delights us."*

181. Being the highest kind of life, the Religious is that to which Scripture chiefly alludes. Jesus, in particular, rarely speaks of man's animal, organic life; he concerns himself with what vitalizes the soul, and introduces it to immortality in heaven. When life in the sense of the future state is referred to in the Bible, it always implies antecedent religious life on earth; *necessarily* so, because no man can live in heaven who has not first lived religiously here. Religion is a marriage in the soul, and in heaven there is neither marrying nor giving in marriage. It must

* *Elia*, "Grace before Meat."

be consummated in this life, if at all. No one who is accustomed to peruse the Word of God attentively is a stranger to these things. For completeness' sake some few illustrations may nevertheless be adduced, *i. e.*, of the word "life," as used in its sense of the religious. "He that hath the Son, hath *life;* and he that hath not the Son, hath not life." "Keep my commandments and *live.*" "He that followeth after righteousness and mercy findeth *life.*" "To be carnally-minded is death, but to be spiritually-minded is *life.*" "In the pathway of righteousnesss is *life;* in the pathway thereof there is no death." The same is meant in all such expressions as "enter into *life,*" "light of *life,*" "word of *life,*" "bread of *life;*" where it is plain that something is intended far higher, far more transcendental, than can be identified or connected with mere animal, temporal vitality. Every such passage must of course be interpreted on its own basis and by its own context; to read them aright, however, we should act on the admirable maxim of Bishop Heber, that the best means of understanding any single passage of Scripture is to acquire an intimate and long acquaintance with the whole of the sacred volume. It is instructive to observe that the terms used to denote life in the original languages of the Bible, announce on the very face of the matter, that different ideas of it are intended. Thus, in the New Testament, while the animal, temporal life is called ψυχὴ, the religious life, both as enjoyed here and as continued hereafter, is distinguished, almost uniformly as ζωὴ. Those who are interested in the Scriptural usages of the word life, will do well to consult a fine old volume, curiously and immensely learned, by Richard Brocklesby—"An Explication of the Gospel Theism, and the Divinity of the Christian Religion," Book iv. chap. 10, sect. 12, pp. 975—993. (1706.)

CHAPTER XVIII.

LIFE REALIZED BY ACTIVITY—ACTION THE LAW OF HAPPINESS.

182. As the operations and phenomena of physical life resolve universally into MOTION, so do those of the spiritual life into ACTIVITY. The reason is that the soul, like the body, and nature universally, is a subject of continual change, and depends upon its changes for all its energy and pleasures. Like the body again, it acts both secretly *within* itself, and externally, upon what environs it. The externalized activities are fulfillments of the inner, and are possible only as effects of them; the secret or interior ones form that sleepless life of desire, memory, and imagination, which gives so beautiful an assurance that we are immortal. Whatever we may seem to ourselves to be, we are never in reality unoccupied; the thinking powers and the affections may appear to be at rest, we may be quite unconscious that they are otherwise, but they never cease from action altogether; the spiritual heart, like the physical, is in ceaseless throb. That which we commonly call activity is thus only pictorial, and but a part of what we effect; the essential transpires beneath, in the silent chambers of the soul, and so restlessly that no exertion of body can ever set forth the half of it. To think is virtually to act; so are to love, to hope, to muse. Men are not to be considered idle because we do not see them incessantly working with their hands. That idleness exists there is no doubt, and that not a little

of it is utterly shameful; but we should be cautious how we charge idleness upon any man too hastily, for it often happens that the idlest to appearance are precisely those who work the hardest. Before a man is set down as idle, it should be asked what is his aptitude for *seeing;* for never since the world began, did an indolent heart and mind dwell in the same body with open eyes. The truly idle man is the selfish and unintellectual one, "spinning on his own axis in the dark." Still, it is by the vigor and effectiveness with which this essential activity of the soul is played forth into the world around that it is to be estimated; and unless we see signs and tokens of it in the shape of deeds, we are justified in slowness of acknowledgment. In fact, it becomes *real* only by impersonation into deed, for until thought and affection utter themselves on society, they are only inutile visions. As a man's health and strength are not determined by the bare circumstance of our knowledge that his blood is circulating, but by the energy with which we see him use his limbs and organs generally; so the life of the soul is to be judged of, not by its invisible dreamings, but by its outward, sensible manifestations. Reverie, though most wholesome services are sometimes wrought by it, is but the *phyllomania* or running to leaf of the soul; the exclusively right purpose of spiritual life is the blossom and fruit of external act. "By their fruits shall ye know them." We tell what a man *is*, or as it is well-phrased, what he is "made of," by what he *does;* not, however, by what he does once, or occasionally, fine as the deed may be, but by what he continues to do, and persists in doing, spite of all hindrances. Cleverness, parts, talent, so called, can be taken no account of till they come out. A man of mere "capacity undeveloped," as Emerson says, "is only an "organized day-dream with a skin on it." Genius itself is no genius if it stay in-doors. "Genius unexerted is no more genius than a bushel of acorns in a forest of oaks. There may be epics in men's brains, just as there are oaks in acorns, but the tree and the book must come out before we can measure them." A thing of names and definitions innumerable, Genius, whatever its particular attitude or features, is the highest development of the energy of the soul; its certificate and office, as with the great function of the body which corresponds to it, or the procreation of offspring, which is the highest development of physical energy, is that it again *imparts life;* but until life has sprung up under its mighty impulse, till we feel the world the richer for it, to call it genius is ridiculous and false. Genius is known by its *activity;* dumb and unprolific genius are but appellations of the want of it. Let none, then, stand still in the supposition that because the soul works, and works diligently, of its own accord, a lofty spiritual life will necessarily be present; nothing is vital and substantial till it be ultimated into body or performance. So completely is action identified with life, that it is the natural metaphor for its lapse and progress. *Agere,* to act, is used by Tacitus for "to live;" and to say that a person has lived thirty years, is the same as saying that he has *acted* thirty years.

183. That which is the truest sign of a thing is always its chief ornament and blessedness. Life, accordingly, is a delight just in the degree that it is consecrated to Action, or the conscious, volitional exercise of our noblest capabilities. Action and enjoyment are contingent upon each other; when we are unfit for work we are always incapable of pleasure; work is the wooing by which happiness is won. The exercise even of our most ordinary bodily functions is a source of pleasure—breathing, for example. If not directly recognized as such, it is simply because of its uninterruptedness, beautifully illustrating that in order to the complete sense of happiness in the soul, there must be *con-*

sciousness of being employed. All physical pleasures depend for the maximum of their delightfulness, on continual cessation and recurrence, often on slight movements and undulations, just sufficient to give keener edge to their renewal in the next instant; similarly, but in a far higher degree, all our spiritual, or mental and emotional pleasures, come of constant action, unceasingly recapitulated. So inseparably connected are the ideas of action and enjoyment, that whenever in nature we behold free movement, it awakens agreeable emotions; when, for example, in the calm air of a summer's evening we watch the insects weaving their mazy dances, we exclaim instinctively, how happy they are! In many languages, happiness and fruitfulness, both of them results and indications of activity, are denoted by the same word, as when the Latin poet calls the apple tree *felix*, the unproductive wild olive *infelix oleaster*. The proximate cause of this great interdependence is that man is a creature of unbounded Wants. It is Want that spurs us on to activity, in order that we may satisfy the want; were it possible for us to appease all wants as fast as they arise, we should be the most miserable and forlorn of beings. This is why we find such keener pleasure in the chase of an object than in the capture of it; why possession satisfies only in the degree that it is a new beginning. It is not, says Helvetius, in the having acquired a fortune, but in the acquiring it; not in having no wants, but in satisfying them; not in having been prosperous, but in prosperity, that happiness essentially consists. The miser grows old enjoying rather than wearied of life; the heir who comes into possession of his hoard dies of *ennui*;—unless he know beforehand, it should be added, wherein the advantage of wealth mainly consists, namely, in the power which it gives to an intelligent possessor to diversify and dignify his pursuits, and thus to multiply and ennoble his emotions, or practically, his wants.

184. In order that good and honorable wants shall always require a certain amount of exertion to appease them, and thus that our zeal shall be kept burning, all those things which humanity most needs are by a wise and benevolent Providence made the most difficult to procure. The silver is hidden and the gold is buried; every gift of the field requires man's coöperation before he can enjoy it; every truth, even of the most universal interest and the most practical tendency, has to be patiently and perseveringly inquired for. Nothing in the world that is worth having is gratis; everything has to be met half-way between God and ourselves; and the more our experience of Divine Providence enlarges, the more deeply do we feel how beneficent is the ordinance that it should be so; how inglorious and negative would be our destiny were there nothing left for us to effect as of ourselves. "Ask, and ye shall have," is equally true in its reverse; neglect to ask, and ye shall *not* have. Whatever God's awaiting privileges, everywhere the law is that they must be sought. Directly a tree neglects to assert its arboreity, it ceases to be a tree, and lapses into mould. Directly that a man falls into idleness and inactivity of soul, ceasing thereby from the true exercise of his human nature, he sinks into infelicity and animalism. A very simple formula comprises the whole matter; the re-action of man in response to the primary action of God, constitutes the vast blessedness it is to Live. "Did the Almighty," says Lessing, "holding in his right hand Truth, and in his left Search after Truth, deign to proffer me the one I should prefer, in all humility, but without hesitation, I should request Search after Truth." The most blessed of men is he who, working with his own hands for his daily bread, reaps delight from the exercise of his intelligence upon his toils, and feels a holy harmony between the munificence of God and the duties which pertain to himself. The dream

of an existence perennially workful, and yet sweet, free and poetic, such as has visited men in every age, is not so visionary as they have fancied, but it rests with the dreamer to clothe it in reality.

185. Without action there can be no cheerfulness—the prime need as well as token of a true and happy life. Doubtless there is a native, spontaneous cheerfulness of spirit, but that which keeps cheerfulness alive is nothing else than activity, sedulously addressed to some worthy end. This is a secret worth knowing, since without cheerfulness neither the intellect nor the affections can expand to their full growth, which is for life never to reach its proper altitude; while nothing is more surely fatal to it than gloom, moroseness, and discontent, unless it be the petty envyings, jealousies, and suspicions, the toadstools of the human heart, which sprout from the same foul soil, or indolent inactivity. Who are the people most generally given to talking scandal? Those who for want of some enlivening occupation become peevish and impatient, and know little or nothing about cheerfulness. Having nothing to agreeably engage the mind, the temptation to assume the office of censor over their neighbors is too strong to resist, the whole heart becomes tainted and purulent, and the very occupations that make others lively become an eye-sore. Every one has noticed the cheerfulness which comes of a little bustle in which all parties are concerned; how ill-tempers subside, and crossest faces become bland. A result as much more solid and graceful as the instrumentality is nobler, infallibly follows regular and solid devotion of the soul to aims that demand its best imaginings. The beginning of idleness is an *ignoble ruling love.* The wants which come of such a love are few and soon satisfied, since that which is lowest is always easiest to reach, and hence it is incessantly left destitute. Nothing so effectually prevents idleness as a noble

sympathy. The indolent rich, who fancy themselves weak and invalided when they are simply stagnant for want of a great purpose, would become sprightly and well directly, did they but enter on some genial and generous love, which would impel them into varied occupations. The very restlessness which frets them shows that action is the soul of life. Do something they *must;* this is a necessity they cannot evade, for absolute inactivity is impossible: it is nature's law that employment shall go on with every one in some sort; but in the degree that the inevitable something is mean and indeterminate, the end of the pursuit is mortifying and vain. God knows the means to make us work soberly and usefully. Do you see any one at a loss how to spend his time, undecided where to go, walking through dry places, seeking rest, and finding none? Be assured that individual finds existence a burden, and is a total stranger to its bloom and true emoluments. Many sights are melancholy, but none are worse than the listless, jaded countenances of those who have nothing worthy to devote their energies to. Yet these faces *could* beam with intelligence. Every man is happy by birth-right. It is his power to be happy that makes him able to be miserable; the capacity for *ennui* being, in fact, one of the signatures of his immortality. Why brutes never suffer *ennui* is simply because they are incapable of noble delights. How inexcusable it is, if not shameful and disgraceful, to have nothing but what is low and transitory to think about, and thus to fall into such a state of dullness, scarcely needs an observation. Were the world empty, were it a silent, barren waste, without a tree or a blade of grass, there might possibly be an excuse; but overflowing as it does with the most beautiful curiosities, nothing is so utterly indefensible as to let a single waking hour die blank. Thanks be to God, as soon as a man desires to seek, he is always enabled to find; directly he feels his heart and mind swell with a great desire, he finds the world ready and waiting to supply him. Even though busily engaged throughout the day in commercial or domestic avocations, the *dolce far niente* which our poor weariness is so apt to plead in the evening, and which no wise man ever refuses to listen to altogether, is a principle only to be admitted under the protest that the proper rest for man is *change of occupation*. There are few kinds of business which fatigue both body and mind at once; while one toils, the other almost necessarily reposes; when the one ceases work, nature rules that the other shall be fittest to begin; and that is a rare case indeed where either body or mind is debarred all opportunity of healthful and useful occupation when its turn to work comes on. Man is not so imperfectly constituted, nor is the world so defectively framed, as for him to be constrained to look for pastime and relaxation anywhere but in change from one improving employment to another; it may be questioned whether the sweetness of Home can ever be truly enjoyed where the leading recreation does not take the shape of some intelligent and pretty pursuit, such as the formation of an herbarium, or the use of the microscope or pencil. Boys would not incessantly be in mischief and trouble were they encouraged to study natural history; girls would be far livelier and companionable, and also enjoy better health, were they trained to fixed habits of mental employment. The delight of a single hour of recreation in art or science, outweighs a whole life-time of mere frivolities; before the picture of this delight, could it be brought home to him, the mere trifler would sink in dismay. Finding our pastime in such pursuits, we render ourselves independent of the casualties of time and place, and secure an arbor of our own, where none can molest. Accustoming ourselves to live in *ideas*, sorrow and misfortune lose their sting. We discover that though disappointed of our greatest and most cherished hopes, that is no reason why we should be impatient, or unhappy, or no longer given to pleasant wishes and desires. We get to live rather in that same kind of well-tempered hope and contentedness both in one, which leads men to plant trees for the future. "To have always," says D'Israeli, "some secret, darling idea to which we can have recourse amid the noise and nonsense of the world, and which never fails to touch us in the most exquisite manner, is an art of happiness that fortune cannot deprive us of." Many things may furnish such an idea; we have shown where they may be found. Nepenthe still grows plentiful and green; the world is full of sweet places where we may rest ourselves, and eat of the lotus. We have no need to court gaiety in order to be happy; nor yet a large circle of acquaintance. Few would longer trouble themselves about mere "diversions," were they once to feel what it is to possess the art of self-recreation among the untaxed gifts of nature.

186. While our leisure is honored and agreeably occupied by such pursuits, materials are acquired also for that most invaluable of the Fine Arts, the art of Conversation, destitute of which, no family or social circle can be thoroughly happy. Not that mere dry scientific facts of themselves can serve its purposes, because the best, most living part of conversation is emotional, imaginative, bird-like. Moreover, the richest conversation may be and often is wholly independent of such facts. But where brothers and sisters have each their tale to tell of something curious or interesting seen in the day's progress, and have a common interest in each other's discoveries and acquisitions, the imagination soon finds wing, and the heart soon warms. To learn how to talk, let people learn how to *do* something, and get those about them to do the same. Of all the unbecoming things which true education would seek to anticipate and prevent,

that weak gossip about persons and clothes, eating and *faux pas*, which generally passes current as conversation, is the first that demands to be corrected. With the lover of noble employment, leisure indeed, either for trifling talk, or for trifles of any kind, exists no longer. No one ever wants to "kill time" who has fixed, intelligent work in hand. He very soon discovers that to kill time is to kill *himself*. The time-killer, the mere trifler, condemns it in his own looks, for he always seems *ashamed*. We never find him, like Archimedes, shouting *ευρήκα!* Such declarations of honorable joy are the privilege of the wisely active in liberal arts; no man, says Plutarch, was ever heard to cry out after a luxurious meal, *βέβρωκα!* or after another form of sensual pleasure, *πεφίληκα!* Briefly, to make itself happy is a duty which every created being, in proportion to its capacity, owes to itself and to God; one of the chief characteristics of moral health, Lord Bacon tells us, is a "constant quick sense of felicity, and a noble satisfaction;" felicity, in its highest signification, implies all that can ennoble, while it excites our minds; idleness and trifling, though they may excite, can never by any possibility ennoble; hence are the workers on intelligent pursuits, at once the dutiful to God, the healthy in soul, the happy ones of their race. *Si non ingentem*, as Virgil says, "if they have not vestments curiously embroidered with gold, and if for them the white wool is not stained with the Assyrian dye—

At secura quies, et nescia fallere vita,
Dives opum variarum,—

"Yet theirs is peace secure, and a life of solid, unfallacious happiness, rich in various opulence."

187. Scientific and artististic recreations, pursued either purely on their own account, or with a view to agreeable

intellectual intercourses, by no means demand the intense application that many suppose. Neither is a little knowledge the dangerous thing which others often fear. The infirmity is not to have only a little, but to fancy that that little is a great deal. Neither are brilliant talents wanted; a very moderate capacity will soon carry us out to sea. Nor, again, is there that incongruity between scientific recreations and the ordinary duties of life which is not infrequently alleged. "Business must be attended to," is one of the best and safest maxims in the world; a man, as Dr. Johnson said, is never more usefully employed than when earning money. There is another maxim, however, fully as important, and founded upon as great a principle, and that is, the *intervals* of business must be attended to, implying that there is none of the incongruity supposed. No one can sharpen his intellectual faculties, or widen the range of his knowledge, without becoming more skilful and successful in the business or profession in which he is engaged. Whatever tends to cheer the understanding in leisure moments, so far from being in antagonism to business thoughts, is complementary to them, and gives them zest. It is doubtful whether any man can heartily enjoy the country who does not spend a large part of every week in town-work; and no less questionable whether any one so thoroughly enjoys business as he who turns to it as a change. The same principle applies to literary recreations. How long is the list of men distinguished in commerce, who have also shone in letters, even in literature sparkling with imagination! The late Mr. Roby, of Rochdale, author of the Traditions of Lancashire, is a memorable example. Mr. Roby, says his biographer, "was not inapt for the addition sum of the banker because he delved into legendary lore, or rushed into the realms of the imagination. He showed in his various performances that the poetic temperament is not in antagonism to the duties of life; a truth the sooner recognized the better. Many of our best writers are not professionally so; they sweeten a life of physical labor by intellectual activity, and society reaps the double harvest. In his ordinary life the author is but an ordinary man, and it is a monstrous exaggeration to suppose as many do, that he is always walking with his head among the stars and his feet among the flowers. It would not be difficult to show that the man who is engaged during the day in what are commonly called unintellectual employments, or in semi-intellectual ones, such as buying, selling, and casting accounts, has a decided advantage in his leisure moments, *cæteris paribus*, over him who has wholly to *think*.

188. Employment, therefore, does not mean no amusement; the workers, or those who use their time instead of wasting it, have more holidays than any one else, for every change is a going out to play. When rational and unsophisticated, play, commonly so called, is still work; at all events, no man ever played genially and heartily without gaining something by it, and thus gathering from it a fruition of work. Play, moreover, is perfectly compatible with work; let no one suppose that art and science disallow it, or that they render play uninteresting and distasteful. Pastime and fun are as great a need as occupation, and as great a luxury. He who refuses to play is but a stately fool; to sport and gambol with children is one of the sweetest lyric songs of life; grown people, however, should remember that as the end of all exertion, even the slightest, should be profit, play should always be based upon an intelligent idea. People may be mirthful without being silly, just as they may be grave without being gloomy; a mind in right order can descend into frolics as readily as it can soar into magnificent ideas; for it is the characteristic of well-disciplined intelligence, and of purity and earnestness of the affections, that

they are universal in their capacity. It is this which makes the *philosopher;* the true idea of whom is that of an amiable and pious man, who with the profound and scientific combines the lively and the droll. "My idea of wise men," says some author, "needs that they shall be very lively: I don't call dull men wise." Plato and Aristotle were not always seen in their long robes, dignified and serious. No; they were good-natured fellows, who enjoyed a laugh with their friends like the rest of the world, and who loved, and hoped, and listened to a good story with as much zest as the least learned. "As much" did we say? Culture of mind enables us to enjoy far more intensely when enjoyment is afloat than when our heads are ill-provided. Love-poetry owes to Plato a more exquisite stroke of nature than ever was penned by a mere writer of songs and valentines:—"While kissing Agathon, I had my soul upon my lips, for it came, the hapless, as if about to depart." Many persons, it is true, live *without* amusement; grave, dull, would-be moralists and sages; and certainly, pastime is not so indispensably necessary after the mental and physical constitutions have arrived at maturity, as before. It by no means follows, however, that such persons would not live happier and more useful lives if they resorted occasionally to the ordinary sports of mankind. None ever decry play and fun but those who are strangers to their value. The love of them is one of the signs of a great nature. All true genius is in its very essence, a *joyous* faculty; "wit" originally signifies the very highest efforts of mind. It is only by looking around as well as upwards that a large and just conception of life is attainable, and therefore that life is truly realized. "A mind charged with vitality, and sustained by trust in God, will not only look cheerfully to the goal of its pilgrimage, but have ample stores of gladness to expend upon the journey. The Muses have left no diaries, or doubtless we should find that they had their gipsy-parties and lively games; that they danced and sang for pure enjoyment; and visited mortal dreamers not only in inspiring vision, but sometimes to

'Tickle men's noses as they lay asleep.' "

In a word, though recreation with science and literature be the most solid and unfailing kind of play, it is not the only kind we need. With all his toil, and care, and penury of time, the man who devotes himself to learning, or science, or business, is no gainer in the end, if he do not take part sometimes in lively entertainments. For a while he may seem to suffer nothing; but the belief of his being able to dispense with such playing is only a delusion; there is a heavy reckoning going on against him, which sooner or later will have to be paid in suffering and premature exhaustion. Work and play are reciprocally advantageous. While without due play, there is no effective working, on the other hand, in order to play heartily with the body, we must learn how to play heartily, in privacy, with the soul. No man thoroughly enjoys play, or knows what play really is, who cannot spend hours of solitude in comfort.

189. In the degree that we employ ourselves, we acquire Power. As nature, ever shifting and transforming, is most beautiful and delicious when it is not strictly either spring, or summer, or autumn,—morning, noon, evening, or night; so, all the potency we ever possess, is referable to our moments of action, or when we are experiencing or effecting Changes; the period of *transition* is that in which power is developed; to acquire and to wield it, we must be forever seeking to quit the state we are in, and to rise into a higher one. Power, accordingly, which is only life under another name, is resolvable, essentially, into constant progression. It never consists in the *having been*, but always in the

becoming; we flourish in proportion to our desire to emerge out of To-day. It is often asked concerning a stranger, Where does he come from? The better question would be, *Where is he going to?* Never mind the antecedents, if he be now in some shining pathway. Other people are continually heard wishing to be "settled." It may be useful to be settled as to our physical resources; but to be settled in any other way is the heaviest misfortune that can befall a man, for when settled, he ceases to improve, and is like a ship stranded high and dry upon the sand. Who is the man from whose society and conversation we derive soundest pleasure and instruction? Not he who, as it is facetiously said, has "completed his education," but he who, like a bee, is daily wandering over the fields of thought. The privilege of living and associating with a person who knows how to think, and is not afraid to think, is inestimable; and nowhere is it felt more profoundly than in the intimate companionship of wedded life. Rousseau finds in this need a beautiful argument for inspiring one's beloved, during the sweet, plastic days of betrothal, with a taste for the amenities of nature, such as shall provide a source in after years, of lasting and mutual delight. How pleasing, when many summers of married love have thrown those hallowed days far into the rear, to note again the uncurling ferns of spring, wrapped so comfortably in their curious brown scales; the pretty scarlet hedge-strawberries gathered for her hand, the delicate mosses, and the hundred other objects then first noticed, objects which set both mind and lips in action, invoking currents of sweet converse, kindling looks from which we turned to the sunshine for relief, and opening the way to long trains of agreeable and profitable contemplation, enlarged with every new impulse to mutual tenderness. The being *afraid* to think is the chief reason perhaps why the majority of people are so disinclined to think—to think, that is, beyond the little circle of their bodily wants. There can be few who are positively *unable* to think; otherwise thought and happiness would not bear the close natural relation which they do. Put a grand idea before the generality of people, and it seems to them like looking up a ship's mast from the deck. Yet it is not that they cannot ascend, using the proper means; they let themselves be terrified away, fancying they are unable, when they are merely self-distrustful. Doubtless there is a difference in aptitude, but every one may become stronger if he will; the worst unbelief is unbelief in one's self; it only needs confidence and a start; whatever we may get from others, or from the world, has grown from germs such as we have also in ourselves—whence it is that in our reading we are so continually coming up with ideas that we feel to be our own; nor is there anything more beautiful in creation than each man's own private soul, when fairly dealt with and elicited. Helen, when she explored nature for a model of a golden cup that she should offer upon the altar of Diana as perfectly beautiful, found nothing more exquisite than her own bosom.

190. Practically then—for to bring us to some practical conclusion is the sole use of such considerations—we learn from the great law of Action the spring of Happiness, that to encourage love of work is the first article of sensible Education. In effect, this is the stimulating of the Intellect and the Affections which has already been adverted to under other heads. All action, to be efficacious for good, must rise into a certain intensity; it must also be regular and determinate, and it is only training and culture that can make it so. As in the structure of plants and animals, where any organ is deficient, or there is departure from symmetry, it is uniformly referable to a weakening of the vital energies, or to restraint or diversion of them away from their proper office; so when our experience of life is

infelicitous and unrewarding, it is because the natural activity of the soul has either been repressed, or neglected, or turned astray in early youth. The unhappy are those "who from want of practice cannot manage their thoughts, who have few to select from, and who, because of their sloth or weakness, do not roll away the heaviest," and these are precisely the individuals whom observation would perceive to be laboring under imperfect discipline of the spiritual activities, dating from the very commencement of education. Ordinarily, to the young, work is rendered so unattractive, and the idea of pleasure so entirely dissevered from it, that the first wears the semblance of a penalty, and the latter of the true object of existence. This is to completely neutralize the design of work, and to despoil life of its highest luxuries. Pleasure is not bestowed on us to be made a *motive;* still less is it to be deemed, as by many, a *right* of human existence, and its non-arrival an exhibition of Divine injustice. What we ought to let reign in our minds, is primarily, *work*, which translates itself, in every true soul, into the *duty of development.* Let the præludia of stem and foliage be made the business, and the flowers will come of their own accord, and fill the air with fragrance. "In teaching," says the good Jean Paul, "accustom the boy to regard his future, not as a path from pleasures, though innocent, to other pleasures; nor even as a gleaning, from spring-time to harvest, of flowers and fruits; but as a time in which he must execute some long plan; let him aim at a long course of *activity*—not of pleasure." Then he shows how privileged is such a course: "That man is happy, for instance, who devotes his life to the cultivation of an island, to the discovery of one that is lost, or to the extent of the ocean. I would rather be the court-gardener who watches and protects an aloe for fifteen years, until at last it opens to him the heaven of its blossom, than the prince who is hastily called to look at the opened heaven. The writer of a dictionary rises every morning, like the sun, to move past some little star in his zodiac; a new letter is to him a new year's festival, the conclusion of an old one a harvest-home." Bodily health, as well as spiritual, depends on work. Very many of the complaints so frequently heard from the delicate young women of our day, as want of vigor, inability to bear exposure, deficiency of strength to walk far, may be traced to other and earlier causes than supposed, settling at last into absence of well-trained mental power, such as would seek an outlet in useful and agreeable occupation. But mental power, let them understand, is not to be gained from *senseless fiction*, which leading, as it is almost sure to do in the end, to discontented dreams of what might have been, or should be, keeps the heart away from thankful perception and enjoyment of what *is;* it is to be got from no such miserable waste of time as this; but from steady and well-directed reading of stories *not* fictitious, and from steady and systematic contemplation of the works of nature. Seeking to improve themselves as intelligent beings, our young ladies would not half as often want the doctor. Rational work they would find, moreover, less fatiguing than the very pastimes which they fancy true enjoyment. Under proper management, work never becomes irksome. When prematurely fatigued, it is not the action that has tired us, but want of ingenious and orderly methods. Work never killed or hurt any man who knew how to go about it. See what order there is in nature! Along with sublimest activity, what smoothness and ease! How still the growth of the plant, yet how rapid! How peacefully the stars of midnight seem encamped; yet before morning whole armies have disappeared! So much is achieved, because everything is done in order, at the right time, intently, yet deliberately, and the minutes never wasted in indecision. In work, then, consists the true pride of life. Grounded in active employment, though early ardor may abate, it never degenerates into indifference; and age, as we have said before, lives in perennial youth. Life is a weariness only to the idle, or where the soul is empty, and better than to exist thus vacantly, is it for longevity as to birth-days to be denied.

191. The consideration of this great principle, Action the spring of Happiness, though it is in regard to the present life that it practically concerns us, belongs as largely to right estimates of the life to come. Doubtless, the means by which we secure enjoyment upon earth, instruct us as to the proximate source of the enjoyments that will be felt in heaven, a subject that cannot be uninteresting to any man who reflects for a moment how long he hopes to live there. That the same re-action of man, in response to the primary action of God, which *here* makes life and happiness, will similarly engender it hereafter, we may gather, indeed, most plainly, from the divine oracles themselves. When we are told so consolingly, that to die is to go to rest, and that "Blessed are the dead who die in the Lord, for they rest from their labors," it is not meant that by entering the future state we enter on a state of passiveness. There can be no happiness or holiness, even in heaven, if the life be one of mere quiescence. Do we not see, even in this world, that those who would have us understand by Remember the Sabbath-day to keep it *holy*, Remember to keep it *idle*, i. e., idle as regards everything but religious discipline; do we not see, even in this world, that they prescribe a course against which all nature rebels, and which fails from its very absurdity? How much more impossible will it be to keep holy the everlasting sabbath, except by supplementing its peculiar duties of praise and worship with useful and benevolent occupations. The labors which will be "rested from"

are the resistance of temptations, the endurance of trials, the struggles with evil, which incessantly harass our temporal existence; all our chosen and happier activities will continue, in a more glorious manner, and with the *perfect* results which on earth are unattainable. The best and wisest of mankind have always had a conviction that it will be so. "He felt," says the memoir of Dr. Gordon, "that there would be no interval of unconsciousness, no cessation of activity, no intermission of enjoyment; that though the mode of existence would be changed, the existence itself would be neither destroyed nor suspended."* We may learn much from the very term that Scripture employs. It is never said that we shall rest from our *work*, only from "labor." Labor is that exertion which is irksome and painful; work that which is congenial, welcome, a delightful exercise. Labor is the toil of the soul and body upon things in opposition to them; work is the bestowal of their best energies on what pleases and recompenses. Work, rightly understood, is divine, and nothing that is divine can ever cease. It is divine because it comes out of the inmost spirit of goodness and love, and thus, primarily, from God, whereas indolence and laziness come of the very essence of evil. Who is the greatest workman in the universe? He who works, from out of His infinite Love, for the smallest insect as well as the immortal angel. That the wicked are often diligent, more diligent, possibly, than many of the good, is no objection; because the diligence of such does not come of their evil, as to its own intrinsic nature, but of its *necessities;* work must be done in order that the means may be procured whereby the appetites of the evil shall be indulged. The idea of an idle heaven is a very low and unintelligent one: it could only have arisen with the indolent upon earth; and

---

* The Christian Philosopher triumphing over Death, p. 177.

wherever found, we may be sure there is an indolent spirit underneath. Heaven, like the Lord himself, who to the pure appears pure, who to the merciful appears merciful, is measured by each man according to his own character and inclinations, and if we would ask which view is nearer to the truth, we may be sure it is that which most exalts us. If true life consist in well-directed activity while we are here, assuredly the continuation of our life in heaven will derive its blessedness, in no slight degree, from the new and magnificent opportunities it will there enjoy. There will be an external world of nature to study, consisting of that inexhaustible store of spiritual objects and phenomena which forms the scenery of the spiritual world, and which is the prototype of the material worlds and their contents, and inviting us to endless research and contemplation; there will also be good uses to fulfill, the prototypes of practical charity and affection upon earth, and which will be largely directed, there is every reason to believe, to the spiritual needs of the successive and interminable generations of men. Angel, literally "messenger," is not so much a designation of nature, as commonly supposed, as a title or name of office; and no office can be conceived more superb than that of aiding and protecting souls still upon their pilgrimage. That such functions are exercised, in other words, the doctrine of the "ministration of angels," has soothed and encouraged the virtuous of every age; the Grecian belief in δαιμονες or invisible attendant *genii*, was itself a recognition of the guardianship of that celestial fraternity, the "bright band" which gave cause to Archdeacon Hare to say so beautifully, that while it is blessed to have friends on earth, it is yet *more* blessed to have friends in heaven. Leigh Hunt, speaking of Shelley (whose virtues we should do well to remember before his failings), acknowledges this fine sentiment in the most exquisite manner; "Alas! and he suffered for years, as Ariel did in the cloven pine; but now he is out of it, and serving the purposes of Beneficence with a calmness befitting his knowledge and his love." Thus is our destiny, even in this world, sublime, if we will but serve God, and not Mammon. For the "spirits of just men made perfect" then come into company with us; they "encamp" around us, and "minister" to us, even as they themselves are ministered to by the Lord. It is no mere fancy of a fond mother that the smile of her sleeping infant comes of the angels' whisper. So lovely an idea would not live among the hallowed ones were it not the reflection of a heaven-sent truth; when the heart in its thankful musings lifts itself towards the skies, it is never sent away with a falsehood in it. Wonderful has been the effect upon mankind even of this little ministry. It was the smiling in her sleep of Benjamin West's infant niece that led him, though quite a boy, to use the pencil. He was placed to watch the cradle, and struck by the innocent smiles of his little charge, drew her as she lay.

CHAPTER XIX.

DEATH IN RELATION TO THE SPIRITUAL-LIFE.

192. If life be realized only in the degree that it is happy, then is an infelicitous existence only a kind of death; and the man who experiences it, though he may walk about, eat, drink, and sleep like other men—virtually, and as regards all the true idea and design of life, is dead. It sounds strangely, but if there be a state of spirit which it is right, preëminently, to call Life, by reason of its excellence and exaltation, the contrary condition can be no other than what we have said. Life is where there are hope, faith, reverence, sense of the beautiful, the sentiment of religion; death is where these are absent or extinguished. Death, in fact, like Life, is no unitary thing; there are as many ways of dying as of living, and as the highest kinds of life are those which belong to and express themselves in the Soul, in the Soul, too, are suffered the bitterest of deaths. In childhood we do not know this. Death's heaviest shafts seem to be those which fall on things external to us, as parents, friends, companions; but as our experience enlarges, we discover that no death is so sad, no death so momentous in its consequences, as the death of the things which die *within*. So true is this, that often the greatest epoch in a man's life is by no means the day of his physical death, but the day in which he has died to something more important to him than the whole world. "That which has died within us," says Hare, "is often the saddest portion of what Death

has taken away—sad to all, sad above measure to those in whom no higher life has been awakened. The heavy thought is the thought of what we were, of what we hoped and purposed to have been, of what we ought to have been, of what but for ourselves we might have been, set by the side of what we are, as though we were haunted by the ghost of our own youth. This is a thought the crushing weight of which nothing but a strength above our own can lighten." Death, accordingly, in its most sorrowful sense, is not the death of the body, but the death of feelings and ideas—the death of our *love.* For when men say that they have no "spirit" for a thing, or no "heart" for it, it is only another way of saying that they have no "love," which is practically to have no "life" for it. Spirit is breath, and the heart is figuratively the blood, and by the breath and the blood all life is circled in. So with the expressions "dead to hope," "dead to enjoyment," "dead to enterprise." Those who are thus lifeless are they who, having lost their property, or their animal pleasures, or who, having had their worldly schemes defeated, and have found no better things to set their affections on, have *lost their love,* for life is union with the object of our love. "Nabal's heart died within him, and he became a stone." How sublime a contrast where those better things have been acquired!

Soft was the voice of the priest, and he spoke with an accent of kindness,
But on Evangeline's heart fell his words as in winter the snow-flakes
Fall into some lone nest from which the birds have departed.

* * * * *

So was her love diffused, but like to some odorous spices,
Suffered no waste nor loss, though filling the air with aroma.
Other hopes she had none, nor wish in life, but to follow
Meekly, with reverent steps, the sacred feet of her Saviour.

Of all sad things in the world, the saddest yet is that which, living to appearance, in soul is dead. Not only in human beings is it witnessed: towns, countries, institutions, may lie dead, though alive, as pictured in that wonderful passage in the Giaour, so beautiful in the midst of its inexpressible mournfulness, where the still and melancholy aspect of the once busy and glorious shores of Greece is compared to the features of the dead,—

> Ere the first day of death hath fled.
>
> * * * *
>
> Such is the aspect of this shore,
> 'Tis Greece, but *living* Greece no more!

Every man experiences a measure of such death. Every "mortification" we endure is literally "a death." Secularly, at least, if not in the higher sense of the words, like the flowers of the Cistus, we "die daily;" and the more that the temporal is loved, the more does the death afflict. For it is of attempting to love the transitory and perishable—so far as it is capable of being loved—and thus of loving what is only a continual vicissitude, that death of spirit comes. That which undergoes vicissitude has only a seeming life in it, and therefore the love of it, so far as it is worthy the name of love, can never uphold itself into a true and felicitative life, for this comes only of loving the unchangeable. "Before the eye of Truth," says Fichte, "all life which finds its love in the temporary, and seeks its enjoyment in any other object than the eternal and unchangeable, is vain and unblessed, because it loves only death."

193. What we have chiefly spoken of is the death of feelings having relation to temporal and external things; far more solemn and momentous is the death of those which have relation to morals and religion. Both kinds might be contemplated as to the place of their *beginning*, which is

likewise twofold, *i. e.*, in the intellect or in the affections. The duality in the springs of life involves duality in the place of death. As physical death is referable either to the heart or to the lungs, so is spiritual death referable either to the will or the understanding, and is marked by correspondent phenomena. "The ἀπολιθώσις or petrifaction of the soul," says Epictetus, "is double; in the one case it is stupified in its intellectuals; the other is when it is dead in its morals. He who is thus dead, is not to be disputed with." But there is no need to analyze so minutely. It is sufficient to distinguish between death to what is good, and death to what is bad, whether of an intellectual or an emotional character. The Scriptural expressions of being "dead *in* trespasses and sins," and of being "dead *to* sin," exactly illustrate the difference. In every age there has been a perception that real death consists in loss of wisdom and virtue. "It is a doctrine of immemorial antiquity that the real death pertains to those who on earth are immersed in the Lethe of its passions and fascinations, and that the real life commences only when the soul is emancipated from them." Evil and falsity bring spiritual life to an end, just as diseases do animal life. "What then are we to say?" concludes Philo. "Surely that death is of two kinds—the one being the death of the man; the other, the peculiar death of the soul. The death of the man is the separation of the soul from the body; the death of the soul is the destruction of virtue and the admission of vice."* Aristophanes, in a well-known passage, calls the depraved citizens of Athens "dead men," and founded, no doubt, on the correspondence thus acknowledged, was the belief among his countrymen and other ancient nations, that to see or touch dead bodies was a great pollution. Jodrell gives numerous

---

* Allegories of the Sacred Laws, Book i., end.

illustrations, both from historical and poetic sources, (iii. 15.) In the ancient Jewish law, for the same original reason, it was one of the things required to be followed up by "cleansing." "This is the law, when a man dieth in a tent, all that come into the tent, and all that is in the tent, shall be unclean seven days." * Vice as identified with death, is not necessarily vice in its baser forms, or crime; it is wilful violation of the laws of God, whether externalized into criminal act or not; and it is this which is chiefly intended by "death" in Scripture. "Life" is attainment of union with God, founded on reconciliation with one's self; "death" is secession from truth and goodness. When, for instance, Christ says that he shall come to judge "the quick and the dead," the meaning is, all mankind, both good and evil. So when David exclaims, "In death there is no remembrance of thee," he intends, those who cease to obey God, cease also to think of God. "Lighten mine eyes, lest I sleep the sleep of death," is a prayer to quicken the soul with new aptitude for sacred things. It is the very same death which is intended in the parable of the Prodigal Son—"For this my son was dead, and is alive again;" and which the Apostle alludes to when he says, "We know that we have passed from death unto life." In its direst degree, this is the death which on the other side of the grave becomes "hell," and which begins it even in this world. It is by no metaphor that men who have steeped themselves in iniquities, cry out that they suffer the tortures of the pit. As no man enters heaven after the death of the material body, but he who has received heaven into his soul in this life; so "hell" is an intensifying and consolidating forever, of infernal states that

* Numbers xix. 14. See also chap. vi., and Leviticus, chaps. xv., xxi., &c.

have already been sunk into. "Though this a heavenly angel," exclaims Iachimo, looking at Imogen asleep,

> "Though this a heavenly angel, *hell is here.*"

Death, in Scripture, when signifying death to virtue, potentially means also the eternal perdition of the soul, as in James v. 20, whence it is that we are so earnestly urged to fly from it, seeing that after the dissolution of the material body, ability to escape is at an end.

194. Death to what is evil is *rejuvenescence.* Though consecrated by use in Scripture, it is a mode of expression, therefore, which an exacter rhetoric would supersede with "life to good." A man cannot properly be said to "die to evil," because evil is in itself death. He can only die to that which is essentially Life, or good. "Death to evil" is like "Blessed Life," a phrase which, "according to the true view of the matter," says Fichte, "has in it something superfluous, to wit, life is necessarily blessed; the thought of an *un*blessed life carries with it a contradiction. Death alone is unblessed. What is unblessed, does not really and truly live; but in most of its component parts is sunk in death and nothingness." By whichever name we call it,—death to evil, or return to youth and life,—nothing ever occurs in the soul of man which more deeply and vitally affects him: for it carries with it the change which it is the office of religion to promote, or what Scripture terms regeneration. Hence it is the true "resurrection." That which is commonly so called, is simply the exchange of one's sphere of action, induced by the dissolution of the material body;—an exchange which in no way affects or alters the moral character, and is nothing more, essentially, than removal from one country to another is in this present life. The place of abode is new, but the man is the same. Resurrection is *rising*, not remaining *as we were.* It is not barely to enter the

spiritual world, which is the destiny of all, both good and evil, but to rise into a loftier and diviner state of soul, such as must be attained in this life, if at all. "He that is unjust, let him be unjust still; and he that is filthy, let him be filthy still; and he that is righteous, let him be righteous still; and he that is holy, let him be holy still." The *ανάαστασις* of the wicked, as Olshausen remarks, is only a part of the *θάνατος δεύτερος*. The resurrection, popularly so called, like every other great fact in the economy of the universe, is thus a *representative* occurrence. Attaching to all mankind, both good and evil, it is not a doctrine peculiarly of theology, but one of the simple laws of nature; and therefore an intimation and exponent of a truth yet grander than itself, and ready for all to realize who will. When man disengages himself from his earthly vesture, and passes from the temporal into eternity, he presents a picture of the soul which detaches itself from evil, and ascends into the high and lovely life of Christianity. That the true resurrection is the regeneration of the soul, is shown by our Lord's own divine words—"*I* am the resurrection." Doubtless, in his ascent from the tomb, we have the type of man's immortality; but this is not so much the doctrine intended in the words in question, as that resurrection is to acknowledge and follow him while we are yet on earth.

195. Such also is the resurrection which alone is represented and foreshadowed in the beautiful phenomena of the Spring, so enthusiastically pointed to by preachers of every creed and age. When the seeds vegetate, and cover the earth with leaves and flowers; when the trees bud, and foliage takes the place of snow and icicles, the resurrection that goes on is a rejuvenescence of life, beauty, vigor; no dead thing reappears; nothing that is defaced comes up again; there is no portraiture of the re-animation of mere dead material bodies, only of the deathlessness and energy

of moral excellence. Nowhere in the whole scope of nature is there ever seen resurrection of what is dead, or emblematic of death; all its revivifying processes attach to things which are alive and representative of life. It is only where the principle and power of life have never been for one instant interrupted, that resurrection takes place; resurrection of that which has altogether perished and decomposed, as the material body, which in itself is neither good nor evil, is never in the least degree illustrated; and from this single circumstance, the current doctrine of the resurrection, or that which regards it as a return of the soul into the material body from which it had been separated—the latter being transmogrified into a "spiritual body"—may be regarded as much in need of revision. The expectation of such return is in reality no more than a varied shape of the doctrine of the old Egyptians, which led them to embalm the corpses of their dead, to be, they imagined, in course of time re-animated by the relenting soul. Any theological dogma which is not illustrated by the Divine economy as it works visibly in the material creation, may legitimately be demurred to. There is no truth vouchsafed to man but is inscribed over again in the beautiful volume of the earth and sky; and conversely, the point where nature no longer speaks, is the point where truth also is at an end. The test of truth is that nature mirrors it.

196. With this right understanding of the word before our eyes, we see what is meant by "Blessed and holy is he that hath part in the first resurrection." The *second* is simply to enter the spiritual world, which all men do in due course; some to the "resurrection of life," some to the "resurrection of condemnation;" but that which is "blessed and holy," is the resurrection which the soul has already experienced in the body. It is this "first resurrection" which is referred to in the encouraging and consolatory

verse—"Precious unto the Lord is the death of his saints." Some think that this means the death of the body. Nay; what God rejoices in, is the death of selfishness and bad passions. There can be no resurrection, either real or representative, except contingently on death; hence it is said, that a man must "hate his own life," and "except he lay down his life." "Life" here denotes that particular, selfish, temporal love by which every man is animated while unregenerate, impelling some in one way, some in another, and which must be subordinated to a higher one if he would rise. *This* death, therefore, does it behoove us strenuously and unceasingly to contemplate; and not only so, it needs that, with the Apostle, we "die daily," that is, that we *rejuvenize* daily, exchanging what is unlovely in our affections for some diviner attachment, and replacing our childish, foolish, and unprofitable knowledges with wisdom at once comely and substantial. Every day that something is not effected towards these two ends, is a day ill-spent. Few, very few, are the truths and emotions which, however relatively excellent, do not require to be replaced by still superior ones, or at least to be rectified and expanded; and nowhere is the necessity more urgent than in those which have reference to religion and theology. If the first and greatest of existing evils be indifference to practical religion, want of enlarged understanding of spiritual things is unquestionably the second. People grow up, live and die, in the rudimentary knowledge of religious truths communicated to them in their childhood, and think their little leaf is all the forest. Inquire if they have read the last new novel or review, and it is considered a reproach to have to say "No." Ask what new fact they have learned in geography, or other physical science, and a reply is ready. But inquire, even of "religious" people, what new idea they have of heaven, or of God, or the human soul, or the prophecies, and they wonder what you mean, or what there can be to learn. Some abstain from search for fear of their "faith" becoming weakened. Faith in Christ, says Vater, can be no hindrance to critical and philosophical inquiries; otherwise he would himself impede the progress of truth. The best token that genuine rejuvenescence of the soul is going on in us, is, that the Word of God becomes daily a richer mine to our intelligence.

197. Death implies a place of burial, and as death in Scripture denotes, on the one hand, declension from virtue; on the other, escape from the power of evil, or regeneration; so do the words grave, tomb, and sepulchre. The unregenerate man is not only dead, but as truly entombed as a corpse beneath the sods. In the prophets there are many examples, as when Isaiah, speaking of the "rebellious," says that "they remain among the graves." Similarly, in the New Testament, dwelling "among the tombs" denotes living in the shades and negations of irreligiousness. The "lunatic" loved to dwell among the tombs. *He* impersonates the man who is dead to spiritualities. If it be "madness" to act recklessly in secular things, surely it must be "madness" to forget God. Properly regarded, insanity is of two kinds; one comes of the brain being diseased, so that the soul, healthy in itself, cannot use it; this is insanity commonly so called: the other is when it is the soul that is diseased, albeit the brain be perfectly healthy; this is infidelity and irreligiousness. The Pharisees of the human race our Lord calls whited sepulchres, because, making a fair show on the outside, within they are full of dead men's bones. In the sense of regeneration or newness of life, there is no more beautiful instance than that in Ezekiel xxxvii. 12, "Behold, O, my people, I will open your graves, and cause you to come up out of your graves, and bring you into the land of Israel, and ye shall know that I am the Lord,

and I will put my spirit in you, and ye shall live." St. John records how the promise was fulfilled: "I say unto you, the hour is coming, and *now is*, when the dead shall hear the voice of the Son of God, and they that hear shall live." (v. 25.) A moment's reflection will show that these words can in neither case refer to the resurrection after the death of the body. They can mean nothing else but the "quickening to grace." The raising of Lazarus by the Lord, and of the widow's son at the city of Nain, were intended as signs that the same power should revive men who had been long "dead in trespasses and sins." It was because the Jewish religion was so essentially and minutely representative, or prefigurative of the Christian religion which was to "fulfill" it, that the Jews were so desirous of burial in the land of Canaan, the Scriptural symbol of heaven. Interment in that country was emblematical and prefigurative of resurrection into Paradise. The inhumation of the material body is the resurrection of the spiritual, and where the former is symbolically deposited, the latter symbolically becomes an inhabitant. It is for the same reason, though it may be unsuspected, that Christians bury their dead either in or closely adjacent to their churches, the representatives of the temple not made with hands. Every observance and ceremony of this nature is founded on the relation of things physical to things spiritual. If, then, a man would vitally experience what resurrection is, what it essentially is to rise from the grave, let him, with God's help, "die unto sin." That he will survive the death of his material body, he may assure himself, for it is not given him to choose, but whether he will rise or not, he himself must elect.

CHAPTER XX.

*REJUVENESCENCE.**

198. MORE than once in previous chapters we have spoken of REJUVENESCENCE; it now becomes important to treat the subject independently and connectedly. The most glorious principle of nature, impressed upon its every object, Life and Death themselves are only other names for Rejuvenescence; the history of the world and of its contents, in all their variety and phases, is no more than the history of its operation; the one great poetic idea of the universe, all phenomena and splendors, spiritual as well as material, are but parts and elements of it, illustrating and adorning its different modes. Everywhere, since the first morning, has youth been incessantly bursting forth, and creation beginning afresh. "The universe, open to the eye to-day, looks as it did a thousand years ago; the morning hymn of Milton does but tell the beauty with which our own familiar sun dressed the earliest fields and gardens of the world;" all things, says the apostle, "continue as they were from the beginning of creation." True, there is continual dismemberment and disintegration; the flower fades, the animal falls to dust, but this is not *death*—it is merely the casting away of worn-out vestures, in order that the new may be put on. The form, the idea, the actuality, lives forever; the

* Literally "Return to a state of youth."

end always reverts to the beginning; from the plant comes the fruit, and from the fruit comes the seed, which again contains the plant within itself. Look at that sculptured pine-apple! Nature in miniature; upon its yellow ripeness ensues a beautiful tufted crown of leaves, promising and beginning the whole history over again, the true Phœnix of creation.* The fabled Palm is only a metaphor of the world. Turn which way we will, we find no "killing principle" in nature, only a vitalizing and sustaining one. Throughout its whole extent, Nature is LIFE; in all its forms and modifications, one vast and infinite LIFE—subject, no doubt, to the extinction of particular presentations, but never to absolute and total death, even in its least and weakest things. Anything that looks like death is a token and certificate of life being about to start anew and invigorated. Every end is also a beginning. "All things in the world," says Lynch, "are striving to begin as well as to finish." Marriage once more is the type and exponent. So far, therefore, from being the *destroyer* of life, death, rightly viewed, is its nourisher and aliment. A thing does not perish in order that it may no longer exist, but that another of the same or similar kind may enter fresh and beautiful upon the scene, and thus virtually perpetuate the original. "All death in nature," says Fichte, "is life, and in death appears visibly the advancement of life. It is not death which kills, but the higher life which, concealed behind the other, begins to develop itself. Death and birth are but the struggle of life with itself to attain a higher form.†

---

* The same beautiful onward growth appears conspicuously in several of the New Holland genera of Myrtaceæ, as Melaleuca, Metrosideros, Beaufortia, &c.; and a similar phenomenon in the cones of the Larch, from the apex of which occasionally extends a leafy shoot.

† Destination of Man, p. 127.

Granted, we do not perceive it to be so if we look at things merely with the outward senses—we perceive it in the degree that our own minds are alive, and apt, from culture and sincere and fervent aspiration after truth, to rejuvenize in themselves. Everything is alive to the living mind. Death is abundant in proportion as the mind is dead. To estimate our intellectual vitality, at any given time, we have but to ask ourselves, How much life are we conscious of? We speak, in ordinary converse, of youth and age as *distinct epochs*, and as a matter of appearance, correctly so. It results, however, from this great law, that so far from being separate and successive, they are cotemporaneous and concurrent. Youth does not cease, and age begin. Throughout life their phenomena run side by side, revolving each upon the other, age succeeding youth, youth succeeding age, in the most varied conditions of exchange, and often crowding into the same region. Everywhere in nature we see youth and senility intermingled, presenting themselves alternately, and altogether irrespective and independent of annual birthdays. If decay attend upon age, so does it upon infancy; if youth is a beginning, so, too is maturity. Life rising out of death was the great "mystery" which in old time, symbolism delighted to represent under the thousand ingenious forms preserved in mythology and ancient poetry, as in the lovely fable of Cupid and Psyche. Nature was explored in her every realm for attestations to it, the results giving to religion new sanctity and illustration, to philosophy new dignity and grace. Sleep was beautifully called "the minor mystery of death;" since the seeming suspension of life during the stillness of slumber, is the pathway to restoration of its powers, and thus a prefigurement of what death is designed for. "Death, like sleep," says the illustrious Herder, "cools the fever of life; gently interrupts its too uniform and long-continued movement; heals many wounds incurable before, and prepares the soul for a pleasurable awakening, for the enjoyment of a new morning of youth. As in my dreams, my thoughts fly back to youth—as in my dreams, being only half fettered by the bodily organs, and more concentred in myself, I feel more free and active—so thou, revivifying dream of death, wilt smilingly bring back the youth of my life, the most energetic and pleasing moments of my existence."*

199. When, then, it is said that *death* takes things away, it is said wrongfully. It is done by Life, the constant aim of which is to obtain a point of departure for renewed progress, pushing out of the way whatever may obstruct. See what curious and striking illustrations are furnished in the physiology of our own bodies! The teeth of the child drop from its little gums, that the teeth of manhood may take their place; the blood, by its particles, supersedes itself as fast as it is formed; every molecule of muscle, and bone, and brain, is an ephemeron; our entire fabric is taken to pieces and rebuilt some seven or eight times before we leave it. The bodies of all other animals similarly rejuvenize during the period between birth and dissolution, some, in addition to the molecular renewal, having periodical and most curious replacements of entire organs. Birds renew their plumage; lizards and snakes their skins; the crab even replaces its stomach, forming a new one every year, and casting away the old. Plants also rejuvenize, exemplified in the annual renewal of their leaves and flowers. In the higher kinds of vegetation the phenomena are at once so marked and intelligible, as to have called forth the first, and as yet the only treatise, expressly devoted to this mag-

---

* Outlines of a History of the Philosophy of Man, book v., chap. 4.

nificent science.* Philo beautifully uses them to illustrate the "unbounded wisdom of God:" "The wealth of that wisdom is as a tree, which is continually putting forth new shoots after the old ones, so that it never ceases growing young again, and being in the flower of its strength."

200. As a phenomenon of physiological or organic life, Rejuvenescence appears under two great general modes, namely, first, Return by the individual, either as a whole, or in its molecules, to an earlier condition of existence, securing thereby a point of departure for renewed progress; secondly, Repetition in a new being, under the law of procreation by male and female, of the entire course of organic evolution. The first has for its object, the *completion* of the form; the second has for its object, the *repetition* of the form. Rejuvenescence in order to Completion is exemplified in the growth of a child, leading it on to puberty, and thence to manhood; that which has Repetition for its end, appears in the phenomena of generation and birth. It follows that it is the power of Rejuvenescence which mainly distinguishes organic bodies from inorganic, since in the latter there is neither a graduated development of the individual, nor renewal by procreation. Without rejuvenescence there can be no organic development, nor where organs are absent can rejuvenescence ever occur. The distinction between the two kingdoms of organized beings themselves as regards rejuvenescence, is that while in animals there is a perpetual dissolution and rebuilding of the entire substance, the devitalized atoms being ejected, plants never rejuvenize

---

* The Phenomenon of Rejuvenescence in Nature, especially in the life and development of Plants. From the German of Dr. A. Braun, by Arthur Henfrey. Ray Society's Volume, 1853. One of the most important of modern contributions to the philosophy of Botany.

a part once completed, but provide for the stability and regularity of the vital processes, by developing *new* parts. The stem once formed and consolidated, never alters in the least; the leaves and flowers when done with, are disengaged, and absolutely new ones are unfolded in their place.

201. Rejuvenescence in order to the Completion of the form, has, accordingly, for its chief process in Animals, the decay and renewal of the tissues; in Plants, the unfolding of new organs. Both involve a variety of minor and contributive activities, but most especially is this the case in the rejuvenescence of the animal, where the full effectuation of the molecular renewal requires and is secured by the grand supplementary process of Sleep—in effect a periodical return of the animal to its ante-natal state, beautifully corresponding with the resumption of that state in lactation, which is a living over again of the life of the womb, on a higher plane. During sleep, the inner formative processes by which the body is preserved act undisturbedly and concentratedly. Every one knows how sweet is the restoration derived from one's pillow when in health; more wonderful even yet is that which we derive when sleep occurs at the crisis of severe diseases. The nocturnal refreshment of the physical frame induces a similar restoration of the spiritual. Relaxed from the tension in which it is held towards the outer world while awake, during sleep the mind sinks into a condition comparable to that in which it lay before consciousness commenced; all images and shapes it is cognizant of by day, either vanish, or appear only as reflected pictures; unexcited from without, it "gathers itself up into new force, new comprehension of its purpose, much that crossed the waking thoughts, scattered and entangled, becoming thereby sifted and arranged." Hence is it that "our waking thoughts are often our truest and finest; and that dreams are sometimes eminent and wise; phenomena incom-

patible with the idea that we die down like grass into our organic roots at night, and are merely resuscitated as from a winter when we wake. Man is captured in sleep, not by death, but by his better nature; to-day runs in through a deeper day to become the parent of to-morrow, and he issues every morning, bright as the morning and of life size, from the peaceful womb of the cerebellum." The most remarkable illustration of the bearing of sleep upon rejuvenescence is supplied perhaps in the chrysalis period of Insect-life. Here takes place that grand retreat and gathering-in of vital power which enables the unsightly grub to expand into the lovely, completed and expressive form we call the Butterfly, so exquisite a symbol of the Spring, when winter, the grub and chrysalis era of the vegetable world, is emerged from and superseded. The analogy is important to consider, because of the common but mistaken impression that the charming green exuberance of the vernal season is no more than the work of the few days during which it appears. That beautiful display is in preparation all the winter, just as the butterfly is in preparation in the grub and chrysalis; Spring merely brings the concluding steps before our eyes, as the rupture of the chrysalis the painted wings of the perfect insect. Not a little of the Spring begins in the previous autumn, and even in the previous summer. The rudiments of the future leaves of the alder may be found in August; the leaves and even the flower-buds also of the lilac; the catkins of the hazel make their appearance with the asters and golden-rod; in the bulbs of the hyacinth, the tulip, and the crocus, long before they manifest the least sign of vegetation, the future blossom may readily be discerned. Insect-life, as a whole, is the most perfect example we possess of Rejuvenescence having for its aim the Completion of the Individual. The true idea of what is so improperly called the "metamorphosis" or "transformation" of insects, is *development into a perfect state.* It is no change of one creature into another. The caterpillar contains within itself the rudiments of the future butterfly in all its parts; it becomes the butterfly—not, as commonly supposed, by a monstrous and supernatural mutation—simply by *casting its skin,* and unfolding parts previously concealed and immature, first the limbs, by and by the wings, opening more and more, till the idea of the perfect insect is attained. No less striking and beautiful than the analogy of the Butterfly with the opening leaves and flowers of spring, is the rejuvenescence at that season of the Birds. They blossom in the Spring, like the trees and plants, glossy and tinted in their plumage, and like the plants again when they shed their petals, lose their peculiar spring and summer lustre immediately the process of hatching is completed. To return, however, to the Butterfly. We have a lesson in the insect's history of another kind. From time immemorial the butterfly has been the emblem of the resurrection. Anciently, as with the Egyptians, we find it drawn either in its proper form, or as a lovely female child with butterfly's wings. "Employed, subsequently, by the Fathers of the Church, the beautiful symbol shone on their ponderous pages like a beam of sunlight falling through a painted window on the gloom of a cloister." The beauty and truthfulness of the emblem lie, however, in exactly the opposite direction to that ordinarily supposed. Not only is the usual idea of the resurrection, or that of a decayed body recomposed in its elements, and reunited after a certain interval to the soul, not represented in the natural history of the insect, but altogether contrary to it. What the history *does* teach is that which is also the *true* idea of the resurrection. As the caterpillar becomes the butterfly by no supernatural transformation, but simply by the casting away of outward coverings; so does man become an angel, not by any imaginary transmogrification of his "natural" body into a "spiritual" body, but by the latter, which he always has, laying down and departing from the former, expanding its matured organs, and ascending into that higher and lovelier mode of life which is poetically represented under the name of wings. Only with such an understanding, does the name ψυχὴ properly apply to the beautiful creature it denotes. Reaumur, that great and good naturalist, when he discovered the real structure of the caterpillar, and pointed out the discrepancy between the truth of nature and the dogma of the preachers, was denounced as an enemy to revelation.

202. Occasionally, but rarely, there is in man a resumption, when old, of the *external* signs of youth. Cherished from the remotest ages, the idea of a restoration of youthful health, and strength, and bodily shape, by some beautiful stroke of magic, is not altogether remote from fact, though the magic is in nature rather than Art. The basis, probably, of the story of Medea and Æson; it figures in the fables and national poetry of every period of the world; its most beautiful embodiment, the Fountain of Rejuvenescence, is found in the tales of the far East, in the romances of Chivalry, and in the Mysteries: in the middle ages it was the symbol of Christianity renewing the moral strength of the world after the corruptions of pagan Rome; and now we have it in a fine picture by one of the best of the French pre-Raphaelite school.* The Alchemists thought to secure such rejuvenescence by the aid of the Philosopher's Stone, which was not only to ward off sickness and infirmities, but to replace men in the vigor of early youth. Vincent de Beauvais attempted to show that Noah's having children

---

* M. Haussouiller, "La Fontaine de Jouvence." See the engraving in the "Illustrated London News," September 20th, 1856.

when five hundred years old was owing to his possession of this precious secret, whereby he had had restored to him the freshness of his ancient puberty. Vain expectation! though man may certainly please himself with the reflection that he alone ever steps in the grateful path. The lower animals begin to decay almost immediately after the decline of their propagative power; in man, life is prolonged more or less after virility has ceased, and now and then operates over again some of the most characteristic phenomena of his earliest days. The cutting of new teeth in old age; return of the power of suckling; growth of hair similar to that of the young, and several other such phenomena are abundantly on record, as may be seen at one view in Dr. Mehliss, whose curious work, *Ueber Viriliseenz und Rejuvenescenz thierischer Körper* (Leipsic, 1838), has raised the matter into a branch of physiology. Of new dentition, for example, he cites not less than thirty or forty authentic instances, many of them octogenarian. For the appearance of these phenomena it is necessary, he tells us, that there should exist complete energy and integrity of vegetative life, and probably also local excitement.

203. The second great form of physiological Rejuvenescence, or that by which man, and all other living creatures, together with plants, renew themselves as to race, is expressed in the phenomena of procreation.

> Like leaves on trees the race of man is found,
> Now green in youth, now withering on the ground;
> So generations in their course decay,
> So flourish these, when those are passed away.

Here it is that we most clearly understand that death, so called, is the operation of Life. The particular aggregations of material elements, carbon, oxygen, nitrogen, and so forth, drawn together and consolidated by the immortal idea of each plant and animal, and by the spiritual body in man, break up and disappear after awhile; but the Form remains with us still; its old apparel only parted with, in order that new may be put on. Wonderful as are the processes of sustentation and repair in the individual, those of procreation, or the sustentation of the species, incomparably transcend them. No trifling work is the elaboration of a body which shall feed and grow, move and exchange offices of friendship; but to construct one which, in addition to all this, shall be able to engender new beings like itself, is the very acme of skill and miracle. So excellently has the subject been dealt with by other hands, so extensive also is its detail, that here we need only advert to it as one of the most solemn considerations of life, a subject never to be approached without reverence and awe. The unthinking part of mankind look upon procreation as no more than one of the common impulses of nature, and consider the slightest allusion to it improper. Many even of those who ought to know better, regard it as ignoble and degrading, and its alluring incidents only as palliative and reconciliatory. There cannot be a lower idea. In the whole range of delegated offices there is none more honorable and noble than to act for the Father of all, as perpetuator of the objects he has created "for his pleasure;" wherefore also the depth and fearfulness of its responsibility, since of all situations a man can place himself in, that of Father is the most serious and manifold in duties. Large indeed should be the faith in heavenly succor of him who adventures upon progeny. The same is the ground of the brilliant delights which enter into its history, since outward circumstance is always made commensurate with the dignity of that which it accompanies and invests. The Beauty which attends on the period when with the complete evolution of the system, the power is attained of reproducing the species, is one of the most admirable phenomena of nature. The principle is universally set forth. See how the plant, at its nuptial hour, adorns itself with bright flowers! See how the glow-worm trims its lamp; how the butterfly spreads its gallant pinions! In fishes, birds and mammals, puberty is again characterized universally by the development of ornaments more or less striking, such as brightly-colored scales and plumage, horns, manes, and beards, the last-named enhancing the manly beauty attained at this period in our own species, the female of which is even more largely embellished by the growth of the hair, and the development of the mammæ, and of the subcutaneous tissues of the body in general, giving to the limbs their matchless "lily roundness." Not only are beauty of form and color now most exquisite. Flowers smell the sweetest during the union of the sperm-cell with the germ-cell, especially in its central moments, losing their fragrance rapidly when it is completed; in the animal kingdom, during the same period, *sounds* are emitted, pleasing, undoubtedly, to the ears they are designed for, and taking in man, the form of poetry and music. The ballad "to his mistress' eyebrow" of the lover is the exact analogue of the song of the bird, and the chirp of the grasshopper and cicada.* That the song of birds has immediate reference to their loves, is generally understood. Like the beauty of their plumage, it rises to its highest degree during the pairing season, and is lost at the time of moulting. All our resident birds that renew their song in the autumn, probably have broods at that time; the thrush, and the blackbird, which are heard from the middle of January to October, generally have two broods in the course of the season, and not infrequently

---

* Abridged, in part, from Dr. Laycock. British and Foreign Medico-Chirurgical Review, July, 1855.

three. But it is not merely a pairing cry, being continued till the young birds break the shell, and in many cases till they are able to fly. Probably it produces general excitement in the female bird, while sitting, so as to increase the needful warmth, and a power of more energetic performance by both parents of the various duties of the nest. We all know that there are sounds, especially from those we love, which make the heart beat, and the bosom thrill, and the whole body glow, inspiring us magically and beautifully, and doubtless it is the same with the feathered dwellers in the trees.

204. Holding this sublime power of self-renewal as a part of its very nature, every animal, bird and insect, every tree and herb, down to the humblest moss, is in its procreant capacity an emblem and prefigurement of Eternity. Forever rolling onwards, the truest and grandest idea of the Divine life is unfolded to us in the phenomena of reproduction. Hence that beautiful custom of the ancients, of placing seeds in the hands of the dead, and in their tombs and sarcophagi. They perceived that the renovation of a plant, by its seeds, year by year, and from age to age, unchanged in the least of its essential characters, is a picture in little of immortality. The rites of religion always have reference to the theory; wherever religion has existed, the offices of the living to the dead have invariably formed a part of them; and as all religious rites are of necessity symbolical, their beauty and intelligibleness show the quality of the faith which employs them. The custom alluded to thus testifies in itself to the antiquity of man's persuasion that he is to live forever.* With mankind, elevation to capacity for the

---

* The early Christians also put seeds in the coffins of the dead, but in their case it was in acknowledgment of the imagery of St.

privileges and rewards of procreation is the effulgent Aurora of existence. Youth begins over again, on a higher and more beautiful plane; whatever talents there may be in the soul, now they make their appearance. Early or late, whenever it may be first felt, love, the high-priest of procreation, always leads the way to rejuvenescence of our entire nature; no pleasures are so sincere and so enduring as those which come late in life through renewal of one's youth under the sweet agency of a happily-placed affection, nor are any so thankfully enjoyed.

205. The rejuvenescence which the *entire organic garment of the earth* has undergone, and will not improbably undergo again, is the poem of Geology. This rejuvenescence consists in the development of successive *suites* of animals and plants; enduring, as to their species, for incalculable ages, and then disappearing, or nearly so, to make way for newer and higher kinds, to endure for as long, and in turn be themselves superseded. Four times, at least, says Lyell, do these changes take place in the course of the tertiary era, and to an extent which leaves hardly a species of the first period extant among the species now living. This is not inconsistent with the previously noticed kinds of rejuvenescence. It is rejuvenescence of organic nature *in the mass*, the particular genera and species being but subordinate incidents in the great onward and upward current of terrestrial Life. "Newer *and higher* kinds" is not to be understood as implying that the new appearances are *all* of higher grade. "Geology affords no ground whatever for the hypothesis of a regular succession of creatures, beginning with the simplest forms in the older strata, and ascending to more complicated

---

Paul. See an interesting article on the subject in Hooker's "Companion to the Botanical Magazine," vol. 2, p. 298.

in the later formations. The earliest forms of life known to geology are not of the lowest grade of organization; neither are the earliest forms of any of the classes which subsequently appear, the simplest of their kind." It is in the *aggregate* of forms, large and small, higher and lower, that the progressive improvement is shown, and this is one of the proudest facts of natural history. It is proper to remark, however, that there is a difference in this respect, as regards plant and animal remains. While the vegetable kingdom has *always* had representatives of highest as well as of lowest forms; in the animal fossils of the earlier ages, there are, on the other hand, no vertebrates. But this difference, as Alphonse De Candolle remarks, "need not excite much astonishment, when we think of the vast distance which separates the inferior and the superior animals, and the comparatively homogeneous character of the great classes of vegetables." Neither does geology give any countenance to the idea of "progressive development," in the sense of transmutation of one species into another. We mention this because of the importance of distinguishing the idea in question from that of gradual improvement as a characteristic of successive creations. It is a very different thing for an organism to improve into one of higher nature, by elevation of its own qualities and powers, and for that organism to cease altogether, and be replaced by a superior one. The changes in the plants and animals of our earth, as regards its successive periods, have uniformly been wrought in the *latter* way. The evidence of it is plain and abundant; whereas there is none whatever to support the hypothesis of the superiority having resulted from change for the better of earlier individuals. That such improvement in the successive sets of organized beings has been made, and is visible to us, is a strong proof of the existence and the activity of God; "improvement" of course being understood, when predicated of the Divine work, not as a coming forth of *results of experience* in creating, but simply as a term denoting that Divine wisdom saw fit to disclose less elaborate forms in the first place, and more elaborate ones subsequently. The halting of nature at given periods in the world's history, and in the intervals between one set of species and another, producing (as at present) only the like, is but the same phenomenon, on a grand scale, as that of the repetition of its leaves by a plant, perhaps hundreds of times, before the development advances to the stage of flowers. Looking at the world as a grand scene of organic evolution, every new step in its rejuvenescence bringing it nearer and nearer towards completion, we cannot but recognize how beautiful an image of it, in little, is presented in a youthful TREE, with its successive sets of leaves, more and more perfect and abundant in each new unfolding (so well shown, for example, in young sycamores), the last and fairest era being, in the one case, Man and the magnificent nature cotemporary with him; in the other, Blossoms and Fruit. Blossoms and humanity are ideas which invariably go together; the pre-Adamite plants were almost without exception flowerless; fossil bees do not occur till the period of the earth's preparation as a home for human beings. "The first bee," says the late talented and lamented author of The Testimony of the Rocks, "makes its appearance in the amber of the Eocene, locked up hermetically in its gem-like tomb—an embalmed corpse in a crystal coffin—along with fragments of flower-bearing herbs and trees. The first of the Bombycidæ too—insects that may be seen suspended over flowers by the scarcely visible vibrations of their wings, and sucking the honied juices by means of their long slender trunks—also appear in the amber, associated with moths, butterflies, and a few caterpillars. Bees and butterflies are present in increased proportions in the latter tertiary deposits; but not until that terminal creation to which we ourselves belong was ushered on the scene, did they receive their fullest development." Examining the curious and beautiful relics to which Miller alludes, how striking appears the contrast between the tombs of these ancient and inconsiderable insects and those which the dead receive at our own hands! Instead of the gloom which surrounds the last habitations of mankind, here is brightness; instead of being loathsome and painful to look upon, here is something to admire and covet. How insignificant and bungling seem the best efforts of Art to embalm and preserve the corpse of a departed friend, compared with this simple and elegant method of Nature, so profound and perfect even in what may appear most fanciful and trifling in her works!

206. Not only were the *species* new, in the successive rejuvenizings of the earth's surface, but in many instances, the entire families. Rosaceous plants, for example, do not belong to the earlier periods of the world's history. Hence may we infer the higher nature of their correspondence in regard to the spiritual principles of which they are outbirths and representatives, a presumption already afforded in the apple—a leading member of this tribe—being the most perfect realization of a fruit, whether regarded as to its botanical structure, or its uses. In the same generous family are comprised the almond, the strawberry, and the medlar; the plum, the peach, the nectarine, the apricot, "shining in sweet brightness of golden velvet," together with innumerable charming flowers, every one of them, without doubt, of a fine spiritual origin and significance. That these plants were not placed upon the earth until the period of its occupancy by man, because he alone could esteem their produce, and that they were specially destined for human nourishment and satisfaction, may certainly be assumed as the reason of their late bestowal. Doubtless,

there is an exact relation between the races of animals and plants, and the epochs at which they have been placed upon the earth; since the whole matter of the succession of organized beings is the realization of an infinitely wise plan—whence, also, the impossibility of attaining grand and accurate ideas of nature without the aid of geology;—the profounder reasön lies, however, in the correspondence of nature and the soul, the order in which, of growth and efflorescence, is in every point the same. Quite unlike the Rosaceæ are the FERNS. In these, so far from a comparatively recent family, we have the inheritors of one of the most ancient and noble titles in vegetable peerage. Glorious in all periods of the world's history, while the leaves and branches of its genealogical tree are green and vigorous with rills of current life, its roots strike deep into the remotest records of the past. Honorable in the olden time, beautiful to-day, the Ferns are the *beau-idéal* of a patrician family. Their value is commensurate with their charms. Like the Rosetta stone, they speak at once a familiar language and a primæval, helping thereby to interpret the vast and sacred mysteries of extinguished ages. Less interesting, only because exotices of small numbers and variety, are those other curious relics of antiquity, the Cycadeæ. Memorials of a class of plants whose day is past, they seem to linger with us not so much for themselves as to "make former times shake hands with latter."

207. Let us pass on to the renewals that pertain to the Spiritual degree of life. In the changes of our feelings we have rejuvenescences quite as beautiful as those of nature. The decay and retrogression which we see in autumn among the plants, providing the means of a charming palingenesis in the spring, is not more regular and universal than are the declensions we are subject to in ourselves; nor does nature rebound more freely and improved. Whenever there is a

return of the heart from unsatisfying, selfish, or ignoble pursuits, to a taste for the pure and uncloying charms of virtue and nature, there we have the restoration of our youth; wherever there is advance into new and delicious fields of thought and feeling, under the influence of new scenes, or the advent of new friends, or the passing away of what is painful, or distasteful, life starts anew in all its plenitude of powers and sentiment. How charmingly does D'Israeli describe the rejuvenescence in old age, of well-cultivated literary taste! "The steps of time are retraced, and we resume the possessions we seemed to have lost. We open the poets who made us enthusiasts, and the philosophers who taught us to think, with a new source of feeling acquired by our own experience. Adam Smith confessed his satisfaction at this pleasure to Dugald Stewart, while reperusing with the enthusiasm of a student, the tragic poets of ancient Greece. The calm, philosophic Hume found death only could interrupt the keen pleasure he was again receiving from Lucian. 'Happily,' said this philosopher, 'on retiring from the world, I found my taste for reading return with even greater avidity.' Lord Woodhouselee found the composing anew his Lectures on History so fascinating in the last period of his life, that it rewarded him, Alison informs us, with 'that *peculiar delight* which has been often observed in the later years of literary men, the delight of returning to the studies of their youth, and of feeling under the snows of age the cheerful memories of their Spring.' In the solitude and night of human life, is discovered that unregarded kindness of nature which has given flowers that only open in the evening, and bloom through the night season."* As morning and sunshine come back in the Hes-

* "The Literary Character," chap. xx. See also an original and beautiful "Account of the state of the body and mind in old age," in

peris, the evening primrose, and the night-flowering cereus, so do fancy and imagination rejuvenize with the man of taste.*

208. There is abundant illustration of this great law also in civil, scientific, and literary history, especially the last; and it is worthy of observation that the precursor of a new era is always one who refuses to follow the slavishness, extravagances, and caprices of exhausted invention, and returns to the freedom, simplicity, and integrity of nature. This is why men of true genius, who illumine the world with something new and glorious, are always accused of "violating the rules," *i. e.*, refusing to dwell among the tombs. What shallow-minded bigots call "heresy" and "heterodoxy" is often nothing more than the rejuvenescence of a devout and healthy soul, too far elevated above themselves ever to care for their censure and wrath. The great Sydenham, with whom the science of medicine rejuvenized, as it did with Harvey and Hunter, was conspired against with intent to expel him from his College, as "guilty of medical heresy." Death, in its blindness, always thinks that its contrary, or Life, is the dead condition; as evil always pities the good, and would fain persuade us that itself is the *sum-*

---

the Medical Inquiries and Observations of that most interesting writer, Dr. Rush. Volume 2. (Philadelphia, 1793.)

* The number and variety of the flowers which expand, or only become fragrant towards evening, show how deeply seated is this beautiful correspondence. Besides the familiar species above mentioned, there are the Marvel of Peru, the tuberose, several species of the Germaniceæ, as Pelargonium triste; several of the Caryophylleæ, as Silene noctiflora and vespertina, and Dianthus pomeridianus; many tropical Convolvulaceæ, as Ipomæa bona-nox; additional Cruciferæ, as Cheiranthus sinuatus; together with various Orchideæ, Malvaceæ, and Thymeleæ. Bartonia ornata, and Barringtonia speciosa are also beautiful congeners.

mum bonum. When another kind of rejuvenescence was transpiring under the genius of Lord Bacon, Sir Thomas Bodley wrote to him remonstrating on his "new mode of philosophizing." New doctrines always displease the small and stagnant-souled, who may be known by their having nailed themselves to given opinions, and considering novelties vicious and illegal. Given to fancying that the world has been losing wisdom instead of gaining it, since the period when *they* contracted their views, they must work by precedent, or not at all, and hence are never anything but mimics. Not so the men of life and power. "The great men never know how or why they do things. They have no rules, cannot comprehend the nature of rules. The moment any man begins to talk about rules, in whatsoever art, you may know him for a second-rate man; and if he talk *much* about them, he is a third-rate." As Goethe said, all great men produce their works *as women do pretty children,* without either thinking about it, or knowing how it is done. All great epochs are epochs of resurrection. Not one of our modern institutions is purely an establishment of To-day. That which is, has already been, only under another and cruder form. The mode may be different, but the principle is the same; the truths we delight in as our own, were pleasures to our forefathers; if we do not recognize them in our readings in history, it is because the ages in their spiral rise have lifted them to a higher level, as a building becomes different when we are close beside it, from what it appears while in the distance. Ideas never die. Out of fashion for awhile; lost, perhaps, for generations, they bide their time, then revive, as Ovid says, *in nova corpora mutata,* "changed into new bodies." No fragment of truth has ever been really lost. Immortal as its origin, every particle is sure to rise again, its resurrection the result of its immortality. All the great "Revivals" of the present age partake of this character, and result from this mighty law. Let us be careful then how we ridicule even the least of them. Resuscitations can only happen where there is life; the absurdity may prove to be in ourselves, rather than in the things. What the many are, such is the individual. The parallel between the soul of man and that of society is exact. "Every man," says Sir Thomas Browne, "is not only himself; there have been many Diogeneses, and many Timons, though but few of the name; men are lived over again; the world is now as it was in ages past; there was none then, but there has been some one since that parallels him, and is, as it were, his revived self." We often cast our eyes towards the *future*. If we would speculate on it rightly, we must first comprehend the *present*, and that is best done by contemplating the *past*. True, in our retrospect we seem to see little more than Destruction; but in the eyes of the naturalist this indicates Renewal, transition into a new, upgrowing Time. Not a few of our greatest riddles have their solutions in ancient history; yea, even in the fables of mythology; for mythology is not, as foolish people fancy, profane romance, and nothing more, but sound and living prophecy, a sort of secular inspiration suited to the times to which it was given, and intended to receive fulfillment in later days. We talk of the golden age as *gone*. Not so; the golden age is both with us, and to come.

209. The highest rejuvenescence of all is man's return to youth in heaven. Some people think, weakly, that "death is the only reality in life; happier and rightlier-minded are those who see and feel that Life is the true reality in death." Why, then, call it death? and why mourn and weep for those who return to the spring-time of existence? Why complain that we ourselves seem to be so soon taken from this land of tombs, and replaced in the golden country of our pristine hopes and imaginings?

CHAPTER XXI.

HEALTH AND DISEASE—RATIONALE OF MIRACLES.

210. INTIMATELY allied with the idea of Rejuvenescence, is that of HEALTH, the synonyme of Life, the delicious spring of all animal enjoyment, and the finest light whereby both to think and to love. Without health, the larger part of our time is at once wretched and unprofitable. Sickness, which, in its intenser degree, is disease, turns existence from a blessing into misery; it makes us "go mourning all the day long," and if not checked in its inroads, soon ends in the death which it foretells. "The excellences of the body," says old Charron, "are health, beauty, sprightliness, agility, vigor, dexterity, gracefulness in motion and behaviour. But HEALTH is infinitely before all. Health is the loveliest, the most desirable, the richest present in the power of nature to confer. One thing only is more valuable, and that is Probity." Vigorous health is the chief secret of Good Temper. Fretfulness, petulance, irritability, come oftener of bodily ailments than of natural unloveliness of disposition, as proved by the change which supervenes with relief. No one of any considerateness will ever deal harshly where such states of feeling are developed from such a cause, though none are more likely to be betrayed into impatience with them than the hearty and robust, who having no experience of the aggravations of physical pain, deem that moral offences can have no other than a moral origin. As with the individual, so with Communities. Study the

temper of the people who live in marshy districts, of those who encounter an annual tropical fever, or who are subject to goître, and contrast them with the dispositions of the dwellers on mountains, and in dry prairies; what selfishness, apathy, and discontent we find in the former class; what kindliness, cheerfulness, and hospitality in the other! A curious parallel might be instituted between Health and MONEY. Health is the less envied, but the more largely and thoroughly enjoyed; money is exactly the reverse, or a thousand times less enjoyed than it is envied. The superiority of Health becomes evident, nevertheless, when we reflect that the poorest man would not part with his health for money, whereas the invalided rich would willingly buy health.

211. True of the body, all this is even more true of the soul, which has likewise its health and its ailments; and in no less intimate connection with its vitality, and happiness, and death. Far more emphatically does the ancient proverb apply to the soul than to the body—

Non est vivere, sed *valere*, vita.

"Let no man deceive himself," say the incomparable Petrarch, "by thinking that the contagions of the soul are less than those of the body. They are yet greater; they sink deeper, and creep on more unsuspectedly."* To talk either of life or health, whether of soul or of body, is thus virtually to talk of the other; and the same of their negations, or death and disease. Spiritual disease is not to be confounded, however, with "mental disease," or insanity, lunacy, idiotcy, dementia, &c., in their various kinds. Not one of

* De Vita Solitaria, I. 3, iv., *Opera*, p. 233. One of the best portions of what Coleridge so well calls "the inestimable Latin writings of Petrarch."

these conditions implies, necessarily, a diseased soul, seeing that they may and do most frequently come of mere disease of its material instrument, the brain. "Circumstances not only environ essentials, but alter their seemings. Brains may be born into inconvenient cases. Good human minds, veritable immortal children, may be born into idiot brains, which will represent them badly, as a poor gift of speech may choke the utterance of a rich heart."* Spiritual disease is where the brain itself is healthy, but its owner and master distempered. Spiritually, we are well when we feel ourselves diligent in the pursuit of intelligence, and have "a conscience void of offence toward God and man," when we are earnest to keep God's law, and thence tranquil, and sensitive to whatever is beautiful; we are sick when these conditions are absent or reversed. The correspondence of physical disease with spiritual is most exact. By reason of it we speak of a healthy tone of feeling, a morbid imagination, sickly sentimentality, ill-nature, ill-temper; also of being sick at heart, ill at ease, cured of bad habits. Prudent, well-timed words, Homer calls ὑγιής, healthy. (Il. viii. 524.) From the Latin *sanus* and *sanitas*, we have the equivalent expressions, sanitary, sanatory, sanative, sane, insane, sanity, insanity; the three first applied to bodily, the

---

* In ascribing lunacy, insanity, &c. to diseased *brain*, we must take care not to do so unreservedly. Cases are not infrequently met with of patients who have been mad for years, and yet whose brains, on dissection after death, present no appearances different from those of persons who have died in all the vigor of sound intellect. On the other hand, all morbid appearances of the brain (except those which supervene upon general paralysis) are found as frequently in persons who have died sane as in those who have died mad. The sudden cures of the mad, their temporary restorations, and many other facts lead to the belief that insanity may probably be a disease of the *blood*.

others to intellectual health. *Sound*, which is the same word as *sanus*, is applied to a "sound judgment," as well as to a "sound constitution."

212. It is because of the spiritual diseases that the physical ones exist; or rather, they are both of them outbirths of the same infernal cause, namely, the circumstances and principles of hell. Whatever is good, beautiful, and enjoyable upon earth, is by derivation from heaven, or the bright and angelic portion of the spiritual world; whatever is evil, offensive, and ugly, comes, similarly, from the regions of darkness. Disease belongs to the dark catalogue. In its moral forms, it is directly inseminated and sustained by evil spirits—the door to their agency being the "fallen nature" inherited from our parents and ancestors; for, that man is exposed to the incessant, though secret and silent seductions of evil spirits, is no less certain than that he is blessed by the ministration of angels;—its physical forms appear among us, because of the universal and immutable ordinance that all things and conditions spiritual, shall issue into material representatives. *Proximately*, these latter are induced by infraction of the laws of the physical world. Though all such afflictions are referable, ultimately, to the providence of God, it is no direct supernatural influence that casts a man into rheumatism or fever, but carelessness of something purely natural. This is the *immediate* cause of physical suffering; else man would not be the free agent that he is, in matters of health and self-protection. Disease, accordingly, is no part of the proper nature of things, as death is, but a declension from it. Disease destroys, but death is sanative. Disease is to the material body what sin is to the soul; a condition it is liable to, but so far as it is given to man to judge, apparently by no means inevitable. A distinction is clearly drawn in Scripture between those who "kept not their first estate," and those whom the sense

of the passage implies to have retained it. Decay is natural, because nature is finite, such decay always having reference to Rejuvenescence, or the renewal of life; but disease—understanding by this name, painful and virulent affections—is *not* natural. At least it is impossible to conceive of it as in any way compatible with a state of moral and physical purity, such as that which the Bible teaches regarding our first parents, and which alone is a true state of Nature. The hundred wretched maladies which *now* infest the world, entered it, there is every reason to believe, with man's gradual, and deeper and deeper lapse into sin, or the *un*-natural state. While the "corruption of nature by the Fall" is unquestionably much exaggerated by theologians, in whose commentaries it is far more largely dwelt upon than in the Scriptures—neither our Saviour nor any of the New Testament writers who profited by his oral instruction ever making mention of it—it cannot for a moment be doubted that there is an awful and unrecalled literal truth in what it is customary to call the "curse." Thorns and thistles shall the earth produce unto thee, in sorrow shalt thou bring forth; and the other similar intimations of evil to come, carry with them the intimation, though this is not specifically stated, that disease also would now begin to afflict. It would enter the world, like the thorns and thistles themselves, and like the creatures which are noxious to man—expressly taught by Luther, Kirby, and many others to have been unknown to this earth till after the Fall;—it would now enter the world because the latter had become an arena, through the sin of its inhabitants, into which infernal principles and circumstances could project themselves; each thorn and thistle, and noxious animal and disease, being the physical embodiment or playing forth of some element of hell; the virus of a long anterior sin, infusing itself into a fresh country of the universe. The common origin of the two forms of disease of course does not imply that they shall exist in the *same person*, or that moral disease necessarily engenders physical, or physical disease, moral, in a man who suffers from the other. It is in the *total* of the world and its inhabitants—some experiencing the spiritual, others the physical, that the representative fulfillment is effected. Physical disease visits the most virtuous, if they neglect to take sanitary precautions; and the man who attends to them, though he be a thief and a liar, probably has not a day's sickness in his life-time. Permitted thus to enter the world we dwell in, like all other evils, it still comes under the supervision of divine love. To exhibit this great principle as regards sickness, has been the happy office of Dr. Duncan, in his commendable little work, "God in Disease, or the manifestations of design in morbid phenomena." "Throughout every department of the various forms of physical suffering," says he, "are scattered in profusion, proofs of care, of tenderness, and of design." By well-chosen illustrations, embracing many different kinds of disease, the Doctor shows most conclusively, that though infernal in its origin, all the subsequent history of disease is a history of infinite benevolence, and this whether it afflict the wicked or the good. This book is of peculiar value as being the first step in a very useful direction, namely, the collection of the evidence of a personal and merciful God in the disorders and irregularities of the universe.

213. Connected thus intimately, it follows that the best and shortest way to diminish physical disease, is to strive to diminish that which is spiritual; seeing that wherever there is most scope afforded for underlying spiritual forces to express themselves, the physical outbirths of those forces will most abound. So long as mankind surrender themselves willingly to the malignant seductions of infernal spirits, thereby opening the way for aggravation and extension of

spiritual disease, so long will physical disease continue in full force. The principle is daily becoming verified. Though the names, and thence the apparent diversities of disease, are multiplying, disease itself, with the advance of civilization, is steadily decreasing.* While knowledge is power, it is also bodily health. As arts and sciences, social economy and refinement, move onwards, all these things being essentially connected with moral or Christian advance, the means are increased by which life is defended, and pain alleviated. How much more, then, may be anticipated from the direct warfare with the very fundamental causes of disease carried on by the extension of religious principle and motive, in other words, from the gradual evangelization of the world. Intelligence assails disease proximately, because it teaches what are the physical laws of health, and the implicit obedience they require; improvement in morals helps to subvert its very basis. To get a vicious man to amend his morals, is similar to burying a corpse. For as the latter diffuses malaria of physical death, so do the wicked among mankind diffuse those of spiritual death. Innocence and purity are corrupted by them; health is lost, and disease takes its place.

214. The miracles performed by our Lord consisted chiefly in healing, for the very reason that bodily diseases represent the more awful ones of the soul, which it was the object of his life and death in the flesh to remove. "Jesus went about all Galilee, teaching in their synagogues, and preaching the gospel of the kingdom, and healing all manner of sickness, and all manner of disease among the people." Every cure which he wrought represented the liberation of the soul from some particular kind of moral evil, or some specific intellec-

* See Marx and Willis, On the Decrease of Disease effected by the Progress of Civilization. 1844.

tual error. "Bless the Lord, O my soul," says the psalmist, "who forgiveth all thine iniquities, who healeth all thy diseases." Thus were the miracles in question performed not merely as indications of a Divine power to command, but as media of spiritual instruction. To the more intelligent Jews who witnessed them, they must have been peculiarly attractive, seeing that an especial function of their Scriptures—the Old Testament of our Bible—and of the entire ritual of their religion, had been to train them to look for lessons of spiritual wisdom in things physical and objective. Under this discipline, the love of signs and wonders became eminently characteristic of the Jewish mind, as a taste for philosophic speculation and discussion was peculiarly distinctive of the Greek;* so that, from disposition as well as habit, they must have been prepared—or at least the pious and better part, who had eyes to see—to perceive in those acts of divine cure the benignest and most godlike of promises. No man rightly appreciates the miracles who does not interpret them after the same manner. That such is the true and the *prescribed* intent of the miracles, is shown by the very word used to denote them, which is almost uniformly *σημεῖον*, "sign," implying that they are to be regarded as *significant, i. e.*, significant of something interior to and higher than the bare physical performance. The value of a thing is always in proportion to its significance, to the truth which it representatively teaches; the spectacle of the world is the grand, permanent source of sound and sublime instruction which we find it, entirely by virtue of this great quality; as the chief effect of female beauty depends on expression, so the value to our minds of the material universe comes of our being able to perceive in it the expressive cha-

* "The Jews," says St. Paul, "require a sign, and the Greeks seek after wisdom." 1 Cor. i. 22.

racters of Divine intelligence and love. When, in daily converse, we would speak of a thing as utterly worthless, we say that it is *in*significant, it teaches nothing but what we see in its blank outline.

215. Whatever may be the theological importance of these miracles, their value in helping us on towards a right philosophy of the universe, is at least equal to it. We are introduced by them, and indeed by the miracles universally, to new and more enlightened perceptions of those admirable methods of the Creator which men call Nature, and thus to enlarged understanding of the Life which it is one of the splendid functions of nature to assist in expounding, so far as it is capable of exposition. A notice of them is here, therefore, quite in place. Miracles, as wrought by our Lord, and by certain of the prophets and disciples, are not, as many suppose, at variance with nature, but only with unexpanded notions about nature. To assert them to be at variance with nature, is to assume, in fact, to know everything, both about God, and his universe, and his mode of managing it. Nothing can be really inconsistent with nature. It is a first principle of true philosophy that events, apparently the most unnatural and incompatible, admit, nevertheless, of classification, when taken into some higher synthesis;—that in the long run, everything is referable to Law. "Every ultimate fact is only the first of a new series. Every 'general law' is only a particular fact of some *more* general law, presently to disclose itself. There is no outside, no finally enclosing wall. The principle which to-day seems circumferential, to-morrow appears included in a larger. Our life is an apprenticeship to the truth, that around every circle another can be drawn; that there is no *end*, but that every end is a new beginning." Physical science is continually revealing, or at least pointing to such wider, more comprehensive, laws, within which the familiar

ones are contained; its progress "is constantly towards larger and larger generalizations, towards generalizations, that is, which include the generalizations previously established." Miracles, for their part, however widely they may be at variance with the ordinary course of things, come under a law which comprises both themselves and the daily phenomena which surround us, a law of which the sight is not withheld from the inquirer. Everything is a miracle when for the first time witnessed; it is our ignorance of the cause of the phenomenon which gives it the miraculous aspect. Gaining clearer knowledge, we refer it to its place.

216. By taking an example or two from physical science, we shall see this great principle without difficulty;—the laws, for instance, under which, in the first place, the *leaves* of plants are produced, and subsequently the *flowers*, which are yet but two different operations of *one* law. Watch a plant during the spring and early summer, and to appearance it lives for the sole purpose of multiplying its leaves, and enlarging its general fabric; and were we ourselves to live no longer, we should conclude, and allowably, that it was its nature to do no more. Presently, however, the production of foliage is found to be only a part of the scheme of plant-life. As the season advances, our attention is invited to another process. The development of stem and leaf abates, and the plant covers itself with blossoms. Now did we not annually witness the beautiful show; did the carrying out of the *whole* of the plan of plant-life, which is for flowers to be superadded to leaves, at a certain time, for a purpose of their own,—did this, we say, take place but once in a thousand years, how little short would it be of all the external characteristics of a miracle. But the exigencies of organization require that it should be incessant, so it is depreciated into one of the common, spontaneous acts of nature. If not absolutely a miracle, it is at least a *picture* of what miracles

are. The flower is from the first, in preparation,—an integral part of the idea of the plant; though to the unobservant it comes suddenly, the practiced eye can discern its embryo even when the leaf-buds have scarcely begun to open; beautifully representing in finites what miracles and their laws are to the Infinite. For could we see the entire scheme of the universe as He alone can see it, we should perceive them, unquestionably, bearing a relation to its symmetry and inviolable Order, similar to that which, in miniature, the flower bears to the plant. So with the phenomena of astronomical science. The "natural law" of the visible heavens is for the planets to move in certain, well-known orbits; for the constellations to change their apparent positions with the circling of the hours and seasons, and for various other phenomena to transpire, familiar and intelligible enough to their student. Yet how many others take place in the depths of space which seemingly are altogether anomalous, such as most of those connected with comets. Compared with the ordinary occurrences, they are miracles. But no; whatever the ignorant may suppose, the astronomer is satisfied that they are merely phenomena waiting explanation;—phenomena referable to some wider law, which controls our solar system, and the constellations, and the comets alike, and which science may some day put in the same rank as to intelligibleness, with eclipses and the morphology of plants. Again; "the anomaly that water is at its greatest density at about 40° Fahr., and below that, *expands* with decrease of temperature, is held by some to be a marvelous and outstanding fact, setting all theory at defiance. Yet no truly inductive philosopher for a moment doubts that it is really a part and consequence of some higher law, of which the ordinary law of expansion is a part."* Much of what it is customary

* Baden Powell, Unity of Worlds, &c., p. 96.

to call, in reference to miracles, the "suspension" or "violation" of natural laws, is disproved by the phenomena attending the operation of *counteracting* laws; also by such as come of the simultaneous operation of two *different* laws. For instance, it is "a natural law" that fire shall burn; but at the 1861 meeting of the British Association, M. Boutigny passed his bare hand harmlessly through a mass of molten metal, showing that fire may be prevented from burning, although to the spectator who is unacquainted with the scientific reason of the prevention, there is no apparent reason why it should not burn. The freezing of water in a red-hot platinum crucible, which every dextrous chemical teacher now shows to his pupils, curiously exemplifies the miracles which come of two or more laws acting at the same moment. The very notion of an "interference" with natural law is foolish, since every effect in nature must necessarily be the result of a law instituted to ensure it. In whatever department of nature they may occur, all such anomalies will unquestionably be found some day, to be included under grand and harmonious laws. "Nature," in the words of the great master, "pursues its course, and what we take for an exception, is but in accordance with law." As to anomalies, says the acute writer just quoted, "the philosopher will always fall back upon the primary maxim that it is in every case more probable that events of an unaccountable and marvelous character are parts of some great fixed order of causes unknown to us, than that any real interruption occurs."* When we speak, accordingly, of the "laws of nature," and define miracles, as we suppose, by means of the contrast, we do no more than speak of some few laws that lie on the surface. Familiar with a certain number of them, we are prone to look upon ourselves as admitted into the sanctuary of the

---

* Baden Powell, Unity of Worlds, &c., p. 108.

temple, when in reality we are only in the porch. When science shall be able to explain the miracles, it will be time, and not before, for men to catalogue the "laws of nature." That smaller things and principles, perfect in themselves, are yet contained within larger ones, is shown as well in the *forms* as in the laws of nature; of which latter, indeed, objective forms are only so many exhibitions. However widely objects may vary in configuration and structure among themselves, a common idea is found to pervade them all. Everything is but a part of a wider complex. In all their insatiable variety there is yet contained a permanent and unmistakeable unity. The idea of any given "species of animal is only part of the idea of the whole animal kingdom; and this again is only part of a still more enlarged idea, which comprises both the animal and the vegetable kingdoms. This again is a part of the whole idea of the earth, which appears at first sight an exclusive little world of itself, but is, notwithstanding, only a part of a vast system of worlds."

217. It does but require then that we should carry this great general principle to the consideration of the miracles, to find them, as affirmed in the outset, at once a portion of nature, and one of its most valuable and instructive portions; differing from the familiar portion only in the circumstance of their having been so *timed* in the general plan of creation, as to subserve specific religious purposes. The difference does not consist, as commonly supposed, in the putting forth of a greater *amount* of divine power; it is a difference only in the mode of the manifestation of that power; or consisting in the unaccustomed shape or formula in which, at particular eras, it has been exhibited to men. To say that an event such as that of the sudden healing of the sick was a "miracle," is strictly nothing more than to speak of it as an anomaly in our experience. Whatever

else the miracles may prove, the first thing they make us sensible of is our *ignorance;* the first benefit we derive from them is impulse therefore to new intellectual effort. There is nothing about the miracles to put them absolutely out of the pale of our understanding. True, nature has an accessible and an inaccessible, and it is our wisdom to find out where the division lies. But it is also true that nature is a vast *promise.* Though there are thousands of things not yet understood, he would be a bold man who would enumerate what things are absolutely incomprehensible. Darkness, for the most part, is not so much the darkness of night to an eye that is open, as of day to an eye that is closed in indifference. The contentment of the world in general with the light they possess, is no reason with the Fountain of Wisdom for withholding enlarged supplies from those who ask for more. It comes therefore to a mere question of intelligence and desire to know. There is every encouragement to hope and strive. How small a part even of the ordinary laws of nature is yet open to the profoundest philosopher; yet how clear are the ideas already attained from the index which that small part furnishes! How many wonderful processes are going on in secret which we know nothing of! How many are there which this age was first acquainted with; how many that we are ignorant of will be discovered when our memory shall be no more! We have but to abide by the principles which guide us in scientific research. With every step upwards, we learn to think more of the "common" arrangements of the world, and to lay less proportionate stress upon occurrences which are rare, because all are found referable to a central spring, rendering none more peculiarly strange than another, and taking even from the strangest that seeming of an "interference" with law, or of "suspension" of law, which at first is all our thought. The brute is scared by the lightning, and the untutored mind is aghast at the storm; both are unobservant of the stars and their movements, while all these things are to the intelligent as much a part of nature as daylight. "The difference between the wise and the unwise is, that the latter wonder more at what is *un*usual, the former more at what is *usual*." In reality, what we pass by so indifferently as "common," is for the most part, in the highest degree extraordinary, habit alone dulling the sight to what we should otherwise wonder at as "miraculous," just as we are apt to overlook many of the greatest of God's mercies, because with us always.

218. The function or instructive purpose of a miracle is Rejuvenescence. Wrought in all cases, either directly or indirectly, by Him who "upholdeth all things by the word of his power," the miracles, whether judicial, creative, or restorative, were acts uniformly bearing a definite and positive relation to the highest and heavenliest condition of things, the everlasting Eden of Life. How beautifully is it told of Naaman, that when miraculously cured of his leprosy by washing seven times in Jordan, "his flesh came again, like unto the flesh of *a little child*." What could show more strikingly that miracles, rightly understood, so far from being arbitrary deeds in contravention of nature, consist in the removal of hindrances to its proper, harmonious activity? All, without doubt, were indications to man, that by his moral degeneracy he is in an abnormal state; that sickness, want, evil, are the *un*natural condition; that the state of Nature is Excellence, Youth, Life; that these, as we have said before, are the one grand, comprehensive idea of the universe, and other things mere accidents and phenomena of their history and promotion. "A miracle," says Dr. Cumming, "is not, as some have tried to show, contrary to nature, but is above and beyond what we call nature. For instance, when we read of our Lord's healing

the sick, and raising the dead, we hear it said that it is contrary to nature. It is no such thing. We call it contrary to nature, because we say that sickness is natural. Sickness is *not* natural; it is an *un*natural thing—a discord in the glorious harmony. So with death. Death is the unnatural thing, and the natural thing is putting an end to death, and bringing back glorious and everlasting life. Healing the sick, and raising the dead, are the perfection of nature; they are the bringing back of nature to its pristine state; the restoration of the primæval harmony, the augury of future happiness; they are demonstrations to us that all the prophecies which describe paradise are possibilities. Every miracle of our Lord is a specimen of that new genesis under which there shall be no more sickness, but wherein former things shall have passed away, and all things shall be made new."*

219. What maladies of the soul are specifically represented by given diseases, it is easy to perceive. Those which are mentioned in the Bible furnish a clue to all. Leprosy, for example, corresponds to profanation; or the knowledge of what is right, but contempt and neglect of the practice of it. Reverence for divine truth, and obedience to it, is the very first step in regeneration; hence, the first person cured after the sermon on the mount was one afflicted with the disease in question. The next was one "sick of the palsy;" the condition of the paralytic exactly represents the infirmity of the human will. Fever represents anger, rage, and fury in their various degrees, whence its frequent meta-

---

* Foreshadows, vol. i. Lectures on the Miracles of our Lord, as earnests of the Age to come, p. 9. In saying that *death* is unnatural, Dr. Cumming of course is influenced by the low and popular notion respecting death which we have had occasion to correct above.

phorical use alike in poetry and colloquial converse. Further illustrations may be seen in the Rev. Isaac Williams' "Thoughts on the Study of the Holy Gospels," and in Dr. Duncan's little work just now spoken of.

220. Because of the correspondence we are considering, our Lord is called the great Physician and the Saviour. The former name signifies one who restores to a state of nature; the latter, the healer or health-giver. "Salvation" is derived from the Latin *salus* health, *salvus* healthy, which in French reappears as *sauf*, the proximate root of *save*. Salvation, accordingly, is that which, as the work of God saves or heals our souls. Hence the cry of David—O Lord, heal my soul! and the prayer of the prophet—Heal me, O Lord, and I shall be healed; save me, and I shall be saved. Jesus Christ, as the Sun of Righteousness, is said to bring healing on his wings. Etymologically, "heal" and "save" are the same word, as readily seen by grouping together the several collateral forms, as "whole," and the Greek ὁλος. The *hale* man is he who is whole; health is literally a state of wholeness. Primarily, the words heal and save thus mean to make sound or entire, as when a wound is healed, and the new skin grown over. The numerous sad pictures in Scripture of the depraved moral state as one of wounds, laceration, and bleeding, give to these words, as there used, an unspeakable beauty and appropriateness. How sublimely it is ascribed to the Lord, that "He healeth the stroke of their wound!" Derived from the same primitive root, through another channel, and denoting the same idea, are the words solace, console, consolation. An incurable grief, the wound of heart that remains open till death, Ovid beautifully calls *vulnus inconsolabilis*. Life and health, or wholeness, imply unity, integrity, perfection; hence we find the earth, "the firm, round earth," called *solum*, and whatever is like it in its integrity, sol*id*, whether material or

spiritual. We speak of a solid understanding, as Horace of *mens solida*, a fixed resolution. To consolidate is to make perfect or entire. The idea of such entirety is the ground of the adjective *solus*, alone; and reappears also in ἥλιος, or Sol, the sun. Helios was the same as Phœbus Apollo, the god of day and of light, and the father of Æsculapius, the god of medicine, if not the god of medicine or healing in his own person; for though in later times there were as many as four Apollos distinguished, this was probably but in keeping with the tendency of the Grecian mind to change the several attributes of a deity into as many distinct gods. The primitive idea was the sun, the fountain of light; to this, as a matter of course, followed life and health; and by another beautiful perception, the same deity presided over music, one of the soul's chief comforters and healers, whence its medicinal fame from time immemorial. "The poets," says Lord Bacon, "did well to conjoin music and medicine in Apollo, since the office of medicine is but to tune this curious harp of man's body, and to reduce it to harmony." Apollo was the pagan aspiration after Christ; one of his surnames was σωτὴρ, Saviour. His worship, his festivals, his oracles, all had more weight and influence with the Greeks than those of any other deity they worshiped. They would never have become what they were without the worship of Apollo; in him was the brightest side of the Grecian mind reflected. He who is the True Light, the Light which is the life of men, reveals himself also as Healer of the nations, in his "lovely song of one that playeth well upon an instrument."

221. The profound and beautiful relations indicated in the above ideas are acknowledged alike by theology and philosophy, by science, poetry, and language; all of which testify that like the Bible in its multiplicity of translations, the great, primal truths of creation are yet but varied pre-

sentations of One truth. Every cluster of human knowledge is consanguineous with every other cluster, like the bunches of grapes upon a vine, and our highest and most delightful intellectual exercise is to realize their unity, and their common origin. How beautifully, for instance, does science illustrate the correspondence of Light and Music, as regards the fundamental tones of the musical scale and the prismatic colors! The colors thrown by the prism upon the wall are the sounds of music, in a different sphere, so that whatever is representatively expressed in Light, is representatively expressed also in the harmonies which please the ear, the difference being only in the method. The correspondence is not a *discovery* of science; strictly speaking, science discovers very little; its function is rather to *confirm*. We speak intuitively of the "harmony of colors;" the poet in every age finds music in the lovely variegations of natural scenery, and equally detects in music that exquisite interweaving and melody of tints, which contributes so largely to the objective picturesque. The harp of Memnon is not a fable; the glow of the rising sun is a song wherever it may shine; "every lover of nature who, seated on a mountain or by the ocean, has witnessed the sun casting his first golden beams across the earth, has had his soul stirred by its heavenly music;" heard faintly and from afar, as it is in towns, still how divinely glad and animating are its strains! Sunrise may well have been deemed the return of a god: it is not merely the awakener of the world to life; the whole idea of life is representatively summed up in it, as in a happy and beautiful child descending upon the household as its morning-beam. Thus is it with all knowledge; the wider and higher the laws of nature we can discover, the more admirable and extended is our insight into nature, and the more of it do we enjoy at any given moment, as by grasping the stem on which they grow, we secure a whole posy of flowers at once. Far, we can never penetrate, yet may every man more deeply than he does. Isis still presents her countenance veiled as of old; but while she with disdain rejects the mere dissector and nomenclator, who cares only to inspect her as an anatomist; to him who would look upon her with the eyes of a lover, she will grant divinest glimpses. That heavenly face is hidden from the world only that rude profanity shall not stare at it; it is in wise encouragement that it should be so; for if, according to the inscription, no mortal may uncover it, we must seek then to be *im*mortal. He whose heart faints because discomfited while on earth, is no true disciple at Saïs.

CHAPTER XXII.

MORTALITY AND IMMORTALITY.

222. WITH so solemn and inevitable a destiny as Death forever looming in the future, it is not surprising that the leading text of the moralist and preacher in every age should be preparation for it; or that, viewing the changes which it works, and contemplating them only in their mournful aspect, the verses of the poet should be strown so profusely with elegiacs. Laments over the evanescence of the beautiful constitute some of the richest poetry the world possesses; and were even prose literature to be sifted for its gems, they would probably be found in connection with the same grateful but melancholy theme, as the loveliest hours of the summer are those which are wet with the tears of Eos. There are no monopolies in the kingdom of thought and feeling; the spirit by which modern or Christian meditations on life and death are often thought to be distinguished from those of the ancients, is itself cosmopolite, as well as cotemporaneous with all eras; for although the particular phraseology which the New Testament has supplied, is in the writings of pagan moralists necessarily absent, those writings breathe nevertheless, along with their sadness, a serene and earnest piety, which may be found if there be disposition to acknowledge it when met with. That the ancients' moralizings on life and death are comparable with those of Christian writers, it is by no means meant to assert. Unhappily, there is but too much room

for censure, especially as regards that ample portion where the scantiness and transiency of our temporal opportunities are made an argument for sensual indulgence—when they cry—"Let us eat, drink, and be merry, for to-morrow we die." The verses ascribed to Anacreon and other Greek poets, those likewise of Horace, Propertius, and Catullus, inciting to such indulgence, are well known to every lover of classical literature. Yet even these have their better, perhaps their redeeming aspect, and this, in merest prudence, should be considered first. Nothing is ever lost, while much is always gained, by attending to the good of a thing before its evil. Catullus' address to Lesbia, for instance, beginning

Vivamus, mea Lesbia, atque amemus,

which beautiful little poem may be taken as a type of all its class, has in it something so exquisitely tender and affecting that we can readily suppose the poet to have laid so much stress upon the certainty of never returning into the sunshine of terrestrial life, in order to encourage mankind to value that life as it deserves, and to enjoy it as intensely as the Creator desires we should. As the perishableness of the rose quickens our sense of its beauty and fragrance, so the picture of Joy, with Death in the distance, inspires us with new interest in our innumerable temporal delights, given us, as they are, "richly to enjoy." We need such reminders; men weaken in soul as well as body; the glow and ardor of love for the beautiful and true die from out of them, like strength from the limbs, if not watched and fed; the high and glorious function of the poet is, that he comes to us with his stronger soul, and sets us growing and living afresh. Such restorative, invigorative influence it is the nature and utility of all true poetry to exert upon us, and the degree in which it vitalizes is the token of the poet's genius. And though his particular theme, as in the song referred to, which dwells wholly upon kisses, may seem trite and poor, still he is none the less faithful to his mission if he awaken lofty and amiable sentiments. The physical images with which he deals, are so many figures and representatives, which it is for ourselves to translate into their significance, making out a new poem in our own minds. The opposition of ideas, so remarkable in the opening lines of the song spoken of, has a beautiful reflex in the Arcadian landscape of Poussin, representing rural festivity, the charm of which would be sensibly diminished, were it destitute of the monument and inscription.*

223. Be it Catullian or not, the sentiment that we should make the most of life; that as we go along we should enjoy every gift of God as ardently and as copiously as we can, consistently with sobriety and order, is a perfectly right and proper one—it is more, it is one of our first and highest duties. To sell one's self to sensuality is one thing; thankfully to accept, and temperately to enjoy the honest pleasures of the senses, is quite a different matter. Sight and hearing, taste and touch, were bestowed for no other end than to be exercised on things congenial to them. The true way to enjoy most of heaven is previously to strive how much we can enjoy of earth; not, however, by striving to enjoy it exclusively as an earthly thing, still less as a sensuous one, to the neglect of the moral and intellectual; neither again by laying ourselves out for pleasure, purely *as such*, but by taking as our ruling motive, in our search for enjoyment, the higher development of our humanity. The golden rule of all is to connect, as often and as closely as we can, the terrestrial with the heavenly. The highest delight of

---

* For a variety of beautiful commentary and quotation upon this subject, see Dunlop's History of Roman Literature, vol. 1, p. 470.

which human intelligence is susceptible is that which comes of the habit of translating the ordinary circumstances of daily life into ideas that lead ultimately to God; there are no truly beautiful and nourishing ideas but such as are felt to gravitate imperceptibly towards Him, while none are so practical and efficacious, as ingredients of happiness, as those that are sucked, honey-like, from the merest trifles of existence. So in regard to the *time* for enjoyment. Though we may rely upon the recurrence of some few sources of pleasure, the greater part are so fitful, the total of the circumstances is so unlikely ever to be the same again, and our own changes of emotional state are so frequent and extreme—what enraptures to-day often becoming distasteful and even bitter on the morrow—that if we would realize life in its fullness, we must let no chance, not the slightest, escape, though at the moment it may seem utterly insignificant. Life is made up of minutes, and its happiness of corresponding little pleasures; the wise man secures the atoms as they flit past him, and thus become owner of the aggregate. Making every circumstance of life, sensuous, moral, and intellectual, and every day and hour, contribute a little something, he finds that though a brilliant and memorable pleasure may come but twice or thrice, the secret of a happy life is nevertheless his own. That fine secret is not so much to lay plans for acquiring happy days, as to pluck our enjoyment on the spot; in other words, to spend that time in *being* happy which so many lose in deliberating and scheming how to *become* so.

> Non est, crede mihi, sapiente dicere *Vivam;*
> Sera nimis vita est crastina, *vive hodie.*
>
> I'll live to-morrow, 'tis not wise to say;
> 'Twill be too late to-morrow,—live *to-day.*

To accomplish this, we have only, as said before, to make the most of each little incident and opportunity, contemning and repudiating nothing; always remembering, however, that the way to make such incidents and opportunities most prolific of enjoyment is so to humanize them that they shall flower into thoughts of heaven. Wilfully to let opportunities go by, is a wickedness and an inexcusable folly; whence the still more foolish regrets which tear the heart that has been so unjust to itself—for folly is only another name for thorn and prickle seed;—but a greater folly yet, is to stand waiting and wishing for opportunities, when in fact they circle us, if we will but keep on the *qui vive.* As the best school in respect of high duties is the practice of the little ones of common life, so the best and shortest road to happiness and true philosophy is to make the most of what lies beside us, and enjoy all we can of the life we have, leaving it to God to determine what fortune shall attend our steps. *Dominus providebit.* If we trusted more in his spontaneous generosity, we should seldomer be disconcerted by the failure of our own preparations, and should find that the Divine intent is that life shall be felicitous. The same, did we ask ourselves more frequently what we *have*, rather than brood so ungratefully upon what we have *not.* Though we may be poor and afflicted in comparison with some, in contrast with others we are opulent and blest. Life has a prize for every one who will open his heart to receive it, though it may be a very different one from the spirit of his early dreams. "There is no greater mistake," says a thoughtful writer, "in contemplating the issues of life, than to suppose that baffled endeavors and disappointed hopes bear no fruits, because they do not bear those particular fruits which were sought and sighed for.

"The tree
Sucks kindlier nurture from a soil enrich'd
By its own fallen leaves, and man is made

In heart and spirit, from deciduous hopes,
And things that seem to perish."*

The disproportion in men's inheritances is far less than we are prone to think. If one hand of the universal Giver be closed, the other is expanded; no one is left without his meed of compensation, only in our weakness and unthankfulness we look more at the darker side of our own lot, and at what appears to us the brighter side of our neighbor's. Epictetus explains the mystery in part; "it is not Fortune that is blind, but ourselves." Whatever be our lot, if man will but just concede that that must be best for him which the Best of Beings has ordained, life thenceforward has a solace which no fortune can wrest away.

224. Thankful, hopeful, happy as we may be, Death comes at last, and familiar as we may have made it in thought as a general proposition, always so strangely and solemnly as to be incredible and unexpected; in the case of those we love, as an impossibility suddenly converted into a reality. Immortal until taken away from us, now for the first time we become aware that they were only lent, and mourning and grieving seem to be the only real and permanent things of earth. There is no wrong done in giving way to such emotions. To be troubled at the death of those we love, and to shrink from death on our own part, are equally in obedience to heaven-implanted instincts, and the former is always the sign of an amiable and tender disposition. Luther thought that the punishment of Adam partly consisted in his long life of nine hundred years, seeing that in the space of it he would lose so many friends. They are emotions, nevertheless, which require to be controlled, and which demand, no less, that they shall not be perverted.

---

* Henry Taylor, "Notes from Life."

Our moral and intellectual knowledge we should ever allow to remind us of the high purposes they are intended to serve, and to lift us out of useless and ungrateful regrets. The Creator disposes us to be grieved at the decease of our friends, in order that all humane and kindly feelings may be awakened and deepened. It is for the sake of the survivors that he leads us to sorrow for those who die; that the wretchedness it is to be bereaved of those we love, with the inevitable reflection that enters into it of how much we have left undone that would have contributed to their happiness, may incite us to be more generous to those who are with us still. True mourning for the dead is to live as they desire we should do, and as we feel most pleasure in having others live towards ourselves. Any other is little different from selfishness. "We do not honor the dead by withdrawing our sympathy from the living, or neglecting occasions of being as useful to *them* as we were to the individual we mourn. No man loses by death the whole of his friends and acquaintance, and can say that his generation has left him alone. The place of those who are gone will be supplied by others; the circle perpetually renews itself; to determine that none can or shall be so good in our eyes as the departed, is at once to behave uncharitably to mankind, and to refuse the compensations which God provides." Thus does the death, so called, of those of our friends and companions who precede us in the return to youth, provide us with the most favorable opportunity of testing how much life there is in ourselves. For the value and reality of a friend consist, essentially, in his influence on the development of our affections, charming them, as with a song, into love of the Good and Beautiful, and this, to the soul that is in right order, the mere dissolution of the body but little hinders. All that is dearest and loveliest in those who go first, all that makes it good for our souls to possess such treasures, remains with us, if we love truly, after they are gone. Friends, parents, children, brothers, sisters, though they may quit their accustomed places, and be no more seen, die to us only when in our inconstancy we forget them. Life is love. So long as we love a thing we retain it. It is only when we cease to love it that it dies. "To me, indeed," says Cicero, speaking of his lost friend Scipio, "though he was suddenly snatched away, Scipio still lives, and will always live, for I love the virtue of that man, and that worth is not extinguished. If the recollection of these things had died along with him, I could in nowise have borne the loss of that most intimate and affectionate friend. But these things have *not* perished; nay, they are cherished rather and improved by reflection and memory."* Rightly regarded, the death of a friend is one of the greatest mercies God bestows upon us. Not only does it operate upon the development of the affections; but "through the gap which it makes in the visible, we gain a vision into the awful, invisible life of which it was for a moment the semblance. We see what we had forgotten, or never properly known, that the life we lead in the flesh is only the appearance, and that the hidden life of the spirit is the reality, and thence are we warned from walking "in vain show;" for it is no other than walking in vain show, to surrender ourselves, as we are so prone, to matter and material things, and turn deafly from the message of the spiritual." In its purity, sorrow for the dead is a part of that elegant sentiment of our nature which leads us to sigh at the ruin of the beautiful, wherever it may pertain, or however it may appeal. The heart of that man is not to be envied, who can see the leaves wither and the flowers fall, without some sentiment of regret, or who can pass unnoticed the

---

* *De Amicitia,* at the end.

dried-up fountain, or the time-worn, roofless, silent abbey. The tender interest which every rightly-ordered mind feels in the frailty of the beautiful, alike of nature and of art, is only a slight tribute of becoming grief and affection, seeing that it is under its benign and humanizing influence that we grow in wisdom, and become conscious of delight; our sorrow for the dead, so lovely as they were to our hearts, is this self-same tribute, only deserved infinitely better. Far, accordingly, from our thoughts should be the idea of *misfortune* in connection with death. "To have laid a strong affection down among the dead, may be a great sorrow, but is not a real misfortune. Whatever one's after-goings may be, there is a deposit for the future life, a stake in the better country, a part for the heart which the grave keeps holy, in spite of the evil that is in the world. The living may change to us, or we to them; sin may divide, strife may come between, but through all times and fortunes, the dead remain the same to our memories and loves. The child taken from us long ago is still the innocent lamb that was not for our folding; the early lost friend is still the blessed of our youth, a hope not to be withered, a promise not to be broken, a possession wherein there is no disappointment."

225. If it be inconsiderate, or unkind, or unwise, to mourn for the dead merely in the shape of regret for their departure, it cannot be wisdom to complain if part of our own time seem withheld. That a man should lament at having to die, be it soon or late, indicates neither philosophy nor religion. No one who is in a right state of mind ever even thinks about death. He thinks only of his *life*, knowing that if this be properly regulated and developed, death, come when it may, will but invigorate and renew him. It would be difficult to find a greater or more pernicious error than that so often propounded as "religion," that men should be always looking forward to their "end." They

should never be looking forward to their *end;* they should be too intent upon their *present.* True religion does not concern itself as to how and when men die, but as to the quality of their current life. Men are not saved according to how they die, but according to how they live. Death takes no man unprepared, whenever it may come, wherever he may be, or however employed. Neither could he die at a better time, were he allowed even to choose and arrange for himself; because God, who fixes it, is the only competent judge of our spiritual condition, and causes us to die at the precise moment when it will be best for our eternal welfare, whether we be tending upwards or downwards. Even to the most wicked, death is an operation of mercy, seeing that it is of Him who maketh the sun of his love, no less than that of nature, "to rise both on the evil and on the good, and sendeth rain both on the just and on the unjust." If to one man life be "providentially spared," the life of another is providentially taken. The only ground on which we can properly lament the ending of our sojourn on earth, is that it prevents our being any longer corporeally useful to others. But in thinking only of life, and never of death, we are not to think only of our *time*-life. We should think of our life as a stream, which commencing in a wilderness, presently leaps from it in a waterfall, and thereafter pursues its endless course through a country infinitely rich and beautiful with nature, art, civilization, and religion, reflecting in its serene and softly gliding depths, each heavenly scene it visits. Darwin remarks that we are less dazzled by the light on waking, if we have been dreaming of visible objects. Happy are they who in this life dream of higher things than those of earth! They will the sooner be able to see the glories of the world to come. Living *here* the true life of the soul, we shall start at once from the slumber of temporal existence into shining and intelligible morning.

> To me the thought of death is terrible,
> Having such hold on life. To thee it is not
> So much even as the lifting of a latch;
> Only a step into the open air
> Out of a tent already luminous
> With light that shines through its transparent walls.

Wisdom, then, dictates that life should be our great and only regard. For the first office of wisdom is to give things their due valuation, to estimate aright how much they are worth; and the second is to treat them according to their worthiness.

226. The *fear* of death is quite another matter. As said above, it is the simple emotion of nature, the play of a divinely-implanted instinct, and thus conformable to the just order of things. Virtually, it is the impulse to *self-preservation*, the profoundest instinct of the whole animal creation, seeing that without it, every species, man included, would soon become extinct. The innumerable physical perils which endanger life; and in man, the mental sufferings superadded to them, would lead, in different instances, either to its accidental loss, or its willing surrender, almost as soon as possessed, and thus to the depopulating of the world. How rapidly does life even now become lost, despite the desire to preserve it! Save for the great impulse within, to Live, whatever it may cost, the world would cease to be replenished, and "Be fruitful and multiply" have been an impractical command. Men differ about arts and sciences, about their pleasures, fashions, ornaments, and avocations, but all are agreed in the love of life, and hate, and fear, and flee from death. "We do not all philosophize," says Clemens, "but do we not all follow after life?" "This temporal life," says another venerable writer, "though full of labor and trouble, yet is desired by all, both old and young,

princes and peasants, wise men and fools."* Virtue, wisdom, poetry, the Bible, are matters which from intellectual slow-pacedness, or moral disrelish, excite only moieties of interest, but life is the central, universal, indomitable solicitude.

> The weariest and most loathed worldly life
> That age, ache, penury or imprisonment
> Can lay on nature, is a paradise
> To what we fear of death.

Man needs, in truth, to love life, if only from the immensity of function which he is qualified to perform ; and doubtless it is in order that he may avail himself of his opportunities, if he will, and build up his futurity, that the love of the merely animal life is made so strong in him ; for this is the first essential to the incomparable privileges of existence. It is by reason of the great excellence of life, as a *spiritual* necessity, that the deepest injury that can be inflicted is to kill, and that the highest philanthropy and goodness is to preserve alive. To lay down one's life for another implies the most ardent of all possible love, because it is the relinquishment of our richest treasure.

227. The man, accordingly, who affects to regard death *without fear*, must not expect to be believed. He may not anticipate it with horror; he may have learned, by secret and silent preparation of the heart, and by accustoming himself to see God as infinitely just and merciful, how to meet it cheerfully; he may be perfectly resigned to it when he sees its approaching shadow; but still he dreads, and were the spirit not withdrawn by him who gave it, would never part with it of himself. When death is actually about to happen, the fear of it is in great measure lost. At all

---

* Lactantius, Book iii., chap. 12.

34

events it is not common, as well known to those whose professions lead them to the pillows of the dying. This, again, is a vast mercy and providence of God, both to the individual and to the bystanders. Given to us when it is proper we should live, it is mercifully taken away when we are going to depart. When we fear death most, supposing that is, that there is no sufficient physical reason for the fear, we are probably entering on our highest usefulness to the world. When fear does manifest itself at the period of approaching death, it is rather as the result of some diseased or enfeebled state of mind, usually induced by spurious religious teaching; or of vivid presentiments of what a wicked life is about to lead to; than as a part of the animal instinct which previously had ruled. As a rule, death, at the last hour, like Satan, appears only to those who have reason to be afraid of him, and rarely even to these. Nothing is more deceptive than the manner in which a person dies, though often made so much of. The wickedest die "in peace" no seldomer than the righteous, though it is the peace of torpor in one case, of piety in the other. The inmost ground of men's fear of death is consciousness of severance from God, through disobedience to his law. Brutes fear to die simply because of their instinct to preserve life, or from the purely animal feeling. Men fear to die from a twofold ground; superficially, from the same instinct as that of the brutes; interiorly, from consciousness of this severance from their Maker. God desires that all men should be united to him, and to this end has given them adequate spiritual faculties, wherein they shall exercise the life which conducts to heaven. In proportion as they do this, and thereby attain to consciousness of union with Him, the idea of death departs from them, because they are living with the Fountain of Life; the less that they feel united, the more do they think of death, and fear to die. While, accordingly, the righteous man views his physical death with no alarm, the unrighteous carries his fear with him even into the future state. Fear of death is not so much according to the *place* a person is in, as according to the condition of his heart. It is its own dissolution of which the soul, in its secret chambers, is afraid; and the sense of dislocation from God which gives the real agony to the expectation of death here, will constitute a similar but infinitely severer torment hereafter; as in heaven the greatest blessing will be the sensation of coherence with God, or Life. To fancy, as many do, that death is not only terrible and affrighting, but physically painful, is quite a mistake, being to look for sensibility in the *loss of* sensibility. Death is a sleep rather than a sensation, a suspension of our faculties rather than a conflict with them; instead of a time of suffering, a time of deepening unconsciousness. Dr. Baillie tells us that his observation of death-beds inclines him to the firm belief that nature intended we should go out of the world as unconsciously as we come into it. The moment, says Mrs. Jameson, "in which the spirit meets death is probably like that in which it is embraced by sleep. To be conscious of the immediate transition from the waking to the sleeping state never, I suppose, happened to any one."

228. *Why* is man immortal? Not simply because the soul is non-material. We must not suppose, remarks Warburton, that because the soul is immaterial, it is necessarily imperishable. Though it does not dissolve after the manner of matter, that is no reason why it should not be susceptible of extinction in some other way.* To suppose otherwise would be to esteem it of the same substance as the Creator, instead of one of his creatures, as it is. Of all the arguments for the immortality of the soul, that of its being "immaterial"

---

* Divine Legation of Moses, Book ix., chap. 1.

is unquestionably the weakest. "The immortality of the soul," says Dr. Knapp, in the Christian Theology, "neither depends for proof upon its immateriality, nor from the latter can it be certainly deduced." To the same effect is the remark of Mr. Isaac Taylor:—"As to the pretended demonstrations of immortality drawn from the assumed simplicity and indestructibility of the soul as an immaterial substance, they appear altogether inconclusive."* It would be easy to show indeed, that he who affirms man to be immortal simply because of the immateriality of the soul, is bound to affirm likewise the immortality not only of the nobler animals, but even of the microscopic animalculæ, which would be contrary alike to reason and revelation. Bishop Butler's argument for the immortality of the soul, namely, that in fatal diseases the mind often remains vigorous to the last, though commonly esteemed one of the strongest, is actually of no more worth than the argument of immateriality. Any function will remain vigorous to the last if the organ of its exercise be not the seat of the disease. Immortality inheres in the soul of man not because it is immaterial or spiritual as to substance, but by virtue of the "breath of lives" which God breathed into man in the beginning; the life of intelligence to *know* him, and the life of power and adaptedness to *love* him. It is through the possession of these two faculties that man lives forever, in happiness or in misery, according as they are honored or abused, and not merely because he possesses a soul or spiritual body. They remain with him, and thus keep him alive forever, because given by infinite, divine, *unchangeable* Love, which, whatever it gives once, it gives everlastingly. Were God to withdraw life from man, even for an instant,

* Physical Theory of another Life, page 254.

he would not be the Faithful and the True. The very object of the creation of man was, that a being should exist competent to receive and reciprocate this love. Love lives by reciprocity. Its most exquisite satisfaction and delight is at once to love and be loved back again by the chosen one of the bosom and the offspring of the body. Not simply to exhibit his power or his skill, did God create the universe, but that his love might have an arena, and that happiness inexpressible should animate innumerable hearts. To think of God aright, we must think at the same moment of a universe of intelligent and feeling creatures, for each idea is needful to the true reading of the other. Any idea of God which does not include man, is low and imperfect. Banish then the fancy that man is immortal because he has an "immaterial" soul. It needs to be something more than "immaterial;" it must be adapted to religious exercises; just as it avails nothing to the Ourang Outang to be organized, he must be adapted to talk and to manipulate, if he is to enter the ranks of humanity.

229. It is because these two faculties—intelligence to know and adaptedness to love—are *not* possessed, that brutes are only temporal. They cannot entertain heavenly ideas—they cannot feel religious emotions;—as Wesley beautifully expresses it, they are not "creatures capable of God." Unprofitably indeed has the time been spent by those who have sought to show that brutes are immortal, or even have any claim to be. The chief argument with those who have espoused the notion, has been the "justice of God," which requires, they contend, that brutes should live over again, in order to be recompensed for the evils they suffer here. This, indeed, is the only argument, as there is nothing in brutes which shows them to be placed here for probationary and preparative discipline, as man is; such discipline being not only needful to heaven, and the reason of man's being

made a free moral agent, but one of the best natural proofs of the destiny of him who is subjected to it. Brutes have none of the pains, anxieties, and disquietudes arising from moral causes, to which man is subject. They have none of his love of virtue, thirst of knowledge, or intense and constant longing after such a degree of happiness as this life not only never gives, but is absolutely incapable of affording. The plea above-mentioned is therefore the only one. But is it a reasonable plea? That the infliction of cruelties on brutes by man must one day be accounted for by him is certain, because of the great and shameful wickedness of ill-treating and giving pain to the defenseless. Probably, however, all these cruelties and pains appear to brutes as so many *accidents*, devoid of meaning or intentional harm, and no more than the fall upon them of a tree or a house. That they suffer with the *intensity* commonly supposed, may also be seriously doubted. In reasoning concerning the feelings of the lower animals, we are too apt to reason from *our own*—a course which cannot but lead to error. That which so enormously aggravates physical suffering in man, is the operation of his *imagination*. Brutes, being destitute of this faculty, perceive only by moments, without reflecting upon past and future, and time and life without reflection are, as we all know, next neighbors to *no*-time and *no*-life. Suffering, alone and definite, is incomparably less afflictive than when combined with various and indefinite trouble of mind. Let none suppose that divulging this to mankind at large would be to the prejudice of the brute creation. The gentle and kind will always treat brutes gently and kindly, whatever their feeling or want of feeling; while the cruel will always treat them cruelly, as they do their own species.

230. Whether or no, that pain, hunger, thirst, and other such "evils," (which are all that brutes can be seen to endure,) require compensation in another life, is after all, no

argument, because it has yet to be proved that these *are* evils; and query, is not the physical enjoyment of all creatures quite a balance against their physical sufferings? The enjoyment of the brute creation is immense. We cannot turn our eyes in any direction, but we witness an exuberance of it. Earth, air, and water alike swarm with beings full of the delight of living, and collectively, perhaps experiencing as large an amount of agreeable physical sensation as does the total of the human race. No small part of this happiness is of man's own bounty to them, though certainly for his own interest in the end. "He spreads the verdant mead, and lays out pleasure-grounds for the horse, the ox, the sheep, and the deer; and the pang that deprives them of existence is as nothing compared to their antecedent life of luxury. Were there no men to till the ground, the earth would not maintain a thousandth part of the animals it does at present, and the want of cultivation would also unfit it for the mass of living insect enjoyment with which it now swarms." Besides, in the lower grades of animals, whose numbers compared with those of the higher kinds, or quadrupeds and birds, aré as the sands of the sea, physical suffering is little, if at all experienced. As regards these, accordingly, the plea of recompense cannot stand, and this is enough to condemn the whole hypothesis. When we see fishes and insects apparently writhing in pain, it is not that they are in a state of agonizing torture, but that they are *struggling to be free.* Those vehement efforts come simply of impatience of control, a desire common to every living creature. Nothing that has life but rebels against captivity. Imprison even a plant, and it becomes as restless, in its sphere of being, as a chained animal. Pain, in fact, is so slight in the humbler classes of animals as in no way to admit of comparison with what it is in man and the creatures he has domesticated. Every entomologist knows how indifferent are insects to mutilations that would be instant death to a quadruped; Mr. Stoddart, in his entertaining little volume, "Angling Reminiscences," has put it beyond all possibility of doubt that fishes feel no hurt from the hook.

231. The doctrine of the immortality of brutes is an exceedingly ancient one. The Indian, whose blissful heaven consists of exhaustless hunting-grounds, does but reflect from the forests of the West, what is thousands of years old in the Odyssey: "After him I beheld vast Orion, hunting in the meadows of asphodel, beasts which he had killed in the desert mountains, having a brazen club in his hands, forever unbroken." Virgil, in his sixth book, enumerates animals seen by Æneas in the kingdom of Pluto; Hercules, in Theocritus, finishes the narration of his great exploit of slaying the Nemean lion by saying that "Hades received a monster soul." The same belief existed among the Druids, though doubtless a transplantation from the East; the warrior shades, celebrated in song by the son of Fingal, love all the amusements of their youth; they bend the bow, and pursue the resuscitated stag. Authors who have left treatises on the subject are Crocius, Ribovius, Aubry, Gimma, &c., and in our own country, Richard Dean, Curate of Middleton in 1768. "As brutes," says the latter, "have accompanied man in all his capital calamities, (as deluges, famines, and pestilences,) so will they attend him in his final deliverance." Southey, Lamartine, and Miss Seward have written beautiful verses expressing their belief in the immortality of brutes. The "Penscellwood Papers" (Bentley, 1846) may be consulted for an essay to the same purpose; Mrs. Jameson's Common-place Book (pp. 207–212) for selected opinions; and Bonnet's *Palingénésie Philosophique; Idées sur l'état futur des Animaux,* (Œuvres, Tom. vii.) for a long and minute argument. Dr. Barclay (Inquiry, &c., p.

399,) pleads that for aught we know, brutes *may* be immortal, "reserved as forming many of the accustomed links in the chain of being, and by preserving the chain entire, contribute, in the future state, as they do here, to the general beauty and variety of the universe, a source, not only of sublime, but of perpetual, delight." It is true that the forms of animals will be thus needed; it is true also that they will appear in the scenery of the future world, but it is *not* true that those forms will be there by resurrection from earth.

CHAPTER XXIII.

THE RESURRECTION AND THE FUTURE LIFE.

232. Concerning no subject of vital interest to the human mind are theoretical doctrine, and familiar, practical belief, so widely discrepant, as in regard to that most solemn and awful event of human life, the Resurrection after death. We say "of life" because life and immortality, rightly viewed, are not two distinct things, any more than time and eternity are. Life runs on into immortality, partitioned from it only by a thin, dissolving veil of flesh and blood; Time is simply that part of Eternity in which we exist now. Man *is*, not *to be* immortal. Although the true idea of the Resurrection has been incidentally stated in other places, a distinct chapter upon its philosophy and phenomena becomes of the highest importance to our present inquiry. As with many other topics, it has been impossible wholly to postpone it; some of what we have now to present in a connected form may in consequence want the air of absolute novelty; but by concentrating the whole, perhaps even the points already touched upon will become more intelligible, and thus render the new allusion to them not unwelcome.

233. Doctrine says the Resurrection is to happen in the remote future; Belief says it occurs simultaneously with dissolution. Who ever speaks of a departed friend except as having "gone to heaven," that is, of living there as a glorified human being, in the enjoyment of every bodily member, and every mental faculty and emotion, needful to

the realization of celestial happiness? Who ever speaks, we say, except of their having *gone*—mark, not as *to go*, at some indefinitely distant period, but as having already and absolutely *gone?* Unwilling as men may be to allow in words that the soul is a spiritual body, independent of the material body, and capable of complete existence after parting with the latter; to believe that the departed is "in heaven" is *necessarily* to believe it; also to believe in immediate resurrection, and what is of no less importance, in immediate "judgment." In every age has that great unimpeachable intuition of the spiritual body, and of its immediate resurrection, been the faith of sorrowing men. Whatever light Scripture may have thrown upon death, to this the human heart cleaves with firm, undeviating affection. However opposed in other things, in this, Pagan and Christian are agreed—death is immediate entrance into the Better Land. How beautiful is the monody of the old Greek poet—

> "Protè, thou art not dead, but hast removed to a better place, and dwellest in the Islands of the Blest, among abundant banquets, where thou art delighted, while tripping along the Elysian plains amongst soft flowers, far from all ills. The winter pains thee not, neither does heat nor disease trouble thee, nor hunger nor thirst; nor is the life of man any longer desired by thee, for thou livest in the pure splendor of Olympus."

Cyrus, on his death-bed, desired the Persians to rejoice at his funeral, and not to lament as if he were really dead. The Arabs regard it impious to mourn for the deceased, "that is," say they, "for those who are with Mahomet in Paradise." "Dear Sir," writes Jeremy Taylor to Evelyn, in 1656, "I am in some little disorder by reason of the death of a little child of mine, a boy that lately made me very glad; but now he rejoices in his little orb, while we think and sigh, and long to be as safe as he is." Here, indeed, is the mourner's consolation. When the loved and lost are thought of by the calm light of the great and sacred truth that "there is a spiritual body," they cease to be dead; their resurrection has already taken place. The mind that is in a right state recoils from the chill ideas of the coffin, and putrefaction, and inanimateness, and fastens on the sweet conviction that the vanished one is alive, and in the enjoyment of serenest happiness and rest. It thinks of the corpse in the grave merely as an old garment, consecrated indeed by the loved being who had used it, but of no value in itself, and soon to be the dust from which it was moulded. Never was there a more lovely illustration of this faith than the epitaph on the mother and her infant in the Greenwood Cemetery at New York: "Is it well with thee? Is it well with the child? And she answered, It *is* well." (2 Kings iv. 26.) That part of the great mystery which concerns the souls of little children who die, and their development in the future life, is the most pleasing perhaps of all for our contemplation. Whether do they remain little children, or expand to the full, beautiful, noble human stature? Either way, those who have lost such a one, are never without a little child to love and nestle in their hearts. The others grow up and become men and women, but this one stays with them forever.

234. In order to a true idea of the Resurrection, it requires accordingly, first that we should have a true idea of what the soul is; second, a true idea of what constitutes Death. The soul, as we have seen above, is no mere appendage to man, formless and insubstantial, but man himself. Death, as we have also seen, is simply the departure of man from his temporal, material body, and his consciousness of the *material* world; and entrance upon full consciousness of the *spiritual* world. The fundamental truth of the whole matter simplifies therefore into this—the dis-

tinctiveness of *ourselves* from our *material bodies.* "It is the soul," says Hierocles, "that is *you*, the body that is *yours*."* What we *are* is one thing, what we have, or some time have had, round about us, is another. We must not confound them. It is because they are confounded, that people cannot see how the soul can be independent, and live and act separately and apart. As we cast off our clothes at night, and wake to the world of visions, so is it at death—we cast off our temporary material bodies, which are only so much apparel, and become conscious of the world of spirits. A man never really *dies*. A change comes over us, but life is never really extinguished, nor for one instant suspended. The dead, as we call them, are no more dead than we ourselves. Solemn is the thought, but *somewhere* our departed friends are every one of them alive, consciously, vigorously, actively alive.

235. Further, as the soul is the man, and the material body only his house while upon earth, a man is never really *buried*. No human being, since the beginning of the world, has ever yet been buried, no, not even for a few minutes. Buried! How can a living soul be buried? Man is where his conscious being is, his memory, his love, his imagination; and since *these* cannot be put into the grave, the man is never put there. So far from being our "last home," the grave is not a home at all, for we never are laid in it or go near it. "How shall we bury you?" said Crito to Socrates, before he drank the poison. "Just as you please," replied Socrates, "if only you can catch me!" Socrates knew better than that he should die. He saw through death as a

* *Σὺ γὰρ ἔι ἡ ψυχὴ· τὸ δὲ σῶμα, σον.* Commentaries on the Golden Verses of Pythagoras, (Ed. Needham, 1709, p. 114). Many other observations of the same tenor occur in this truly philosophical writer.

vapor curtain, through which he would burst into another life. "I shall not die; I shall never die," is what every man ought to say, and energetically to think. "I shall never die; I shall never be buried; bury me if you can catch me!" Burying, as commonly spoken of, is a gross, material idea, thoroughly vulgar, unpoetical, and unscriptural, the result of materialism in theology, and a striking proof of the small amount of spirituality current in the popular religious creed. To talk of a man being "buried," put into the earth, and lying there, while his soul is somewhere else, is no less false and illogical to the understanding than it is offensive to the feelings. "We ought to rise above the use of such base phraseology. We ought even to teach our children, from the earliest, that there are no men and women really in the grave; and truly they better understand and receive this great truth than many of their elders. How difficult to make a child believe that its mother, or father, or brother, is below the sods! And how foolish the efforts sometimes made to force it to believe the degrading falsehood! Leave it alone to its heaven-born thoughts. Why attempt to destroy the being of one who is merely absent to us, as we shall all be, ere long, to others?" The very tombstone is inscribed falsely. It says "Here lies the body of ——." Rather should it be, "Here lies the *last* of the bodies of ——," since the body we depart out of at death is only the concluding one of a long series, every one of them quite as worthy of commemoration. The earth, let us remember, too, does not itself open the grave we deem so frightful. It is man who digs it, and who peoples it with the horror which he charges on it. People talk again of the "worms" which devour the dead. Here is another falsity. Our bodies moulder and decay, but they are not *eaten*. Worms are engendered, not by corruption, but by flies, who must lay the eggs from which they issue, and no flies have power to penetrate so far into the earth as the depth at which the dead are usually laid. Wrong feeling about dead bodies and the grave does more than anything else to vitiate religious teaching, to hinder consolation for the loss of friends, and in general, to mar faith in immortality. Happy the day when all shall learn that the corpses of the departed are no more than relinquished garments of living men and women—temples of God in which divine service is over and finished, the chanting hushed, the aisles deserted, and to be contemplated with as little terror and revolting as we gaze at the silent ruins of Rivaulx or Tintern before altogether "wede away" by Time.

236. The conviction of our departed friends being alive in heaven, fashions our own secret expectations. No one ever imagines from his heart, that he is to lie indefinitely in the earth, but rather that death will be to greet and be greeted by old, well-known faces, shining in the sweetest lineaments of love—that as we were received when as little infants we entered *this* world, with tenderness and affection, so shall we be when as men and women we enter the next; that, in short, all pleasant things and states will immediately supervene, the same, yet inexpressibly more bright, all the dreams found, and only the sleep lost. It is enough that we have a spontaneous hope of it, for the hopes of the heart are rarely deceptions.

> My sprightly neighbor, gone before,
> To that unknown and silent shore,
> Shall we not meet as heretofore,
> Some summer morning?
>
> When from thy cheerful face, a ray
> Of bliss hath struck across the day,
> A bliss that would not go away,
> A sweet forewarning?

Intuition is worth volumes of logic. "Where, in the plan of nature," says the German writer Reimar, "do we find instincts falsified? Where do we see an instance of a creature instinctively craving a certain kind of food, in a place where no such food can be found? Are the swallows deceived by their instinct when they fly away from clouds and storms to seek a warmer country? Do they not find a milder climate beyond the water? When the May-flies and other aquatic insects leave their shells, expand their wings, and soar from the water into the air, do they not find an atmosphere fitted to sustain them in a new stage of life? Yes. The voice of nature does not utter false prophecies. It is the call, the invitation of the Creator addressed to his creatures. And if this be true with regard to the impulses of physical life, why should it not be true with regard to the superior instincts of the soul?"*

237. Holding such views in their hearts, and daily reading the book wherein they are confirmed, is it not strange that Christians should use for the symbol of death, the unconsoling, not to say disgusting and disheartening, skull and cross-bones? What a Sadducean usage compared with the beautiful custom of the ancient Greeks, who, though "pagans," saw death imaged rather in the living, glossy, Evergreen tree, and planted accordingly, beside their tombs, the cypress and the yew. In ancient funeral ceremonies were used, for the same reason, branches of myrtle and arbutus, as shown by the beautiful allusions in the Electra of Euripides, and the 11th book of the Æneid. Certainly the former custom is still extant, but not so its intrinsic significance, or whence the dull surmises that have been set forth to explain its retention? That which is perennially

* The Principal Truths of Natural Religion Defended and Illustrated, in Nine Dissertations.—*English Trans.*, 1766.

fair and cheerful is the true emblem of death; not that which is dolorous; the tree green throughout the winter, and the Amaranth, rather than the decaying old bone. How elegantly and appropriately the Amaranth is associated with immortality by the poets; and practically, under the name of *Immortelle*, in the cemetery of *Père la Chaise*, is familiar to accomplished minds.* No less so the fine similitude of life and its interlude of death, presented in those mysterious rivers which, like the Guadalquiver, after flowing for some distance, lucid and majestic, suddenly hide themselves in the ground, but a little further on burst out again, as pure, and bright, and grand as ever. It is not a little curious that the only personification of death which has come down to us from antiquity, represents it as a skeleton dancing to the music of the double flute;† the charming old fable of the singing of the swan before its death, is but a poetic rendering of the same idea. Jerome Cardan, the famous physician of Milan, in the sixteenth century, concludes his

---

* The Amaranth or "Everlasting" is not, as commonly supposed, a flower *sui generis*. There are many species, and even genera of flowers which by reason of their juiceless and scariose texture, retain their color and form indefinitely. Such are different species of *Elichrysum, Gnaphalium,* &c. among the compositæ, in which family the Amaranths chiefly occur. Oddly enough, the genus botanically called *Amaranthus*, least merits the name. Those who would cultivate these beautiful flowers should on no account omit *Gnaphalium fulgidum*, golden; *Aphelexis humilis*, crimson; *Rhodanthe Manglesii*, rose-color and silver; *Ammobium alatum*, white; and above all, the incomparable *Astelma eximia*, resembling clusters of ripe raspberries. The chaplets, &c. used at Père la Chaise are made of the *Gnaphalium Orientale*. No garden need be destitute of the *Elichrysum bracteatum*.

† On a gem preserved in the Medicean Gallery at Florence, and figured in the *Musæum Florentinum*. Gemmæ Antiquæ ex Thesauro Mediceo, &c. Plate 94, fig. 3.

beautiful book on Consolation, with a comparison of death to marital love. "Cum itaque stremem àgonem anima superaverit, tam quam amans amanti copulata, eâ dulcedine ac securitate fruitur, quam nec scribere, nec cogitare possumus, &c." "When, therefore, thou hast taken thy last leave of life, thy soul, like unto a lover embracing his love, shall enjoy that sweetness and security which we can neither write of nor conceive."—*Opera*, tom. i., p. 636. This beautiful composition, the choicest work of its extraordinary author, ranks second only to that of Boethius on the same subject.

238. The transplantation of our consciousness, at the period of death, from the material to the spiritual world, has its image in the suspension of our external senses during Sleep, and the wakening of that mysterious sensibility of which we become conscious in certain modes of dreaming. "We are somewhat more than ourselves in our sleep," says Sir Thomas Browne. "The slumber of the body seems to be but the waking of the soul. It is the ligation of sense, but the liberty of reason."

> Strange state of being! For 'tis still to be;
> Senseless to feel, and with seal'd eyes to see.

Doubtless the majority of dreams are what Macnish asserts all to be, namely, "the resuscitation of thoughts which in some shape or other have previously occupied the mind." Experience and revelation attest, however, that at times, the struggles of the chained spirit to employ, and thus to enjoy itself amid the glories of its proper clime, are not in vain. Such are the occasions when strange, beautiful pictures open out before our sleeping sight, rich in all the colors and reality of life. It will be said that these are creations of the imagination. Probably so. But then what is this imagination?" Barely to assign a phenomenon to the "imagination" is to get no nearer to its cause. It is to evade the question, rather than to resolve it. The "imagination," as usually referred to in such matters, is just one of those useful entrenchments behind which perplexity is apt to shelter itself, and nothing more. The imagination belongs less to the material than to the spiritual world; or at least, it is like the *Janus bifrons* of the Roman mythology,—provided with a twofold face and senses. What the populace say about imagination presenting images that we mistake for realities, is like popular philosophy in general, pure nonsense. No man ever imagined or can imagine anything that has not reality *somewhere*, and this whether waking or sleeping. That which we call imagination in reference to dreams is what in the day-time we call our poetic faculty,—and probably the play of each is in definite ratio to the other—the prime characteristic of the faculty being unswerving allegiance to Truth and fact, and one of its chief privileges, insight into the spiritual world. In sleep we are conscious of beholding objects as distinctly, and hearing sounds as plainly, as in our waking state, yet with an eye and ear wholly different from the outward organs; and which can have reference therefore only to a sphere of nature and mode of being likewise entirely different, a sphere which can be no other than the Spiritual world. Dreams, in a word, rank with the highest phenomena of the spiritual life. "Dreams," says Addison, "give us some idea of the great excellence of a human soul, and its independency of matter, They are an instance of that agility and perfection which is natural to the soul when disengaged from the body. When the organs of sense want their due repose and necessary reparation, and the body is no longer able to keep pace with that spiritual substance to which it is united, the soul exalts herself in her several faculties, and continues in action until her partner is again qualified to bear her company. Dreams look like the amusements and relaxations of the soul when she is disencumbered of her machine; her sports and pastimes when she has laid her charge asleep." Bishop Newton's remarks on dreams are little less than argumentative for the spiritual body. "It is very evident," he writes, "that the soul is in great measure independent of the body, even while she is within the body; since the deepest sleep that possesseth the one cannot affect the other. While the avenues of the body are closed, the soul is still endued with sense and perception, and the impressions are often stronger, and the images more lively, when we are asleep than when awake. They must necessarily be two distinct and different substances, whose nature and properties are so very different that while the one shall sink under the burden and fatigue of the day, the other shall still be fresh and active as the flame; while the one shall be dead to the world, the other shall be ranging the universe." Lord Brougham's Discourse of Natural Theology contains reasoning to the same effect, and almost in the same words. A most clever and interesting little book on this subject, and one which nobody curious in the phenomena of man's inner life should fail to peruse, is Sheppard's "On Dreams, in their Mental and Moral Aspects, 1847."

239. But leaving aside such dreams as those alluded to, even the ordinary kind claim to originate in a spiritual activity, similarly concurrent with the ligation of external sense. For "the resuscitation of thoughts which in some shape or other have previously occupied the mind," is nothing more or less than a prelude to what will unquestionably form a chief part of our intellectual experience of futurity; namely, the inalienable and irrepressible recollection of the deeds and feelings played forth while in the

flesh, providing a beatitude or a misery forever.* Ordinarily, this resuscitation is of such a medley and jumbled character, that not only is the general product unintelligible, but the particular incidents are themselves too fragmentary and dislocated to be recognized. But it is not always so. There must be few who have not experienced in their sleep, with what peculiar vividness, unknown to their waking hours, and with what minute exactitude of portraiture, events long past and long lost sight of, will not infrequently come back, showing that there is a something within which never forgets, and which only waits the negation of the external world, to leap up and certify its powers.

O, wondrous Dreamland! who hath not
  Threaded some mystic maze
In its dim retreats, and lived again
  In the light of other days?
  * * * *
There the child is on its mother's breast
  That long in the grave hath lain,
For in Dreamland all the loved and lost
  Are given us again.

In the whole compass of poetry, perhaps there is nothing more touching than the allusion in the Exile of Erin:—

---

* Martineau carries out this view, in a piece of great power, in the "Endeavors after the Christian Life." Vol. 1. Coleridge, in *Biographia Literaria*, (vol. 1, p. 115. Ed. 1817,) suggests that the "books" which are to be opened at the last day, are men's own perfect memories of what they have thought and done during life. In relation to the quickening of the memory at death, it is full of solemn interest that persons so nearly drowned as to lose all consciousness, and all sense of physical pain, see, during the moments preceding their restoration, the whole of their past life in mental panorama. Of this there are many well known instances on record. Forgetting, absolute forgetting, asserts De Quincey, is a thing not possible to the human mind.

Erin! my country, though sad and forsaken,
In dreams I revisit thy sea-beaten shore;
But alas! in a far foreign land I awaken,
And sigh for the friends I shall never see more!

That which so vividly remembers is the Soul; and if in the sleep which refreshes our organic nature, it utters its recollections but brokenly and indistinctly, it will abundantly compensate itself when the material vesture which clogs it shall be cast away. Much of the indistinctness of dreams probably arises from physical unhealthiness. If a sound body be one of the first requirements to a sound mind, in relation to its waking employments, no less must it be needful to the sanity and precision of its sleeping ones. Brilliant as are the powers and functions of the spiritual body, the performance of them, whether sleeping or waking, so long as it is investured with flesh and blood, is immensely, perhaps wholly, contingent on the health of the material body. If the material body be improperly fed, or the blood be insufficiently oxygenated, the brain and nerves are imperfectly nourished, and the spiritual body can but imperfectly enact its wills. However little it may be suspected, the great practical question of our day, the health of towns, thus involves, to a less or greater extent, the moral and intellectual interests of the community. For a soul that is debarred from acting freely and vigorously, through a defective or vitiated condition of its instrument, cannot be expected to act nobly and religiously.

240. To enter the spiritual world, or rather, to become conscious of it, requires no long journey. Man, as already observed, is from his birth an inhabitant of it. Wherever there are material substances and material worlds, there likewise is the spiritual universe. Could we be transported to the most distant star that the telescope can descry, we should not be a hair's breadth nearer to it than we are at

this moment, nor should we be a hair's breadth more distant from it. So far from being infinitely remote and unconnected, as vulgarly supposed, the invisible or spiritual world is immediately contiguous. It circumferences us like the air we breathe. It is only to unintelligence that it is distant, and thus, like the Beautiful, at once quite close, and far away. It is near to our souls, which alone have concern with it, as the sweet kiss of true love; far from our bodies as such love is from the vicious. The notion that heaven is somewhere beyond the stars, a country on the convex side of the firmament, merely an elevated part of space, has long since been neutralized by the discoveries of Astronomy alone. "Above" the physical earth, and "below" it, are conditions which are changing every moment. If heaven be above our heads at noon, it is beneath our feet at midnight. The blue, radiant, infinite sky is the material *emblem* of heaven, but heaven itself lies nowhere in material space, because it does not belong to such space. This is the very letter of Scripture. When the shepherds were watching their flocks on the eve of the nativity, the angels had no long distance to traverse in order to come into view. They were not seen first as a bright speck in the sky, gradually taking shape as they drew nearer. They were beheld "suddenly," indicating that they were close by all the while, and that for them to be seen it was merely needful that the spiritual eyes of the shepherds should be opened. It was "suddenly" also that Moses and Elias disappeared after they had been seen on the mount of the Transfiguration; implying a similar closing of the spiritual eyes of the three disciples. So when "the angel of God called to Hagar out of heaven, and said unto her, What aileth thee, Hagar?" the words could have been uttered in no distant realm, or they would have been inaudible. At death, accordingly, there is no migration to some distant region of space; the avenue to our eternal abode is simply the casting off the "flesh and blood" which "cannot inherit" it, and heaven and hell are near and distant according to each man's moral state.

Death is another life. We bow our heads
At going out, we think, and enter straight
Another golden chamber of the King's,
Larger than this, and lovelier.—*Festus.*

241. What are the landscape features of that "golden chamber," of course we cannot know till we enter it, "neither hath it entered into the heart of man to conceive." But the inspiration which promises it says also that "the invisible things of God are clearly seen by the things which are made," signifying that the splendors of futurity, though in their fullness unimaginable, are nevertheless pictured in those of earth. Heaven is the permanent *εἶδος* of creation; earth is its dim *εἴδωλον*. The spiritual world is the universe of the essences of things; the material one is the theatre of their finited presentation; to such extent, and in such variety, that is, as it is necessary or desirable that man should know them during his time-life. Doubtless there are millions of spiritual things which are never ultimated into material effigies, but reserved as the privilege of the angels. Yet whatever we *do* see that is excellent and lovely, we may be sure is a counterpart of something in every sense celestial. The flowers of the spring yearly delight us by their return, because of prototypes in the spiritual world which are immortal, though their material emblems, like the beautiful Dissolving Views, come but to flee away; and tried by the Sensational standard of the real, seem to be gone and lost forever. The rose seems to wither, its petals scatter, and its loveliness is only a recollection; but the real rose can never perish. The real rose abides where it always was, in the

spiritual world; and there it will subsist for ever; and when we cast off our own leaves, we shall find it there in all its deathless beauty, along with all the other loved and vanished. God takes care of all that is truly beautiful and precious, and reserves it for us, provided we will go and take possession. We have but to cross the dark river confident in his trustworthiness, and we shall not be disappointed. God loves to be trusted. Then, too, we shall behold the spiritual sea, and islands, and rivers, and sun, and stars, and trees, just as St. John beheld them when God opened his eyes so that he might tell us of them in the Apocalypse, and as we continually express our own personal hope in respect of, in that beautiful anticipative hymn beginning

> There is a land of pure delight,

and proceeding—

> There everlasting spring abides,
> *And never-withering flowers;*
> * * * *
> Sweet fields beyond the swelling flood
> Stand dressed in living green.*

We all came into the world for something; we shall all go

---

* Other scenes in nature may be grander, but lovelier there are none than the view, on a fair summer morning, from the eastern shores of the upper part of the Bristol Channel. Seated on the thymy hills of happy Clevedon, sloping so delicately to the edge of the wild, seaweed-mantled crags, upon whose feet the impetuous waves, dashing and tossing, seem never weary of flinging their white beauty—as we gaze upon the opposite coast, the picture in these verses is completely and most exquisitely realized. There rolls the "swelling flood;" there lie the "sweet fields beyond," dressed in their "living green," and dotted with hamlets and white cottages which show conspicuous in the bright revealing sun. Borne to this beautiful presence, the heart learns how to understand the heavenly Jordan, and swells with new delight of pious hope.

out of it for more; just as when daylight is exchanged for starlight, we lose our consciousness of the terrestrial in the superber consciousness of the universal.

Mysterious Night! when our first parent knew
  Thee, from report divine, and heard thy name,
  Did he not tremble for this lovely frame,
This glorious canopy of light and blue?
Yet, 'neath a curtain of translucent dew,
  Bathed in the rays of the great setting flame,
  Hesperus, with the host of heaven came,
And lo! creation widened in man's view.
Who could have thought such darkness lay concealed
  Within thy beams, O Sun? or who could find,
Whilst fly, and leaf, and insect stood revealed,
  That to such countless orbs thou mad'st us blind?
Why do we, then, shun death with anxious strife?
If Light can thus deceive, wherefore not Life?

242. But, because of these prospects, we are not to think slightingly of the present life and its arena. Each sphere of being is divine, for each is the work of God, and if not felt sacred, it is the observer that is in fault. Many think that because heaven, which is the sunny part of the spiritual world, is above all places holy, therefore the material world, this earth, is vile—the devil's kingdom. Not so. The world, properly regarded, is GOD's kingdom, not the devil's. Hell only is the devil's kingdom. True, Jesus said, "My kingdom is not of this world." But it is quite wrong to infer from this, as many do, that he neither felt any interest in it himself, nor desired that man should feel any. To fancy our Lord to have promulgated Christianity upon earth solely with a view to man's future happiness in heaven, is one of the fatalest errors we can fall into. The true office of religion is to teach us so to live in *this* world, and so to enjoy it, that we must needs live in and enjoy the

other. "If thou wilt rightly understand and love eternity, learn properly to understand and love terrestrial life. The true preparation for heaven is to learn what we have on earth, and to be glad in it." To say that there is "nothing true but heaven," that all below is unworthy a wish or thought, is the very opposite to what Christ really taught. Certainly, the world we live in is full of trials and deceitfulness, and blessed is the promise of solace and compensation in a brighter sphere; but it is God's world still, therefore abounding in good and beauty, and impossible to be all worthlessness and illusion. The tendency to neglect and too little appreciate the advantages of the present life, encouraged by the incessant dwelling by many of our spiritual teachers on the prospects of the life to come, is a result which every thinking Christian man cannot but deplore; for that cannot be a true spirit of Christianity which deems our beautiful world a mere "vale of tears," the mere passage to a better, or which thanks God not so much for what he has already given, as for what we consider we are and ought, to receive. What our Lord really meant in those memorable words, "My kingdom,"&c., was, that he came to introduce an order of things based on other principles entirely than those of the humanly constituted kingdoms then existing—principles of love, charity and mercy, instead of selfishness, cruelty and aggression. Hence the angels sang not only Glory to God in the highest, but on earth, peace and good-will. There is something truly grand in the spectacle of a man in the enjoyment of health, prosperity, and reputation, looking forward nevertheless to a future life, with hope and thankfulness. Far more admirable, however, is the spectacle of him who feels this hope and thankfulness, not by reason of dissatisfaction with the world, but by reason of its ministry to him of wisdom and delight. "The fact," says a great and original writer, "that the sky is brighter than the earth is *not* a precious truth unless the earth itself be first understood. Despise the earth, or slander it, fix your eyes on its gloom, and forget its loveliness, and we do not thank you for your languid or despairing perception of brightness in heaven. But rise up actively on the earth, learn what there is in it, know its color and form, and the full measure and make of it, and when *after that*, you say 'heaven is bright,' it will be a precious truth, but not till then." (Ruskin, Modern Painters, iv. 39.) Constant dwelling upon death and what will follow it, too often confounded with religion, and even mistaken for it, is not only not healthful to the soul, but injurious. True, the way to live pleasantly is to learn to die hopefully; "fine ideas," says Goethe, "must needs fill the soul that in any way outsteps the boundaries of terrestrial life;" but we must not think *only* of dying; it is more religious to seek to preserve our life as long as we possibly can, and to exert ourselves as far as strength and opportunity will permit, than to *estrange* ourselves from God's gifts. Anything which too powerfully attracts us away from the duties of the present life, cannot be regarded as beneficial. While here, the living should belong to life, and adapt themselves to it. God has shown us that it is his will that we should do so, by withholding from us every clue as to the time of our departure. A truly noble soul loves both heaven and earth, falling neither into fanaticism nor terrestrialism. The functions of our temporal life are as noble in their degree as those of eternity can be. Our relations to God can never be more intimate or grand. "It is a poor mistake to think that we compliment God's heaven by despising his earth, and that we best show our sense of the great things the future man will do yonder, by counting as utterly worthless all that the present man can do here."

CHAPTER XXIV.

THE ANALOGIES OF NATURE—LAW OF PREFIGURATION.

243. A TRUE philosophy of Life includes the great phenomena of ANALOGY. In order, therefore, to the completion of our subject, it is proper that they should receive an independent and methodical consideration, over and above the passing allusions that have from time to time been made. Analogy as it exists among natural objects and appearances, is not, as often supposed, mere casual and superficial resemblance, though it is perfectly true that such resemblance exists. It is a part of the very method, order, and constitution of things. The evidence of the Unity of creation resides in its analogies; in these also we realize the noblest and most ennobling knowledge that is open to us after Scriptural truth, namely, the dual glory and blessedness of our position in the universe, or as regards Nature on the one hand, below, and God upon the other hand, above. Lord Bacon, who calls them the "respondences" of Nature, fully alive to their value, thus urgently enforces it in the Advancement of Learning. "Neither," says he, "are those of which we have spoken, and others of like nature, *mere resemblances* (as men of narrow observation may possibly imagine), but one and the very same seals and footsteps of Nature, impressed upon various subjects and objects. Hitherto this branch of science hath not been cultivated as it ought. In the writings emanating from the profounder class of wits you may find examples thinly and sparsely in-

serted, for the use and illustration of the argument, but a complete body of these axioms no one hath yet prepared; *though they have a primitive force and efficacy in all science, and are of such consequence as materially to conduce to the understanding of the Unity of Nature;* which latter we conceive to be the office and use of PHILOSOPHIA PRIMA." All philosophy goes to establish this high claim. No portion of Nature is truly intelligible till its analogies with the other portions are investigated and applied; the man who disregards them can never be more than a sectarian, while he who uses them—not in the way of a trifler, as the end of his inquiries, but as a philosopher, for their efficacy as a means—proves that it is they alone which can render the mind cosmopolitan, and truly instruct us in the arcana of creation. A man may be a very good chemist, as to acquaintance with salts and acids; he may be a very good botanist, as concerns the names and uses of plants; but this is only to be a *savant;* he is no philosopher till he can gather new insight into his chemistry or his botany by virtue of its analogies with other shapes of truth, and feel the centrality, as to essentials, of every science. For the true analogist, wherever he may be, however he may shift his standing ground, always finds himself in the *middle* of nature, his particular object for the time being, the clue and text-book to the whole. The characteristic of the true philosopher is his large consciousness of what is proper to the race in general, and of the varied circumstances which pertain to its expression in the individual. Analogy as it exists in the world of material nature, or as we are now treating of it, must not be confounded with Correspondence. "Correspondence," in the strict and proper sense of the word, and as ordinarily used in this volume, denotes the relation of the material and objective, to the spiritual and invisible, that is to say, the relation of inmost Cause to outermost

Effect, all causes belonging primarily to the spiritual world, and the phenomena of material nature being so many final effects of them, as shown in our chapter upon this subject. Correspondence, accordingly, can properly be spoken only of that first, governing analogy of the universe which involves the relation of a *prior* principle to a *posterior*, of a noumenon to a phenomenon, or *vice versâ*. The analogies of the material world are secondary, and are *not* correspondences. They are analogies of one natural effect with another natural effect; of one natural cause with another natural cause, and so forth; while Correspondences rest on the relations, not of two natural things to one another, but of natural things to spiritual things.

244. The value of the study of analogy, even in its simplest applications, is impossible to be over-rated. There is not a single science from which difficulties have not been removed by the certainties of a kindred science, when analogically compared with it, or which, on similar comparison, does not furnish new hints and illustrations. "It is curious," remarks Sir David Brewster, tacitly vouching for this principle, "how the conjectures in one science are sometimes converted into truths by the discoveries in another." Structures, forms, and phenomena, moreover, which are incomprehensible, considered locally and specifically, and which often seem positively useless and incongruous, become, by reference to a higher synthesis, based on an extended and philosophic consideration of analogies, not only comprehensible, but fraught with meaning of the finest order. Such, for example, are the organs which in man seem meaningless mimicry of the female bosom. Viewed by the light of analogy, there is nothing in the world either capricious or inconsistent. The mistake which too often prevents the full realization of the use of analogy, and tends even to engender distrust and prejudice, is the waywardness which so

commonly persists in contrasting that which is highest with that which is lowest—the *extremes*, in a word—and rejecting all that lies between as anomalous. Relations, like causes, that are not immediate, are discovered by such as are *intermediate*. When divested of the arbitrary disguises with which fancy may choose to clothe them, the highest and the lowest reflect each other's looks, and a common brotherhood becomes everywhere apparent. Because of this grand consanguinity of all knowledge, arising from the unity of nature, comes also the lofty opinion which the votaries of any particular department entertain of it. To the geologist there is nothing nobler than geology; to the chemist than chemistry; to the florist than floriculture. Each man feels the throbbing of the mighty heart, and, like the true analogist, seems to himself to stand in the middle.

245. Analogy accordingly, true, inductive, poetic analogy, constitutes the highest exercise of philosophy, "the science," as Adam Smith well defines it, "of the *connecting principles of nature.*" Not that perception of analogies is itself philosophy, but that all true philosophy rests on large and brilliant generalization, the means to this latter being fine and lively aptitude for the former. "The excellence of a philosophy," says Ruskin, "consists in the breadth of its harmony, or the number of truths it has been able to reconcile." That powerful capacity of abstraction which seizing the points of agreement in a number of otherwise dissimilar individuals, marshals the related, and separates the alien, is in fact, the highest prerogative of the human mind. "To generalize," says Mackay, "to discover unity in multiplicity, order in apparent confusion; to separate from the accidental and the transitory, the stable and universal; this is the great aim of human Reason." Not only is it the strongest evidence of Intellectual greatness. "The tendency to connect and harmonize everything is one of the eminent conditions

of a mind leaning to virtue and beauty, just as the tendency to dismember and separate everything is that of a mind leaning to vice and ugliness." The finest part of Originality is *combination*, or the power of generalizing and uniting, discovering new harmonies among familiar elements, and showing us gracefully and eloquently how to see them for ourselves. Originality therefore, instead of being, as many suppose, nearly exhausted, instead of becoming rarer, will become grander every day, and go on delighting us forever, seeing that with increase of facts and principles to generalize and combine, *pari passu* will there be scope for the power of generalizing. Essentially, this great power is innate and intuitional; hence it is classed by Plato with the divine or Promethean gifts. Forming, as it does, an integral and vital part of "Genius," or that which we are born with, if genius be acknowledged a boon from heaven, the part must of necessity be of the same origin as the whole, and the sage of the Academian garden be in the right. All men are competent to it, for all men's intuitions are alike, however different may be their development into living force under the influence of education and self-culture. Genius is not so rare as many suppose. Let a man assiduously apply himself to Nature and Analogies, and he will find in his own heart, however unexpectedly, hidden stores of the envied power, ready to burst into lifelike seeds. The achievements of genius, even the very highest of them, come not of something peculiar to *the man*, but of something common to *all men*. The man of genius, restrictively so called, does but set forth, clearly and beautifully, what all the world knows already, and what every true reader of him feels to be equally *his own*. Other people differ from him not as being ignorant, but as having their knowledge confused, vague, and inarticulate. This is the reason why in the land where a great genius lived and wrote, we always feel *at home*.

Though we may never have quitted our own shores, reading Virgil we feel that our native soil is beyond the Apennines. To the Englishman who loves him, Goethe makes Germany England; to the German who has a heart, Shakspere makes England Germany. Generalization, accordingly, is not to be deemed purely a *gift*, a power vain to aspire to; what is intuitive, even in the greatest, is simply the *capacity* to generalize. Whatever its particular bent, genius cannot do without study and culture, and these will often lift a man to the level of the reputed "Genius." In no department of life do men rise to eminence who have not undergone a long and diligent preparation; for whatever be the difference in the mental powers of individuals, it is the *cultivation* of them that alone leads to distinction. Though few may even by culture be able to express, all can in some measure learn to *feel and understand*. This, if nothing further, is in the power and will of every man, and peculiarly of the analogist. He may begin where he pleases; Nature has everywhere a portico; Truth, like the world, is a sphere; dig wherever we may, we shall surely come to the centre if we dig deep enough.

246. That Nature is a magnificent Unity has long been perceived; also that its parts form a vast Chain or series, beginning with the atom of dust, and extending through minerals, plants, and animals up to man. Associated with these great principles, and springing out of them, is a third, the beautiful principle of PREFIGURATION. Everything in nature is a sign of something higher and more living than itself, to follow in due course, and in turn announce a yet higher one; the mineral foretells the plant, the plant foretells the animal, all things in their degree foretell mankind. "Nature," says Henry Sutton, "before she developes the human being, prophesies of that her grand and ultimate performance, and gives pictures and shows of her unborn

man-child, hinting at him, and longing and trying to realize him, before the time has come for his actual appearance." As the Poet is not of one nature, but of Two, one concerned with the present, the other reaching forwards into the future, so is it with the phenomena and forms of Life. Over and above their ordinary present use and meaning, they tell of other and greater things to come, anticipating them, and pointing to them. Ordinarily, the resemblances subsisting between the three kingdoms of nature are deemed *mimicries;* the higher manifestation is said to be "imitated" by the lower, the phenomena of the vegetable being considered a degradation or humble copy of those of the animal, and those of the mineral world a degradation of those of the plant. This is wrong altogether; it is viewing the column as commencing with the capital, and ending with the pedestal. Properly understood, there is no such thing as *mimicry* in nature; it is an inverted mode of observation that makes it seem as if there were; the motto is everywhere Excelsior: the likenesses are not those of the living, smiling child and the wooden doll, but of the artist's pencilled outline and finished picture in colored oils. "In the inferior orders of creation it is not that the lamp of vitality is *going out,* but that we catch the first kindlings of that spark which glows with so noble a flame in the Aristotles, the Newtons, the Miltons, of our heaven-gazing race." So full of interest are these prefigurations, so serviceable to a right conception both of the unity and of the chain of nature, that it will be best for them to receive our first consideration, letting the former and greater truths come after. None of these matters, it may be hinted, are for closet study; they concern nature as it flows fresh and immaculate from God, and only by conversance with nature can they be justly apprehended. The man who would be truly instructed in her ways must seek them, not by pursuit of his fancy in a chair, but with his eyes abroad.

247. The Mineral kingdom, as the common basis of material nature, is also the first seat of prefiguration, which begins in the beautiful objects known as Crystals, including both the minerals proper, as the amethyst, lapis-lazuli, and emerald, and the infinite variety of chemical salts, as sulphate of copper, prussiate and bichromate of potash. These, in the symmetry of their forms, the purity and often translucent brightness of their colors, and their clustered mode of growth, give promise of the flowers of the plant, and are the blossoms of inorganic nature. Many substances in crystalizing, so dispose themselves as to predict the branching and general arrangement of the stems and foliage of plants. This we may see in native silver and native copper, which frequently assume most beautiful arborescent and frondose figures. In the freezing of water it is shown so strikingly, that while it transports the true lover of nature with delight, even the dullest are attracted and pleased by it. The delicate silvery lace-work on the window-panes on frosty mornings is something more than a pretty accident. By no means a mere *lusus naturæ*, (a very unmeaning expression,) not without a cause do we find it anticipating the forms of certain mosses, as those of the genus *Hypnum*, and in particular the soft, feathery *Hypnum proliferum* of sylvan pathways, giving not only the contour, but the very size. Nature places it there because in her least as well as greatest works there is nothing so incongenial as an abrupt beginning, and nothing so grateful as to sound a "herald voice" of coming glory. Certain sea-weeds are prefigured by the frost-work no less strikingly than the mosses; in the *Ptilota plumosa* we have a remarkably beautiful instance, every pinnule of this charming plant ramifying at a given angle, and originating smaller ones of the same character. Sometimes the tracery

is curvilinear instead of angular, when it points to the luxuriant wavy leaves of the Acanthus, as chiselled for the crown of the Corinthian pillar. No branches of trees, or foliage, however graceful, can exceed the freedom and variety with which these lines are drawn. In other cases, when curved and frondose, they foreshadow the rounded masses that give such richness to the umbrageous elm and courtly chestnut. Jones of Nayland gives plates of some of the latter varieties in his *Philosophical Disquisitions* (p. 244). Scheuchzer, in that curious old book, the *Herbarium Diluvianum* (tab. 8, p. 40,) figures a specimen of another variety, singularly presignificant of the club-moss, or Lycopodium clavatum, formed, he tells us, on the inner surface of a glass globe in his museum, during the severe winter of 1709. Prefigurements of vegetable forms occur likewise on the pavement in winter mornings, decorating it even in the heart of foggy towns, with graceful arching sprays in *basso relievo* of brown ice. In their earlier stages these remind us of the foot-prints of the sea-gulls upon the sand. On the surface of very shallow water, as at the bottom of tubs, congelation not seldom repeats, on a grand scale, small portions of the flowerage of the window-panes. The prefiguration is then of the larger pinnate-leaved ferns, as the *Polypodium aureum*, especially as they appear when pressed and dried for the Hortus Siccus. In fossil ferns, from these latter having more the appearance of drawings, we may observe it more plainly still.* In the animal kingdom these forms are recapitulated in the flat, white, pectinated skeletons of such fishes as the sole; just as

* An extraordinary example, singularly like the *Pecopteris gigantea*, occurred on the premises of the author, during the intense frost of February, 1855. The pinnæ were fourteen inches long, and the entire ice-leaf five feet in circumference.

the angles and geometrical nicety of the proportions of single crystals, reappear in the honeycomb of the bee, and the hexagonal facets of insects' eyes. The *stems* of plants, or at least those of exogenous structure, are prefigured in that curious stalactitic variety of sulphate of baryta, called in Derbyshire "petrified oak." The horizontal section of this mineral, when polished, presents a rich brown, circular disk, and gives an exact picture of the concentric rings and medullary rays. Flowers are foretold again in Snow. Walking over the white mantle of mid-winter, we little think that at every step we annihilate a tiny garden. But so it is. Scattered over the surface of snow are innumerable glittering spangles, composed of six minute icicles, spreading starlike from a centre, the rays themselves often provided with smaller, secondary filaments, so as to resemble microscopic feathers. In the less developed stage we see Nature planning in them such of the lilies and other flowers of Endogens as when expanded are flat and radiate, the *Ornithogalum unbellatum*, or Star of Bethlehem, for instance: in the latter or more developed stage they are harbingers of that dainty little blossom of the Canadian woods, the *Mitella nuda*, the petals of which are fimbriated and of the purest white. In the animal kingdom, the idea culminates in the star-fishes. The beauty of these unregarded little diamonds of the snow, though lost upon most men, has long been a delight to quick observers. Descartes gives rude drawings of them in the *Meteora*, and the ingenious but unfortunate microscopist, Robert Hooke, in his *Micrographia*. (Plate viii., 1675.) Dr. Grew, author of that immortal work, the Anatomy of Plants, contributed a paper upon them to the Philosophical Transactions for 1673, and there is a notice of them somewhere by Linnæus. It remained however for Scoresby, the arctic voyager, to point out their astonishing *variety*. His figures amount to nearly a hundred, and look as if designed from a kaleidoscope, all referable, nevertheless, to the common six-rayed star as their fundamental form. It is from these figures that the Cyclopædias and Galleries of Nature have all copied. The impression commonly entertained that the large diversity found by Scoresby in the Polar regions belongs only to such latitudes, is not correct. In the "Illustrated London News" for February, 1855, and again in the "Art Journal" for March, 1857, there are drawings by Mr. Glaisher, of the Greenwich Observatory, of no less than thirty-two varieties discovered in his own neighborhood, and doubtless many more may be found, and in any part of the country, if diligently sought, providing a Christmas and New-year's pleasure for the intelligent such as will outweigh whole nights of the mere temporicide popularly esteemed the *beau-idéal* of winter pastime. They were no common eyes that first espied the snow-flowers. Most men can see large things, but it takes clever ones to see the little. Nor were they common *minds*. To take the simple, the homely, the unheeded, and show mankind how to find in it a source of new, rational, and unsophisticated enjoyment, is not the least of the benign functions that belong to Genius. To learn how to see and delight in *little* things as well as large, is in fact, to make no slight progress both in true intelligence and in aptitude for genuine pleasure. Many laugh at the idea of being pleased with little things. "Little things," they say, "please little minds." They should remember that the great mass of the population of our planet consists of the merest pigmies, diminutive birds and fishes, tiny insects, animalcules only visible with a microscope, so that to turn away from *little* things is to be indifferent to almost everything the world contains. Besides, with Uranus eighty times greater than the whole earth, Neptune a hundred and fifty times greater, Saturn more than seven hundred times, and Jupiter more than fourteen hundred, it is rather inconsistent to talk about *littleness* in the objects of a world itself so puny.

248. The enterprise of PLANTS is one of the most wonderful things in nature. Irrespectively of their immense presignificance of Animal life, which infinitely exceeds that of the mineral world with regard to the vegetable, there is a continual and ardent emulation of all higher parts and forms by those which in function or development are lower. Leaves, for example, which, as we all know, are ordinarily of some shade of green, in many species paint themselves with the most vivid and beautiful colors. The leaves of several kinds of Amaranthus, as the Prince's-feather and Love-lies-bleeding, even when they first creep out of the ground, are brilliant red, announcing the blossom from afar; those of the *Caladium bicolor*, *Cissus discolor*, *Physurus pictus*, *Anœctochilus argenteus* and *setaceus*, *Plectranthus concolor*, and many others, are variegated with all the hues of summer gardens, and outshine tens of thousands of actual flowers. In the genus *Tillandsia* they are often striped as if with rainbows. It is not implied, or at least it is not a rule, that richly-tinted leaves predict richly-tinted flowers as coming by and by upon the *same stem*. Prefigurement may or may not refer thus particularly; its tidings are for the most part of a future glory in nature as a whole. The flowers of plants are foretold also by the bracteas and even by the calyces of certain kinds. Such is the case with the *Euphorbia splendens*, several species of Salvia, the Hydrangea, and the white-winged *Mussænda frondosa*. By means of their veins and other peculiarities, leaves in other cases apprize us of the very configuration of the tree they are building up. The angle at which the veins diverge is often the same as that which the branches make with regard to the trunk; where the leaves are sessile, the stem is usually set with branches down to the very ground; where they are

petiolate, the stem is also naked to a considerable height. "So far," say Dickie and McCosh, "as we have been able to generalize a very extensive series of facts before us, we are inclined to lay down the provisional law that the whole leafage coming out at one place on the stem corresponds to the whole plant, and that the venation of each single leaf corresponds to the ramification of a branch."* In certain mosses, as the Hypnum dendroides and Hypnum alopecurum, may be found miniatures of every tree in an arboretum.

249. The presignificance of Animal forms and economy by plants extend to the whole of their organic functions, many of their very organs, even to their spontaneous movements, their habits and qualities. As regards structure, the soft parts of the animal body are foretold by the succulent portion of the plant; the veins and blood by the ducts and vessels, with their rills of sap; the bones by its strong skeleton of woody fibre.† What is the nature of vegetable Feeding has been shown in a former chapter. It may be added that the eating of *organized* food, esteemed so peculiarly distinctive of animals, has its prefigurement in the *Drosera* and *Dionæa;* those curious little plants already mentioned on p. 63, which by means of appendages to their

---

* Typical Forms and Special Ends in Creation, Book 2, chap. 2, (1856.) See which excellent work for abundant illustration of the facts adverted to.

† Nowhere in nature are there more finished examples of skeletons than occur in plants. Those furnished by the capsules of the Stramonium, the Henbane, and the Campanula, and by the leaves of the holly, poplar, and Indian fig, when grouped and glass-shaded like wax-flowers, are fit ornaments for the most *recherché* drawing-room. The best are obtained by artificial maceration, but singularly beautiful specimens often occur among the natural relics of the autumn. The Indian fig-leaves are those imported from China.

leaves, entrap the smaller kinds of insects, as flies are ensnared in spiders' webs, and then appear to suck and absorb their juices. From June to August, when the English species of these vegetable carnivora are most active, there is scarcely a leaf in which we may not see either a recently-caught victim, or the desiccated relics of a former one. Vegetable Sleep is that relaxation of the vital processes which is indicated by the folding together and drooping of the leaves as night approaches, prefiguring the listlessness and supine attitude of the dormant animal, and further, in the beautiful phenomenon of the closing, eyelid-like, of the petals of the flowers, so charming to watch in the stillness of summer twilight. All plants do not exhibit these phenomena, but there are probably none which do not experience a periodical repose (at least when they are in a state of growth and inflorescence), eminently beneficial to their health, whether marked by external change or not. It is not to be understood that there is *actual* sleep in plants. Real sleep occurs only where animal functions are superadded to simply vegetative ones. The classes of plants wherein the prefiguration of sleep is chiefly conspicuous are the Leguminosæ and the Compositæ, the former closing their leaves, and the latter their flowers. Strikingly beautiful examples occur also in the water-lilies, the crocus, and the poppy, lulled as it were by its own Lethean balm. Those plants which do not open their flowers till sunset, as the Evening-primrose, or until night is far advanced, as the *Cereus grandiflorus,* seem to be the harbingers in the vegetable world, of those nocturnal birds, animals, and insects which are active only after dark, when all others are asleep. The Night-scented stock, and other flowers which are *fragrant* only or chiefly in the evening, are the heralds of the nightingale. Certain other plants agree with certain other kinds of birds in being peculiarly *matutinal.* Go out as early as we will, we find the delicate white bells of the wild convolvulus in the dewy hedge, and the rich imperial purple and crimson ones in the garden, just as we are never too soon for the chaffinch, the blackbird, and the lark. More wonderfully yet is Procreation foretold by plants. The apparatus, the mode, the circumstances, the results, all are delicately, but explicitly and fully announced. The lower kinds of plants, as fungi and lichens, wherein distinctness of sexual organization is imperfect, point to sponges and their congeners; the higher kinds, as roses and apple-trees, which have male and female as plainly marked as in mankind, prefigure in this respect, mammals, birds, insects, and all the nobler animate beings. Every individual flower on a given plant is a fore-shining of the nest of the bird, and the lair of the quadruped, and consummately, in its beautiful, silken, shielding petals, of the inmost curtained sanctuary of married love. The very colors and the fragrance perform a part in the exquisite proëm, being to the flower what sensation is to the creature, and emotion and sentiment to man. It is by reason of what it foretells, that the flower is so lovely. So near is the plant lifted towards the animal world, during the period of its sexual activity, that it becomes illuminated by the light of human love, reflecting the loveliness of the higher nature, like woods made musical by the descent into them of the singing birds. As with Sleep, there is no *genuine* sex in plants; this belongs purely to the animal world. The hymeneal hour gone by, and fertilization accomplished, the rudimentary seed begins to form, giving a presage of antenatal existence, followed in turn by a prefigurement of parturition in the bursting of the pod, and the escape of the ripened seeds. Finally, the seed itself, while in course of formation, is connected with the ovarium by a funis; when detached, it is marked with an umbilical scar Even lactation is prefigured in plants. The germinating embryo of the seed, too small and tender to live by itself, has vegetable mammæ provided for it in the cotyledons, which, white and rounded, nourish it with their sweet, milk-like contents. In the two large white symmetrical halves of the almond, the filbert, the acorn, the bean, we see this exemplified in perfection. They are no part of the future plant, which grows entirely out of the little hinge-like body lying at the point where they unite. Everywhere in nature the mother's bosom is foretold. The streams which "give drink to every beast of the field, where the wild asses quench their thirst," are its adumbrations in the great world of inorganic nature; to "flow with milk and honey" is the poetical or natural metaphor for the irrigation of a thirsty land with nutrient rivers. Rocks and towering mountains have a terrible and romantic grandeur, but the beauty of earth lies in those round, gently-swelling hills and eminences which the French so appropriately call *mamelons*. Not that the figure is a modern one. The Greeks termed such hills τιτθοι and μαστοι. A mound of this form at Samos, Callimachus calls "the breast of Parthenia."

250. The special prefigurations of animal ideas by plants are no less striking than the general. Thus, in the large, white, ovoid berry of the *Solanum Melongena* or "Egg-plant," we have the egg of the domestic fowl; in the pods of certain leguminous plants, bivalve shells, with their occupants; in the stem of the Testudinaria, a tortoise; in the seed of the Ophiocaryon, a coiled-up serpent, with glaring eyes, ready to dart upon its prey. The caterpillar is seen in the pod of the Scorpiurus; the antlers of the stag in the leaves of the *Acrostichum alcicorne;* the cocoa-nut gives tidings of the round brown head and comical visage of the monkey. Fishes are not the first beings to be clothed with scales; they are anticipated on the leaves of the *Hippophae* and *Elæagnus;* the hair, wool, and fur of terrestrial crea-

tures are similarly announced by the vestures of the *Gnaphalium* and *Verbascum*, while many ferns have their stems covered with *quasi*-plumage. The unexpanded buds of the great Shield-fern, Mr. Gosse compares to the shell of the *Trochus magus*. (Aquarium, p. 70.) The names Lagurus, Bird's-foot, Cock's-comb, Echinocactus, Phytelephas,* and a hundred others, refer to foreshadowings of the same character. So with the title of the large and beautiful family called *Papilionaceæ*, literally, "the Butterflies," typically represented in the Sweet-pea. In these we see Nature's first step towards the Insect-world, or at least towards the lepidopterous class. "The insect-world," says Coleridge, "taken at large, appears an intenser life, that has struggled itself loose, and become emancipated from vegetation. *Floræ liberti et libertini!* If, for the sake of a moment's relaxation, we might indulge a Darwinian flight, we might imagine the life of insects an apotheosis of the petals, stamens, and nectaries round which they flutter." There is no need for this; there is ample delight in the simple truth of the prefiguration, which ranks with the loveliest in nature. In that charming book, "Episodes of Insect Life," there is a long discourse upon the subject, to which the interested in it should not fail to refer.† It is not a little curious that the moths called from the time of their appearance "night-flyers," are generally of a subdued tone of color, corresponding with that prevalent in the nocturnal flowers. More prefigurative even than the Papilionaceæ are the Orchids, which present

---

* "Phytelephas" is the appropriate name of the palm, the seeds of which, commonly known as *Vegetable ivory*, have now so extensively superseded the tusk of the elephant, as regards parasol and umbrella handles, and the numberless little articles of the toy-shop and ladies' work-boxes.

† Vol. 1, p. 306. See also Vol. 2, pp. 294, 295.

the forms not only of insects, but of birds, and even reptiles. Even our indigenous species, next to the ferns the most attractive of British plants, mount so high towards animality, that we discern in different kinds the bee, the wasp, the butterfly, and the spider. The European Orchids are terrestrial plants, but the tropical and principal part of the family are *epiphytes*, that is, instead of anchoring in the earth, like the mass of vegetation, they perch upon other plants, and usually upon trees, in the clefts of which they lodge. Thus lifting themselves away from the earth, they beautifully presignify the aërial life, as well as the forms of bird and insect; and in the tenuity of their flower-stems, whereby the blossoms seem to flutter in the air, predict even the animal freedom from all bonds, and preëminently the living liberty given by wings. The inclinations which prompt both the Orchids and all other epiphytes to forsake the earth, and seek the friendly support of stronger plants, are the first prophecies and signs of volition and social sentiment. Actual motion is prefigured in the Sensitive-plants, described on page 18. As regards the natures, habits, and peculiar phenomena of animals, vicious and poisonous ones are foreshadowed in the nettle;* the sharp and rending teeth of wild beasts in thorns and thistles. There are grasses which anticipate the camel in providing against drought; the phosphorescence of the glow-worm and the fire-fly is a brightening of the light which first shines in the Rhizomorpha and the luminous Agarics; the juice of the Sanguinaria is like blood; that of the *Palo de Vaca*, or Cow-tree,

---

* The Nettle-plants, says Schleiden, are "the serpents of the vegetable kingdom. The similarity between the instruments with which both produce and poison their wounds is very remarkable." See his minute account of the apparatus, and a drawing of the nettle-sting, in "The Plant, a Biography," Lecture VIII., pp. 199, 200.

is like milk, not only in color, but in fitness for human food. In a few cases the prefigurations point directly towards mankind. Such are those which occur in the Orchis mascula, the Uvularia, the Phallus, and the Clitoria, names sufficiently descriptive of their extraordinary nature. In the walnut is a hint of the human head. The shell is the skull; the kernel, white, oval, convex, curiously convoluted, and enclosed in two delicate membranes, is the brain. Because of this resemblance, this fruit is in its native Eastern countries, called the "brain-nut." The stems of the Balsam, the Stellaria, the Carnation, and their allies, prefigure, in their long slender shafts and peculiar joints, the bones of the leg and arm. "The stalk which supports the leaflets of a species of Æsculus (the Horse-chesnut) exactly resembles a bone of the hand or foot; while in the Manna ash we have four or more pieces of like shape, forming the main stalk of the compound leaf, separating at the joints, and resembling a series of phalanges, as in a finger or toe."* Far above all, is the exquisite presignificance conveyed in the pomegranate, which, newly ripe, and before the crown has expanded, is a perfect representation of the full-grown virgin breast. Some varieties of apples bear a similar resemblance, furnishing one of the most beautiful metaphors of Greek poetry: in Theocritus, for instance, *μᾶλα τεὰ χνοάοντα*, "thy downy apples." (xxvii. 48.) In that truly elegant descriptive pastoral, hardly inferior to any in Theocritus, "The Garden of Phyllion" of Aristænetus, apples floating down the stream in which she is bathing, are mistaken for Limona's breasts by her companion:—

> But my love's bosom oft deceived my eye,
> Resembling those fair fruits that glided by;

---

* Dickie and McCosh, p. 185.

For when I thought her swelling breast to clasp,
An apple met my disappointed grasp.*

In the poetry of the Orientals, we find the pomegranate furnishing similar allusions. The temple of Solomon, which in its every circumstance and particular, was representative and antetypical of the Christian church, was, on account of the correspondence of the female bosom, largely adorned with pomegranates of gold.

251. The presignificance of mental and moral qualities by plants is fully as extensive as that of organic structure and configuration. This arises, of course, from the correspondence which subsists between the material and the spiritual worlds. The former, as the representative of the latter, must needs prefigure it. Thus the box-tree foretells stoicism; the chamomile-plant energy and patience in adversity; the ash and mulberry prefigure prudence; the nettle is a presage of spitefulness; trees like the Hernandia, that make a great display of foliage, but produce no fruit of any value, apprize us of pretentious but empty boasters. It was not from their mere commercial value that the dowry of a Greek bride was paid in olive plants, any more than it is from mere fancy that the English one wears a wreath of orange-blossom. It prefigures the virtues and the aptitudes which adorn and should appear in the wife. The leaves are green

---

* Compare Aristophanes, *Lysistrata*, 155; and *Acharnenses*, 1198; also the allusion in that charming little poem in the fourth book of the Anthologia (De Bosch, vol. 2, p. 420), beginning τὰν ἐκφυγοῦσαν ματρος, and descriptive of Venus rising from the sea. See likewise, Wharton's Theocritus, vol. 2, pp. 296–299; 4to., 1770. Why, in ancient times, the apple was sacred to Venus, is easy to understand. The curious may read concerning its symbolic use, the *Hieroglyphica* of Pierius, Lib. LIV., cap. 1–14, *de malo* (pp. 573–577), and Alciati, *Emblemata*, p. 814.

all the year round; flowers white and fragrant, fruits full grown, and others in youngest infancy, are always to be seen on this beautiful tree. We may gather from Scripture why the ancients placed palm-branches in the hands of their statues of Temperance and Cheerfulness, and why in Egypt a vine was the hieroglyph of intelligence. Many plants are social, or often found in each other's company. Between others there exists a kind of discord or enmity; that is, they do not flourish when in proximity, and seem even to render the soil unfit for each other's support. Others again inflict injury by their peculiar twining and constricting mode of growth; others by the deep shade they cast. "Orobanche," the name of a well known genus of parasitic plants, means literally the "vetch-strangler." In the tribe of grasses, which invariably grow in company, we see the gregarious instinct foreshadowed. In other cases, there is love of solitude and seclusion.

252. Chiefly of this latter nature are the prefigurations which occur in the last or ANIMAL kingdom. The mineral having foretold the plant, and the plant the animal, this last can do no more than point to Intellect and Affections. All that is presignified by plants with regard to human character, is reiterated, and with new emphasis, by animals, in their various habits, economies, and instincts. Language is foretold in their various cries; singing in the warbling of the birds—next to the voice of woman, the sweetest melody in nature. To this no doubt is owing that peculiar and striking adaptation to the human ear of the music of birds which makes it the most tender and beautiful relation by which man is connected with the external world. Human Art is preceded in the fabricative instincts, as of the bee, the wasp, and the beaver. Democritus contended that men learnt weaving from spiders, and architecture from the nest-builders. Citizenship and social compact are prefigured in

the gregarious animals, as the antelopes and the deer. Parental affection, anger, vanity, courage, cowardice, mildness, fidelity, grief, artifice, rapacity, all have their first shows in different creatures, and after the same manner; *i. e.*, only as *shows*, inasmuch as they remain, like the architecture and the warbling, the same from age to age and everywhere, whereas in mankind they are local and elastic. In the canine race is prefigured even the sentiment of veneration. To a noble-spirited dog, a kind and generous master is a god.

CHAPTER XXV.

THE CHAIN OF NATURE.

253. The Chain of Nature, one of the most beautiful of philosophic truths, is at the same time one of the most defectively understood. It would seem to be the fate of all great truths to be most familiar to the world under the guise of some mistaken apprehension. As popularly regarded, it has its likeness in Bishop Berkeley's celebrated book called *Siris*, which begins with the medicinal virtues of tar-water, and insensibly mounting upwards, through every variety of learning, ends in a discourse upon the Trinity. The genuine Chain of nature is another thing altogether. Plants are higher in the scale of being than minerals, and animals than plants, and in each kingdom there are series of forms, successively more and more complex; but there is none of that complete and absolute progression from the lowest mineral to the highest animal, which is ordinarily supposed. Such a sequence is not only not consonant with the true principles of harmony and symmetrical disposition, but at variance with them; certainly it is not borne out either by analogy or facts. The appearances, as we shall see presently, in which the popular belief originated, and which are esteemed its evidence and verification, prove, not as most frequently happens in matters of testimony, too *little*, but *too much*. They prove, not that there is *a* chain, but that there are thousands, nay, millions of chains. The idea is an exceedingly ancient one. Macrobius thinks it in-

tended in the famous "golden chain" of Homer. "Since all things," says he, "follow in continuous succession, degenerating in order, to the very bottom of the series, the more attentive observer will discover a connection of parts, down from the Supreme God to the last off-scouring of nature, mutually linked together, and without any interruption. And this is Homer's *golden chain*, which he tells us Jupiter ordained to be let down from heaven to earth."* In the 27th Dissertation of the accomplished and delightful Maximus Tyrius, it is adduced with a view to illustrating the nature of Socrates' *δαίμων* or guardian angel, the subject of this and the preceding discourse. In nature, he tells us, there is a regular gradation of being, commencing with God, and terminating with plants, each rank of existence being connected with one above, and one below, by the union of different qualities in the same body. The *δαιμονες* partake of the divine nature on the one hand, and of the human on the other. In modern times the idea has had the support of Addison, Locke, and Dugald Stewart. "Nature," says Addison, "is filled up with divers kinds of creatures, rising one above another by such a gentle and easy ascent, that the little transitions and deviations from one species to another are almost insensible." (Spectator 579.) Locke's account occurs in the Essay on the Human Understanding, (Book iii. chap. 6,) finishing with a rather amusing allusion to "*what is confidently reported of mermaids.*" Dugald Stewart's may be found in the Outlines of Moral Philosophy, section 109. To no one, however, does the hypothesis owe so much as to the enthusiastic Genevese naturalist, Charles Bonnet. In his work entitled "Contemplation de

* Cumque omnia continuis, &c. In Somnium Scipionis Comment., Lib. I. cap. xiv.

la Nature," he takes up the proposition of Leibnitz, that everything in the universe is connected, and that nature makes no leaps. This—unlike the German philosopher, who confines its application to successive events, having the relation of causes and effects, or at most to the reciprocal action and reaction of cotemporary beings—Bonnet extends, with astonishing ingenuity, to the *forms* of those beings. Commencing with the consideration of the ruder and more simple substances of our planet, he successively introduces us to minerals, plants, and animals, mounting through the various species of the latter up to man, and exhibiting his conclusions, at the last, in a kind of thermometrical table. At the bottom we have *matieres plus subtiles*, then *feu*, then *air*, then *eau*, and at the top *l'Homme*.* Unfolded with the sprightliest eloquence, the enchanting picture could not fail to gain many admirers, and for a long period naturalists busied themselves in filling up the vacancies which the want of observation, in their view, still left in Bonnet's scale, the discovery of an additional link being an object of their greatest interest and delight. In Applegarth's Theological Survey (p. 270) we are treated to a panorama still more extensive, namely, a scale of being of which the foot is the magnet, and the apex the cherubim. This last carries out the idea entertained by many, both before and after, that man himself is only an intermediate; in other words, that there are as many varieties of animated existence *above* him as there are below, successively nearer and nearer to the Almighty. There is no more substantial ground for such a

---

* The table in question forms the frontispiece to Vol. I. of the collected works (Neuchatel, 1781), the "Contemplation" being in Vol. IV. The original publication, in 2 vols. 8vo, was seventeen years earlier.

belief than for the hypothesis of an exact sequence of terrestrial things. There are only three orders of being in the universe, the Absolute, the rational finite, and the irrational finite, or God, man, and what is inferior to man. Degrees of celestial intelligence and authority we may readily suppose, as "one star differeth from another in glory;" there are men who are greater than man as he is *here*, but there is no *form* superior to the human. If the human form be as Revelation intimates, "the image of God," there can be no room for intermediate forms. The name of "angel" as said before, is a designation, not of difference of nature, but of *office*. The angels themselves are both in the Old Testament and the New, called indifferently "angels and men." Compare verses 1 to 16 of Genesis xix., and verses 4 and 23 of Luke xxix. The correct rendering of the only text in Scripture which seems to countenance the opinion that angels are nobler in the scale of being than mankind, teaches, not as the common version has it, that man is "a little lower than the *angels*," but "a little lower than *Elohim*." The Psalm in which the words occur is a kind of *resumè* of the Mosaic history of the creation, and simply repeats in other terms, that "God created man in his own image."

254. It is possible, unquestionably, and easy, to pick out a series of forms which can be placed, as by Bonnet, so as to stand in a seeming natural sequence. But to effect this as many more must be left aside, which cannot be incorporated either into the same, or into any linear scale. A true "chain of being" would not only provide places for all things without exception, but demand them as indispensable to its construction. Things are related by so curious and vast a variety of particulars, that if we attempt to arrange them in an exact series and gradation, violence is done at every step to some close affinity, one point of resemblance being necessarily neglected for the sake of another, and the

determination where each species shall be located becomes almost entirely a matter of fancy. Which are the plants, for example, best deserving to be placed next to animals? Nothing is more like an animal than the Sensitive-plant, as regards its power of movement, yet the Sensitive-plant is the very furthest removed from what naturalists universally call the "zoophytes." Even a chain-like classification of the forms belonging to the separate departments of nature becomes practicable, if attempted on a scale of any extent, only by such artificial and conventional methodizing as the thirteen *andrian* classes of the botanical system of Linnæus. Natural orders, classes, &c. do certainly follow one another *seriatim* in books, *as if* it were so in nature, but this is purely an exigency of the pen. In writing, we must needs begin with something, and go on, and finish with something, just as in order to survey the world, we must start from a specific point. The real relation of natural orders and classes, and no less so of species, is that of the provinces of a great empire, every one of which is in marginal contact with many others. It is under the influence of this insight that those grand theories of classification have been conceived which arrange the objects of nature after the manner of solar systems, the highest forms being placed as centres, and the lower ones round about them; these latter gradually approximating towards other centres. "This radiation, as it were," says Kirby, "from a typical form as a centre, by various roads towards different tribes, seems to prove that the world of animals, as well as that of heavenly bodies, consists of numerous systems, each with its central orb. . . . . From the genus *Patella*, among the molluscous animals, by different and diverging routes, we may arrive at almost any molluscan group or tribe." (Bridgewater Treatise, p. 275.) In the vegetable kingdom it is the same. Families most unlike in the total of their characters, consociate by means of planets which, though remote from their respective suns, are in close proximity with one another. On the other hand, while immense number of species, both of animals and of plants, are so closely allied as to furnish naturalists with "genera," not a few species stand completely isolated: on account of their very distinct and peculiar forms, they cannot be associated with any others. To place the whole in one grand continuous line would obviously require that sometimes a solitary species should be taken, at other times vast suites of species. The genus *Erica*, for example, the four or five hundred species of which are all upon a level in point of excellence, would have to be esteemed as a single species. Legitimately, there is no place in the hypothetical chain of nature for many even of the *families* of living things—Birds for instance, which by reason of their two wings, two feet, a bill either partly or entirely horny, and a body covered with feathers, are distinguished so entirely from all other animals as to constitute an absolutely independent class of beings, merging into no other class, either above them or below. Blumenbach, who is as fond of citing objections to the hypothesis of the single chain as Bonnet is devoted to the assertion of it, remarks to the same purpose concerning the Tortoises: "The very peculiar and distinct form of this isolated group," says he, "constitutes a strong proof of the non-existence of the supposed gradation of objects in nature."

255. That there are mixed or transitional beings in nature, is as much an hypothesis as the Chain, being, in fact, a part of it. Doubtless there are many curious organisms which from some peculiarity of structure, *appear* to be combinations of two other kinds; the whale, for example, which in an arbitrary and popular sense, conjoins fishes to mammals. But it is no mixture in the strict sense of the word, any more than such aquatic plants as the *Ranunculus aqua-*

tilis and the *Sium inundatum*, with their seaweed-like foliage, conjoin terrestrial exogens and algæ. Connection, to a certain extent, there is also, both in plants and animals. No two species are so closely allied, but that there is room between them for a third, as proved by the frequent discovery of such intermediates in countries newly explored. But this is a very different thing from mixture or insensible transition. Lithophytes, zoophytes, phytozoa,* are mere names. None of the beings so designated are really twofold. Nowhere in the world is there an object which may be referred with equal or even plausible propriety, to the mineral kingdom or to the vegetable, to the vegetable or to the animal; or which, as used to be said of the fresh-water polypus, is at once "the last of animals, and the first of plants."

256. In thus criticizing the doctrine of the Chain of Being, it is not intended to imply that it is current in modern science. No one who is conversant with the writings of Cuvier, Swainson, or Lindley, believes in that universal συνέχεια which the authority of Aristotle was for centuries sufficient to certify. "May we expect," says Rymer Jones, "as we advance from the lower types of organization to such as are more perfect, to be led on through an unbroken and continuous series of creatures, gradually rising in importance

---

* The vermiform filaments contained in the antheridia of Charas, Mosses, and other cryptogamous plants, are by some authors called "phytozoa." It is scarcely necessary to say that the term is used above as by Ehrenberg, or in its proper, etymological sense of "plant-animals," which should never have been departed from. The German naturalist Horaninow, who divides the organic world into vegetables, "phytozoa," animals and Man, gives to the word a still greater ambiguity, by including under it the fungi and the algæ.

and complexity of structure, each succeeding tribe of beings presenting an advance upon the preceding, and merging insensibly into that which follows it? A very slight examination will convince us to the contrary." All, however, are not scientific botanists and zoologists, and so long as popular authors continue blindly to re-assert it, Bucke, for example, in the "Beauties, Harmonies, and Sublimities of Nature," so long must the error be met with new exposure. Besides, it is by acquainting ourselves with the defects and inconsistencies of the popular idea, that we become best able to appreciate the genuine. Those who, with Bonnet, sought so ardently to establish it would have escaped their pleasing illusion had they applied themselves to the diligent examination of SPECIES, in Natural History the very basis of accurate knowledge. Bonnet himself appears to have participated in that unwise contempt for the minute discrimination of individual forms which at the time he lived was proscribed under the name of "nomenclature," and like other men of merit never to have imagined its immense value.

257. The true idea of the Chain of Nature has for its centre the law of DISCRETE DEGREES,*—a law which has been several times alluded to, and which the time is now come to illustrate specially. "To-day," says M. Victor Cousin, "two great wants are felt by man. The first, the most imperious, is that of fixed, immutable principles, which depend upon neither place, nor time, nor circumstance, and

---

* The reader to whom "discrete" may be a new word, must receive it as signifying "parted" or "severed." The term belongs originally and properly to the philosophy of the illustrious Swedenborg, the first to discriminate the two-fold nature of Degrees. See, for his exposition of the subject, the volume on the "Divine Love and Wisdom."

on which the mind reposes with unbounded confidence. In all investigations, as long as we have seized only isolated, disconnected facts, as long as we have not referred them to a general law, we possess the material of science, but as yet there is no science. Even physics commence only when universal truths appear, to which all the facts of the same order that observation discovers to us in nature may be referred."* In the law of Discrete degrees we realize one of these sterling principles. Intelligently applied, it clears away difficulties that are insuperable before; it puts us on our guard against merely apparent truths, and ratifies and shows the rationale of the genuine; and while it exposes what is false in our preconceived ideas, becomes a means and highway to new and accurate ones. It is not too much to say that it has been the want of an enlarged and philosophical recognition of the law of Discrete degrees which has mainly led to many of the grossest errors of materialism,—that spirit, for example, is only matter attenuated and etherialized;—to the weary, iterated and reiterated, but still fruitless controversies concerning instinct and reason, with the varied evils that have followed in their wake; to the popular misconception of the Chain of Being; and though last, not least, to the mischievous hypotheses of "progressive development." The law of Correspondence, which is another of the sterling principles desiderated by Victor Cousin, and the law of Discrete degrees, taken together, and properly developed and applied, would form the most efficient of all possible aids to the discovery of that grand philosophic *ultimatum*, the System of Nature. Thence they would tend, more than anything else, to draw the conflicts of the various schools of human thought and speculation to a close, and to

---

* Lectures on the True, the Beautiful, and the Good, p. 33.

supersede them with a noble unanimity; and bearing as they do, on the spiritual no less than on the material, would become preachers of holiness and religion. The long-looked-for, long-prayed-for reign of God upon earth, cannot begin till the reign of the true science of creation, which will be at once its harbinger and the plane for its establishment.

258. Looking abroad upon the external world, we find everywhere two great modes of special arrangement, Latitude or extension, and Altitude or elevation. Exactly accordant with this duality are the relations and the properties of all the organisms and forms of nature, and of all the powers and principles of life. Those which are represented in latitude or extension are relations of Continuity; those represented in altitude comprise the relations we term Discrete. The difference may be illustrated under the image of a splendid mansion. Discrete degrees are represented in its successive floors; Continuous degrees in the suites of apartments which they severally comprise. Let us move about as much as we will on a given floor, we are still on the same level; it is only when we ascend to a higher or descend to a lower, that we essentially change our position; the change is then, however, absolute and complete. So is it in nature. First, we have vast platforms, one above another; secondly, on every platform innumerable chambers and noble galleries, respectively adapted and appropriated to some special use, possessing their own peculiar interest and attractions; also their lowest, superior, and most honorable places; pointing, moreover, to the platform next above, and prefiguring and presignifying its contents, but never actually merging into or coalescing with it. To define these two kinds of relation more particularly, let us take examples from familiar nature, and first, as being the simplest, the relations of Continuity.

259. Continuous degrees are those which intervene be-

tween the extreme phases or conditions of which any given subject or object is naturally susceptible, and which mark its development and historic progress up to the period of its consummation. Thus, the progress of the day is by continuous degrees; the night melts into the dawn, the dawn into the morning, the morning into noon. The influx of the tide upon the shore is by continuous degrees; from low water to high, is one long, unintermittent flow, and the same when the waves retire. The march of the Seasons is by continuous degrees; Spring glides imperceptibly into Summer; summer as softly wanes into the year's beautiful old age, like human life, every day a little, and without halting for a moment. The tinting of the leaves in autumn, commonly called the *fading* of the leaves, is again by continuity. From the full, bright, living green of June, to the not-always "sere and yellow," but oftentimes rich crimson of October,—as when a monarch gathers his robes about him that he may die royally,—it is like the painting of the sky at the close of a summer's day, when the molten gold boils up behind the purple cloud-mountains of the west, and the very zenith and farthest east are tinted with virgin rose,—one long, soft, lovely transfiguration, such as the eye in vain essays to follow. Nowhere in nature is there a more beautiful analogy than this of sunset with the "many-colored woods" of the year's eventide. Everything in plants is more or less illustrative of continuity. We see it most remarkably in what botanists call Varieties, all of which are sports within a given circle. The Broccoli and the Cauliflower are but modifications of the coarse marine cabbage. From wild sour crabs, scarcely larger than boys' marbles, have arisen all varieties of apples, not excluding the pippin and nonpareil; the austere and uneatable sloe is the source of the luscious plum; even wheat appears to be the culmination of an obscure grass, the *Ægilops ovata*. So with many of our choicest flowers. The innumerable varieties of carnations, fuchsias, pelargoniums, &c., are all resolvable into some simple and original form, from which they have arisen under the stimulus of culture, and to which, in the course of a generation or two, they relapse if left to themselves. The choicest pansies in a flower-garden, if neglected, return in a very few years, in their descendants, to the inconspicuous *Viola tricolor* of the fields. Were another example needed, we might point to the various conditions of which water is susceptible. According to the amount of caloric present in it, we have ice, water properly so called, or steam. Between the solid glacier and the white clouds from the locomotive, there is an exact continuity and gradation, and either extreme is convertible into the other. In degrees of Continuity, it will be observed, then, we have relations merely of *state*, not of kind, every new appearance and condition being developed out of its immediate predecessor, and limited to externals. Whatever the amount of sport, whether in color or configuration, in density or in texture, the absolute internal nature remains the same, just as in regard to the human race: whether we take Caucasians or Ethiops, Bosjemans or Feejee islanders, all are resolvable into the zoological species Man.

260. Where things are differentiated by a *discrete* degree, the commencement of the new one is not, as with continuity, where the inferior or prior one left off, but on a distinct and higher level, and under the influence of new principles. Every ending is absolute, and every beginning *de novo*, initiating an altogether nobler mode of existence, which culminates after its own manner, and is then succeeded by another. This is most strikingly displayed in the relations of the three great kingdoms of nature, Minerals, Plants, and Animals. So far from being true, as supposed by Continuity and the "Vestiges," that the ending of one joins the

foundation of the succeeding, it is here that the affinity and resemblance are the very slightest. The humblest forms of plants are those which are least like arborescent crystallizations; and the humblest forms of animals those which have least in common with the Mimosa. Each kingdom of nature, as it ascends towards its maximum, instead of approximating closer and closer to the next above, and eventually passing into it, in reality becomes more and more remote from it. They may be compared to three beautiful temples; the first of Doric architecture, the second of Ionic, the third of Roman. Each temple is built on a plan of its own; the foundations have a measure of uniformity; but while the Doric pillars are simple shafts, the loftier and fluted Ionic are crowned with graceful, curling volutes, and the Composite, loftier still, with all the ornament that tasteful luxury can engraft. Each kingdom starts on a platform of its own, as physiology will some day demonstrate beyond dispute; growing more distinct with every step, at last it enjoys a per fection no less peculiarly its own. That perfection does not reside in the forms which seem to be connecting links with the kingdoms next above; the perfection and termination of each realm, as of each tribe and class, is in the maximum realization of its archetype. Quadrupeds, for example, do not termimate with the monkeys; their maximum is the *lion*, the acknowledged king of beasts from time immemorial. So in the vegetable world. Endogens do not terminate with the Smilax, though it anticipates the netted leaves of the Exogens overhead; but with the princes of their archetype, the stately Palms. Though the several perfections are so unlike, there is still a fine harmony between them. The perfection of the mineral kingdom in the lucid and brilliant Crystal, harmonizes with the perfection of the plant in the odorous and glowing Blossom, and both harmonize with the perfection of the animal, which resides in its vast powers of body and external sense. Brutes are possessed of these vast powers, because the ascent of the brute creation towards its maximum is *away from* man rather than in the direction of him, just as the mineral series divaricates from the plant, and the plant series from the animal. For man, though the head and archetype of all things, is no part of a specific chain, but a series in himself, at once a beginning and an end. Everywhere the maximum of the lower realm is more glorious than the minimum of the next above; man is excelled by the brutes he rules over, in swiftness, in eyesight, in delicacy of touch and smell,* because these things, though the perfection of the brutes, belong to the mere basis of humanity;—all creatures, however, in his *own* maximum, he transcendently excels, vindicating the supreme majesty of Intellect. In every maximum, it is further to be observed, all the forces of nature that have reference to it, are concentrated. Chemistry is at its acmê in the moulding of the crystal; vitality in the fashioning of the flower.

261. When, therefore, we would rightly contemplate the great kingdoms of nature, or any of their subdivisions, we should begin by comparing summit with summit. The keys of knowledge are the *perfections* of nature. Descending from the capitals to the pedestals, we learn that the animal differs as widely from the vegetable, as both differ from the mineral, This should be our rule even in the comparison and estimate of species. "Every species is higher in some respects, and lower in others; there are many scales of perfection in *different respects*, running, as it were, parallel with one another; so that in defining the degree of elevation of any particular species, we must take into account the posi-

* Smell seems to be most acute in the predaceous mammalia; sight in the predaceous birds; touch in the antennæ of insects.

tion it occupies in the several scales jointly." The criterion of excellence is *combination* of properties. Man, for example, as just observed, is inferior to the dog, as regards smell, and to the elephant, as regards bulk, but in neither of these creatures, nor in any other, are so many properties *combined* as in himself; this at once places him immeasurably above them all. In regard to "lower" or "inferior" forms, and in general to *maximum* and *minimum*, as spoken of the separate departments of nature, it is essential to remember carefully that there is no such thing as *defect* in the works of God. "Higher forms" are simply such as are more complex in their organization than certain other forms. To the simple organization of the plant, for instance, in the Animal are added nerves, endowing it with the sensation which the plant has not. Instead of "lower" and "superior," it would be better therefore to say "simple" and "complex," only that usage has established the former terms. So with the epithet "perfect" as applied to natural structures. Nothing is positively or absolutely *im*perfect. The tender moss is as perfect in its little sphere as the lordly forest-tree. "Perfect" is used by the naturalist simply in a *technical* sense, to express "the degree in which those peculiarities are developed which characterize a particular group. Those peculiarities of structure, for example, which make an insect what it is, and not a worm or a crustacean, are found to be present in their greatest intensity, and in the fullest combination, in the *beetles;* hence we say the beetles are the most perfect of their class. A beetle is not more perfect *as an animal* than any other, but it is more perfect as *an insect*." It is at once the most permanent and the most elaborate of insect forms.

262. Not only is there no succession of one kingdom of nature above another by the *maximum* of the lower gradually sliding into the *minimum* of the superior; the law of

discrete degrees precludes intermixture at any other point, even at the foundations. The common opinion regarding the animal and vegetable worlds is, that at their commencement they are united. It is true that between the first animalcules and the first vegetalcules there is a seeming identity, and that the embryo human organism itself does not perceptibly differ from the earliest forms of plants; true, moreover, that the two classes of beings retain a kind of parallelism for a considerable distance. Both begin with the simple vesicle, the globe in miniature, the cylinder, and the disc, seeming to measure with their fine geometry the space which they are by and bye to fill so admirably; experimenting more boldly as they proceed, the bells and vases of the polyps and the coral-creatures pair with the cups of the lichen and the thecæ of the mosses, even to their peristomes; the divergence, however, rapidly becomes so wide, and the culminating extremes are so far asunder, as to prove them wholly distinct ideas of Almighty wisdom. "To suppose," well observes Dr. Harris, "that because it is difficult to assign the boundaries of the two kingdoms, therefore there are no boundaries, would be as irrational as to conclude that, because material atoms disappear, first from our unaided sight, and then even beyond the reach of microscopic power, there is a point at which they graduate into nothingness. A moment's reflection will show us that between that supposed point and the point beyond, there is all the difference between body and space, something and nothing, an infinite difference. In the same manner, however slight the *break*, where the vegetable appears to graduate into the animal, such an interruption there is; and it is nothing less than an interruption in *kind*, a transition from identity to essential difference."* The dispute, not yet settled, as to

* Pre-Adamite Earth, pp. 245, 246.

whether those beautiful little specks of life, the Desmidieæ, are animals or vegetables, merely shows that we are still in ignorance of their essential nature. It is but a little while since opinions were similarly divided as to the sponges, Corallines, Sertularias, and even the fungi. Natural history, like theology and every other great system of truth, always has its mysteries, though they are not always the same mysteries, either absolutely or relatively.

263. The three great primary platforms of nature, minerals, plants, and animals, though they are the chief seat and illustration of discrete distinctiveness, by no means exhaust it. Each of these three principal platforms comprises many minor ones, and each of these latter a multitude of still finer. The first are occupied by the various tribes, classes, and families of beings, the last by genera and species, organs and organic tissues. Doubtless, the more minute our analysis, the more difficult becomes the determination of the relative rank of the objects compared; as when we compare, for example, the various genera of a "natural order," or the various species of a genus. Ordinarily they are so alike in apparent excellence, that, as said above of the species of *Erica*, fancy and taste alone can graduate their merits; that there is a discrete difference, we may nevertheless be assured, since Nature in the principles of its least things, is invariably the same as in those of its greatest. The difficulty in nature is to see the law where it hides itself from us, and not to be led astray by appearances. Many things in nature which are contradicted by our senses, are nevertheless, true, and chief among them are these seeming equalities of things. To their discrete separateness is referable the *constancy* of species. Primarily dependent, as well said by Agassiz and Gould, "upon im-

material nature,"* that is to say, upon pre-existent forms in the Spiritual world, the fixedness of species rests proximately in the distinctiveness of their platforms, from which they are incapable of moving, either upwards or downwards; and which prevents them, at the same moment, from intermarrying, and thus defacing and disordering the world with hybrids. The great mass of the organic forms commonly deemed hybrids are in reality mere *varieties; i. e.*, sports of a given single species, rather than intermixtures of two different ones. Purely and entirely by reason of this absolute separateness, does it become possible to classify material objects into scientific systems, and to impersonate them with names. The boundaries being unalterably fixed, we are enabled, first to discriminate, and subsequently to recognize them. Were there no discrete degrees, the world instead of *Κόσμος*, would be *χάος*. St. Paul tells us of the discrete degrees of the animal world, when he says: "All flesh is not the same flesh; there is one flesh of men, another flesh of beasts, another of fishes, and another of birds." Flesh is only consolidated blood. Not only hath God "made of one blood all nations of *men*;" all things discretely separated, are of their own peculiar blood; the differences in the vital fluid, (which, homogeneous and uniform as it is to the eye, is one of the most varied substances in nature,) are the inmost seats of all distinctions. Here, in the blood, *begins* the difference of creatures one from another; the Teeth, which are the last and completing effort of the vital energy, as the blood is the first, completing also the distinctions, and standing as the Omega to the Alpha of the crimson stream which originated their own material. The structure and form of the teeth constitute so important a

* Outlines of Comparative Physiology, p. 86.

particular in the discrimination of species, that if any tribe of human beings were found to differ materially in their dentition from the rest of mankind, it would justify a strong suspicion of a real specific difference—as strong a one as would arise from a difference in the form of the blood-discs. Discrete difference prevails as profoundly in the saps of plants; and closely as they resemble in some points, between the vegetable and the animal tissues. Vegetable cells are discretely below animal cells; no vegetable tissue could associate with animal tissue; "it would be the sport of activities which it could neither share nor reciprocate." So with the vital functions. What are called the "vegetative functions" of animals are not vege*table*. An animal is not, as to its physiology, plant *plus* animal, but wholly and absolutely *sui generis*. There are feeding, respiration, reproduction, &c., in both, but they are never *the same* feeding, nor the *same* respiration. Every function, on the higher platform, is as totally different from those of the lower ones, as are the forms and organizations. Plants, for example, take carbon from the atmosphere, while animals take oxygen. Were the various properties which are distributed among the members of the vegetable kingdom to be concentrated in a single individual, that individual would still be inferior to the ignoblest brute. The discrete degree pronounces once for all, Thus far and no farther. A long procession of discrete degrees, it may be added, often has the *look* of continuity, as in the case of the successive steps between the hoof of the quadruped and the human hand. They are shown to be *discrete* degrees which intervene, by not a single hoof having ever become anything *more* than a hoof, during the twenty centuries that naturalists have studied animal history; the hand of man similarly remaining the same from age to age.

264. Along with discrete degrees it is important to con-

sider the great companion law of *promotion*. Nature, in her ascent, leaves nothing behind; she subordinates, but never disuses; the past is always brought forward into the present; every degree of ascent is marked by new powers and new forms of apparatus, but with these are always essentially recapitulated all things that have previously been employed. The properties, moreover, which exist in the lower or anterior stages, are not only carried on to the superior, but are there applied to new and higher purposes. The physical laws which in the mineral world induce cohesion and affinity, and achieve their highest in the production of crystal flowers, these do not *cease* with the crystal; brought forward into the vegetable, they are as active as they were in the mineral, only that now they are no longer the rulers, but subordinated to the higher authority of the vital forces. These in turn move forward into the animal, where to chemistry and vitality are superadded senses and locomotion; all finally move forwards into man, where they lie under the new and crowning magistracy of reason. Man, as said above, is not like lower natures, contained on a given platform, but a platform in himself, discretely separated from all below by his vertical attitude and consummate nervous system,* as a material organism; by his intellect and affections as a vessel of life. He is all that has gone before, and Man besides. He feeds and sleeps with the vegetable; builds and procreates with the animal; talks, dresses, worships, hopes, laughs, and imagines, in virtue of

---

* The most striking illustration of this occurs perhaps in relation to the human voice. It is not so much in the mere *organs* of the voice, as they are commonly called, the larynx, &c., that man differs from the inferior animals, and by which he is enabled to speak; it is in the nerves rather, by which all the parts are combined into one simultaneous act. This is peculiar to him.

his own original and unique humanity. In man all the operations of nature are concentrated and perfected. He is the continent of the world rather than contained in it; the aggregate of all properties, phenomena, and uses; thus the summary and mirror of the whole of God's creation. He never ceases to be the lower natures, and cannot, for they are the basis and factors of his perfection. There are times when he is, practically, nothing else, and it is good that it should be so. "The master-piece of creation," says Lichtenberg, "must for a while, on his pillow, become a plant, in order that he may *be* this same master-piece."

265. The promotion of *physiognomies* is one of the most curious things in nature. As the crystal is a mineral flower, so is the flower a vegetable crystal. The geometry of the former reappears in flowers as their numerical proportion; the angles and faces of the one, become the outlines and symmetry of the other. Flowers, however, have a greater variety of forms than crystals, and some of them are unknown to the mineral world, as the pentagonal. The trigonal and tetragonal are plentiful in both. The cube is recapitulated in that pretty little blossom of early Spring, the Adoxa moschatellina; on the cone of the fir before it opens we have the most beautiful rhomboidal figures; and in the delicate little organisms called Desmidieæ, triangles, cylinders, and ellipses.

266. The renewal, in the animal kingdom, of the features of plants and flowers, is divided between the arborescent polypifera, and those lovely marine productions, the Actiniæ, popularly known as the sea-anemone, the sea-daisy, &c. The resemblance of these curious organisms to the rich, double, and many-colored varieties of the Anemone hortensis, and the Chrysanthemum, is most extraordinary. The Actinia equina, says Lamouroux, may be seen, when the tide retires, "ornamenting the sea-rocks with its beautiful

colors, purple, violet, blue,* pink, yellow, and green, like so many flowers in a meadow." The Actinia Dianthus, or sea-carnation, the Actinia Calendula, or sea-marigold, and the Actinia crassicornis, perhaps the finest example of the whole tribe, are miracles of beauty. Besides these, there is the exquisite genus Lucernaria, one species of which, the Lucernaria Auricula, transcends even the Actinias in its lovely renewal of the flower. No one who has collected Sertularias can have failed to observe their beautiful resemblance to slenderly-branching trees of the cypress kind. "The polypidom," remarks Mr. Gosse, "of that very elegant species, the Sertularia cupressina, fine specimens of which are eight to twelve inches high, forms a taper-pointed spire, the numerous component branches of which are fan-shaped, and arch gracefully downwards, so that the resemblance to a tree of the pine tribe is neither fanciful nor remote." In no department of nature do we see more strikingly illustrated the indifference to large and little in the workmanship of the Almighty; in a cluster of these delicate little polyp-trees, with their inhabitants, without the slightest voluntary effort of the imagination, we live over again among the noblest elements of the forest. But the great zoophytes of the tropical seas eclipse all. Ehrenberg was so struck with the magnificent spectacle of the floriform polyparia of the Red Sea, that he exclaimed, "Where is the paradise of flowers that can rival in variety and beauty these living wonders of the ocean!" Many species, Mr. Dana tells us, "spread out in broad leaves, and resemble some large plant just unfolding; others are gracefully branched, and the

---

* When Lamouroux speaks of *blue* sea-anemones, he refers merely to the variegation of certain species. An Actinia wholly blue seems as unlikely a wonder as a blue dahlia or blue rose.

whole surface blooms with stars of crimson, purple, and emerald green." At Macao, says another, "dendritic zoophytes, having their branches loaded with colored polyps, like trees covered with delicate blossoms, richly uprose from the clear bottom of the bay." (Adams, "Voyage of the Samarang.") The star-fishes recapitulate the various kinds of radiate flowers, and other stelliform products of plants; the bilateral animals, or those in which the external members are in pairs, remind us of the configuration of the Labiatæ. How beautifully even the simplest forms and phenomena of lower platforms are brought forward to the higher, is shown in the ice-plant, which recapitulates the hoar frost, and in the Drosera, gemmed with unforgotten dew.

267. Understanding the law of promotion, we first begin to read truly, the great lessons inscribed on lower natures. Were there no animals man would be a thousand times more incomprehensible than he is; animals, in turn, are similarly illustrated in the plant-world; in either case because the lower nature shows in detail and prominently, what in the higher nature is obscured by subordination. Seeing that all things are mute predictions and prefigurements of Man, it follows again, conversely, that in the laws and phenomena of our *own* being, we have the keys to all phenomena beneath. All lower things derive their intelligibleness from higher ones; we learn the nature of the world only by viewing it in the sunshine. The true science of nature we shall never become possessed of till it is studied, in every part, by the light of humanity;—till the naturalist looks more narrowly to the congruity which subsists between the world and himself—"the world of which he is lord, not because he is the most subtle inhabitant, but because he is its head and heart."

268. Now that we have seen how the various parts of nature stand related, viz., according to Discrete degrees and Continuous degrees; also what is the meaning and the teaching of Prefiguration; the way is opened to a clearer and more comprehensive survey of the Analogies of nature, the phenomena which in their total, declare its UNITY. As to the broad, general fact of this unity, there is nothing new to be said. Since the world is the work of God, and He is ONE, its constituent parts must needs correspond, not only with Him as their Designer and Creator, but likewise, in some way, with one another. In other words, the world as a whole cannot display its Maker without its several parts doing the same, and to this end they must necessarily be alike. Such, accordingly, is the fact. "Everything in nature contains all the powers of nature. Each new form repeats not only the main character of the type, but part for part, all the details, aims, furtherances, hindrances, energies, and whole system of every other. There is something that resembles the ebb and flow of the sea, day and night, man and woman, in a single needle of the pine, in a kernel of corn. Every occupation, trade, art, transaction, is a compend of the world, and a correlative of every other. Each one is an entire emblem of human life, of its good and ill, its trials, its enemies, its course, and its end." We speak of the "physical geography" of the world. That

which we find in the whole, we find over again in every scene and portion. The sea, for example, has its mountains and valleys, in the waves; its rivers, in the currents; its forests and "ocean-gardens," in the densely-planted and luxuriant algæ which adorn it as with trees and flowers. Descending to the special provinces of nature, we find animals intimately analogous with plants, plants possessing analogies with minerals—each particular form, whether organic or inorgantic, being a miniature representative of the class to which it belongs, and all its factors representatives again of itself; the members show more or less, the essential properties of the total, the total is a vast expansion of the atom. Because of this unity, it follows that, absolutely, there is only one Science, at least only one physical science, just as in the doctrine of a celebrated school of ancient philosophy, there was only one Virtue. That one science has various departments, whereby the incommensurableness of nature is brought down to our capacity; still it is only one science essentially, as we prove every day. Occupy ourselves with whatever province of it we may, we soon become sensible of its interconnection with others, and are frequently at a loss to determine the actual area that it covers. "The unity of science," says one of the profoundest thinkers of our day, "is the reflection of the unity of nature, and of the unity of the Supreme Reason and Intelligence which pervades and rules over nature, and from which all reason and all science are derived." It follows again that in all our investigations of natural phenomena, if we would justly comprehend them, we should more and more vigilantly look for likenesses. The beginning of philosophy is the study of differences, but we climb to that beautiful Olympus where simple and essential Truths reside, the heaven of all the other spheres of knowledge, by comparing, and deducing *resemblances;* just as we rise in moral and religious life by seeking and valuing Christianity above sectarianism.

269. In organic nature, to which alone is it expedient to give attention at present, Three kinds of analogy are observable. First, analogies of organization, which are the profoundest; second, analogies of external configuration, with or without similarity of internal structure; third, analogies of qualities, habits, instincts, &c. Frequently one kind of analogy presupposes and brings another, but it is by no means necessary to the existence of analogy that all three kinds, or even two of them, should be associated. The analogy between the different species and tribes of organized beings as to their *internal structure*, is the subject-matter of one of the grandest of natural sciences. If one thing more than another attests the unity of creation, it is Comparative Anatomy. Different as are the outward seemings of bird and quadruped, fish and reptile, and more different even yet those of the boneless creatures, leaving plants, for the time, altogether out of the question, nothing is plainer to the tutored eye than that all these varied beings are utterances of a single Divine idea. The likeness in the higher classes, the Vertebrata, is unanimously acknowledged in their name. The lower classes, negatively distinguished as the *in*vertebrata, differ unquestionably, in respect of that hard framework we call the skeleton, which in these no longer appears as a set of internal bones, but is replaced by a solid outer covering, well shown in the lobster and the crab. In regard to the viscera and the organs of sense, the analogy, however, is obvious enough; and since so many affinities have been already demonstrated between these invertebrata and the higher classes, all pointing moreover to a common archetype; the circumstance of their unlikeness in the matter of skeleton, and thence of configuration (as in the case of the star-fishes compared with birds,) stands only as a mys-

tery to be cleared up.* The advances which science has already made towards the solution, are sure in their promise; as the stars and the compass tell the mariner his prow is homeward, though the land be yet invisible.

270. *Homology* is the name of the science which seeks to determine these deep affinities. The more usual application of the word is to the science of skeletons and their parts; but properly, it applies to all parts whatever of the animal structure, whether hard or soft. The idea intended to be conveyed by it is, that specific organs of animals, to appearance quite distinct, do nevertheless directly answer to one another, and are derivations from a common archetype or model. The arm of the human body is "homologous" with the fore-leg of the brute, with the wing of the bird, and with the pectoral fin of the fish. Essentially it is the same part which we see in each, but being intended to serve a different purpose in each different animal, is modified accordingly. The homologies just alluded to are called by Owen "special." He gives this name to all such affinities of different parts or organs, in *different* animals, as demonstrably answer one to another. The least acquainted with animal structure may understand them, by comparing the hoof, the paw, the talon, and the human foot. "*General* homologies" form another and yet profounder class. These are the relations which the total of the structures of animals, in all their variety, bear to that grand, universal type of which Man is the proudest fulfillment,—the type termed the Vertebral, but though in the vertebrated animals most consummately set forth, cer-

* The bilateral symmetry of those curious shells cast upon our sandy shores, commonly known as "mermaids' heads," (zoologically *Spatangus,*) beautifully points from afar to the vertebral idea. See for an account of it, "Annals of Natural History," vol. 1, p. 30.

tainly not confined to them. Every one may see the general quality of this type, by comparing the skeletons of quadrupeds, the bird, and the fish. No animal has all the parts of the common archetype expressed in their *maximum*. Some have one part more highly developed, some have another; always, however, in a fixed degree, neither more nor less, whereby the specific identity of each is preserved pure. The wing, though an organ of the same archetype as the arm, never changes to an arm; nor does the fin of the fish ever assume the character of a wing. Thirdly, Owen discriminates "*serial* homologies." These are the relations which the several parts of an animal bear among themselves. Comparing, for example, the bones of the leg with those of the arm, we pursue "serial" homologies; and again, when we compare the bones of the spinal column with those of the skull, which latter the acute Oken has demonstrated beyond dispute, to be itself a chain of vertebræ, the various elements of the several bones being so modified, expanded, or contracted, as to convert them into a fitting cavity for the brain. Homology is thus to analogy in general, what grammar and etymology are to the science of language,—a finer, more recondite, and more exact determination of its fundamental truths. Obviously, without a careful and extended study of all three of its departments, our apprehension of the Unity of Nature can be no more than superficial and vague. Happily, this grand science is now kindling a literature of its own, the light of which points and illuminates our way.*

---

* See, for instance, Owen's Works "On the Homologies of the Vertebrate Skeleton," and on the "Nature of Limbs;" and the masterly article on the Skeleton in Todd's Cyclopædia of Anatomy and Physiology, by Maclise. For a talented *résumé* of the subject, see the London Quarterly Review, No. viii., July, 1855.

271. Botany has its Comparative Anatomy as well as Zoology, all sound and scientific classification resting upon the resemblances of the different organs as to their essential nature, however widely diversified in seeming. Viewed homologically, the parts of which plants are composed are, like those of animals, exceedingly few. The flower, with its various members, is only a fasciculus of leaves, similar to those of the stem, only more delicately fashioned, and beautifully colored; the fruit is no more than another such fasciculus, curiously folded together, and distended or covered in with juice or pulp. The proofs of this are furnished, partly by the phenomena of double flowers, partly by the comparison of a large number of different species. In the double white water-lily, the double tulip, and often in the double camellia, every shade of transition may be traced between petal and stamen; in the double cherry-blossom, instead of a pistil, there grow two little leaves, exact miniatures of the ordinary foliage; sometimes, even in single blossoms of the Anemone nemorosa, leaves similarly stand in place of ovaries. The identity of the petals and the calyx, and of the calyx and the stem-leaves, is shown by the polyanthus, in its different varieties; the latter also by the gentianella, and a variety not infrequently met with, of the common white clover. It is not that any given flower or fruit ever actually consisted of green leaves, and was formed from them by direct transmutation, but that the essential elements both of flower and fruit are varied and elaborate developments of a single organic form, which in a lower state of development would have been a simple twig of leaves. Every leaf in its embryo state is potentially a petal, potentially a stamen, potentially the carpel of a fruit, and it expands into one part or another according to the impress given it at birth, by the directive vital power. The term "metamorphosis," as applied to floral development, becomes,

therefore, incorrect. An organ once framed and determined is never converted into a different organ; there is simply a capacity on the part of the original germ to develope into one or another of many different shapes. The homologies disclosed by the different *species* of plants are most strikingly illustrated in the origin and structure of Fruits. In the apple, for example, we have five carpellary leaves, united and enclosed in pulp; in the fraxinella and the star-anise a similar combination, but without the surrounding pulp; in the pæony, three or four such leaves, at once destitute of pulp, and instead of being united, perfectly independent and distinct, and apt, when withered and dried, and the seeds have fallen out, to expand into a close likeness of the green leaf. The flowers of the different genera of Ranunculaceæ are scarcely less instructive. Only by the laws of homology do we rightly understand Anemone, Clematis, Caltha, Trollius, Helleborus, &c., and learn that what seem to be petals, are in reality exalted calyx-leaves. Botany and Zoology will some day be found of singular mutual service in regard to their comparative anatomy. The homologies of the Vertebrata will be illustrated by those of the higher orders of plants, those of the invertebrata by the less perfect kinds. Nothing is plainer even now than that the general model of plants is upon the vertebral archetype. We find it in what is *essentially* the Plant, namely, the LEAF. It is in the leaf that the vegetable energies are chiefly exercised; it is from the leaf that all the floral organs are developed, and to the leaf that all parts are reducible by homology; the Leaf therefore may be regarded, as above said, the essential and prototypical Plant.* Taking, then, the essential plant, the

* That a leaf is a *perfect* plant we by no means intend to say. A perfect plant is a highly complex organism, a structure built up of

simple green leaf, its normal and highest form is found to consist in a strong, central axis or midrib, giving rise to numerous lateral ribs, which diverge from it at certain angles, and establish the general figure. The interstices are filled with pulp, and the whole organism is enclosed in a skin. The essential parts of the flower, and of the fruit, the maximum stages of vegetable development, consist of this identical green leaf, folded vertically upon its axis, as on a hinge, so that the edges come in contact, each being a miniature of the cavity formed by the spine, the ribs, and the breast-bone. In the cavities thus formed, the highest energies of vegetable life are concentrated, and the ends of that life accomplished. The stamens supply pollen; the pistils, or organs of female function, contain seeds. Looked at, accordingly, from the plant, the body of a vertebrated creature, or at least of any of the mammalian tribes, is seen to be an infinitely perfected Leaf; looked at from Man, the carpel of the fruit (the pod of the pea, for instance), folded with such fine symmetry on its little spine, is the miniature idea of the human frame, which is also folded, as it were, on the spinal column. Everything in nature shows more or less of the spinal column, a right and a left, standing side by side, and vertically united, since everything flows from the Good and the True, as conjoined in the Divine, and receives their dual and undivided impress.

272. Guided by the light of these great principles, we see, then, that the kingdoms of organized nature are but manifold repetitions and modifications of one grand ruling arche-

---

many distinct pieces, each with an allotted office of its own. It is in no case merely a leaf, nor even a twig, *per se*, because to the full and complete idea of a plant is needed not only distinct nutritive and sexual apparatus, but a descending axis or root, as well as an ascending axis or stem.

type of structure, divaricating on the one hand, into the idea realized in the perfect Animal, on the other, into that of the perfect Plant, the several members of each kingdom being allied, remotely to those of the sister kingdom, intimately and definitely to one another. Begin, as in former surveys, with the Vegetable Kingdom. In its aggregate, this is in reality the distributed exhibition of a *single* plant—a plant existing nowhere as a fixed, tangible individual, but everywhere as a theoretical or ideal one, having its parts or factors diffused over the whole surface of the earth, in the infinitely-varied figures we call "species." Some species show one part in perfection, some show another, the ideal total being best represented where the largest number of parts occur in most symmetrical combination. It is not the more thorough completeness or excellence of any one organ in particular that gives superiority to a vegetable form, but the collocation of the largest number of *distinct* parts, well balanced and proportionate, and in nowise defective or confused. That such an archetype governs the forms of the vegetable world, appears not only in completed parts, but conspicuously also in the *quasi*-abortive or rudimentary development of certain organs in given species, which in other species expand to high perfection, and serve highly important purposes. It appears again in what are so viciously miscalled "monstrosities," as when the Linaria vulgaris, the pretty yellow toad-flax of our autumnal hedge-banks, makes those curious efforts to rise from the usual unsymmetrical corolla into the regular five-leaved form. Rightly regarded, the vegetable kingdom is thus—not what it appears at first sight, an assortment of discrepancies—but a grand whole, formed of an innumerable quantity of smaller parts, the mass presenting nothing different from what may be discovered in the individual, and the individual reflecting all the qualities of the mass. Every leaf on a tree is a tree in little; the tree, in its turn, is a leaf, as it were, enlarged; every variety in outline and structure, whether of bud, or leaf, or flower, or fruit, is only another utterance of one primitive and ubiquitous idea. The very cells of which a plant is built are so many plants in miniature, having their own seasons, life, death, and renewal, and performing within themselves the whole series of vital functions. Thousands of plants consist of nothing more than a few such cells as in septillions make up an oak tree, mere microscopic threads, yet in all the characteristic phenomena of vegetable life they are on a par. Such are the red-snow plant and its congeners, the various species of Palmella and Protococcus. "Whether," says Mohl, "they consist of a single cell, or as in the Confervas, of rows of cells united into a thread, each cell is capable of an independent existence. It absorbs fluids from the surrounding medium, respires, and assimilates the absorbed substances; in short, the simple vesicle suffices for the accomplishment of all the various functions which must coöperate in the nutritive processes of the plant." According to the closeness or otherwise of the analogy between particular *forms*, we have species, genera, tribes, classes, and so forth; the skill of the botanist largely consisting in his ability to collocate such as to the less observant and sagacious appear alien. Where there is the greatest amount of *real* affinity, there is often the least *apparent* affinity, and *vice versâ;* the progress of genuinely scientific Botany, as of every other department of natural history, consists in seizing the deep and permanent resemblances, and passing by the superficial and occasional. Narrowly looked at, the smallest mosses are found analogous with the tallest tree; the most insignificant of weeds with the choicest flowers; Lycopodiums disclose analogies with firs and pines; the gourd and cucumber plants with the passion-flowers; water-lilies with poppies and Magnolias. Every great platform of plants is found in close analogy with every other platform. Looking from the outside, the throne of difference, to the inside, the throne of likeness, the same old, old fashion is ever present. There is nothing in Exogens which we do not find, prefiguratively, in Endogens, as when we compare the pine-apple with the cones of the fir tree; nothing in flowering-plants which we do not find among the flowerless. In the curious Brazilian family Podostemaceæ, especially in the genera Lacis and Mniopsis, we see liver-worts and sea-weeds as it were in bloom. Twining plants have their forerunner in the fern called Lygodium; the Casuarinas of New Holland their precursors in the Equisetums. Nothing is more interesting than the simple resemblance of large and little. The Mucedines or mildew-plants, comprising the genera Penicillium, Botrytis, Aspergillus, &c., form sometimes in the space of a square inch an immense forest of little trees from one to ten lines high, varied, but always elegant in their ramification, and bearing at the extremities of their whorled, umbellate, or panicled branches, bunches or heads of seed, producing the most exquisite effect. Growing on all sorts of substances, and in all latitudes, if they do not attract the eye, it is because without the microscope they are scarcely visible. What a new world do we owe to this wonderful instrument!

273. The Animal Kingdom, like the vegetable, is a grand whole, of which the smallest polyp is a perfect representative. None are ignorant that every living creature eats, drinks, and propagates; that it is born, grows, lives, and dies, and has more or less means of intercourse with the external world. A moment's reflection makes it self-evident that such conformity of history implies a generally concurrent likeness as to organization. Animalcules, a thousand of which do not exceed the bulk of a grain of sand, are essentially not different from the largest quadruped. They

are composed of members equally well suited to their mode of life. Their actions display all the phenomena of instinct; they move with surprising speed and agility, directed evidently by choice, and with a specific end in view. They eat and drink, and must therefore be supplied with a digestive apparatus; they exhibit muscular power of the most extraordinary amount; they are susceptible of the same passions as the superior animals, though differing in degree; and the satisfaction of those passions is attended by the same results as in our own species. These and many other phenomena of the same nature indicate, beyond question, that they must be as highly organized, in their degree, as the Mammalia themselves. So full and exact are the analogies which unite the various provinces of the realm of animals, that while every inhabitant of a given platform is in general affinity with the whole, it is in immediate agreement with particular forms occupying the platforms above and below. Every quadruped, that is to say, is in direct analogy with some bird, fish, reptile, and insect; partaking, it may be, more of the structure of one, more of the habits of another, more of the qualities of a third, but in every case definitely. For, as said above, we must never think of analogy as a matter purely of *organic structure.* Nature does not confine herself to a single mode of alliance; structure is one method, others consist in economy, to which, however, structure is always co-ordinated and predetermined. To the lowest members of the animal kingdom, as the sponges, Sertularias, and other "zoophytes," one great attribute of animals seems, however, to be denied, viz., the power of *locomotion.* But the unity of plan is only curiously varied. All the fixed animals are *aquatic,* so that the constantly changing element in which they live, incessantly brings new objects into contact with them. Unable to move personally, their world, which is the water, moves for them, as the atmosphere does for the trees.

The sea-anemone, glued to a rock upon the shore, bathed by a thousand waves that come but once, is far more of a traveler than the worm crawling in the soil.*

274. To illustrate the particular analogies of animals, we may adduce first, those existing between Mammals and Birds. The analogies in question have been noted from very early times. Naturalists were not long in finding out that the Quadrumana or monkey-family have their parallel in the Scansores or climbing birds; the Carnivora in the Raptores or birds of prey; the Cetacea, or whales, in the Natatores or swimming birds. Mr. Newman, in his treatise on the "System of Nature," sums them up most felicitously. Thus:—"The parrots among birds emulate the monkeys among placentals; they eat all kinds of food that they can procure; they obtain it in the same situations; they seek it in the same way—by climbing—for a parrot does not run or leap like other birds, but like a monkey, climbs slowly and solemnly from bough to bough. Its foot is constantly used as a hand for conveying food to the mouth; its chattering voice is also similar; its large brain and peculiar tact in imitation are still additional similarities." No less striking is the agreement between the carnivora and the birds of prey. What the lion and the tiger are among the former, the same—and in many more points than the thirst for blood, and the pursuit of living quarry,—are the eagle and the vulture among the tenants of the air. So with the birds denominated the Insessores or Perchers, such as the sparrow, the raven, and the thrush. These are the feathered analogues of that class

* The Actinias are not *absolutely* fixed. Ordinarily so found, they have the power, nevertheless, of detaching themselves, and moving away. They do this either by slowly gliding along; or by reversing the body, and using the tentacula as feet; or by inflating the body with water, and committing themselves to the waves.

of quadrupeds to which the mouse and the squirrel belong. "Many of them are remarkable for their attachment to the residences of man; they perforate our walls, make their nests and bring forth their young in holes and crevices of our roofs; they are remarkable for boldness yet wariness; they are forever intruding, yet constantly on the watch; they are of small size, and infinite in number; they are merry, active, and playful. Who is there that has not compared the sparrow to the mouse?" Passing to other families, we see in the wryneck a feathered ant-eater; the camel and the giraffe remind us of the stork and the ostrich; the penguins and the sea-gulls of the seals. Birds in general are to the rest of the vertebrata what Insects are to the invertebrata. Both tribes of beings are remarkable for the lustre and variety of their colors: for their power of rapidly sailing through the air; for their high degree of respiration; and their extraordinary amount of instinct. In beautiful and ingenious architecture, the birds, the bees, and the wasps, have been competitors since the world began.

275. In the inferior tribes of animals we have analogies precisely similar, as in the likeness of the shell-bearing mollusca, such as the snail, to certain members of the tribe of reptiles. As it slowly crawls along, with head and tail alone protruding, we see over again the general figure and proverbial slowness of the tortoise. The fish called the Tansy, or *Blennius pholis*, is remarkable for its skill in building nests like those of birds. "What makes this fish," says Mr. Gosse, "more than usually interesting is, that it is one of those species which construct an elaborate nest for the deposition of their eggs and the hatching of their young—

Atque avium dulces nidos imitata sub undis!

In Mr. Couch's "Illustrations of Instinct" (p. 252 *et seq.*)

the construction of the little dwelling, of fragments of coralline and other sea-weeds, interwoven by silken threads, its suspension from an overhanging rock, the deposition of the amber-colored eggs, the habits of the new-born young, the danger they incur from predatory enemies, and the vigilant care of the affectionate parent, are well described." From the same author may be cited another curious history. "The Strawberry-crab (Eurynome aspera), so called from its being studded all over with pink tubercles on a white ground," he tells us, "is a *climber*. If it were a terrestrial animal, I should say its habits were *arboreal*. True, it now and then wanders over the bottom of its abode, with slow and painful march, but generally it seeks an elevated position. We usually see it in the morning perched on the summit of some one of the more bushy weeds of the Aquarium, as the Chondrus or Phyllophora rubens, where it has taken its station during the night, the season of its chief activity, as of most other Crustacea. While watching it climb," he continues, "I was strongly reminded of the Ourang-Outang at the Zoological Gardens; the manner in which each of these very dissimilar animals performed the same feat was so closely alike as to create an agreeable feeling of surprise."* This crab resembles the monkeys also in *its great length of arm*, obviously an adaptation for climbing; seen also in the Sloths of South America, which are almost exclusively arboreal; in the Longicorns among beetles, which are essentially tree-insects; and in the perpendicular web-makers among the Spiders. The Cephalopoda or Cuttle-fishes are preëminently the Felidæ of the ocean. Lying in wait for living prey; lurking in secrecy to spring upon it; feeding chiefly in the twilight or at night; their

* The Aquarium, pp. 127–131.

strength and rapidity of movement render them formidable enemies to many of their fellow-inhabitants of the waters. They are, moreover, the chamæleons of the deep, having the power of rapidly changing the color of the skin as emergencies require. The Pteropoda (wing-footed), so called from the peculiar lateral appendages which constitute their principal means of progression, are the moths and butterflies of the sea. Insects in general, are represented there by the Crustacea, a tribe nearly allied to them. No true insect ever occurs in salt water.

276. Fossil species no less than living ones attest the unity of organic life. Whether antediluvian or recent, there is only one system of structure, either for animals or for plants. "Throughout all formations, the grand truth to which every accession of geological discovery bears witness, is the principle of unity of plan. Even the most seemingly monstrous and incongruous forms of animated existence in past times, are all, without exception, constituted according to regular modifications of a common type, and with parts, organs, and functions, related by the closest analogies to one another; so that no sooner is a new specimen detected than it immediately finds its proper position in the scheme of nature. Whether an absolutely new form, or offering appearances intermediate, a place can be assigned to it, and this invariably too in such a manner that it either tends "to supply a link of affinity between orders of beings already related, or indicates some new and unexpected point of analogy."* Take a few examples. No living species of animals have wider intervals between them than those belonging to the Pachydermata, or family of the rhinoceros and elephant. But in the ages when the tertiary strata were deposited, this

* Baden Powell, "Philosophy of Creation," p. 337.

tribe of quadrupeds was far more abundant than now; the fossil species supply the links which are needed to unite the existing kinds, and complete the series. Of the reptilian creatures we now similarly possess only a remnant. This earth was for thousands of years the abode of numerous species no longer to be found alive, the Ichthyosaurus, the Plesiosaurus, and the Iguanodon; the fossil and the living taken together, make up the series to which they are mutually indispensable. The same with fossil plants. The Calamites of the coal-formation take their place in the existing family of Equisetaceæ; the Lepidodendra are intermediate between living Lycopodiaceæ and Coniferæ, approaching, however, more nearly to the former; and even the Sigillarias find, as far as the particulars of their organization are known, a definite place in the living flora that surrounds us. NATURE, we thus learn, knows nothing of past and present. The relics of bygone ages are not relics of extinct systems, simply of extinct species. The trilobites and pterodactyles, the Sigillarias and the Lepidodendra, are as much a part of the chain of being as the zebra and the camel, the oak and the myrtle-tree, and are fully as essential to its completeness.

277. That Animals and Plants taken together, form a whole, is a fact no less obvious than the unity of either kingdom considered separately. As organized beings, formed of solids and fluids, maintaining, and maintained by, an incessant cyclical action, born of a parent, or rather of parents, growing to a given bulk, feeding, sleeping, reproducing their kind, and on the expiration of their lease of life, dying, and giving place to their descendants; the members of these two great realms are perfectly and in every point analogous. Every function in the one is so closely imaged in the other, that although in no case identically the same, it is impos sible not to recognize them as determined by a common law.

Physiologically, they are *one*. The wide difference in the general *configuration* of the two classes of beings takes nothing from the integrity of the principle. The unlikeness in general form which on a superficial contrast, would keep asunder the quadruped and the tree, would on the same reasoning keep even further apart the mammal and the polyp. The unlikeness, after all, is not so great as we are apt to suppose. There is little resemblance, it is true, between the totality of plants compared with animals; we must not expect that, because analogous, a menagerie and a flower-garden will be like seal and impression; taking, however, one object at a time, and though no analogue be straightway found, instead of throwing it on one side, patiently and sanguinely persisting in the search, knowing what we look for, there is nothing in the world of animals for which a parallel may not be found in the world of plants. Examples of these parallels were cited in the chapter on Prefiguration, leading, as we there saw, to the transfer of animals' names to plants, and of plants' names to animals. It will suffice to add, that while plants, as a whole, occupy a platform beneath animals, so do their particular races, and even species, occupy specific places, each higher kind of organism standing, as it were, virtually above the next inferior, the mammal at the summit, the plant underneath, and probably a mineral below the plant. As the parrots, for instance, answer to the monkeys, so do the epiphytic Orchids to the parrots. They reside, like both classes of creatures, not upon the ground, as other plants do, but upon the boughs and branches of trees; the gaudy plumage of the parrots they almost surpass in the brilliant coloring of their petals; the aptitude for mimicry in the monkeys they parallel in their extraordinary counterfeits of the shapes of insects, birds, and reptiles. It may be remarked here that Nature has her mountain-families, her sea-families, her river-families, and so forth, in every department. The monkeys, the parrots, and the epiphytic Orchids are peculiarly her threefold *forest* family, at least as regards the tropics. In the torrid zone the parrots are the principal of the birds which make their dwelling in the woods; they rarely descend to the ground, and numerous in individuals, fill the forest with their disagreeable cries. Similarly, the monkeys, so well adapted for a life in the woods, by the structure of their bodies, and the nature of their food, numerous also both in species and individuals, live almost entirely in the trees. In the forests of tropical South America, the Orchids are described as growing in myriads, adorning the living trunks as it were with jewels, and rendering the prostrate beautiful even in death.

278. In no light does the analogy of plants and animals appear more striking, than when we compare the great natural groups into which they are scientifically divided. In both there is a common archetype, but in both there are many sub-types, the latter being the ground of the distinctions of tribes, orders, classes, genera, and so forth. Ordinarily, the animal world is divided first into Vertebrata and Invertebrata; or animals with a spine, and internal skeleton, such as man; and animals destitute of a spinal column, and with their bony part on the *outside*, as in the case of the crab. Plants, after the same manner, are primarily distinguished by almost all, into the two great classes of Phænogamia and Cryptogamia, or flowering and flowerless, the former distinguished by their conspicuous stamens and pistils, or reproductive apparatus; the latter by the apparent absence of these parts. The Cryptogamia comprise the ferns, sea-weeds, lichens, and similar plants; the Phænogamia include all kinds of trees, shrubs, and the remainder of the herbaceous vegetation of our planet. In both cases the negative is intensely deceptive. We might as reasonably

divide animals into radiate and non-radiate, or plants into fungoid and non-fungoid, as say "vertebrate" and "*in*vertebrate," "flowering" and "flowerless." The invertebrate tribes of animals, and the flowerless tribes of plants, are in no sense natural, coherent, and symmetrical groups. So far from it, they differ among themselves quite as widely as in the collective from the vertebrated and the phænogamous. The true distinction to begin with is the *quadruple*, namely, of Animals into Vertebrata, Articulata, Mollusca, and Radiata; and of Plants into Exogens, Endogens, Cormogens, and Thallogens.* The Vertebrata comprise man, quadrupeds, birds, fishes, and reptiles: the Articulata, insects in all their variety, together with the crustacean animals, such as the crab and lobster; also the centipede, the earth-worm, and similar creatures: the Mollusca comprise the slug, the snail, and the inhabitants generally of *shells*, whether fresh-water or marine, univalve or bivalve: to the Radiata belong the star and jelly-fishes, the sea-anemones, the coral-creatures, and most kinds of animalcules. These last are all of them aquatic. The four great provinces of the Vegetable Kingdom are equally intelligible, even to the least practiced. "Exogens" comprehend all those trees and plants which have the wood forming their stems deposited in concentric layers, so that the section shows beautiful rings; the veins of their leaves are netted; their flowers and fruit are constructed on a quinary type; and the embryo of the seed is provided with two seed-leaves. Such, for example, is the structure in the oak, the apple, the olive, and the rose; the first, the most perfect realization of a forest-tree; the second of a fruit-tree; the last of a lovely flower. "Endogens" are

* The two latter groups together form what some authors call the *Acrogens*, but to view them as *one* is certainly incorrect.

of lower development. The section of the stem presents dots instead of rings; the stems are rarely provided with branches, and instead of bark have only a hardened surface; the veins of the leaves are straight and parallel instead of netted; perhaps the leaves themselves are in general only the parts which in Exogens are simply the petioles, the lamina being here undeveloped; the plan of the flowers and fruit instead of quinary, is ternary; and the embryo has a solitary seed-leaf. Lilies and grasses of all kinds are endogenous, and in the tropics, the number is swelled by the stately Palm-trees. "Cormogens" have their noblest representatives in the Ferns; plants destitute for the most part of aërial stems; destitute also of true flowers, but provided with elegant green "fronds," which serve at once for leaves, and to bear the fructification, the curious and characteristic brown bars or spangles developed on their under surface. To the same province belong the Lycopodiums, the Equisetums, and the Mosses. Fourth and last, the "Thallogens" comprise the singular, universally diffused and familiar plants called Lichens, Fungi, and Sea-weeds. None of these plants have proper stems, leaves, or blossoms. They are simple masses of cellular tissue, and are scarcely ever of a green color; gray, yellow, red, purple, or white, replace the verdure we find in every other race.

279. Now these four great classes of Animals, and four great classes of Plants,—acknowledged by all the best systematists to be strictly "natural,"—*answer to one another exactly.* The Exogenous plants are the vegetable analogues of the Vertebrata; the Endogens of the Articulata; the Cormogens answer to the Molluscous creatures: and the Thallogens to the Radiate. The details of the several analogies would require a volume; a word upon each is all that can here be given. The agreement of the Exogens with the Vertebrata is known to most; it is one of the first facts

which the philosophic naturalist finds appealing to him. To illustrate that of the Endogens with the Articulata, which is little less conspicuous, it will suffice to point once again to the insectiform flowers and the aërial habitats of the Orchideæ. The analogy of the Mollusca with the Cormogens is not so palpable till scrutinized;—it is hard to think that the shells upon our mantel-pieces can have anything in common with ferns and mosses. When, however, we compare the *naked* molluscs, such as the slug, with the *essential* part of the fern,—which is not so much the frond, as the rhizome or root-stock from which the frond arises,—the mystery begins to clear. Take, for instance, the rhizomes of the different species of *Davallia*, and of many of the genus *Polypodium*, as they lie, slug-like, upon the surface of the earth. In the *ramosum* they are streaked; those of the *vespertilionis* crawl over the edges of the flower-pot. The analogy becomes further evident when we compare the fronds themselves with the peculiar respiratory apparatus found in the Mollusca, and called their "branchiæ." The fronds of the fern, it will be remembered, are the respiratory apparatus of the plant, and therefore analogous to the branchiæ. These latter, like the ferns, are often delicately branched, and stand to the body of the creature just as the fronds do to the rhizome. Such is the case in the Nudibranchiate molluscs, delicate and fragile little creatures found crawling on corallines, sponges, and sea-weeds, and usually of the most charming and diversified colors. Their branchiæ are beautifully arborescent, in many species doubly and triply pinnate, resembling the fronds of the *Davallia* or of the *Polypodium Dryopteris*, and disposed either in a star-like circle, as in the genera *Doris*, *Polycera*, and *Miranda*, or in a double row down the back, as in the *Tritonia* (or *Dendronotus*) *arborescens*. This most elegant little creature has a body of about two inches in length, supporting seven or eight pairs of its fern-like plumes, those towards the head being the largest, and those nearest the tail the smallest. It is met with on the shore, in crevices of rocks, and upon sea-weeds, &c., almost throughout the north, or from Greenland to the English Channel, and again on the north-east coast of America. The reader interested in knowing more of these curious and unregarded, but exquisite little beings, *theoretically*, may consult the admirable monograph of Messrs. Alder and Hancock, published by the Ray Society. How the analogy between the Radiata and the Thallogens is determined, may readily be understood on a comparison of the higher fungi, such as the mushroom, with the jelly-fishes. Every one who has seen these latter lying stranded on the shore, will remember their circular configuration. We have it markedly also in the opened Geastrum and the star-fishes. Most of the crustaceous lichens, and the fructification universally, show circles and radiations; and how common this is with the polyps is unnecessary to say. In the beautiful white laminated coral, the *Fungia agariciformis*, we can hardly persuade ourselves that we do not see a petrified mushroom; as for the analogy of the Algæ with the Radiata, every one at first sight takes the Sertularias for Seaweeds.

280. While the innumerable facts which disclose these grand analogies, testify, in so doing, to the Unity of Nature, they are unanswerable evidence against the hypothesis of the Continuous CHAIN. Vertebrates unquestionably stand at the head of the animal kingdom, man, considered zoologically, being their *maximum;* and Exogens as plainly stand first among plants; the descent, however, from these down to the lowest, is not by a single line, but by *many* lines diverging in widely separated directions. No tribe, either of plants or of animals, can be said to be *absolutely* at the bottom. Though the Radiata and the Thallogens are placed

there in schemes of classification, a considerable portion of them are far superior in their development to species belonging to the higher tribes. Every tribe, in fact, both of animals and plants, possesses, as said before, an extremely wide range of form, higher kinds and lower kinds, the former always superior to the lower ones of the adjacent tribes. Like the columns of the orders of architecture, they begin in simplicity, but are crowned with sculptured capitals. We may construct a continuous chain by taking the various tribes of beings in their aggregates, and placing them according to the dignity of their maximum developments; but such a course is impossible with subtribes, genera, and species. In short, if we seek to arrange things in a strictly arithmetical succession, we not only depart from the true order of nature, but outrage it. The Radiata have as good a claim to be put second as the Articulata, and the Mollusca as good a claim as the Radiata; similarly in plants, the highest of the Cormogens, or the Tree-ferns, are incomparably better entitled to be placed next the Exogens than many Endogenous genera, the duck-weed for example, which hides the water of stagnant ponds; and the same is the right of the magnificent sea-weeds of the Indian and Antarctic oceans. The *D'Urvillea,* when cut transversely, presents zones, with divisions resembling medullary rays, and a sort of pith; a similar appearance is observable indeed in the well known olive-brown alga of our own shores, the laminaria digitata, or Sea-tangle, one of the giants of the marine forests, as regards Europe. Lamouroux claims four distinct parts for its stem, analogous in situation, organization, and relative size, to the epidermis, bark, wood, and pith of Exogens.

281. The true position of the subordinate provinces of the two great realms of organic nature, with regard to the chief or typical province; also the relation which the subor-

dinate provinces bear towards one another; and the relation again of the whole of either series to its correlative, plants to animals, and animals to plants—the following diagrams will serve perhaps to make plain :—

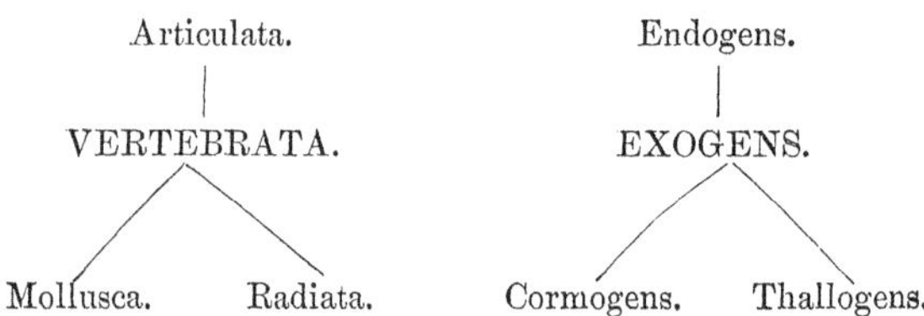

Here we have the Vertebrata and the Exogens the centre of their respective systems, the subordinate tribes equidistant from them, each with its lowest forms on the remote confines, and its highest next the archetype. Each archetype is, as it were, a Sun, transmitting its rays in three directions, and with equal force and effulgence in every one of them. The nearer we stand to the luciferous orb, the more sensible we are of its qualities; the further we travel away from it, the fainter becomes the light. Leaving the apple and the rose, for instance, among Exogens, we come, according to the point of departure, to the palms among Endogens, to the tree-ferns among Cormogens, or to the great tree-like algæ of the southern seas, among the Thallogens. These form, as it were, the inner circle. Next we come to forms of each tribe less elaborately developed, and thence gradually pass outwards to the simplest of each kind, the humble dwellers at the "ends of the earth." The Articulata and the Endogens, the Mollusca and the Cormogens, the Radiata and the Thallogens, may be placed in any one of the three stations; it matters not which lie upon the right, or which upon the left; the essential point is their equidistance from the centre.

282. The distribution into *fours* is not confined to the first

great provinces; every one of these latter is again divisible into a principal and three subordinate, and there is ample reason to believe that it is the same again with every one of *these*. Doubless, the further we push in our inquiries, the greater becomes the difficulty of determining these normal centres, and what characters shall be deemed indicative of superior rank; but it is certain that every principle of nature runs through the *whole* of nature,—that every type and institution is repeated on every platform, though we may be unable to make it out upon the instant. Nature does not disclose all her secrets at once; every generation is allowed its share of insight; an infinite amount is reserved for those unborn. Take, for instance, the Vertebrata. The highest of these are the Mammalia, or animals that suckle their young; the remainder are the three obvious and well-known groups, Birds, Fishes, and Reptiles, all of which stand equally near to the Mammalia in their higher forms, while no one of them is absolutely the lowest. We may repeat here that in the true idea of the Form of an object is involved not merely its *structure*, or that part of its nature which the anatomist is concerned with; it includes also the whole of the qualities and dispositions which pertain to it, and which distinguish it *socially* from other things. And this, in fact, is its *essential* nature, being that which gives it a place and function in the general economy of creation; thus the object and end for which it was created. The End is always nobler than the Means, for the means are only processes whereby the end shall be attained. In all our groupings and classifications, therefore, we should view the organic structure as intermediate between the Artist and the End he has in view. Put in a diagram, the four classes stand thus:—

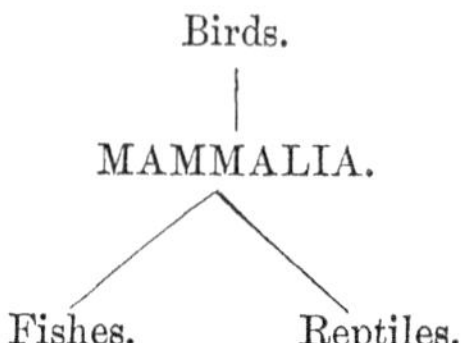

Among plants, after the same manner, the great, primary province of Exogens resolves into

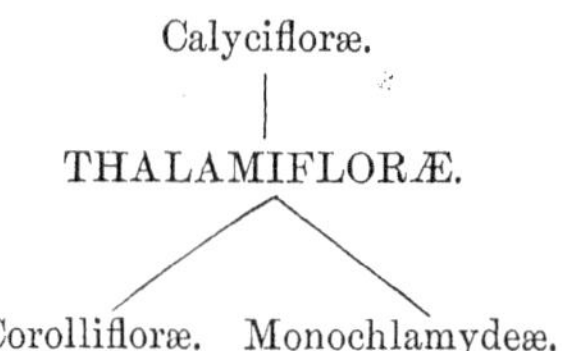

The reciprocal relations are in these minor classes precisely analogous to those of the larger divisions. As Exogens answer to Vertebrata in the first analysis, so, in the second, the Thalamifloræ answer to mammals.

CHAPTER XXVII.

MAN THE EPITOME OF NATURE.

283. In the forms, properties, analogies, and discrete distinctiveness of the three great kingdoms of objective nature is set forth the whole philosophy of Life and Mind. Here are represented and expounded the threefold expression of the Divine life, the threefold composition of the human soul, and all those other sublime trilogies of the universe which declare Him who by wisdom framed the worlds. When, therefore, we would study life, when we would study metaphysics, psychology, or any of the profound and spacious themes which deal with facts not obvious to the senses, our best and shortest way is to begin with studying Natural History, or the science of minerals, vegetables, and animals, their forms, relations, uses, and correspondences. The study of the three kingdoms of nature is in effect the study of Man, who, being the image of God, is the finite archetype and summary of all things, the world over again, at once its lord and its epitome. The world is threefold because man is threefold. In the constitution of human nature is written the rationale of its entire scheme and order—yea, of everything it contains. If man were not what he is, and if he were not the immediate and personal work of God, though there might be a world, it would be as different from the world which now exists, as man himself would be different from what Almighty Wisdom and Goodness have created

him. The primary, essential reason of the world's being what we find it is, of course, the Nature and the Will of God. Every divinely originated object is a result of which the Supreme reason lies far back of man, far back even of his intelligence and imagination. Still, it is man that we must look to as the *explanation* of the world's existence—*he* is the proximate reason, the point at which our inquiries are at once stayed and rewarded. *Why* man is the summary and proximate reason of the world, is that he shall be a happy dweller, in the end, in the mansions of the heavenly presence. He cannot become this unless he have an intelligence commensurate with his glorious destiny, and such intelligence he can only possess by learning the nature and will of God as expressed in material, objective forms. In other words, to realize our sublime destiny we must first learn to know and love HIM who has provided it; but this we can only do through the medium of the finite and material. Only through this medium is God knowable at all. Without an objective world, rich and gorgeous as our own, the idea of God could not be conceived. "As there are no infinite media, no signs that express the infinite, no minds, in fact, that can apprehend the infinite by direct inspection, the One must appear in the manifold; the Absolute in the conditional; Spirit in form; the Motionless in motion; the Infinite in the finite. He must let forth his nature in sounds, colors, forms, works, definite objects and signs."* Not that because of this distribution of the Divine nature, we are to think of it as a congeries of separate and separable elements. No. It is perfect and indivisible Unity, variously exhibiting itself, or in diverse aspects and manifestations, according to the design to be accomplished. We

* "God in Christ," by the Rev. Horace Bushnell, p. 139.

never see only a *part* of God's nature. He is present in his full totality, in every leaf upon the tree; in every little butterfly and shell. Not *personally*, but by the communication of his LIFE. Nature is not God, neither is God nature. Nature is the Divine Art, expressed in material configurations and phenomena; God reigns apart from it, in the heavens. While true, then, that but for the Intellect of God there could not have been a world, it is no less true that the intellect of man is contingent upon the world. In order that as intelligent beings we may appreciate and enjoy our eternity-life, we must abide for a given period in the school of the time-life, or the material world, using it, and fulfilling its duties. This we can only do by being in *unity* with it. Things can only use what surrounds them by virtue of such a relation. Plants can only assimilate mineral matter by virtue of their having a mineral side; animals can only assimilate vegetable matter by virtue of consanguinity with the vegetable; man, were he not both animal and plant, and man besides, could make no use of either. He is competent both to apply the world to his physical use, and to love it, and profit by it, spiritually, because he is its entire nature epitomized and concentrated. It is because they are wanting in this plenitude of relation that brutes are incapable of heaven, and make no use of the world except as a place for eating and drinking. Man would be as short-lived as they are, did not the laws of the world pre-exist in his own nature, and but for this also he would be as blind and speechless. Language, narrowly looked at, is in its every word a spiritual echo and reflection of the world outside; its every atom primarily denotes something objective, or at least physical. "It is only as there is a λογος in the outward world, answering to the λογος or internal reason of the parties, that men can come into a mutual understanding in regard to any thought or spiritual state whatever." For the same reason, every great poem that deals freely and profoundly with external nature, is a "Kosmos" of the spiritual nature of man. None have so largely helped forward the true science of metaphysics as the poets, who have stood face to face with nature, and sung about her splendors.

284. Such is the idea of man intended in his ancient name of *microcosm*, or "little world,"—a name approved by greatest thinkers. "Fantastically strained," as Lord Bacon observes, "by Paracelsus and the alchemists," who made it the ground of their astrological speculations, the idea has to a certain extent lost favor in modern times. There are not wanting even despisers of it. "Paracelsus," says the author of the History of the Literature of Europe, "seized hold of a notion which easily seduces the imagination of those who do not ask for rational proof, that there is a constant analogy between the macrocosm of external nature, and the microcosm of man." Misconceived and misapplied as it was by the arch-mystic, the doctrine has at no time been in the least degree falsified. Rather does it acquire new strength with the growth of science, aided often by those who are least conscious of their services. Dating from the oldest philosophers, it receives its best illustrations from the newest. Every man who seeks to obey the golden aphorism, "Know Thyself," finds in his own nature reiteration of the world at large; he finds it, both physiologically, in his body, and spiritually, in his soul. "Man's body," in the words of a popular writer, "contains the elements of all knowledge." Its chemistry is wonderful, and embraces all chemistry; its geography is equally so; its seas and its rivers are even more wonderful than those of the earth; its temperature contains the whole theory of combustion. All knowledge, all taste, all sense of right and wrong, is comprehended within the sphere of the microcosm, man. He who knows man thoroughly, is both learned and scientific, and what is better than either, he is the

truly wise man." "In man," we are told by another, "all the powers and realities of the universe are concentrated, all developments united, all forms associated. Man is the bearer of all the dignities of nature. There is in nature no tone to which his being is not the response, no form of which he is not the type. The human organism is the whole κοσμος, with its life infused into the individual. Man's organization embraces all; he is the world's self-surveying eye, the world's self-hearing ear, the world's self-enouncing voice. Hence he is termed by Goethe the plan of creation; by Novalis, the systematic index to nature; by Oken, the complex of all organizations."*

285. Of all subjects open to the human mind, it follows that the Unity of man with nature is the most lofty and instructive. If true that he is one with it, then the study of man must needs be the study of all nature, and conversely, as said at the outset, that of nature must be a microscopic view of man, free access to every side and aspect of him. No subject defines so vast a circle. It embraces the whole of metaphysics, and the whole of the philosophy of Language, which is equivalent to saying the entire range of the correspondence of things spiritual with things material. It embraces the whole of zoology, of botany, and the sciences of nature in general, making all things fill with life, and bringing all into an unexpected fellowship. In every sense of the word, it is *self*-knowledge. "The man who does not find in animals younger brothers, and in plants cousins more or less removed, is unacquainted with his own nature." How beautiful the analogy of man with Trees! His physiology is pictured in them; they have members, organs, and tissues; the pendent, flexile branches of many kinds are

---

* Stallo, Philosophy of Nature, p. 107.

transcripts of the locks and ringlets of the head, as those of the silver-birch, called by Coleridge "the lady of the woods;" the gnarled and knotted oak reminds us of masculine sturdiness and muscles. The old botanist, Curtius, has a chapter *De arborum membris, et illorum cum hominis membris conformitate,** imitated by Laurenberg in one *De Analogia plantas et hominem.*† Poetical minds dwell on it enthusiastically, as Sir Uvedale Price, in his book on the Picturesque; "The luxuriance of foliage answers to that of hair; the delicate smoothness of bark to that of skin, and the clear, even, and tender color of it to that of the complexion." Then he shows us how the youth of a tree corresponds with the youth of our own species, each being made beautiful by its freshness, which gives way, however, with lapse of years, to dryness and wrinkles. "By such changes, that nice symmetry and correspondence of parts, so essential to beauty, is in both destroyed; in both, the hand of time roughens the surface, and traces still deeper furrows; a few leaves, a few hairs, are thinly scattered on their summits; the light, airy, aspiring look of youth is gone, and both seem shrunk and tottering, and ready to fall with the next blast."‡ A passage in the elegant "Poetics" of Mr. Dallas, well deserves appending. "Almost every page," he observes, "that Wordsworth has written, bears token of his belief that between man and the flowers of the field there is a close alliance,—that man is indeed a Tree, endowed with powers of self-knowledge and self-movement;—a faith shared by many besides, but entered into by none more entirely, unless by George Herbert; a faith which is nowhere more strongly or

---

* *Hortorum,* Lib. vii., cap. 1—15. 1560.

† *Apparatus Plantarum,* cap. 7—12. 1632.

‡ Pp. 94, 95, Lauder's Edit. 1842.

more frequently affirmed than in the assurances of Holy Writ, and which the legendary lore of Daphnes and Ariels, together with our love for trees, and the way in which we lament their downfall more than that of anything else not human, proves to be deeply seated in every bosom."

286. The unity of man with nature in respect of its three kingdoms is marked, first, in the structure of his corporeal frame; secondly, in the triple action of his life. Begin with the body. Here we have one of the most wonderful analogies in creation. The abdominal region, the lowest part of the body proper, is our mineral kingdom: the chest, with its leafy lungs, and life-giving heart, the source of aliment to every member, is our vegetable kingdom; the head, with its beautifully-moving face, and restless brain, supported by the chest, as the chest by the inferior part, is to the remainder of our fabric what animals are to vegetation and the soil. Every part is needful to the well-being of every other part. As vegetation effects important and salutary changes in the earth and atmosphere; and as animals are at once givers and recipients, in regard both to the plant-world and to the mineral; so is it with the three kingdoms of the human body. The need of plants to the earth in regard to the promotion of rain, and of the earth to plants as an anchorage and source of food, is but a varied utterance of the sympathies of our own organization. Man himself is as necessary to the earth as the earth is necessary to *him;* the same is true of the corporeal members that represent them.

287. As in external nature, by the law of promotion, every superior platform carries with it the essential qualities and powers of all that have gone before, so is it in nature's Epitome. As the plant has the mineral idea in it, the peculiar glory of the vegetable being superadded; and as the animal has the vegetable idea in it, with again a brighter

dignity superinduced, whereby it feels, and moves, and becomes capable of social intercourse; so into the chest, or vegetable region of the human body, are continued the attributes of the earthly or abdominal region; and into the head or animal region, the attributes of both the others. There is nothing either in the structure or the functions of any portion of his body, but is in the Head of man recapitulated and reiterated, and in every case under a nobler and purer guise. The limbs and their activities reappear in the muscles of the face, and that lively play of the features which gives it variety and expression. The digestive system reappears in the mouth, wherein the whole process of feeding is at once begun and representatively completed, the jaws and teeth taking their place as representatives of the hands, —the prehensile organs by which the food has in the first instance been procured. The nose re-enacts in little the duty of the lungs, and the function of the respiratory apparatus in general. On the lips are beautifully spiritualized the idea and circumstances of sexual love.* The eyes in their mighty grasp of total nature, a microscope one moment, a telescope the next, renew and concentrate the powers given by the sense of touch, and the aptitude for locomotion, bringing as it were, the whole surface and whole mechanism of the body to a single point. Hence their beautiful roundness, since whatever in the universe exhibits a totality, is invariably a Sphere. In that wonderful framework, the human Head, are collected accordingly, symbols, representatives, and metaphors of every organ and sign of Life. The body is the first and ruder synthesis, the head the last and finest. Here all the powers and elements of nature converge, as all the light and colors of creation

---

* Καὶ ἡ μίξις αυτη γλυκεία γινεται τῶν ψυχῶν. *Aristænetus*, Epistles, 2, 7.

meet in the grand focus of the Sun. Most naturally is it, then, that in the face are afforded those entertaining disclosures which indicate man's hold within himself of the organization and inmost nature of every creature of zoology. When the features of the monkey, the sheep, the bull, supplant, as we often see them, those of the proper human countenance; when the mildness of the dove, the cunning of the snake, the stupidity of the ass, paint themselves on the physiognomy of our fellows, it is because in man they are all essentially contained; and though their normal and complete realization is outside of him, are yet competent to look forth from the windows.

288. With the three great kingdoms of the bodily fabric correspond, in turn, the three great factors of our humanity, the Sensuous life, the Rational, and the Religious,—forms of activity which have each of them their distinct place and special office in the soul's economy, as minerals, plants, and animals have *theirs* in the economy of the world. The sensuous life is the mineral degree of human nature; the rational life is the vegetable degree; the religious life is the animal. The first, like the solid earth on which we stand, supplies the other with a footing; the rational life is that pleasant green sward of our existence to which belong the innumerable little thoughts and emotions of daily life, amiable and intelligent, worthy and beautiful, but still only secular and temporal; the life of religion is that which, lifting us into the sphere of the heavenly and immortal, crowns and consummates the others, as animals complete the glory of God's creation. Wanting either of these three lives, human nature would be imperfect, nor could we exist without any one of them for a single instant; for though man may refuse to *exercise* the life of religion, the power to do so still flows into him from God, and is an integral part of his vitality as a human being. Neglecting the privileges

of the two higher lives, man degrades himself into the condition of a mere globe of inanimate earth and water; caring only for the sensuous life and the rational, he is a mere world of trees and plants, useless because there is no animal to feed upon them.

289. Between these three lives there are discrete degrees as decided as those of material nature. There is no continuity between them, any more than between mineral and plant, or between plant and animal; each preserves its own plane of beginning and of end. Hence the impossibility of a man ever becoming rational who attends only to the pleasures of external sense; or religious by the mere culture of intelligence and morality. It is no more possible than to procure flowers by sowing crystals, or birds by planting acorns. But though severed by discrete degrees, the three lives are intimately bound together, the highest mediately beholden to the lowest. All, moreover, are good, and excellent in their degree, because every one of them has its own dignifying duty. The religious life is intended to minister to our Maker; the rational to the religious; the sensuous to the rational; each lower life thus, eventually, to ends of piety and the praise of God. There is no greater mistake than to contemn or disparage the sensuous life. Whatever is subservient to delight of sense, is conducive, while used temperately, to the best interests of humanity. The perfection of a Christian character does not consist in ignoring and despising the sensuous, which at no time can it practically dispense with, but in honoring all things in their proper places and degrees, rejecting none, but regenerating all. Educators have much to learn in respect of this. How foolish, for example, the doctrine which would persuade a girl that beauty is valueless, and dress only vanity. It is false altogether. Beauty *is* of value; so is dress, and of great value. The thing to teach is their *just* value; that

there must be something beneath the dress, and interior to the beauty, better than the silk and the rosy cheek, and without which they are truly no more than rags and ugliness. To dress tastefully and prettily is one of the first and finest of the fine arts; elegance of attire is a part of the very method and style of nature; clothed in our very choicest, we are still not to compare with the lilies of the field. Using the sensuous life aright is taking the crystal from the quarry, and converting it into a magnifying lens. Unimpaired in itself, the investiture of it with the new and higher use enhances the loftiest pleasures of our philosophy. Everything in the sensuous life may be made beautiful and poetical if we will bring it *up* into our higher thoughts, instead of sacrificing those higher thoughts to *it;* for the sensuous life, like the world, does not so much want subjugating, as right using. Men say "nature" teaches them to do so and so, and excuse even licentiousness on the plea of following nature. Very good. We can never do better than follow and obey nature. But it must be an enlarged, not a partial survey of nature that we must take. The partial study makes it seem natural to abide in the sensuous; the enlarged study shows that it is infinitely more natural to *come out* of the sensuous, or rather, to value it only as the basis. Nothing is lost of the enjoyment of it, by finding "nature" as much in the rational and the spiritual life. While the sensuous life, thought of for itself alone, too often becomes a sensual, and thence a vicious life; and thence again, full of dangers and anxieties, and usually ends ill, perhaps in rottenness and rags, or at least in a peevish and despicable discontent; the property of the spiritual life, thought of first, and of the rational life, duly honored, is to infuse itself into everything below, giving an unexpected zest to the enjoyment even of the merest animal pleasures, so that the voluptuary, who pities and despises what is above him, after all, misses his own aim and expectation.

290. So with the rational life. If it be foolish to despise the sensuous, a thousand times more foolish is that disesteem of the secular and intellectual which is often thought so helpful to true piety. The Bible requires the abasement of nothing on the part of man beyond his preposterous selfishness and pride. The design of our Lord, in his divine teachings, is to make us, not religionists, but *perfect men.* This he does not propose to do by the suppression of any part of our nature, but by developing the whole. "If it could be proved that Christianity interdicted the exercise of the intellectual life of man in the very slightest degree, it would have as little of the truthful, the heavenly, and the practical in it, as if it forbade the theological element." It never can be religion to contemn and disregard what "God so loved" as to visit in order that he might redeem it. To *forsake* the world is to miss its highest usefulness. The hermit may have few vices, but he can have no genuine and lively virtues, for these are only developed by social congress. It is worthy of note that the most exquisite productions of Art are precisely those which approximate to the representation of spiritual, intellectual, and sensuous beauty in a single subject. The best artists are those who can receive and apply this great truth, that the *beau idéal* of a Christian character is the regenerated triple nature.

CHAPTER XXVIII.

INSTINCT AND REASON.

291. THE brilliant instruction we derive from considering the three great kingdoms of nature as a trilogy answering to the threefold expressions of the DIVINE LIFE, is most largely realized when we turn our minds to the contemplation of Instinct and Reason, a true idea of which forces is not possible until that instruction be listened to and applied. As there are three expressions of life, so are there three great classes of phenomena. Those of the lowest degree of life, or the life of inorganic nature, are the domain of Chemistry and Physics; those of the physiological, or inorganic expression, constitute the Instincts; those of the spiritual degree disclose Reason. The first are identified with the mineral world; the second with plants and animals, including the material body of man, or his temporal and terrestrial nature; the third pertain peculiarly to himself, since he alone is concerned with the immortal and celestial. Each degree of life prefigures the next above; chemical phenomena prefigure instinct; and instinct beautifully prefigures reason; but like minerals, plants, and animals, which are their pictures, they are altogether and eternally distinct, because between each there is the barrier of a discrete degree. Never, therefore, was there a greater mistake than that of Helvetius, Condillac, Smellie, and those other authors who contend that reason is no more than the *maximum development* of instinct; in plain English, that "reason"

means "more instinct," and "instinct" "less reason." This is virtually to deny that there is any difference between man and brute, and thus to pronounce both of them imperfect. The doctrine arose, without doubt, from the false notion of a continuous chain of being.

292. Instinct, accordingly, in its true idea, holds a much larger signification than the performance of certain ingenious works, cognizable by our senses. It does not consist simply in those actions and trains of action which books on the subject of instinct ordinarily confine themselves to, such as the nest-building of birds, and the hunting, by the new-born infant, for the mother's breast. For technical purposes, it may be useful so to restrict the term, but viewed philosophically, instinct is co-ordinate and co-extensive with life itself. The actions commonly called instinctive are exhibitions in a wider form, of the very same formative energy which previously moulds the various organs of the body, and maintains them in their functional activity. This is strikingly illustrated in the operation of the "constructive" instincts, such as impel to the fabrication of coverings, clothing, and the various kinds of dwellings, all of which are a kind of ultimated and externalized organization. God is the organizing framer and preserver of the world of living things; instinct is the method by which his energy takes effect. It is the general faculty of the entire living fabric, underlying and determining all activities which transpire, either invisibly in the organs themselves, or as played forth to observation; thus bearing exactly the same relation to the general structure which the constructive chemical forces bear to the crystal. Instinct, in a word, is the operation of LIFE, whether promoting the health, the preservation, or the reproduction of an organized frame, or any part of such frame, and whether animal or vegetable. "The law of instinct," as Mason Good well puts it, "is the law of

the living principle; instinctive actions are the actions of the living principle, pervading and regulating organized matter as gravitation pervades and regulates *un*organized matter, and uniformly operating, by definite means, to the general welfare of the individual system, or its separate organs, advancing them to perfection, preserving them in it, or laying a foundation for their reproduction, as the nature of the case may require. It applies equally to plants and to animals, and to every part of the plant as well as to every part of the animal, so long as such part continues alive."* Virey uses similar terms—" Internal impulses of life constitute acts of instinct in plants the same as in animals. . . . We distinguish, therefore, two degrees of instinct, first, that of the interior functions, or of the mechanism or organization; secondly, that of the spontaneous outward impulses." Carus also, when he calls upon us to observe how a plant "through *internal instinct,* and under external relations, unfolds itself from an obscure and insignificant seed." To the same effect writes the eminent physiologist, Dr. Laycock. "Inherent," says he, "in the primordial cell of every organism, whether it be animal or vegetable, and in all the tissues which are developed out of it, there is an intelligent power or agent, which acting in all cases independently of the consciousness of the organism, and whether the latter be endowed with consciousness or not, forms matter into machines and machinery of the most singular complexity, with the most exquisite skill, and of wondrous beauty, for a fixed, manifest, and predetermined object—namely, the preservation and welfare of the individual, and the continuance of the species. This *quasi*-intelligent agent works with an apparently perfect knowledge of number, geometry, mathema-

---

* Book of Nature, Series 2, Lecture iv.

tics, and of the properties of matter as known to the human intellect under the term 'natural philosophy' or physics—that is to say, with a perfect knowledge of chemistry, electricity, magnetism, mechanics, hydraulics, optics, acoustics—but as far transcending the limited knowledge of the human intellect as the structure and adaptations of living organisms exceed in beauty and fitness the most finished works of man. . . . . I take it as an established principle that the *quasi*-intelligent agent which operates in the construction of organisms, directs the use of the organs constructed."* Between the work of simple "vitality" or "vital power," as it is customary to call it, and the externalized operations popularly understood by the term Instinctive, there is thus no *real* difference but that of method and proximate object. It is the same force which first clothes the bird with plumage, and then impels it to build its beautiful little nest, and line it with soft feathers. The essential unity of the two classes of phenomena may readily be apprehended by comparing their final purposes, which are in every point alike. Whether we take the operations of simple "vitality," so called, or those of palpable, externalized "instinct," in the popular sense of the word—all have reference either to the temporal welfare of the individual, or to the continuance of the species. Self-maintenance and propagation of the kind, are the two grand purposes for which the mediate or physiological expression of life is communicated by the Almighty to his creatures. From the first moment of their existence, plant and animal alike are actively employed in building up organs, repairing waste, and keeping the whole system in

---

* See for a full and admirable exposition of the views enunciated in the above extract, the article on the Brain in the British and Foreign Medico-Chirurgical Review for July, 1855.

lusty health, unless hindered by extraneous obstacles. A portion of their vital energy is simultaneously directed to such activities with regard to surrounding objects, as shall complement those transpiring within the fabric. No new principle is employed in the effectuation of those activities; they are the application of the one common law and method of life to the furtherance of the same common designs, only on a grander scale, and hence with organs often specially provided. The two kinds of phenomena taken together, form the system of vital economy by which the organism and the species alike endure. Doubtless, man may train and turn the usages of instinct to a different purpose, but wherever it is undisturbed by the influence of human reason, the predetermination is essentially to one or other of the two offices that have been mentioned. The force, called by its right name, is the life of the "Divinity that stirs within us," but for whose continued influx into every organ and cell of plant and animal, they would instantly dissolve. Truly was it said by the philosophers of old, *Deus est anima brutorum.* God *is* the life of the brutes, and no less so of the lilies of the field. Virgil is not so wide of the truth as some have fancied, when he says that the bees have in them a portion of the Divine mind. If "in Him *we* live and move, and have our being," how much more the helpless creatures of the plain, whose dependence, we should do well to note, is an infinitely greater truth than their *in*dependence. Not that the creature is a mere cup into which life is poured despotically though benevolently. Though all creatures depend on God, they are still required to *co-operate* with him. God does one part—He does everything in reality, but one part more peculiarly—the other is appointed to the creature to effect as of itself. To this end are instituted what men call the "laws of nature." Every living thing is put in a certain relation with the external world, and the whole of the external world has an express relation with every living creature; the economy and the very existence, both of the total and every atom, being made to depend on the mutual adaptation, and on the personal activity of every part. The instincts are not played forth purely by the Divine life, arbitrarily swaying and ruling the creature. They are always in response to certain stimuli from without.* We experience every day that impressions made on the organs of sense, or on peculiarly sensitive parts of the body, induce muscular acts, sometimes exceedingly complex, and absolutely independent of the will. Often it happens that such impressions give rise to actions which are not only involuntary, but are performed *unconsciously*. The vital activities which constitute Instinct, whether interior or externalized, are referable to identically the same origin; they are grounded, that is to say, in the process designated by the physiologists, "remote sympathy." The extremities of the nervous filaments, which terminate chiefly on the surface of the body, receive impressions calculated to excite them; thence those impression are communicated, by a succession of nervous influences, to the muscular organs, which acknowledge them, and reply by performing certain movements on a definite plan. The spider weaves its web, and the bee constructs its honeycomb. Briefly, particular impressions, conveyed by nerves to the nervous centre they have peculiar reference to, call forth particular acts, seemingly deliberate, but in reality unconscious. What these acts shall be, and what purpose they

* The well-known opinion of Sir Isaac Newton, that the actions of brutes are under the constant, direct, and *immediate* direction of the Deity, is answered with all the care and respect which it deserves, though with a leaning in its favor, in the Dialogues on Instinct of Lord Brougham.

shall subserve, is no longer a physiological question; they belong to the inmost life of the creature, the seat of the reception of the Divine love. That the proximate source of at least the externalized acts of instinct, is the "remote sympathy" above spoken of, is illustrated by the *errors* which instinct sometimes commits. The moth burns its wings in the flame of the candle; Blumenbach's ape pinched out the painted drawings of beetles from a book on Entomology, and ate them. Such acts cannot be referred to the Deity: they belong purely to the weakness of the finite. The sensational stimuli of the instincts, both in brutes and mankind, may be seen fully described in that masterly performance, the Principles of Physiology of John Augustus Unzer. (Sydenham Society's Vol., 1851.)

293. The particular phenomena of Instinct are referable to four great classes; namely, the instinct of Self-Preservation, the instinct of Self-defense, the instinct of Propagation, and the instinct of Love to offspring. It would be easy to show how these operate in the very inmost economy of organic life, but it will suffice here to speak of them as ultimated into "instinct," popularly so termed. The first is that which leads every living creature to seek and consume food, to sleep and otherwise cherish itself, also, in many cases, to construct dwellings and traps for the capture of prey, and to migrate to milder latitudes during the winter. The skilful artisanship of the industrial classes of the Insect world, as the bee, the ant, and the wasp, illustrates this instinct in its *maximum;* the *minimum* pertains perhaps to the serpent tribe, in which few examples of ingenuity have been noticed. To this instinct, it may be added, belong the greater part of those wonderful and entertaining anecdotes which form the bulk of most treatises on the theme before us. The second instinct, that of Self-defense, is illustrated in the use by various creatures, of those natural weapons with which they

are armed in case of assault, as the sting, the talon, and the teeth. The ejection of poison belongs to the same series, along with the paralyzing shock of the electric eel, and the shrouding ink of the cuttle-fish. Here also are to be referred the anecdotes of pretended death by many of the lower animals when closely pursued, especially insects; and of the hiding of others in retreats of the same color as themselves. Birds, for example, often protect themselves by keeping close to the ground, the color of their plumage rendering it difficult to perceive them till they rise. In the instinct of Self-defense are likewise comprehended all those interior operations of "vitality" which provide the different species of living things with a panoply of protecting skin. The maximum operation of this appears in the scales of fishes, in the armor of the rhinoceros, in the carapace of the turtle and the tortoise, and in the shells of the mollusca. Hair, fur, wool, feathers, &c., are so many varied modes of effectuating the same principle. The instinct of self-defense is much more lively in brutes than it is in man. So serious are their exposures to danger, and so limited their powers of perceiving it, that it is made to operate in them with a force only equaled by its instantaneousness. The most interesting example is presented perhaps in the well-known timid caution of the elephant, which will never cross a bridge without first trying its strength with one foot. The third of the leading forms of instinct, the instinct of Propagation, comprises that long, beautiful, and most interesting episode in the history of life which, beginning with the selection of a mate of complementary sex, underlies all the delights and energies of existence, and is the means, under Providence, whereby "the face of the earth" is "renewed." In connection with this instinct is best illustrated the law of *special instincts*, i. e., the particular modifications of the general or fundamental one whereby the whole of its intent becomes gradually and surely effectuated. Such an instinct is that of *pairing*, one of the most admirable in nature. Every species of animal, where the rearing of the young requires the attention of both parents, is subject to it; all such birds, for example, as build their nests in trees. The young of these birds are hatched blind, and bare of feathers, so that they require the nursing care of both parents till their eyes are opened and they are able to fly; to this end the male feeds his mate as she sits brooding on her eggs, and cheers her with a song. Another of the special instincts belonging to the general one of Propagation, specially deserving notice, is that by which the sexes draw near at such periods of the year as will cause their young to be ushered into the world precisely when their food is most abundant. Though the time of gestation varies so widely in the different species of herbivorous quadrupeds, previous things are so ordained that the young appear early in summer, when grass is plentiful; the lambs and the young goats, which are born after a five months' gestation, come with the first steps of spring, because they love short grass, such as a foal or a young cow could scarcely live upon. The young of pairing birds are similarly produced in early summer, when the weather is warm and genial, and they have a long season before them wherein to grow and become vigorous, and able to resist the cold of winter. With the exception of Henry Home of Kames, who gives a chapter to it in the Sketches of the History of Man, (Book 1, Sect. vi., Appendix,) authors have treated this wonderful instinct with a neglect quite unaccountable. Other special instincts belonging to this class, eminently interesting to contemplate, though like the last-mentioned, commonly overlooked as regards brutes, are those of modesty, chastity, and conjugal fidelity. The last gives efficiency to the instinct for pairing, and is indispensable to the nurture of the young, wherever this devolves upon both parents; modesty animates the same instinct in its beginnings, and gives it delicacy and bloom. The most faithful of the animals below man are the pairing birds; the most modest is the elephant. The last of the four geat Instincts, Love to offspring, is like Self-preservation, one of the principal centres of anecdote. The animal world overflows with that beautiful impulse to which we every one of us owe our being,—that sweet, unworded passion, only in a weaker form, which induces the mother to hold her offspring whole nights and days in her fond arms, and press it to her bosom with silent gladness. If there be one thought more touching than another, when the roll of half a life-time has either given or denied us a pretty little one of our own, it is that of the patient, yearning, unreckoned hours when we lay unconscious on our mother's knees. Poor, tedious, wailing, unthankful little animals, *she* at least cared for us and prized us, and though unsightly and uninteresting to all the world beside, saw in all our little face all the beauty of the angels.

> Our first and sweetest nurture, when the wife
> Blest into mother, in the innocent look
> Or even the piping cry of lips that brook
> No pain nor small suspense, a joy perceives.
> Man knows not, when from out its cradled nook
> She sees her little bud put forth its leaves.

294. The instinct of Plants is similarly played forth in maintenance of the individual, and propagation of the species. To these ends they are endowed with a variety and an elaborateness of curious impulse quite as high, in proportion to their sphere of being, as that which is observable in the Animal Kingdom. Except as objects of nomenclature and classification, plants, ordinarily, are little cared for; they are passed by as destitute of all that makes animals so interesting; feeling, consciousness, volition, undoubtedly they

are short of; their economy is nevertheless so strangely like our own, that it is no wonder a few enthusiasts in every age, as Empedocles among the ancients, and Darwin and Dr. Percival* among the moderns, have fancied them susceptible of pleasures and pains, emotions and ideas. As with animals, there is in plants both an inward vitality and a series of externalized actions, complementing the interior ones, the two together making up the sum of the vegetable economy. Wherever the health and well-being of the individual, or the efficient play of the reproductive forces, may be involved, we find the one grand general principle of Instinct in operation. It is not peculiar to any particular part of the plant; it pertains to the whole, and resides in the whole, operating at every point, according to the exigency. As examples of the externalized instincts of plants, may be cited the ingenious methods whereby such as possess stems too weak to stand upright without assistance, manage, nevertheless, to lift themselves into the air. The sweet-pea and its congeners, the passion-flower, the bryony, the vine, and many others, effect this by converting the extremities of their leaves, or a portion of their flower-stalks, into tendrils, with which they clasp their stouter neighbors, often stretching a long way in order to reach them; the Virginian-creeper puts out curious little organs like hands, having a sucker at the end of every finger, by means of which it attaches itself to its prop; other slender plants are found twining spirally, as the hop, the convolvulus, and the woodbine, each kind adopting the particular method of climbing for which its organization more especially adapts it. The tendrilled plants are destitute of these organs while young,

---

* Memoirs of the Literary and Philosophical Society of Manchester, Series I. Vol. 2.

and at first the twining plants grow vertically; the instinct only comes into operation when the occasion for it arises. The wonderful instincts of certain aquatic plants, as the *Ruppia maritima*, and the *Vallisneria*, are well known to every botanist. The first-named curls its flower-stalks spirally, so as by coiling and uncoiling, according to the changing depth of water, to keep its blossoms on a level with the surface. The other, the Vallisneria, produces its male and female flowers on different plants; at the nuptial season, the former detach themselves, and floating about upon the stream, join company with the females. The innumerable curious facts familiar to the phytologist in regard to the germination of seeds, the sleep of plants, the power of accommodation to adverse circumstances, and other such points in vegetable history are, properly, illustrations of Instinct, and should be treated of in the same way as the *quasi*-reasoning acts of brutes.

CHAPTER XXIX.

INSTINCT AND REASON CONTINUED.

295. INSTINCT, belonging to the physiological expression of life, or that which animates organized material forms, has no other end or function than the maintenance of those forms; whence, moreover, it never operates without manifesting effects in the organic mechanism: REASON, on the other hand, has no relation to the body, except as the soul's lodging and instrument; it belongs to the soul, purely and abidingly, and may be exercised without giving the slightest external token. Instead of framing bodily organs, and originating physical offspring, and inducing the various physical acts on which these two great aims depend for their effectuation, it spans the sciences, sails deliciously through the heavenly realms of poetic analogy, penetrates the significance of things, and looks into the very mind of God himself. The life whose phenomena are the instincts, impels us only to eat, to drink, to propagate, to preserve our fabric safe and sound; the spiritual life, the phenomena of which are forms of reason, gives power, not to do corporeal things, but to think, and to rise emotionally towards the source of life. It is by reason of this supra-instinctive life that man stands as the universal master. God, in creating a being who can be at once cognizant of his Creator and of himself, appoints him vicegerent over all. "Man thinks," says Buffon, "hence he is master over creatures which do not think." With adaptitude for thinking comes power of

spiritual desire. In brutes (that is to say, where the instinctive expression of life is all) there is nothing which reaches further than temporal, terrestrial, purely physical wants; man aspires to spiritual and invisible things; he desires the delights of intelligence, emotion, and imagination; the source and centre of all his desires, however unconsciously it may be to himself, being heavenly and divine. They come of the soul's insatiable and inalienable need of God. "This sentiment," as finely said by Victor Cousin, "the need of the Infinite, is the foundation of the greatest passions and the most trifling desires. It is the infinite that we love, while we believe that we are loving finite things, even while we are loving truth, beauty, virtue. And so surely is it the infinite itself that attracts and charms us, that its higher manifestations do not satisfy us till we have referred them to their immortal origin. A sigh of the soul in the presence of the starry heavens, the passions of glory and ambition express it better without doubt, but they do not express it more than those vulgar loves which wander from object to object in a perpetual circle of anxious desires, poignant disquietudes, and mournful disenchantments." If brutes in any case had spiritual desires (which is tantamount to the possession of reason, seeing that these two faculties are complementary to one another) they would *worship*. The feeblest glimmering of reason among the most ignorant and savage of our race, is expressed, without exception, in acknowledgment and adoration of an unseen power, some "Great Spirit," before whom they bow themselves, whose favor they seek, and whose frowns they fear and deprecate. No brute thus approaches its Maker, nor is it able. The ox, in its rich pasture, never raises its eyes in gratitude towards heaven; it spends its whole existence in purely material satisfactions, and desires nothing beyond herbage and drink. It is from the same aptitude to think of and to love God that man alone is able to appreciate his transcript in the splendor and sweet beauty of outward nature. However exquisite the organs of sense may be in brutes, "eyes have they, but they see not; ears have they, but they hear not." As tersely expressed by the old poet,

νοῦς ὁρᾶ καὶ νοῦς ἀκõυει· τ' ἄλλα κωφὰ και τυφλα.

'Tis *mind* alone that sees and hears; all things besides are deaf and blind. EPICHARMUS.

296. This, it is, accordingly, the spiritual degree of life, peculiarly characterized by capacity for rising to its source, which distinguishes between man and the brute. Man has the instinctive life, the same as the brute; but he has the spiritual life *in addition*. He has it by virtue of his possessing a "spiritual body," so organized as to receive *consciously* the divine love and wisdom, and to be able to reflect them back upon their Almighty giver in the shape of admiration of his works, and worship of him as Father and Saviour. This it is which, establishing a distinction between human nature and the very noblest of brute natures, such as no exquisiteness or complexity of mere physical organization can be compared with for a moment, keeps them infinitely more distinct than animal and plant, or even organic and inorganic substance. Though there is one life,—the instinctive, common to all organic things; here is another, the spiritual, peculiarly and unapproachably human, so that though plants may be charming, and animals beautiful, man alone can be sublime. What glorious privileges attend this life! We do not think of it, but everything superior to the mere gratification of bodily appetite and provision for physical wants, comes of our being gifted with a spiritual organism, receptive of spiritual life; in fact, it is this very same divine gift which separates man,

even as to his *animal* form and nature, from the brutes. How varied and beautiful are the *attitudes* he can assume! No animal can deport itself as man does, nor can any animal but man move in the graceful undulations of the dance. Embodiments, each one of them, of a single and separate principle, brutes can do just *one* thing, concordant with their simplicity; man, as the compend of the world, can do all things. Another striking fact of the same nature is, that while the *eyes* of animals are always of the same color in the same species, the human eye, the symbol of human intellect, is of the most beautiful diversity. The only brute in which there is a tendency to variety in this particular, is the horse, which animal, it will be remembered, is in the Word of God, and therefore in nature, the representative of intelligence.* Man, for the same reason, is the upright animal. While other creatures have their faces turned earthwise, *he* is ἄνθρωπος† "the looker upwards."

> Pronaque cùm spectent animalia cætera terram,
> Os homini sublime dedit, cœlumque tueri
> Jussit, et erectos ad sidera tollere vultus.

(While other animals bend their looks downwards to earth, He gave to man a lofty countenance, commanded him to lift his face to heaven, and behold with upturned eyes the stars.—*Ovid, Met.* i. 84—86.)

Lactantius, in reference to these celebrated lines, contends

---

* That the curious white-haired varieties of many animals, called *Albinos* or *Leucœthiops*, have *pink* eyes, the white rabbit for example, argues nothing to the contrary, because the Albino condition is abnormal. See the article "Albino" in the Penny Cyclopædia, or the article "Eye" in Todd's Cyclopædia of Anatomy and Physiology, p. 161.

† παρὰ τὸ ἄνω αθρειν, according to Plato.

that the erect form of man is palpably a proof of his being designed to look upwards alone, that whatever tends to attract his attention to merely terrestrial objects, is contrary to his nature.* To the spiritual body of man is likewise to be referred his possession of a *face*. Other animals, as Pliny observes, have only some kind of muzzle or beak. Hence, too, that other eminent characteristic of man, the *visibility of the mouth.* "With wild beasts and cattle," says Apuleius, in his Discourse on Magic, "the mouth is low-seated, and brought down to a level with the legs; it lies close to the grass on which they feed, and is scarcely ever to be seen except when they are dead, or in a state of exasperation, and ready to bite; whereas in man you look upon no feature before this, when he is silent; and on none more frequently while he is in the act of speaking." The same is the origin of the variety of the human *voice*, so different from the monotony of that of brutes, and even from the most perfect singing of a bird. The cries and notes of the inferior animals, serve on this account, as the well-known bases of their names, in every language, both ancient and modern; cuckoo, peewit, βους, βομβος, &c. The great distinction between the human voice and the brute is that the former is adapted to *articulation.* No brute can divide its voice as man does, whence the ancient Homeric epithet of "voice-dividing man." All these things are illustrations of Discrete degrees. Whether we take attitude, countenance, or voice, the ending of the brute idea is absolute, the beginning of the human entirely new.

297. Man, it was said in the preceding paragraph, has the instinctive life, the same as the brute; he has it, however, as much more amply as in organization he is superior.

---

* Divinarum Institutionum, Lib. 2, cap. 1.

Flowing, as it does, into a frame so much nobler than that of the brutes, it assumes, in its new recipient, a proportionately nobler nature. The law of *promotion*, above described, whereby principles and faculties lifted from a lower platform to a higher, are there applied to new and greater purposes, here finds not only confirmation, but its most conspicuous example; the very instinct which carries brutes only to physical ends, in man leads to moral ones besides. Hunger, for example, which in brutes impels simply to *eat*, invites man to social gatherings whose object, at least collaterally, is the "feast of reason." The brutes feeding together on the grass, do no more than feed; to men the highest delight of meal-time is their cheerful and salubrious company and conversation. Eating, as such, is at the best, a finite pleasure; it has none of that savor of the infinite which all true and great pleasures must needs possess; but it gives occasion for such pleasures to be developed, and hence becomes in man, a noble function. "I did not calculate the gratification of those banquets," says Cicero, "by the pleasures of the body, so much as by the meetings of friends and conversations. Well did our ancestors style the reclining of friends at an entertainment *convivium*, since it carries with it a union of life."* How marked, again, in respect of the instinct of propagation! The brute fulfills the physical end, and ceases there; man goes further,—he *loves*, and becomes human in proportion as he loves honorably and faithfully. Mere animal love is a very low pleasure; were he incapable of any higher, man would never have become even civilized. "Happily directed and controlled," says Feuchsterleben, "love is the artist of the most exquisite spiritual developments that human nature is susceptible of; whereas he who

---

* De Senectute, Cap. 13.

never loves, becomes egotistical, mean, narrow-minded, covetous, and but too often, an unnatural sensualist." So with the instincts of conjugal fidelity, love to offspring, and that exalted and beautiful one, the love of Home. They lead brute and man alike into states of physical well-being; in man, when properly developed, they are seeds no less of moral, intellectual, and even religious welfare. How many blissful emotions arise out of the instinct of HOME! The bird seeks its nest simply for shelter; man, after the toils of the day, goes homeward, not merely to sup and rest himself but to feel in the bosom of affection, and in the sweet prattle of his little flock, that to *him* it is still the Golden Age. "To Adam and Eve Paradise was home; to the virtuous among their descendants home is Paradise." Many things which *appear* to belong to the spiritual degree of life, are thus, in reality, only high developments of the Instinctive. To distinguish between the two, we have but to ask concerning any particular faculty, Is it possessed both by man and animal? However lustrously a given faculty may shine in man, if we find it anywhere among the brutes, it is still no more than a part of the instinctive life. "We may rest assured," says Sidney Smith, "that whatever principles in the shape of instincts are given to animals for their preservation and protection, are also instincts in man; and that what in them is a propensity or desire, is not in him anything else."* Should we be at a loss to know whether a given faculty be thus shared, the place of its origin and its nature are determinable by its End. For it is not in working for a *purpose;* not in the mere contemplation of results, and adjusting things thereto; not even in the perception of cause and effect,—that man differs from the brute;—it is in working for a

* Principles of Phrenology, p. 123.

purpose having relation to the spiritual and immortal, and in contemplating causes and issues that lie altogether beyond the reach and bearing of the physical. Every instinct, however, in *man*, prefigures and presignifies a sentiment belonging to the spiritual life. Amativeness, for example, the seat of which is the ψυχη (common to all living creatures,) is found over again in the πνευμα (which man alone possesses,) in the shape of spiritual and unsensuous love. It is the same idea, moulded on a higher type. The correspondence between our higher and lower nature is one of the most wonderful features of our humanity. Every man who will watch himself, may see his animal, sensuous, external manhood, duplicated within, in higher workmanship.

298. Instinct, in man, is not only applied to higher purposes; it is expansive and cumulative. These, indeed, are the characters by which it is peculiarly distinguished from the instinct of brutes, which remains the same from age to age, as expressed in every attempt at definition. Why thus expansive, will appear when we consider the especial province of the instinctive life with regard to the spiritual. Though the former may exist without the latter, as happens with brutes, it is impossible for the spiritual life to exist without the instinctive. What sustains us and preserves us as *animals* (which we must needs be if we are to be *men*), is essentially Instinct—not reason. The latter is the source of all our highest enjoyments, as human beings; it is the instrument also of our progression, but it is by instinct that we are rendered *capable of becoming* human beings. "The basis of humanity is *animalism*. Man lives before he thinks; he eats before he reasons; he is social before he is civilized; loves even against reason, and becomes a Nimrod long before he is a Nestor." As the ground on which his spiritual nature is based, the instinctive faculties of man are made capable of a corresponding and adequate expansiveness.

Throughout the universe it is a law that higher principles shall descend into the next inferior, infusing into them a dignity and excellence which is neither native to them, nor attainable, except by communication from above; God gives first effect to it by imparting his glory to his nearest image, "crowning" him with his divine "majesty and honor;"—all things in their turn pour a largess of their nobler nature on those beneath. Reason, under this great law, impregnates and ennobles instinct; the instinctive life similarly descends into the inanimate world, so far as the latter is competent to receive it. "Of the qualities," says Philo, "which the soul has received from God, it gives a share to the irrational portion of our nature, so that the mind is vivified by God, and the irrational part by the mind." The spiritual life can only expand by having a plane beneath it on which to rest; this plane is furnished by the instinctive life, every enlargement of which in power and empire offers so much new scope and opportunity to the soul. The lower animals have no spiritual life thus to grow and dilate in them; their powers, therefore, instead of being expansive, are determinate. They work, but only within the confines of their little circles, and after a thousand years' employ, are still where they began. In man on the other hand, by virtue of the inflowing spiritual life, they are capable of indefinite extension, and grow and spread like watered trees. Every year sees some new application of them, and the fruits of their exercises fill the earth. Nothing so plainly distinguishes between man and brutes as the absolute *nothingness of effect* in the work of the latter. Unless the coral-islands be esteemed an exception, of all the past labors of all the animals that ever existed, there is not a trace extant: we see only what is accomplished by the individuals contemporaneous with ourselves.

299. Instinct, being thus co-ordinate with Life, comprises not only "vitality," and the unconscious external acts ordinarily intended by the term—it is the inmost principle also of a large part of Intelligence, namely, all such intelligence, whether susceptible of cultivation or otherwise, as is applied to the effectuation of physical good. It is a higher type of intelligence which seeks *spiritual* good. Intelligence, so far as it relates to material well-being, is not a distinct faculty; it is referable to the instinctive life, equally in brutes and mankind. It is quite a mistake to suppose that instinct has nothing of intelligence connected with it—that it is uniformly and necessarily *blind*. Often it may be so, and in brutes perhaps it is the rule, but there are no tribes of creatures in which intelligence is not largely and most evidently exhibited, over and above their unconscious skill. The books upon instinct undeniably establish this. "Many animals," Spurzheim remarks, "modify their actions according to external circumstances; they even select one among different motives. A dog may be hungry, but with the opportunity he will not eat, because he remembers the blows he has received for having done so under similar circumstances."* All the best writers on instinct concur in this opinion. "One might as well call all the actions of man rational," says the author of the Natural History of Enthusiasm, "as all of the inferior, instinctive." Sir Benjamin Brodie, in his interesting "Psychological Inquiries," expresses his conviction that "if we study the habits of animals, we cannot doubt that there are many which, however much they are dependent on their instincts, *profit also by experience*, though in a less degree than man." Old brutes

* Philosophical Principles of Phrenology, p. 3.

are more cunning than young ones. An experienced fox differs materially from a novice in the chase; he foresees many snares, and endeavors to avoid them. We must remember, further, that brutes in all probability have much more intelligence than we can become aware of, from their want of words, from our own inattention, and from our ignorance of the import of the symbols which they use in giving intimations to one another and to ourselves. In short, neither is intelligence to be attributed to man as his prerogative, nor is the brute to be defined as a being of invariably unconscious impulse. It is important to observe, however, that the understanding of brutes is affected solely through external or sensational stimuli. Human intelligence having reference to physical things, may be excited either by these or by the interior intelligence of the soul: intelligent acts are performed by brutes, on the other hand, only when the external, sensational stimulus which first called them forth, again affects the creature, and in precisely the same manner. That is to say, while Reason, or the intelligence of the spiritual life, may operate independently of external stimuli—after it has once been excited by them—and does not require the aid of the external senses; the activity of the intelligence of brutes depends for its excitation always and wholly upon such stimuli. This is particularly observable in acts where *memory* is concerned. Memory, in the true idea of it, is a faculty of the spiritual life, and can be exercised without any external or sensational stimulus—we lie quietly on our pillows, and in the dead of night can reproduce what we choose. Brutes have no such power; they remember only through the medium of an outward sense—the dog, for instance, largely through the sense of *smell*. It is true that dogs betoken memory in *dreams*, as long ago described in the verses of Lucretius,* but as this is clearly a recollection of mere events, in no way involving memory of *principles*, there can be little doubt that it is susceptible of the same physiological explanation as bears upon their waking acts. Men alone remember principles; brutes simply remember circumstances. In the former, memory is a spiritual function, and involves a complication of ideas; in the latter it belongs to the instinctive life, and refers but to a *single* impression. Other acts of memory in brutes which appear at first sight difficult to reconcile with the principle of external stimulus, such as the return of bees to the hive, and of migratory birds to their native countries, though problems to-day, are referable, without doubt, to the same origin as the dreams of the hounds. "Exceptions of this sort," it is well remarked by Dr. Martyn Paine, "are but few, and if they be admitted to surpass our present knowledge, the probability will be allowed, through the weight of analogies, that even these problems will be seen to be related to the common physiological laws which rule the instinctive principle in its ordinary operations, and more especially so as they refer, in common with the rest, to the wants of organic life."† It is precisely the same with those *quasi*-intelligent acts which are induced in certain animals by training—the various tricks, for example, which the elephant and the monkey are taught to play. Unlike genuine intelligence, or the faculties of the spiritual life, the superinduced conditions of the instinctive are never awakened except under the stimuli

---

* Venantumque canes in molli sæpe quiete
Jactant crura tamen subito, &c.
De Rerum Natura, iv. 988–1004.

† A Discourse on the Soul and Instinct, physiologically distinguished from Materialism: New York, 1849. A very valuable little Essay.

which originally promoted them, and then only in direct relation with those stimuli. So, too, with what some authors call the "moral sense" of animals. Man alone has a moral sense, justly so called, seeing that it can only exist where there is a spiritual organism competent to receive the knowledge of God. The dog, for instance, is sometimes said to act from *conscience*—that it "manifests a sense of wrong when it surprises the game in a manner opposed to its instructions, or does any other analogous acts. But this manifestation happens only under the influence of those physical causes which lead the creature to act more habitually in a different manner. The sense of wrong does not originate from the act, or on account of the act, but is inspired by the presence of the creature's master, whom it associates with the suffering which it endured when its instinct was undergoing discipline."* In thus recognizing the intelligence of brutes, we may seem to be advancing the very doctrine above repudiated, that "instinct" is "less reason," and "reason" "more instinct." Not so. The term Reason, as commonly used, includes intelligence both as to physical ends and as to spiritual ones. With the former kind, instinct undoubtedly *is* identical, passing into it by degrees of Continuity; but from the latter it is separated by a Discrete degree, and is therefore absolutely distinct.

300. It is easy to see that much of what is popularly called "Reason" was in its first exercise purely instinct. Long experience has thrown the early history of human usages so remotely to the rear, and we are naturally so prone to ascribe everything that is wise and good to "Reason,"—as though we were too proud or too selfish to allow

* A Discourse on the Soul and Instinct, physiologically distinguished from Materialism: New York, 1849, p. 112.

that the inferior animals have anything in common with us,—that Instinct not only goes without its fair share of credit, in our estimate of human nature, but is well-nigh ignored. In the infancy of our race, thousands of the acts which we now ascribe to Reason, must unquestionably have been impulses of instinct; destitute of the experience which now guides us, the first members of mankind must have proceeded, in innumerable cases, as the brutes do still; as experience accumulated, the instinctive procedures would gradually be superseded by thoughtful ones, and eventually they would come to be regarded as purely rational. The selection of food, for instance, must originally have been determined by an instinct in no respect different from that which leads the living brute to eat what is good for it, and to reject the unwholesome and the poisonous. *Now*, men may exercise their reason on the choice of new edibles; they have plenty of experience to proceed upon; but if instinct had not directed them at the first, while deliberating what to eat, they would have starved. All arts and sciences may be referred back to simple instincts of the same character; —instincts having physical welfare for their End, and excited by sensational stimuli; their expansion and enrichment, as time has rolled along, they owe to the descending of the spiritual life on to the plane where they begin. Brutes have neither art nor science, because although they have instincts, they have no spiritual life to fertilize them. This latter is the reason also why the instincts of brutes are made to work with such admirable precision from the very moment of birth. As they have nothing further tc receive, they are made perfect at the outset.

CHAPTER XXX.

SUMMARY.—INSPIRATION.

301. If there be any coherence and validity in the reasonings contained in the foregoing pages, the conclusion must needs be that everything of which human intelligence is cognizant, whether animate or inanimate, material or spiritual, depends on the personal support of the Creator, and that Life is One and Omnipresent; in other words, that God is the supra-natural ground of all phenomena, whether physical, physiological, or intellectual; and that all beginnings and endings are displays of his divine life in operation;—life which flowing continuously into his creation, never begins or ends, but always *is*. "Natural laws" there are, plentiful and amazing, through which his Divine wills are effectuated, but God is the great mover and upholder of those laws; there are no laws independently of Him, and all things are sustained by law. He who said "I bring a cloud over the earth," teaches us thereby that he is the direct and personal agent in all natural phenomena, however slight and apparently casual they may be, no less than in all spiritual phenomena. "Even the blind heathen named their supreme deity 'cloud-driving Jupiter;' and shall not we, thus taught by God himself, still more explicitly and reverently own the living Jehovah, the God in whom we live, and move and have our being, as the Creator of every cloud that flings its shadow over earth? We own him in the uproar of the tempest; let us own him in the stillness of the calm. We

own him in the huge billow; let us own him in the ripple that sinks quietly to rest upon the strand. We own him in the whirlwind; let us own him in the placid breeze of evening." It is no trifling source of mere *pleasure* thus to recognize the Creator in the ordinary occurrences of the world. It sweetens every moment of our time; unites us delightfully to the beauties of nature; and associates us with its varied objects as with so many friends and companions.

302. Viewed in this way, the whole earth is a scene of *Inspiration*,—inspiration of sustaining and directing force, as regards its objects and physical phenomena, and of the power of thought and feeling as regards the soul. Life and Inspiration, in fact, go together. Inspiration is literally "breathing into;" Life is that which is inbreathed. Man could neither think nor feel were he not a subject of inspiration; he does nothing purely of himself except *choose*. It is permitted him to elect by his free-will what things he will love and seek to possess, but all the vitality which he brings to bear upon the acquisition of those things, all the efforts which he makes in connection with the object of his love, have their well-spring and maintenance in God,—*πηγὴ πηγῶν*, "the fountain of fountains." Every vessel that is presented to him, God fills with his sustaining life, leaving the recipient to deal with it how he will; whether it be a pure vessel, or a foul, Life is poured into it all the same; the quality is preserved or marred according to the condition of the receptacle. We talk of our acquiring knowledge of what surrounds us by virtue of our *intellect*. True. We do so, nevertheless, only in so far as God first *inspires* our intellect. We know nothing of a single object of creation in a manner absolutely *original*. As finite things in their very nature are derived, our knowledge, as finite beings, must also be derivative. As the light of the sun makes nature, which in its absence is dark, *physically* visible;

so the light of heaven makes it *intellectually* visible, and without that light we could know nothing about it. Man's physical eye does not see by virtue of any inherent property, but by the aid of the sunbeam; so the intellectual eye does not perceive by virtue of innate power to perceive, but through that light which "has come into the world." We know, in short, just so much of things as God inspires us to know;—a slender and fragmentary knowledge at the best,—even in its highest degree, mere *opinion*, since the real nature of things can only be known by the Infinite. Still, it is *enough* of them that we know, being just what is needful to our happiness,—the design of the Almighty in all that he confers.

303. Inspiration, accordingly, in its full and essential sense, comprises every form and every variety of influx with which the Creator animates and instructs mankind. To attribute it simply to the "holy men of God" who "spake as they were moved by the holy ghost," is a mistake. In the inspiration of Moses, the Prophets, the Psalmists, and the Evangelists, Divine illumination is shown in its *highest* and immediate degree, not in its *only* one. There are as many degrees below it as there are grades of physical structure beneath the consummate frame of man. God is continually visiting the souls of all human beings with a certain amount of inspiration; awarding to every individual the kind and quality suited to his capacity and appointed sphere of duty, and replenishing him with new supplies, according to his needs. St. Paul particularizes some of these "diversities of operations." To one is given the word of wisdom, to another the word of knowledge, to another prophecy, to another, divers kind of tongues, to another the interpretation of tongues. Influx or inspiration from God, however, is always in proportion to the out-pouring from ourselves of what he entrusts us with. Now inspiration can

only enter us through our communicating to our fellow-men the good things we have previously received. We must bless *them* with whatever affection and intellect can bestow, if we would ourselves be newly blessed by God. This is what he intended us to learn from the incident of the widow's cruse of oil, which was replenished in the degree that the contents were poured away. Lynch puts the matter clearly and concisely. "The thinking man," he observes, "as another good result of his thoughtfulness, will get to feel how truly and impressively best thoughts and inward visions are gifts of God. When our 'views,' as we significantly say, are most earnest, most solemn, or most beautiful, we are often conscious of *being in a state* rather than of making an effort."* Goethe held similar opinions, as related in his conversations with Eckermann;—"No productiveness of the highest kind, no remarkable discovery, no great thought which bears fruit and has results, is in the power of any one. Such things are elevated above all earthly control; man must consider them as unexpected gifts from above, as pure children of God, which he must receive and venerate with joyful thanks." All men who closely watch their inner life become conscious of these high truths,—at least as that life developes. The sign of growth of the soul is that it gradually loses confidence in its volitional reasonings about best and highest things, and reposes trust rather in what it feels to be *given.* Though it is our duty to think and work with all our might, we lose nothing by "tarrying the Lord's leisure." "Newton confessed that to his patience he owed everything. An apple plucked from the tree was the death and ruin of our race; an apple falling from the tree told the story of the stars."

304. It is from the perception of this universal and con-

---

* Memorials of Theophilus Trinal, p. 14.

stant influx from heaven, that we speak in daily converse of being inspired with hope, inspired with courage, inspired with veneration; also of the inspiration of the musician, the inspiration of the poet. For in using such phrases of course we recognize an *inspirer*, or we mean *nothing*. All come from the same source, and a single principle explains every variety. The relation between the inspiration of the Poet, justly so called, and that of the Bible, is peculiarly important. Before we can properly understand what *biblical* inspiration is, it has been well said, we must understand what *poetical* inspiration is. The two things are more closely allied than many suppose. No intelligent reader of Scripture needs to be reminded that the resemblance of their written results is most intimate and profound; the poetic interpretation of nature stands, in fact, on a level with the interpretation of the symbolic language of Holy Writ. Philology goes no deeper than the surface; the inner arcana belong to Poetry, and it is only poetical minds of the highest order that can bring them forth in their true colors. The poetry of the Bible is one of the features that especially stamp its divine origin; it discloses the composition of the Mind that uttered it; and deserves as keen attention as its simple doctrines. If that God were only Intellect,—if there were only a *head* shown in nature and the Bible, then the scientific and philological interpretation would compass all. But he is Love also. Therefore the world and his word are no less full of *heart*, so that there is endless poetic interpretation needed likewise. Poetry was rightly accounted in old times the language of the gods. To view nature in a poetical, is an approach towards viewing it in a religious, light. The ancients expressed themselves in terms similar to our own, with regard to inspiration. Homer describes his heroes as "inspired with valor" by their guardian deities; and in narrating the famous story of Penelope and her web, piously makes her say that her ingenious schemes were "breathed into her by a god." (Odyssey xix. 138.) He has a passage also to precisely the same purpose as St. Paul's, saying that to one God gives dancing, to another music, to another a prudent mind, to another valor, &c. (Iliad xiii. 727—733.) In the 8th Odyssey he repeats it in a varied and more elegant form,—"One man is weaker, but God adorns him with words, and he discourses with mild modesty; another in his form is like the immortals, but grace is not set as a crown around his speech." (170—177.) Seneca comments upon inspiration in singularly eloquent terms. "Without God," he observes, "there is no great man. It is He who inspires us with great ideas and exalted designs. When you see a man superior to his passions, happy in adversity, calm amid surrounding storms, can you forbear to confess that these qualities are too exalted to have their origin in the little individual whom they ornament? A god inhabits every virtuous man, and without God there is no virtue." (Epistles, 41, 73.) The "paganism" and "polytheism" of such men deserves a milder judgment than is often passed upon it. However vicious and defective in some respects, it rested on a pure and reverent religious feeling, which needed but Christianity to give it a right direction. That which distinguishes Christianity from the moralism of Seneca, is not so much an absolute difference in the principles inculcated, as the power which it brings, by virtue of its immediate origin, to carry them out practically in the life. Polytheism, indeed, regarded in its better aspect, was but the designation under many names, of the one universal Father, just as in Scripture the single Jehovah is styled the Mighty One, the Lion, the Shepherd, and by hundreds of other names in turn. The more philosophical of the ancients were fully alive to the fact of such being the veritable intent of their theological doctrines. "It is of very little consequence," says the author just quoted, "by what name you call the first Nature, the Divine Reason that presides over the universe, and fills all the parts of it. He is still the same God. We Stoics sometimes call him Father Bacchus, because he is the universal life that animates nature; sometimes Mercury, because he is the Eternal Reason, Order, and Wisdom. You may give him as many names as you please, provided you allow but one sole principle universally present." (*De Beneficiis*, Lib. iv. cap. 7–8.) St. Augustin, probably with these passages, and similar ones in the Philosophical Dissertations of Maximus Tyrius, (xxix., &c.) before his mind, puts the matter in the same generous light. "It was one God," he observes, "the universal Creator and Sustainer, who in the ethereal spaces was called Jupiter, in the sea Neptune, in the sun Phœbus, in the fire Vulcan, in the vintage Bacchus, in the harvests Ceres, in the forests Diana, in the sciences Minerva." (*De Civ. Dei.* iv. 2.)

305. Briefly, then, and finally, we must never attempt to think of Life, in any of its manifestations, apart from, or independently of GOD. Life is uncreate, and wherever Life is, HE is. The same grand principles which we find at the summit of creation, or in the intelligence of man, and which we acknowledge, unhesitatingly, to be by influx of the divine life, are embodied in every kingdom *below* man, in another and humbler manner; animals, plants, and minerals severally and in turn presenting them, after the likeness of descending octaves. What are Intelligence and Emotion in the soul, reappear, as we descend, in the shape of Instinct, Vitality, and the physical properties of inanimate matter; the higher the End, and thence the Form, the more noble is the presentation; as the dignity of the End diminishes, and along with it the grandeur of the form, so does the intensity of the life. With every step in descent, there is a decline in

power; some energy ceases, some faculty disappears, yet the essential principle runs the entire length, and is found at the end as perfect as at the beginning. It is by no means the same *manifestation* that we find. Each new manifestation is lower than the next above by a discrete degree; hence while there are innumerable analogies between them, little pertains absolutely in common, save their one, divine origination. The hardest to connect together are doubtless the life of the mineral and the life of the soul. It must be done by the *intermediate* degrees. When we reflect how beautifully the organizing life of the body repeats, on its lower plane, the organizing life of the soul, it is not difficult to see that the operation of the crystalizing force in minerals is analogous to that of the vital force in plants and animals,—that crystalization, in fact, is mineral organization. Both in organic and in inorganic bodies, the atoms are drawn together and disposed with unerring precision, and with the most exquisite symmetry. The lower physical forces prepare the way. By attraction, matter is simply collected together,—one atom held to another, even of the most heterogeneous kind; Chemical Affinity superadds to attraction, the choice of particular atoms, which combine moreover, in definite proportions; Crystalization brings the atoms thus held together into fixed geometrical solids, moulding them, as it were, with the finger of vitality. The correspondence of the life of the soul with that of the body appears most plainly perhaps in what is called Genius. That admirable and wondrous faculty which on the lowest plane constructs crystals, turning the opaque and grimy charcoal into chaste and lucid diamond;—which on the higher plane constructs blood, and sap, and tissues, builds them into organs, and then impels them to achieve beautiful and useful works;—that same faculty reappears on the highest or spiritual plane, as constructive, formative Intellectual force, enabling its possessor, with the help of memory as a handmaid, to become the poet, the sculptor, or the painter. The essential characteristic of Life is its constructive, organizing force, and this is precisely what characterizes Genius.

TIMES AND SEASONS.

PART I.

WHILE to the poet and the thoughtful man the changes of Times and Seasons are in the highest degree beautiful and suggestive, even to the most indifferent and selfish they are surrounded with an agreeable interest. None view their progress without regard, however little they may be attracted by their sweet pictures and phenomena, or moved by the amenities and wisdom of their ministry. This is because the changes incidental to nature are, on the one hand, a kind of counterpart or image of the occurrences and vicissitudes of human life; and on the other, the circumstances by which its business and pleasures are in large measure suggested and controlled. The consummation of the old year, and the opening of the new, brings with it, accordingly, a fine significance, and a pleasurable importance. So, in their degree, the transitions of Winter into Spring, of Spring into Summer, of Summer into Autumn; and so, in their degree, the alternations of day and night. The longer the interval, the more interesting is the change.

The close of the year occupies the foremost place in this universal interest, from its completing a well-defined and comprehensive cycle of natural mutations. It is by this circumstance rendered an appropriate epoch for the measurement of life and being; and hence there fasten on it peculiar momentousness and solemnity, which remain inseparably attached though the season be unknown or forgotten. Days and nights follow too rapidly to serve such a purpose; and the endings of months and seasons are insufficiently distinct, except as regards Autumn, which in its maturity and fruits fulfills the very cycle in question. Only as the result of these mutations does the year exist. Were there no primroses to die with the spring, no lilies to vanish with the summer; were there not sequences of leaf and flower, sunshine and starlight, there would even be no Time. For Time, like Space, pertains but to the material circumference of creation, that is to the visible half of the universe, and is only appreciable through its medium. It is by objective nature alone that the ideas both of Time and Space are furnished, and they are sustained in us only so long as we are in contact with it. The movements of the heavenly bodies contribute the most exact and obvious data, because expressly given "for signs, and for seasons, and for days, and for years."* But the heavens are not our only timepiece. Another is spread over the surface of the earth in its living products. The phenomena connected with plants and the habits of the lower animals, constitute in themselves a complete system of chronometry; indicating not merely seasons, but even days and hours. In the times of the leafing of trees, the blooming of flowers, the ripening of fruits, the appearance of insects, the singing and nest-building of

---

* The fine poetic fancy of the ancients deified the various divisions of time, and placed them as attendants on the Sun, himself a god of the highest rank. See the beautiful description in Ovid's Metamorphoses, ii. 26–30, where they are represented as standing round his throne, and wearing the insignia proper to their offices in the economy of nature. Hence come the innumerable allusions in poetry to "the Hours," as goddesses:—

"The Graces, and the rosy-bosomed Hours."—*Milton*

birds, the departure and return of the migratory kinds, and of every other such incident of unmolested nature, there is nothing chanceful or uncertain. Every event transpires at a fixed point in the series of changes it belongs to. So precise, in particular, are the hours at which different kinds of flowers open, that it is not only possible, but easy to form a "dial of Flora," by planting them in the order of their expansion. A very little botany will enable any one to notice, during the early part of the day, especially before the dew is off the grass, how one flower anticipates another. And not only as to opening in the morning, but as to closing in the afternoon and evening. Nothing is more pleasant to the lover of nature, than to watch their gradual retirement to rest, and the wonderful diversities of mode in which they shut their petals. The curious *coincidences* between many of these phenomena, (as of certain birds returning from their winter quarters at the identical times when certain flowers come into bloom) have an especial interest, seeing that they not only indicate times, but supply striking illustrations of the lovely *sympathies* of nature, for in nature there is nothing without a friend. Celestial and atmospheric phenomena, if they have fewer of the charms of variety, in their splendors compensate it tenfold. How beautiful to note the phases of the moon, the chameleon tintings of the sky, the traveling of the planets, and the circling round the pole of the seven bright stars of the sleepless Bear! With what gladness and enthusiasm, too, in the cold, inanimate winter, we view the rising of Orion, and his brilliant quarter of the heavens. The cheerlessness of the earth is forgotten in the magnificence overhead, and we thank God for unfolding so much glory. Every event, moreover, having its own poetical relations, at once refreshes the heart, and places before the mind some elegant item in the innumerable harmonies of the universe. In the perpetual sparkle of the Bear is presented an image of the ever-wakeful eyes of Providence; and in the alternate waxing and waning of the moon, a beautiful picture of the oscillations in man's fortunes. Hence we find Plutarch using the latter to describe the chequered life of Demetrius; and Dante, to pourtray the varying fortunes of Florence:—

> E come 'l volger del ciel della luna
> Cuopre ed iscuopre i liti senza posa,
> Cosi fa di Fiorenza la Fortura.
>
> (*Paradiso*, xvi., 82–84.)

(As the revolution of the moon's heavenly sphere hides and reveals the strand unceasingly, so fortune deals with Florence.)

The regularity with which the phenomena of nature recur, and their determinate and unvarying character, are expressed even in many names. Spring is literally the season of growth; summer that of sunshine; autumn (from *augeo*) that of increase or fertility; winter that of the "windy storm and tempest." All languages possess equivalent terms. "Zif," the name of the second Hebrew month, or from the new moon of May to that of June, signifies literally, "the splendor of flowers." "Choreph," the name for autumn, in the same language, means "the gathering season," or time of harvest and fruits. The names given to the months by the French Revolutionists of 1789, every one will remember as in deference to the same instinctive principle.

Times, years, seasons, accordingly, are not to be esteemed a *part* of creation, but simply an accident or result of it. Our personal experiences concur with nature in testifying this, for to no two men has time the same duration, nor does any individual reckon it always by the same dial. To the slothful, time has the feet of a snail; to the diligent, the wings of an eagle. Impatience lengthens, enjoyment shortens it. The unhappy and desolate see nothing but weary tedium; with the cheerful it glides like a stream. "The time," says the unhappy poet, in his wretched exile, "goes so slowly, you would think it was standing still. The summer does not shorten my nights, nor the winter my days. Do the usual periods really perform their wonted courses? Everything is protracted with my eyes."* How different when we are satisfied and glad! Let us go amid new and delightful sceneries, such as vividly excite and animate us, and when over, the days seem to have been hours, the weeks to have been days. Let us retire into the quiet, secluded sanctuaries of thought, losing ourselves in memory or hope, and how complete again is the departure of all conception of either time or space. As in Dreamland, distance collapses, and years and life-times contract into a few shining moments. So, too, when pursuing occupations under the influence of deep feeling,—"Jacob served seven years for Rachel, yet they seemed to him but a few days, for the love he had to her." In Milton, Eve beautifully says to Adam,—

> With thee conversing, *I forget all time;*
> All seasons, and their change, all please alike.

Time, therefore, as in reference to material existence it simply denotes change, in reference to the spiritual or inner life, is but another name for emotional states or attitudes. The man who not only feels to, but actually does live longest, in other words, sees most time, is he who, taking God for a sweet, guiding, and enveloping thought, and quick to read Nature, receives from it the greatest number of impressions.

Natural mutations are emblems both of the external or

---

* Ovid. *Tristia*, Book v., Elegy x.

corporeal life, and of the inner or spiritual life. And this is equally the case whether the history of a year or of a day be taken. For nature, though she seems endlessly diversified, proceeds on but few methods, of which her diversities are varied expressions. Whatever department we may select, whether organization, music, or language, the phenomena of life or those of insensible matter, one or two leading ideas are all that can be discriminated. Not that the talent of nature, though great for species, is poor for genera, because nature, as a manifestation of the Infinite, is competent, necessarily, to express his infinite attributes. It is that with a view to presenting a sublime and intelligible unity, such as man's mind shall apprehend with profit and delight, she better loves to repeat, over and over again, a few fixed and elegant designs, than to amaze and confound with an endless multiplicity. When, therefore, from the outward expression, we penetrate towards the interior idea, it is always to find some old, familiar fashion; and to learn that shapes and complexions are but liveries or costumes appropriate to their several occasions. The history and lapse of a day agree, accordingly, with the history of a year, of which the day is a miniature. Winter corresponds with night, summer with noon, spring with morning, whence the beautiful phrase in 1 Sam. ix. 26, "the spring of the day," and in Lucretius, the equivalent *facies verna diei* (i. 10.) The history of a life-time conforms in turn with both the year and the day, as shown in our speaking of life's morning, noon, and evening; of its spring, summer, autumn, and winter; its April, its May, and its December. For all organized beings are but successions of phenomena, commencing, like the year, in darkness and apparent passivity, and ending in surrender to the effacing fingers of decay. "Evening," says Aristotle, "has the same relation to day that old age has to life. Therefore evening may be called the old age of the day, and old age the evening of life, or, as it is styled by Empedocles, 'the setting of life.'" Nothing has more pleased the poets than to descant on the similitudes so strikingly displayed, especially on behalf of the four seasons. Ovid, for instance, in that extraordinary catalogue of mutations, the fifteenth book of the Metamorphoses; Young, in the sixth book of the Night Thoughts; and Thomson, at the conclusion of his "Winter:"—

Behold, fond man!
See here thy pictured life! Pass some few years,
Thy flowering Spring, thy Summer's ardent strength,
Thy sober Autumn, fading into age,
And pale concluding Winter comes at last,
And shuts the scene.

Prose literature likewise affords numerous allusions to these analogies. They are a constant subject also with sculptors and painters, whose highest function is faithfully to reproduce in objective forms what the poetic faculty seeks elsewhere to delineate in words. The famous riddle of the Sphynx, the solution of which by Œdipus cost her her life, will occur to the recollection of every one—"What animal is that which in the morning goes upon four legs, at mid-day upon two, in the evening upon three?" On the identification of youth with Spring was no doubt founded the ancient belief that it was in the Spring that the world was created: a notion supported, among the moderns, by Stukeley, in his chapter called "Cosmogonia, or the World's Birth-day." (*Palæographia Sacra*, p. 44.) It needs no very deep science to perceive that if the world were created in *any* season, it must have been created in *all four*, since it is always Spring *somewhere*, always Summer, Autumn, and Winter, in one part of the globe or another. If it be intended merely to assert that it was Spring in the latitude where our first parents began their lives, then, perhaps, the fancy may be allowed. According to Venerable Bede, the question was first determined at a council held at Jerusalem, about the year 200. After a learned discussion, reported *verbatim*, it is finally decided that the world's birth-day was Sunday, April 8th, or at the vernal equinox, and at the full of the moon! (*Opera*, tom. 2, pp. 346, 347. Ed. Basil, 1563.)

Dwelling as we do, in the heart of the material and fugitive, it is perfectly natural that winter and night should be regarded as representative of the last stage of our existence. Yet their truest agreement is not with decay. It is rather with the darkness and passivity which preliminate life, and out of which life springs. Everywhere in creation the dim and shapeless is prior in point of time. The universal law is that the passive shall precede the active, ignorance knowledge, indifference love. This is why the narrative of the creation opens with saying that the earth was without form and void, and darkness upon the face of the deep; and why among the ancients, Night was finely styled "mother of all things."

> With him enthroned,
> Sat sable-vested Night, eldest of things.

The cosmogony of the Greeks, as given by Hesiod, and of every ancient nation of which any records survive, opens with darkness, out of whose womb presently proceeds light. Such is the order acknowledged, indeed, by all the greatest poets who have ornamented the world. What a fine line is that in Mephistopheles' address to Faust, when he first introduced himself,—

> Ein Theil der Finstermiss die sich das Licht gebar.
> (Part of the darkness which brought forth Light!)

If we would observe a philosophic order, winter, therefore, should stand first, not last, in the scheme of the seasons, as among the ancient Egyptians, with whom harmonies were an exact science, and who drew the sun at the winter solstice as an infant, at the vernal equinox as a youth, at the summer solstice as a man of middle age, and at the autumnal equinox as one in his maturity.* The other seasons would then fall into their rightful places, Autumn, or the period of ripeness, crowning the noble annals. For autumn, in turn, it is far less just to regard as emblematic of bodily decrepitude, than of consummation, maturity and riches. Job gives a beautiful example of its legitimate symbolic use when, recalling the days of his prosperity, he denominates them his חרף (*choreph,*) literally, as above mentioned, his time of gathering in fruits. The authorized version neutralizes this eloquent figure by translating it "in the days of my *youth.*" But that the word here certainly signifies Autumn, is plain from the remainder of the chapter, even without consulting its etymology. Pindar uses Autumn for the perfection of physical beauty. (Isth. 2, 5. Nem. 5, 6.) Sir Thomas Browne applies the same name to the Resurrection. The dating of the year from a day in the depth of winter is itself a testimony to the true position of the seasons in question.

By virtue of the primitive relations which so wonderfully link the spiritual and the material, the growth of the year has precisely the same analogies with the development of the intellect and affections, as with the history of the body. Winter answers to their germ-stage, summer to their flowers, autumn to their maturity. Hence the elegant and familiar metaphors by which the first buddings of the intellect and affections are called their *Spring.* The Greek poets not infrequently put Autumn, in like manner, for ripened intel-

* Macrobius, *Saturnalia,* Lib. 1, cap. 21.

ligence and wisdom, as Æschylus, in his tragedy of the Suppliants.* Gifted with the sight of these fine analogies, few things are more delightful to the accomplished mind than to note the early primrose and anemone, the wood-sorrel, and the young, uncurling ferns. It sees in them, and in all delicate buds, the pictorial counterparts of its own first steps—images of the pretty little flowers of fancy and affection put forth from the heart of a child. The same circumstances originate an important part of the pleasure with which the mind regards the verdure of trees newly-leafed, the activities and the music of birds, and the thousand other fair conditions of the year in its adolescence. It sees reflected in them its own felt progress. In that perfect sea of rich poetry, "Festus," both the physical and the spiritual symbolism of the year are given in a single passage:—

> We women have four seasons, like the year.
> Our spring is in our lightsome, girlish days,
> When the heart laughs within us for sheer joy.
> Summer is when we love and are beloved;
> Autumn when some young thing with tiny hands,
> And rosy cheeks, and flossy, tendrilled locks,
> Is wantoning about us day and night.
> And Winter is when those we loved have perished,
> For the heart ices then.
> Some miss one season, some another; this
> Shall have them early; and that, late.

The soul, as it quickens towards God (which is quite a different thing from growth in the loves and intellectualities of the simply secular life), similarly views itself reflected wherever the vernal is gushing forth, and loves to think how profound is the dependence on Him "who changeth the times and the seasons, who giveth wisdom to the wise,

---

* 998, 1015.

and revealeth the deep and secret things." A more complete and admirable image than is here presented, it would be difficult to find. For like the seeds and roots which lie hidden in the cold, bare earth during winter, full of splendid capacity and life, are the latent desires in the unawakened soul for what is good and heavenly, inherited from the golden age; and when once quickened, nothing can repress their energy, or forbid their shooting into a luxuriant and flowery vesture for the surface late so naked. We should never desire to be regenerated were it not for the remains of original innocence, which thus repose, like sleeping angels, in our hearts. Martineau appropriately opens his beautiful book, "Endeavors after the Christian Life," with sketching this truest spring-time of the soul, this beginning of its real, productive life. "The thoughts which constitute religion are too vast and solemn to remain subordinate. They are germs of a growth which, with true nurture, must burst into independent life, and overspread the whole soul. When the mind, beginning to be busy for itself, ponders the ideas of the infinite and eternal, it detects, as if by sudden inspiration, the immensity of the relations which it bears to God and immortality. The old formulas of religious instruction break their husk, and give forth the seeds of wonder and of love. Everything that before seemed great and worthy is dwarfed; and secular affinities sink into nothingness compared with the heavenly world which has been discovered. There is a period when earnest spirits become thus possessed; disposed to contrast the grandeur of their new ideal with the littleness of all that is actual, and to look with a sublimated feeling, which in harsher natures passes into contempt, on pursuits and relations once sufficient for the heart's reverence." "Pray that your flight be not *in the winter*," means "before the frosts of indifference to God have melted."

The sequence of morning to night pourtrays precisely the same facts, because each perfect and independent day of twenty-four hours is a year in little, and therefore the analogue of the entire spiritual history. We speak, accordingly, of the night of ignorance, the night of superstition, the dawn of reason, the dawn of the understanding. Hence, too, the innumerable beautiful figures in which these things are spoken of under the equivalent names of "darkness" and "light." As with the transition from ignorance into knowledge, so with the nobler progress which introduces us to God. Before we know him, it is night, afterwards it is morning and day. It is in the night that he comes to us, just as it is during the night of nature that the sun approaches (for it is not *morning* till he is risen), whence the beautiful figure in the parable, that the cry of the bridegroom's coming is heard at "midnight." It was for the same reason that the angels announced the nativity to the shepherds by night rather than by day—a ministry sweetly renewed, with all its heavenly light and music, wherever the "flocks" of the heart are seen to be watched and cherished.

To the same class of facts belong the circumstances of our Lord being born into the material world in the depth of winter; and of the crucifixion taking place during chilly, wintry weather, as shown by the people kindling a fire and warming themselves. These are not mere accidents in the history, but representative occurrences inseparably connected with the spiritual ones they accompany. In several ancient languages the name of God is literally "light," or "morning." Such is the case with the Greek *θεος* and the Latin *Deus* (whence the French *Dieu*, and our own word *Deity*,) both of which, together with the name of the old Indian god *Dyaus*, rest on the Sanscrit root *div*, to shine or irradiate. The Greek *Ζευς* and the Latin *Ju*-piter are from the same source, by permutation of sounds, as shown by the inflections *ΔιFος*, *Jovis*, *&c.*, and by the derivatives *divum* (whence *divine* and *divinity*) and *dies*, the day, literally "the shining." *Jupiter*, and the equivalent *Diespater*, *Diespiter*, signify, literally, "father of light." With the same root are doubtless connected the Celtic *di*, *dian*, and the Anglo-Saxon *dœgan*, whence our current *dawn* and *day*.

But more than *one* such day is needful to regenerate a man. He must go through many successive stages, introduced to one day after another, through the medium of many nights of labor and struggle. And that we may be familiarized with it from the first, this is just what is depicted at the very entrance to God's Word. In their "evenings and mornings," and the accompanying serial creations, the opening verses of Genesis sublimely picture the development of the various emotions and perceptions proper to the Christian character, which gradually open out, like the days of a week. For there are no leaps in the history of spiritual progress,—no violent transitions. There can be no seventh day's rest in heaven without six preceding ones of work, which every man must perform for himself, at God's suggestion, and with God's help. "Let there be light" is only the introductory act,—the showing the way. At first man is not conscious how much is needed of him. It seems sufficient that light has broken. He knows not how bare and desolate is his heart, nor that, until a third, and a fourth, and a fifth day shall have clothed it with spiritual counterparts of the "living creatures," the "grass," the "herbs," and the "fruit-trees," it will be only a desert, and can neither "rejoice" nor "blossom as the rose." Of such a course of developments, accordingly, growth in religion is made up, each stage having its own evening and morning, just as each year of life has its winter and summer. For "evening" here signifies, not the twilight of a day that is past, but the whole of the dark portion of the twenty-four hours, and "morning" the whole of the light portion. The two together make up a complete period in the history, just as a night and a day combined, (the latter dating from *midnight,*) make up each of the three hundred and sixty-five "days" of the solar year.

The creation of man comes last, because it is not until such a series of developments has taken place, that the intellect and affections attain that upright and noble attitude in reference to God, which constitutes genuine manliness.

PART II.

Times and seasons correspond with the life of man in a twofold manner. First, there is the image of his *gradual development*, both as to body and soul, presented, as above described, in each complete and independent year and day. Secondly, there is the image of his innumerable *changes and vicissitudes*, presented in the varied qualities and occurrences of seasons, days, and hours in general. For as with winter and summer, light and darkness, heat and cold, rain and sunshine, clouds and azure, music and silence,—for even the wind and the waters are still at times,—so with health and sickness, hunger and content, fatigue and vigor; no state or condition is lasting. Down even to the minute and secret phenomena of what the physiologists call "molecular death," namely, the continual decay and replacement of the animal tissues, Change is the universal condition of existence. And while so marked a feature of the inanimate world, and of the animal life, infinitely more true of the soul, because of its infinitely higher capabilities and senses. At one moment buoyant with hope, at another depressed by disappointment or misgivings; cheerful to-day, mournful to-morrow; in the course even of a few minutes it will run through a long series of intensest emotions. Change, accordingly, has in all ages been the chosen theme of the moralist and the preacher; while, as at once the most solemn yet most animating, the most sad yet most beautiful subject on which the human mind can dwell, poetry and philosophy have ever held a friendly rivalry in describing its loveliness, and interpreting its lessons.* Well styled by Feltham, "the great lord of the universe," all the best charms of objective nature, and all the noblest attitudes of the intellect and affections owe their being to its magic touch. Incessantly at work, transfiguring, dissolving, and recombining, it makes the physical world one vast kaleidoscope wherein new and unthought-of charms are brought to view with every turn of day and season. Changed, not destroyed, our lament for the beautiful as it glides from out our grasp, is but to lament that brighter things are coming. For there is no truth more sublime than that decay, death, and disappearance are not *annihilation*, but simply the attendants on *change of form*. Annihilation is an impossible thing. Nor is there any truth more consolatory. The chrysalis is the cradle of the butterfly at the same moment that it is the tomb of the grub; the flowers of the summer cease to smile, that the fruits of autumn may step forth. So with the changes of the inner life. For as changes and contrasts are the springs of all our happiness and enjoyment in connection with the external life, as well as productive of the most charming aspects and conditions of nature; so is it from changes in our spiritual states that we acquire true wisdom, and that our affections become invited into their loveliest and most sacred channels. No one, for instance, is capable of truly and heartily sympathizing with the troubles of another, until he has himself been touched by sorrow. How beautiful and pathetic, because so faithful to nature, is that passage in the first Æneid

* As beautiful for its succinctness, as the 15th book of the Metamorphoses is remarkable for its detail, on the subject of change, is the fine passage in the *Œdipus Coloneus*, of Sophocles, beginning ὦ φίλτατ' Αἰγέως παῖ, (607–615.) With the former compare Lucretius, "Mutat enim, mundi naturam totius ætas," &c. Lib. v. 826–834.

where the gentle but unfortunate Dido speaks for the genuineness of her sympathy on the ground of her own experience of misfortune. It is, indeed, by reason of this necessity, that the laws and phenomena of the natural world are as we find them. Throughout the universe, whatever exists, exists not so much for its own sake, as for the sake of something higher and nobler than itself. Night does not unroll its shades solely that the body may rest and sleep; nor does winter diffuse its frosts only that the trees and plants may hybernate, and the soul refit itself for feeding them. They have a nobler use than this. They have lessons to give. They exist, like all other natural mutations, that they may be emblematic of the vicissitudes so important to the spirit; and that from studying the glory and beauty which arise from them, we may learn what is the end and promise of our own. "We often live under a cloud," says a thoughtful writer, "and it is well for us that we should. Uninterrupted sunshine would parch our hearts: we want shade and rain to cool and refresh them." If this be true of the secular side of our constitution, how much more so of the heavenly! It shows why Scripture history (which has a didactic intent throughout) is one continuous detail of misfortune and success, trouble and consolation;—the narrative, for instance, of the pilgrimage of the Israelites, universally acknowledged to be typical of the way of regeneration. In this, every one is beset by hindrances and temptations, which, though sorely oppressive while they last, nevertheless give place in turn to triumph. The hunger and thirst, and bitter streams, all show what must be anticipated, but no less so the supply of food, and the sweetening of the waters. It is a happy thing for a man to feel famished, and that the waters are bitter, for it is the sign of an amending nature, and leads him to cry to God for help. If we are not often so impelled, it is a proof that we are but little advanced upon our journey. There can be no virtue or gladness without trial and suffering in the first place. There is no buying corn of Joseph till there has been a famine in the land; nor can any man know what are the green pastures and the still rivers, till he has been in the valley of the shadow of death. God cannot lead him thither till he has felt how weak he is in himself. Until this experience shall have been gone through, they are a mere mirage of the imagination. "It must needs be that the Son of Man suffer before he enter into his glory." In its aptitude for grievances, temptations, and perplexities, conjoined with its free-will, the spirit of man is constituted, accordingly in the very best manner possible for urging him on towards heaven. Though they are painful to him, they are privileges.* That was a deep insight into the economy of Providence which saw that—

Sweet are the uses of adversity.

Had Flavius Boethius never been imprisoned by Theodoric, he had never written his "Consolations of Philosophy." To a prison also we owe the "Pilgrim's Progress."

As with numbers of other splendid truths, we unconsciously express the excellency of alternation in various words of common discourse, as temper, temperament, temperature. For all these terms have an immediate affinity with the Latin *tempus*, "time." Literally, therefore, to "temper," signifies to combine or intermingle different

---

* In reference to these matters may be quoted Lord Bacon's admirable precept that "we should practice all things at two several times, the one when the mind is best disposed, the other when it is worst disposed; that by the one you may gain a great step; by the other you may work out the knots and stonds of the mind." (Adv. of Learning, Book ii.)

states or conditions, just as seasons, days and nights are intermingled by nature. And as the object of such intermingling is to benefit and ameliorate, the idea of benevolence incorporates with it. Thus, "God *tempers* the wind to the shorn lamb." Virgil often uses the word in this way. When the sunburnt land is refreshed by water, he says that "*arentia temperat arva*," "it tempers the thirsty fields;" and a little further on, "*cum frigidus aera Vespera temperat*," "when cool evening tempers the air." The sun, Cicero finely calls *mundi temperatio*, "the temperer of the world." As a substantive, "temper" denotes our general character or disposition, because compounded of various ingredients. According to the predominance of one element or another, it is good temper, or ill temper, mild temper, or harsh temper. To be "temperate" is not to remain in any one season or state, but to give everything its proper meed of attention, in deference not only to the rules of health, but to the instructions of the Preacher, when he tells us that "there is a time for everything," and that "God hath made everything beautiful (or good) in its season." The "intemperate" man, whether in things of body or mind, is he who, bestowing his love exclusively on the spring or the summer, in the morning or the evening, refuses to enjoy more than a single season; and thereby neutralizes both the pleasures he selects, and the kind offices of the remainder of the year. Who so much enjoys the calm, sweet friendship of the summer, as he who has fought with the asperities of winter? "Temperature," in its primitive sense, denotes that agreeable condition of the atmosphere which results from the due admixture of heat and cold.

We use the word "season" in much the same way, and for a similar reason, season being a kind of synonym of time.

"Earthly power doth then show likest God's
When mercy *seasons* justice."

Experiencing the mutations of nature, then, in our own daily history, and vividly so as regards the spiritual half of our being, the names of the divisions of times and seasons become the appropriate metaphors wherein to speak of our varied states of heart and mind. There is no other language for the purpose. Nor are any figures referring to time so frequent, from the circumstance of the present department of the correspondence having been far more largely recognized than that which regards the symbolism of the year in the collective; which arises in turn, from the fact that men are prone to affix their attention to passing events and contiguous objects, rather than to rise to the panoramas of philosophy. Spring, for instance, is everywhere identified with *hope.* Men see that in all their qualities the two things are naturally and inseparably accordant; and this is probably a reason why descriptions of spring are more plentiful than those of any other season. For Hope, the only heritage of many men, and the light, life, and nepenthe of all, is naturally foremost among the emotions, and the most agreeable to think and write about; and it cannot be supposed that the mind ever fastens with a pure and animated affection on natural objects and appearances, simply because they are pleasing to the eye and ear. That in nature always most interests us which bears the closest affinity with the feelings we most prize, and those feelings are most prized which yield us our highest satisfaction and solace. Rousseau pourtrays the symbolic character of the spring in the most beautiful manner:—"To the appearance of spring the imagination adds that of the seasons which are to follow. To the tender buds which are perceived by the eye, it adds flowers, fruits, shades, and sometimes the mysteries they conceal. It brings into one point of view the things that are to succeed, and sees things less as they are than as it wishes them to be. In the autumn, on the contrary, we can only contemplate the scene before us. If we wish to anticipate the spring, our course is stopped by winter, and our frozen imagination expires amid snows and fogs." (*Emile*, lib. 1, tome 1, 448.) Spring, like the morning, is used also as the emblem of peace and gladness after misfortune, and with perfect propriety, because the season of returning hope. Shelley gives a charming example:—

> Thou Friend, whose presence on my wintry heart
> Fell like bright Spring upon some herbless plain,
> How beautiful, and calm, and free thou wert,
> In thy young wisdom!

Pindar also, having first called calamity and bereavement by the name of *νιφας* or "snow storm,"—

> *νῦν δ' αὖ μετὰ χειμὲριον ποικίλω μηνῶν ζόφον,*
> *χθὼν ὥτε φοινικέοισιν ἄνθησεν ῥόδοις.*

"But now again, after the wintry darkness of the changing months, (this happy household) like the earth, has blossomed with purple flowers."—*Isth.* iii. 36, 37.

So in the elegant poetry of Ovid,—

> Nec fera tempestas toto tamen horret in anno;
> Et tibi (crede mihi) tempora veris erunt.

"Bleak winter does not freeze throughout the year; and to thee, too, believe me, the sweet hours of Spring will yet arrive."—*Fasti*, i. 485–6.

In the *Tristia* of the same author, the word *verno*, literally, to be like the spring, is applied to the joyous warbling of the birds over their newly-made nests, one of the most sweet and inspiring accompaniments of the vernal season:—

Prataque pubescunt variorum flore colorum;
Indocilique loquax gutture vernat avis.

"The meadows are decked with flowers of many hues; and the prattling birds carol with their untaught throats."—Lib. iii., El. xii. 7, 8.

Summer and winter accord with prosperity and adversity. Hence the famous lines at the opening of Richard the Third:—

"Now is the *winter* of our discontent
Made glorious *summer* by the sun of York."

Æschylus, in the Prometheus, cites winter with admirable effect:—

——————— *καίτοι καὶ λέγουσ' ὀδύρομαι*
θεόσσυτον χείμωνα, καὶ διαφθορὰν
μορφῆς. (642–644.)

"And yet do I grieve even to speak of this heaven-sent winter, and the ruin of my form."

It is finely introduced, also, in line 1015 of the same play. But fairly to quote examples of these two figures, would be to illustrate the spontaneity with which they have been used by the best poets of all ages. Language finding no terms so fit, they become a part of its current coin. There is, however, one beautiful fact in connection with the emblemism of the seasons which should not be passed over. As in every part of the year some particular department of nature is in its highest glory and perfection, so at each period of life some particular intellectual faculty is in the ascendant, some sentiment is most persuasive, some passion most imperious. Johnson has well treated of the latter circumstances in a paper on the "Climacterics of the Mind." (Rambler, No. 151.) Each season of the year, like each hour of the day, suggests also its own particular themes for thought and conversation; so that when living in our true and proper relations with nature, there springs up a delicious and rewarding sympathy in our minds, which at once embellishes the world without, and gladdens and fertilizes the little world within. Keenly sensible of the operation of this beneficent law, the meditative find it alike easy and agreeable to classify their thoughts and ideas under the names of the months and seasons. The Italian prose poet of the 17th century, Partenio Giannettasio, divides his lively and versatile book, *Annus Eruditus*, into four portions, naming them Spring, Summer, Autumn, and Winter.

Of the particular *months* of the year, May, as the most celebrated for its charms, is also the most frequently used in metaphor. Perhaps the most elegant instances of the latter are those occurring in the minor poems of Schiller, pieces many of them inimitable, except to paraphrase, even in the hands of his most successful translator—Bulwer. Thus—

> Deine Seele gleich der Spiegelwelle,
> Silberklar und sonnenhelle,
> Maiet noch den trüben Herbst um dich.

Literally,

> "Thy soul, like the mirror-wave, silver-clear and sun-bright, still *Mays* the dim Autumn round thee."—(*Melancholie an Laura.*)

As with the four seasons, and with the months, so with day and night. No two days are exactly alike. Somewhere, in the look either of the sky or of the earth, there is sure to have been a change. Even the *nights* differ in kind. What a contrast between an atmosphere choked with black and melancholy vapors, and the transparent sky of a frosty winter's night, when the innumerable stars are glittering, or the round moon is "walking in her brightness." Take but a single portion of day or night, and the minutes themselves are found inconstant. One lovely tint of sunrise or of sunset comes but as the herald of another. While we watch the purpling of the great cloud-mountains of the west, and the surge of liquid gold above their brows, the sprinkled roses of the zenith have shed their leaves and fled. So with the successive hues of the brighter mornings of Summer and early Autumn. He was no poor observer who gave to their heavenly splendors the immortal epithets of *κρόκοπεπλος* and *ῥοδοδάκτυλος*.* Precisely similar, as to their mutability, are the states or attitudes assumed by us in our inner lives. Every one is sensible that there are light and darkness which are not of the sky; and that peace and happiness are in sweet natural agreement with the morning, when the light breaks forth, and everything is glad; sorrow and disappointment with the gloom of evening; and their extremest and bitterest degrees with the darkness of deep night. Hence, in the languages of all nations, we find such similes as the morning of hope, the noon of enjoyment, the night of sorrow; every one of them taking also the briefer and pleasant form of metaphor, and thus resting on our intuitions for translation. What can be more exquisite and touching than when poor Electra, in Sophocles, exclaims to her long-lost brother, the only friend she has in the world—

> ———— *νῦν δ' ἔχω σε· προὐφάνης δὲ*
> *φιλτάταν ἔχων πρόσοψιν.*

"But now I have thee; and thou hast *dawned* upon me with most dear aspect."—(*Electra*, 1285–6.)

In calamity, says the Arabic proverb, there is hope, for the end of a dark night is the dawn.

The life of religion experiences the same vicissitudes. Consisting of six principal evening-mornings, its minuter history records, nevertheless, an infinity of little ones; just

---

* "Saffron-robed" and "rosy-fingered."

as the three-score-and-ten years of the animal life are made up of some five-and-twenty thousand miniatures of years. Involuntarily and strangely to us, there are perpetual oscillations between love and indifference towards what is right. Without knowing how or why, we find every now and then, that we have traveled into the "strange country" of the prodigal son.* Scripture, accordingly, is replenished with allusions to day and night, morning and evening, in these, their particular senses, night and evening being used to denote the sorrow and despondency of the soul; morning and day to express faith, hope, and joy. The context always indicates whether the words refer to stages of the spiritual development in general, or simply to its often-repeated conditions. In the Psalms these figures are especially abundant. Thus—"At midnight I will rise to give thanks to thee, because of thy righteous judgments." Here is shown how under the deepest sense of sin and disobedience, a sincere and contrite heart will yet remember and be grateful for God's mercy. To the same purport is Ps. lxiii. 6,—"When I meditate on thee in the night-watches, because thou hast been my help, in the shadow of thy wings will I rejoice." Out of the cold and darkness of such night, as out of winter, burst light and beauty. No state of despondency or mourning is so deep that in due time it does not give way to hope and rejoicing. Our "youth is renewed like the eagle's." When his sorrows pass into peace, David exclaims, because of this—"I will sing of thy mercy in the *morning*." And elsewhere, that though "weeping may endure for a night,

---

* "Moral epochs have their course as well as the seasons. We can no more hold them fast than we can hold sun, moon, and stars. Our faults perpetually return upon us, and herein lies the subtlest difficulty of self knowledge."—Goethe, *Dichtung und Wahrheit*, book xiii., vol. 3, p. 123.

joy cometh in the morning." And to show again that whatever may be our state, the mind should always be directed towards God, he says of "the righteous man," that "in His law doth he meditate *both day and night.*" All these passages acquire their highest interest and significance from our realizing them within ourselves. It was for this end they were designed. Beautiful and practical as they are in the letter, and affecting as the recorded utterances of an individual, they truly become God's word to us only in proportion that we feel that we repeat them for ourselves, and not so much with our lips, as in the inmost recesses of our being. The history of the ravens bringing food to Elijah while in the wilderness, both "in the morning" and "in the evening," has the same personal relation to us, and is to be interpreted after the same manner. Whenever, like the prophet, we are dwelling "by the brook Cherith,"* God's benevolent remembrance lets no period pass over without giving appropriate supplies of nourishment. All that he asks is faith in him, and then he will cheer the darkest night. It is a glorious privilege to have the power of honoring God by *faith.* Angels can adore and love, but only man, the suffering, self-made exile, surrounded by doubts and error, pain and temptation, tempest and darkness, can honor his God by *faith.*

"Day" is used not only in the senses above specified, but also as a metonymy for time, periods, and seasons in general, and thence as a metaphor for states and conditions of all possible kinds, whether good or evil. "Time," "period," and "season," are similarly used as figures for "day." We speak of days of rejoicing, a day of trouble, times of success,

---

* To dwell "by the brook Cherith" signifies to be in the endurance of temptations. Though the truths of the Word are then in obscurity to man's mind, he is nevertheless supported by them.

seasons of hope, the days of one's youth. "Behold, I will add unto thy *days*, fifteen *years*." (Is. xxxviii. 5.) It is important to note this meaning of the word, because of its frequent use in Scripture to denote states in general, whatever their quality. "Give us this *day* our daily bread," is in its higher sense, a prayer for the spiritual assistance best suited to the condition of our soul at the moment of preferring the request.

So varied is the moral significance of Times and Seasons that they might yet be contemplated in new relations, and with new and agreeable profit. How beautiful, for instance, is the agreement of the morning and the Spring with childhood, in the further respect of its peculiar innocence and purity! It is by reason of this agreement that in Scripture, the innocence and purity so vitally essential to the life of the Christian, are frequently denoted by or symbolized in childhood; as when our Lord placed the little child "in the midst," thereby showing that innocence should be the centre of thought and deed. For every *act* of the Saviour's, as well as every word, has its spiritual meaning and instruction; and if, with His divine help, we do not strive, in every daily duty, to place the little child in the midst, each of us for ourselves, in the principles and method of our actions, we are not truly attending to His behests. Hence, too, His divine warning that unless we become "as little children," we can "in no wise enter the kingdom of heaven." It is for the same reason that the Lord is imaged as "the Lamb." In the unaffected simplicity of all its little ways, in the sharing of its food, for example, with those around, the little child is the sweetest emblem of the Christian, while the exquisite delicacy of its frame is the outward and visible picture of its moral qualities. Hence the deep significance of the history of Naaman, who, when he had obediently washed himself in the Jordan for his leprosy, "became clean, and his flesh like the flesh of *a little child.*" In the future state we shall probably enjoy all the varieties of temporal life at the same moment; the wisdom of age, the vigor of manhood, the grace of youth, the innocence of infancy.

Again, morning is pre-eminently the time of *beauty.* Hence the innumerable similes of "beautiful as the morning," and "fair as the morning." With its added attributes of innocence and purity, it becomes the emblem of female youthfulness. In "Festus," accordingly, we have the "maiden morn," and the "virgin morn." A "*vir*gin" is literally, "one in her *spring,*" both as to time and to moral state. And as the latter is the higher signification of this beautiful word, the Bible applies it to both sexes. "These are they which are *virgins,* which follow the Lamb whithersoever he goeth."

Finally, may be noticed the ancient, pleasing, and universal fancy that heaven is a land of perpetual spring and sunshine.

> "There everlasting Spring abides,
> And never-withering flowers."

In conformity with this belief, the pictures sought to be drawn of the future state of the blessed have in every age used spring and daylight for their unvarying landscape. But it may be questioned if this be right. Milton perhaps is nearer the truth when he makes Raphael tell Adam that in heaven, as on earth, there are changes of times and seasons, morning and evening:—

> "For we have also our evening and our morn."

> "——The face of brightest heaven had changed
> To grateful twilight (for night comes not there
> In darker veil), and roseate dews disposed
> All but the unsleeping eyes of God to rest."

He gives the reason also why it should be so:—

"———For *change delectable*."

There can be no doubt that that grand unity of design which links together every law and item of the visible universe, extends also to the heavenly world; making it a sublime prototype in *spiritual* scenery and phenomena, of what here below is witnessed in *material* shape. Time reigns in the world of matter; state, in the world of spirit, each answering to the other. When, therefore, we enter the eternal country, the golden city of the great King, though we shall have parted from the sweet presence of months and seasons as we now know them, it will be to find that they were only the weak, shadowy representatives of spiritual states infinitely more glorious and inspiring. The times and seasons which here owe their being to the sun of nature, will then be spiritually reproduced by the Sun of Righteousness, who is its life and light; save that what here is winter will be disarmed of all its cold and bitterness; and what is night, of all its dismalness and terrors. It is in *true* nights, when the skies put forth their radiant splendors, that even in this present life we see most of God.

INDEX.

Elements of Art Criticism. Comprising a treatise on the Principles of Man's Nature as addressed by Art. Together with a historic survey of the methods of Art Execution in the departments of Drawing, Sculpture, Architecture, Painting, Landscape Gardening, and the Decorative Arts. Designed as a Text Book for Schools and Colleges, and as a Hand Book for Amateurs and Artists. By G. W. SAMSON, D.D., President of Columbia College, Washington, D. C. (In press.)

The Divine Attributes, including also the Nature of the Divine Trinity and a Treatise on the Divine Love and Divine Wisdom. From the Apocalypse Explained of Emanuel Swedenborg. (In press.)

Addison's Complete Works. Embracing numerous pieces now first collected, and Macaulay's Essay on the Life and Writings of Addison. Edited, with Notes, by Professor GREENE. With a Portrait on steel. Complete in 6 vols., 12mo. Cloth, $9.00; sheep, library style, $10.50; half calf, neat, $16.50; half calf, gilt, extra, $18.00.

Boswell's Life of Johnson. First Complete American Edition. With Numerous Additions by JNO. WILSON CROKER, M.P., and Notes by various hands. 4 vols., 12mo. Cloth, $6.00; sheep, library style, $7.00; half calf, neat, $11.00; half calf, gilt, extra, $12.00.

Chambers's Book of Days. The Book of Days: A Miscellany of Popular Antiquities in connection with the Calendar, including Anecdote, Biography, and History, Curiosities of Literature, and Oddities of Human Life and Character. Edited under the supervision of ROBERT CHAMBERS, LL. D. Complete in two volumes, royal 8vo. Cloth, $9.00; sheep, $10.00; half Turkey, $11.00.

Chambers's Encyclopædia. A Dictionary of Universal Knowledge for the People, on the basis of the latest edition of the German Conversations-Lexicon. Illustrated with Maps and numerous Wood Engravings. Published in eight parts, price, 25 cents each. The whole to be comprised in nine volumes, royal octavo. Price, per volume, cloth, $4.50; sheep, $5.00; half Turkey, $5.50.

Goldsmith's Complete Works. Embracing numerous pieces now first collected, with copious Notes by JAMES PRIOR. With four Vignettes engraved on steel. 4 vols., 12mo. Cloth, $6.00; do., sheep, library style, $7.00; do., half calf, neat, $11.00; do., half calf, gilt, extra, $12.00.

Lippincott's Pronouncing Gazetteer of the World; Or, Geographical Dictionary. Comprising over 2300 pages; giving a description of nearly one hundred thousand places, with the Correct Pronunciation of their Names. Revised Edition, with an Appendix, containing nearly 10,000 New Notices, and the most recent Statistical Information, being about 30,000 more Geographical Notices than are found in any other Gazetteer of the world. Edited by J. THOMAS, M.D., and T. BALDWIN, assisted by several other gentlemen. 1 vol., royal 8vo. 1866. Library binding, $10.00; half Turkey antique, $12.00; 2 vols., library style, $12,00; do., half antique, $15.00.

Footfalls on the Boundary of Another World. With Narrative Illus-trations by ROBERT DALE OWEN, formerly Member of Congress, and American Minister to Naples. 12mo., cloth, $1.75.

www.ingramcontent.com/pod-product-compliance
Lightning Source LLC
LaVergne TN
LVHW021227110826
845150LV00002B/264

* 9 7 8 1 4 2 5 5 6 3 4 1 7 *